Dynamics of Human Communication

Dynamics of Human Communication

Edited by

Sarita Anand and Archna Kumar

Orient BlackSwan

DYNAMICS OF HUMAN COMMUNICATION

ORIENT BLACKSWAN PRIVATE LIMITED

Registered Office
3-6-752 Himayatnagar, Hyderabad 500 029, Telangana, INDIA
e-mail: centraloffice@orientblackswan.com

Other Offices
Bengaluru, Chennai, Guwahati, Hyderabad, Kolkata,
Mumbai, New Delhi, Noida, Patna, Visakhapatnam

First published by Orient Blackswan Pvt. Ltd. 2016
Reprinted 2020, 2023

ISBN 978-81-250-6325-4

037086

Typeset in
Adobe Garamond Pro 10/12
by Shine Graphics, Delhi 110 094

Printed in India at
Rajiv Book Binding House, Delhi

Published by
Orient Blackswan Private Limited
3-6-752 Himayatnagar, Hyderabad 500 029, Telangana, INDIA
e-mail: info@orientblackswan.com

Contents

Tables, Figures and Images

Tables

Figures

Images

FOREWORD

Let us consider what may seem like the most banal of communication acts in India: the practice of saying *namaskār* (or *namastē*) when meeting or parting company. With both hands pressed together in front of the chest, palms touching and fingers pointed upwards, a slight bow is made as the interacting parties audibly utter namaskār. A non-contact greeting, in the same spirit as the Japanese bow, namaskār holds various layers of meanings at multiple levels—literal, cultural and spiritual. *Namah* means paying respect or obeisance, and the accompanying non-verbal actions connote a heartfelt bowing to the divinity and goodness residing in the other. Namaskār is as much an intentional intrapersonal act as much as it is an interactional relational act between people and groups, small or large. It carries with it a feeling of surrender and gratitude—recognition that the world is more than the sum of the interacting parts.

Really? How could a simple namaskār, an act that many of us carry out with a robotic instinct without thinking, hold this multilayered communicative complexity for over a billion people on the Indian subcontinent? Well, such is often the simplicity and complexity associated with human communication phenomenon, something we rarely discern, analyse, delve into, reflect upon and appreciate.

Toward this purpose, the present book, *Dynamics of Human Communication*, represents an invaluable resource—both for a lay reader and an ardent student of communication. It addresses both the simplicity and multilayered complexity of the human communication phenomenon, and especially for those who harbour a deep interest in the Indian or South Asian experience.

As you will experience in the pages that follow, the present book provides a comprehensive roadmap to the study of human communication. Organised by units and chapters, each logically building on the other, the book encapsulates the key tenets, ideas and perspectives in human communication in a highly engaging manner. Its strength lies in its use of easy-to-grasp language, vivid illustrations, and its plethora of examples and cases—all designed to create a namaskār-like experience.

I invite you to delve into the pages that follow. Namaskār.

18 March 2016

Arvind Singhal
Samuel Shirley and Edna Holt Marston Professor of Communication,
University of Texas

PREFACE

Communication represents an essential and important human need. The urge to communicate is primeval and in contemporary civilisation it is a necessity for survival. The ability to communicate makes it possible to exchange views, opinions, agreements and disagreements. So it enables people to express themselves and show their own points of view. Consequently, communication makes people who and what they are and, in the process of doing so, strengthens human dignity.

In today's multicultural societies communication skills are increasingly being recognised as a core competence for successful realisation of personal and organisational goals. It has become quintessential to train, motivate and promote effective use of communication skills among students and professionals. *Dynamics of Human Communication* is an attempt to put together the basic concepts of communication and their application in the Indian context. This book has been specifically designed for students across disciplines studying the basics of communication as well as professionals interested in enhancing their communication competencies. It has been an earnest endeavour of the team to explain the core notions related to the discipline as well as develop critical thinking about the theories and methods of communication in an ever-changing sociocultural and technological environment. The book makes use of simple language, uses applied and implied examples and elucidates ideas with relevant flowcharts, images, tables and summaries to make the various concepts discussed more interesting to the reader.

This book has been divided into four units, with four chapters under each unit to present the contents in a comprehensive manner. Unit I focuses primarily on the understanding of communication as a process. It talks about the aspects and principles/postulates of human communication, deliberates on the types of communication and the different functions communication performs in modern society. This section of the book also delineates the communication elements and the shifts in the conceptual models for understanding the communication process. The unit closes with a detailed description of the possible barriers in communicating effectively and ways to overcome them.

Unit II delves a level deeper and provides insights into how culture and perception influence our communication processes. The unit lays emphasis on understanding the nature of cultural orientations, their consequent implications and manifestations in moulding perceptions and influencing the meanings drawn from our communication. Understanding of diversity and plurality and listening to what others say, respecting the counterpart's attitude and having mutual trust are essential to nurture mutual cooperation and learning. With an explicit analysis of the role and process of listening, this unit presents the intrinsic relationship between learning and communication and the use of audio-visual aids to facilitate communication and learning.

Without communicating, no individual, community, group or an institution would be able to exist or prosper. Unit III is about these levels of communication—the levels of communication transactions, and the aspects influencing effectiveness of our communications at each level. It begins with intrapersonal communication, the foremost of the communication interactions with oneself; moves to interpersonal communication and communication between dyads and triads that form the essential building block for maintaining and sustaining human relationships. The unit additionally talks about small group communication and organisational communication.

We are witness to the world undergoing an Information Communication Technology (ICT) revolution. India was among the first few nations which used mass media sponsored by the central government through regulative planning to support development initiatives. Beginning with the use of rural radio forums to promote rural development, even satellite communication broadcast was promoted to thousands of villages. Communication has a crucial role to play in development as it creates awareness, generates purposeful knowledge and motivates people to utilise the services offered. Communication is thus fundamental to shaping the future of a developing country like India. The communication strategies have become particularly important to both inform and amplify the voices of all segments of populations. Unit IV has been conceptualised to explain and discuss the strengths and limitations of mediated form of communication and lay thrust on the concept of public and mass communication. This unit discusses the forms, types and functions of mass communication in today's fast-changing world. Tracing its advent and historical milestones, the Unit examines mass media's current scenario, changing dimensions and future since the inception of new media.

We hope the book serves as a fundamental resource volume that not only enhances readers' knowledge but also adds to their discernment about communication as a key asset for personal and professional fulfilment. We would like to state that the images and photographs in the chapters of this textbook are for illustrative purposes only, and not meant to imply that the author(s), volume editors or the publishers endorse the brands that may be featured in them.

This book is dedicated to our students.

15 March 2016

Sarita Anand
Archna Kumar

UNIT I

FUNDAMENTALS OF HUMAN COMMUNICATION

Communication is undoubtedly the essence of our lives. We cannot imagine life without communication. This book endeavours to harness your communication abilities by providing you with knowledge of the discipline of communication that will be applicable in making choices in your professional lives in the future.

Unit I of this book is dedicated to the basics of communication as a subject. We shall begin in Chapter One with understanding the nature of communication, look at the history of communication, the principles that govern the communication process and understand the functions and scope of the discipline. Subsequent chapters will deal with the types of communication, discuss the elements in the process of communication, understand the models of communication and finally look at the possible barriers in the process of communication. Thus, Unit I shall set the path for further in-depth engagement with this subject before going into the process and manifestations of communication which shall be dealt with in the units to follow.

1

HUMAN COMMUNICATION
An Overview

HIGHLIGHTS

- Meaning and definition of communication
- Characteristics of communication
- Key aspects of the communication process
- Culture and communication
- History of communication
- Scope of communication
- Principles of communication
- Functions of communication

Before you begin to read and understand what communication is, close your eyes, sit back and think: What is making you read this book? Is it part of your coursework, a teacher's instruction or your own interest that has motivated you? Your answer may vary; perhaps it may not even be any of the options above. Whatever your answer is, do you realise what you just did? You questioned yourself to receive an answer in your mind, you communicated with yourself.

We do not even realise how many times we communicate in a day. We communicate not only with ourselves, but also with our friends, families and members of social groups we are part of or are attached to. Communication occurs not just through words. It is a way to express ourselves, so we do it through gestures, actions, body language, clothing, etc. Everything about us communicates who we are and gives an idea about our personality. Communication inevitably is the essence of living life. Every piece of information we send, receive and share is communication. It is our need to communicate to make us feel loved and belonging to a family, group or an organisation. Communication helps us to maintain and sustain our relationships and to vent our emotions and succeed in our academic and professional ventures. With the recent advancements in technology, communication gadgets have become an essential part of our lives. It is difficult to think how life would be without cell phones today. Every day, more and more people are beginning to use internet technology and social media. Texts, video calls, sharing pictures, are all just a click away. You and your app world are inseparable. Technology has redefined how we communicate, who we communicate with, and consequently has a deep impact on our socio-cultural and economic environment.

MEANING AND DEFINITION OF COMMUNICATION

The word 'communication' is derived from the Latin word, *communis*, which means 'common'. Communication is a process, which involves organising, selecting and transmitting codes in an appropriate way to ensure that the listener perceives and recreates in his/her own mind the intended meaning of the communicator. And, communication is not only important as it facilitates mutual understanding but also because it is the crux of all human relations.

All life forms communicate, however man's ability to communicate surpasses that of all other beings. Human beings alone have the power to express their ideas and feelings in words. Sight, sound, touch, smell and taste are modes of communication. Further, communication is a two-fold process between two parties—the sender and the receiver. It involves exchange and progression of thoughts, ideas, knowledge and information towards a mutually acceptable goal or direction. Communication performs many functions as well; it provides us information, it can influence change, helps in decision making and, most importantly, it becomes the basis of our social relationships.

Communication can be described as a process wherein, one person stimulates an idea in another person's mind; it is not a panacea—that is, it can neither create nor help eliminate problems—but it definitely opens a platform to come out with problems, differences and conflicts, and resolve them. However, when communication is not effective, it can aggravate the problem. You must have observed when you are very angry and upset with someone, your pitch goes up, and your language becomes rude and gets out of control. At such moments, family or friends witnessing the situation may advise the arguing individual to be quiet, move to a different room, drink water or some such solution. After a few hours or days the arguing person may laugh over the matter they argued over, or they may be able to find the reason in the other person's view and may be able to get over that moment of anger. What does this indicate? It means communication in itself is no answer. The content or feeling with which the communication is made is the deciding factor of its usefulness. Therefore, the question is not whether people are communicating or not, but what is it they are communicating about. Hence, the quality of communication cannot be determined by its quantity.

Educationists like to know more about it to make the teaching-learning process more interesting, sociologists and anthropologists use it to understand the process of change in societies and study its role in the power dynamics within groups and communities, psychologists use it to understand human behaviour in different situations and behavioural problems emanating out of communication in relationships.

Public administrators examine the use of communication in designing strategies to change human behaviour—for instance, in promoting the use of contraceptives or prevention of HIV, in promoting immunisation or the use of latrines. Communication is an essential element of participatory governance, as in the case of negotiating with people when their land is proposed to be used for large-scale infrastructure projects like dams and mining. Thus, we find that since a variety of professions use communication as a key element in their endeavour, we find a variety of definitions put forth by them with respect to their perceived understanding of the use of communication in their respective fields.

According to Paul Leagans (1961), an expert in the area of agricultural communication 'Communication is a process by which two or more persons exchange ideas, facts, impressions in way that each gains a common understanding of the meaning, content and use of message.' According to Wilbur Schramm (1954), a well-known communication expert, 'communication occurs when two corresponding systems coupled together through one or more non-corresponding systems assume identical status as a result of a single transfer along the chain, we are trying to establish commonness'. According to John Dewey, an educationist, 'communication is a process of sharing experiences till it becomes a common possession. It modifies the disposition of both the communicator and the receiver interacting in communication'. He emphasised that the shared experience is the key element. According to Patri, a psychologist, 'communication is the mode of transmitting information, culture, mode, emotions, thoughts, reactions as well as data in the form of symbols, figures and diagrams. Good communication reduces friction and promotes positivity'. Dahama and Bhatnagar (2003), specialists of extension education, defined communication 'as a process of social interaction, i.e. in a communication situation two or more individuals interact'. Further, *The American College Dictionary* defines communication as 'the imparting or interchange of thoughts, opinions and information by speech, writing or signs' (quoted in Dahama and Bhatnagar 2003).

We can easily associate the following with the concept of communication from these definitions:

1. Communication is a two-way process. It involves a sender and a receiver and there is a sharing of information among them. The sender or receiver can be an individual or a group.
2. Because of this exchange of information, communication leads to commonness and shared experiences between the sender and receiver. The commonness includes factors like common culture, common language and common information.
3. Communication is basically meant to convey a message. Message can be in the form of information, a directive, an enquiry, a feeling, an opinion or an idea.
4. It provides an opportunity for the receiver to understand the message and share his/her response (feedback) with the sender.

All these definitions of communication help in clarifying the concept of communication, drawing attention to essential features of communication irrespective of the context like whether it is a communication between an agricultural expert and farmers or a leader and her/his followers or a teacher and students. The basics of communication remain the same.

CHARACTERISTICS OF COMMUNICATION

The characteristics of communication is explained below:

1. Communication is a universal process
2. Communication may be formal or informal
3. Communication is a cultural process
4. Communication is purposeful
5. Communication is both an art and a science

Communication is a Universal Process

Every day from the time we wake up in the morning to the time we go to bed, we find ourselves in different situations of communication. Communication is all-pervasive and omnipresent. It is present everywhere, be it at home, at work or at play. Each individual, young or old in formal or informal environment is engaged in the process of communication. When we are aware, 70 per cent of our time is spent in communicating. Sharing and exchanging of information is a continuous process and it continues in all contexts, be it personal or professional.

Communication May be Formal or Informal

Communication may occur formally or informally. Formal or organisational communication follows the principle of scalar chain hierarchy where communication flows through different levels of hierarchy. For example, while applying for a vacant position in an organisation, usually, we have to communicate first with the human resources department and then our letter/mail will be forwarded to the specific department we want to be part of and finally we may have to meet with the head of the organisation. Informal communication does not need an order or official channel for flow of communication. Members of the group feel free to communicate with anyone and are not required to take cognisance of any hierarchy. A group of friends talking among themselves is an example of informal communication.

Communication is a Cultural Process

Culture defines the rules, norms, beliefs and attitudes prevailing in a society. It may be alright in some cultures to call senior colleagues by their first names and in others it may be considered rude. Thus, culture also influences content, style, approach and channels of communication. We adapt our words and symbols in accordance to the prevailing cultural systems. People from different cultures differ in the meaning they assign to words. Effective communication requires that we select appropriate symbols (verbal and non-verbal) in accordance to the other person and the meaning they will derive from it and not what we may think.

Communication is Purposeful

All communication has a purpose. Communication happens because there is a purpose to it; there is meaning attached to it. The purpose may be personal or social gratification, problem solving, decision making or even venting out our emotions for that matter.

Communication is both an Art and a Science

Human beings are social animals and possess an urge to communicate; to express their feelings and thoughts. It was earlier perceived that effective communicators possess these qualities because they have inherited them. This misconception that communication is an inborn quality has now become obsolete. Scientific research into the discipline of human communication has given ground to the theory that communication skills can be acquired through training and practice. The knowledge of various aspects of communication can be learnt to enhance communication skills. Communication is therefore a science; its learning is based on a body of knowledge that the discipline has. Communication theory is based on certain principles which are fundamental to the discipline. The discipline has distinct models that help comprehend communication in all its forms. Systematic learning within the vast body of knowledge of human communication will lead people to enhance their skills and become effective communicators. Which means, for instance, the results of watching the same film or listening to a lecture can be measured to objectively show why one is better than the other.

Communication is an art. Just as how one story can be told by different filmmakers very differently, the same content can be conveyed to students very differently by different teachers. This skill can be learnt with training and practice. As communication is related to the behavioural aspects of the individuals involved, each individual behaves or perceives a situation different from the other. This makes every interaction unique. There is no one best way to communicate. Each individual has her/his own personal style of communicating; which makes her/him different. Even though two communicators may have the same level of knowledge, how they express themselves to explain the same concept depends on their individual selection of words, expressions and examples. Their understanding of the information is manifested in their presentation, which makes one better than the other. You may find a particular teacher better than the others because of her/his ability to explain. You may like any particular actor better than the others due to their acting skills. Although it is difficult to pinpoint one single logical reason for why someone is an effective communicator, there is no denying that the uniqueness of the communicator lends creativity to communication. Many reputed personalities have garnered visibility and appreciation because of the way they articulate their thoughts. Some people can negotiate better than the others. This is the art of communication.

Hence communication is both an art and a science; it has its own approach, its own set of theories, yet it is based on the individual's practical skills and the dynamics that prevail. The art and science of communication are intricately interwoven as both theoretical and practical knowledge are needed by individuals to appropriately respond to situations.

Having understood the nature of communication, it is important for us to look at the misconceptions about communication; which are pre-conceived notions most of us have in our minds about the process of communication and its ability.

1. *Communication is an answer to all our problems*: Communicating has the potential to solve our problems, relationships and apprehensions. Talking it out does make a difference; but it does not necessarily always lead to a solution to the problem. Sometimes it can be futile to communicate, while at others, it may worsen the situation. Again, it is the quality of communication—and not the amount—that affects the potential to solve our problems.
2. *Communication can go kaput*: Letting oneself stop or restraining from communicating does not mean that communication has stopped working or it has collapsed. Communication can never breakdown, while the situation or a relationship can. People may fail to interact, but the potential of communication to foster change does not go down.
3. *Communication is an innate forte*: We are not born with the inherent ability to communicate; we gradually learn and, in the process, excel in communicating effectively. Communication is not a natural instinct; over time we get ourselves trained to communicate agreeably.
4. *Communication is a positive affair*: Communication is neither good nor bad; it is neither positive nor negative as a phenomenon. It is just a medium that can improve or deteriorate through our day-to-day interactions. The final output of communication thus depends on how we use it.
5. *Expression has significance*: It is generally assumed that the way we express ourselves, through words, language, actions and other non-verbal symbols gives out what we want to convey entirely. But, expressions just by themselves do not have much significance or meaning associated with them. The actual meaning is derived by the people or the individuals who we are communicating with.

KEY ASPECTS OF THE COMMUNICATION PROCESS

After having understood what communication is, its nature and the misconceptions associated with it, let us now glance through the various possibilities of communication interactions. Communication can be: (*a*) mediated, when it uses certain technology as the primary channel, or (*b*) unmediated, when it primarily thrives on the interaction between the participating parties without the use of any technology. Communication could also be: (*a*) verbal, when we use words in the form of speech or writing to communicate, or, (*b*) non-verbal, when it involves the use of symbols—such as gestures, facial expressions, eye contact, tone of voice, use of space and touch.

Central to human communication are certain key aspects which help understand the process of communication and the conveying of meaning. Understanding these aspects provides valuable insights about communication and helps understand the variations in our communication and the factors influencing them. The key aspects of the communication process are:

1. *Communication context*: All communication takes place in a context, i.e. the environment in which communication takes place. A change in the context influences the nature of communication.
2. *Source–Receiver*: The communicator or sender is the person who is sending the message, while the receiver is the recipient of the message. The source/receiver can be an individual, group or an organisation and decides not only the content of the message but also its encoding and decoding.
3. *Message*: Message is the key idea that the sender plans to communicate. It elicits the response of the receiver. The message must be so designed that it is easily comprehended by the receiver. The message may take any form as in writing, in speech or signals.
4. *Channel*: The communication channel is the medium through which the message is exchanged between the sender and the receiver. The sender may use any channel depending on availability, convenience and requirement; and it should be chosen such that the message reaches the receiver as expected.

5. *Feedback*: Feedback is the response to the sender's message. Feedback allows the communicator to adjust message and be more effective. Messages sent back to the communicator by the receivers tell the former about the effects of communication on them.
6. *Noise*: Noise prevents a receiver from getting as well as understanding the message a source is sending. Noise acts as a barrier for effective communication and must be reduced as far as possible.
7. *Effects*: Communication always has some effect on one or more persons involved in the communication act. These may include enhanced knowledge and new learning (cognitive effects), change in attitude, beliefs, emotions and feelings (affective effects), and/or learn new skills (psycho-motor effects).

Figure 1.1: The Process of Communication

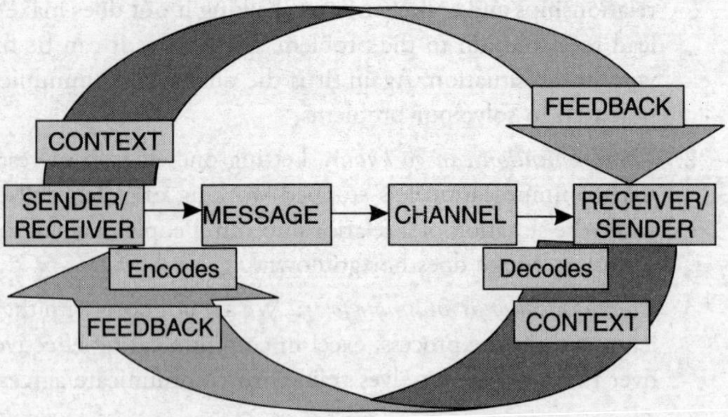

Source: Adapted from DeVito (2006) by the authors.

The key aspects of the communication process make it a cyclic process with the element of feedback incorporated. These key aspects help us to understand the various types of communication using multiple channels for different purposes. We shall study about these in Chapter Three which focuses of the process of communication.

Activity

Identify the various aspects discussed above in this communication situation. Counselling session by teachers for parents of students who did not get good grades in examination at the school premises.

CULTURE AND COMMUNICATION

Culture refers to a pattern of shared assumptions that have been invented, discovered or developed by a given group and are taught to new members as the correct way to think, perceive and behave. Culture shapes our ideas and beliefs, and largely determines our behaviours and actions. Culture is all that is produced and developed by the members of a social group and includes their language, modes of thinking, laws, arts and religion. Further, culture is learnt through communication and is not transmitted through our genes.

We learn and share based on the norms inherent in our traditions and customs and this process of learning and sharing requires communication. Communication also requires coding and symbols that must be learned and shared. Every cultural pattern and every single act of social behaviour involves communication. In today's globalising world understanding the role of culture in communication has acquired even more importance as people, ideas and information move across cultures at much greater speed and frequency. Since culture permeates all forms of communication, understanding its influences on our ability to communicate remains paramount. Further, culture also influences what messages we give importance to, what strategies we adopt for and what channels we give credibility to and select for communicating with and influencing others.

Culture influences what we say to whom, how we say and interact and behave with others, who we give preference and importance in our interactions. For example, how young girls and boys learn to behave differently in different cultures is also an interesting observation to make. Gender is a cultural aspect that varies across cultures. Different cultures socialise girls and boys differently, thus, they differ in their ideas, beliefs and roles they are expected to play, their communication styles and how they interact with others.

Communication across and between cultures is called cross-cultural communication. It has two facets: (*a*) intercultural communication, which refers to face-to-face interactions among people of diverse cultures, and (*b*) intra-cultural communication, which is the communication among different individuals of the same culture.

We will look at these concepts related to culture and communication in-depth in Chapter Five.

Activity

Recall an incident where you found culture to have strongly influenced your communication and interaction and share it with your class.

(For example, when you went to a temple, you were asked by your parents to behave in a specific manner, or when you were asked to dress up in a particular attire for attending a family function)

HISTORY OF COMMUNICATION

The history of communication can be largely attributed to two factors and their intrinsic interplay: (*a*) the prevailing socio-cultural and political factors and (*b*) the growth of communication technology

Each of these factors influenced the other and determined the evolution of each. There is a direct relationship between technologies and the socio-cultural and political ideologies prevailing in a society. The origin of communication can be attributed to nature, where different animals and birds used different signals to communicate. The crackling sound of the leaves, the sound of the breeze, the chirping of the birds, crying of the animals, all were but an example of communication. Even humans at that time used signals and gestures to communicate. Thus at different historical periods of time the progress of civilisations has been shaped by the changing technologies. Let us now look at the various periods and the milestones of communication development within them.

The Classical Period

This period lasted from 5th century BC to 4th century AD. By this period human beings had developed the basic skills and tools to communicate their ideas and the evolution of the human brain had made it possible for the species to master speech—a form of communication much more effective than signs and symbols. Speech meant easier coordination and cooperation, technological progress and development of complex, abstract concepts such as religion or science, and the transmission of information and knowledge down generations. This period also marked the development and focus on persuasion and argumentation as skills.

It was Aristotle, the famous Greek philosopher who was a student of Plato and the teacher of Alexander the Great, who—through his work *Rhetoric* (300 BC)—made an attempt to examine the underlying elements of persuasion through public speaking. He identified five canons of public speaking: invention, arrangement, style, memory and delivery. Invention referred to the idea or subject of an individual's speech, and the discovering of facts and arguments that could lead to sound conclusions. Arrangement was the ordering of ideas in one's speech so that it was effective. Style referred to the selection of words and expressions to clearly convey the message. Memory referred to the memorising of speeches, as without it an oral speech could not be effective; Aristotle laid stress on techniques of memory enhancing. The final aspect was delivery, which included not only the voicing of a speech but also the various non-verbal elements incorporated within it. In addition to this, Aristotle identified three modes of persuasion: 'ethos', using words that indicate a good moral character of the speaker; 'logos', using words that indicate that the speaker thrives on logic and reasoning; and 'pathos', use of emotions in one's speech to sway the audience and gain their confidence.

The Medieval and Renaissance Periods

The Medieval Period lasted from 400 to 1400 AD, while the Renaissance Period spanned from 1400 to 1600 AD. The particular highlight of these periods was that communication was no more limited to merely discovering the truth or clarifying the facts. Instead it went ahead to focus on how communication be expedited. Modes of communication during the Medieval Period were very limited. In the absence of the mass communication methods, postal service and the internet, correspondence took place in the form of letters delivered by private messengers. Letters were written on parchments with the use of ink and quill. Books were written by hand and were expensive. The focus in this era was not on oral communication, but on preaching the principles of spirituality. Rhetoric took a backseat (for further information, see http://educators.medievaltimes.com/1-2-communication.html; accessed 31 March 2016).

The Modern Period

Spanning from 1600 to 1900 AD, this particular period saw the advent of democratic and political reforms with many a powerful politicians emerging during this era. As a consequence, rhetoric, which had been overshadowed by the preaching and teaching practices in the Renaissance Period, was again revived and took centrestage. Public speaking and mass addressing became a norm in this period. According to Patri and Patri (2002), four directions emerged in the area of communication at this time:

> The history of communication can be traced in the following periods:
>
> 1. *Classical Period*: Importance of speech and rhetoric
> 2. *Medieval or Renaissance Period*: Shift from rhetoric to preaching and teaching
> 3. *Modern Period*: Period of democratic reforms, revival of rhetoric and public speaking
> 4. *Contemporary Period*: Thrust on technology for communication

1. The classical approach where insights in terms of truth were ascertained.
2. The psychological approach which sought to understand the link between communication and thought.
3. The belletristic approach where the focus was on writing and due to which speaking was perceived as an art form and standards of judging creative arts like drama, poetry, etc. emerged.
4. The evolutionary approach which tried to look into how verbal and non-verbal presentations can be improved in oratory, through instruction and training.

As a result of these four directions, a lot of thrust was given to the research in communication. Research was done on various fields, from the process of communication to the style of communication and development of tool kits and guides for effective communication. The emphasis thus shifted on making communication effective through the application of these approaches and developing research-based innovations in the area of communication.

The Contemporary Period

This particular period which includes the 20th and 21st centuries thrives on the development of new-age technology. Computer-based technologies have led to the possibility of the transfer and management of data of all sorts (data files, music, videos, etc.), opportunities to network and create new communities cutting across socio-cultural and political boundaries, and the emergence of real-time information systems which gets information as it happens across great distances.

We live in an era of human history where huge changes take place from one generation to the next. Cave drawings were murals that people painted onto walls of caves and canyons to tell the story of their culture. Drums were one way to send signals to neighbouring tribes and groups. The drumming pattern would tell them of concerns and events they needed to know. Smoke signals were another way to send messages to people who were not close enough to communicate via words. But today, one can't imagine living without a cell phone. Internet, social networking, applications, video-chatting, voice routing, e-books are just a few examples of the advancements being made in the field of communication today.

Activity

Recall the kind of programmes you watched on TV or have heard on radio in your childhood. Document the shift in content and style of these programmes and share your views with your classmates.

SCOPE OF COMMUNICATION

All domains of human life are deeply influenced by how effectively we communicate, be it at work (our professional lives), rest (how we relax) or play (entertain, engage in recreation activities and have fun). In today's fast changing world, with newer advances in communication technologies, the communication industry, and hence the field of communication, has seen exponential growth. Further with globalisation and increased intercultural communication people are increasingly feeling the need to understand the value of communicating with people from different nationalities and cultures.

The theory of communication is inter-disciplinary where various disciplines have contributed to the body of knowledge. Recent years have seen various colleges and deemed universities starting formal degree courses in communication. Specialised training is being provided in the allied fields, viz. mass communication and journalism, business communication, organisational communication, development communication, public relations, advertising, media management, media advocacy, audience research, etc. In fact, many NGOs and civil society organisations want communication experts who can devise advocacy plans to bring about a change in the society, or those who are up-to-date with the latest participatory techniques and can bring behavioural change at the grassroots.

Development communication scholars are in demand today. Many national and international programmes demand forte in research in specialised areas such as, C4D (communication for development) studies, and policy planning and M&E (monitoring and evaluation). Professional communication courses endeavour to not only increase the communication competencies of students but also aid in making them professionals geared to the needs of the bourgeoning or expanding communication industry. Figure 1.2 shows the extensive scope of communication, which is not limited to one, but a number of fields.

Various fields require the knowledge and application of communication directly or indirectly. All of these fields—be it advertising, electronic or media communication, public relations, education, or computer technology—require a person to master the theoretical and practical aspects of communication. Worldwide, job descriptions for numerous positions state that excellent communication and interpersonal skills are mandatory. And in these cases even if an applicant is not as much qualified for the post, (s)he may make it in an interview if (s)he has excellent communication skills. Hence the scope of communication is not only limited to these aforementioned fields but also to many others. Besides having the basic skill of communication, creative communication is hugely in demand. Government offices, corporate brands, and organisations big and small want to ensure their products and services are effectively marketed and therefore resort to different and unique ways of communicating to their audiences. Social media, comic strips, theatre, branding through multiple means, use of multiple channels, adopting themes and colours related to the organisation, etc. are the unique ways of creative communication that these entities use. And this work demands individuals who aren't only good communicators, but also creative minds that can research, plan, script, implement and evaluate a particular campaign.

Another emerging dimension of communication is that of development communication that entails development journalism and strategic communication which involves communication targeted at addressing health, environment and global peace issues (such as public health, HIV/AIDS, gender equality, pollution, water security, sanitation, peace and conflict resolution). Here methods of participatory research and appraisal, communitisation and strategic planning of programmes are essential. This requires specialists who are trained in the field of communication and are familiar with grassroots practices and community engagement. Now, with the Corporate Social Responsibility Bill passed in India, demand for development professionals is bound to increase in corporate houses too.

Figure 1.2: Scope of Communication

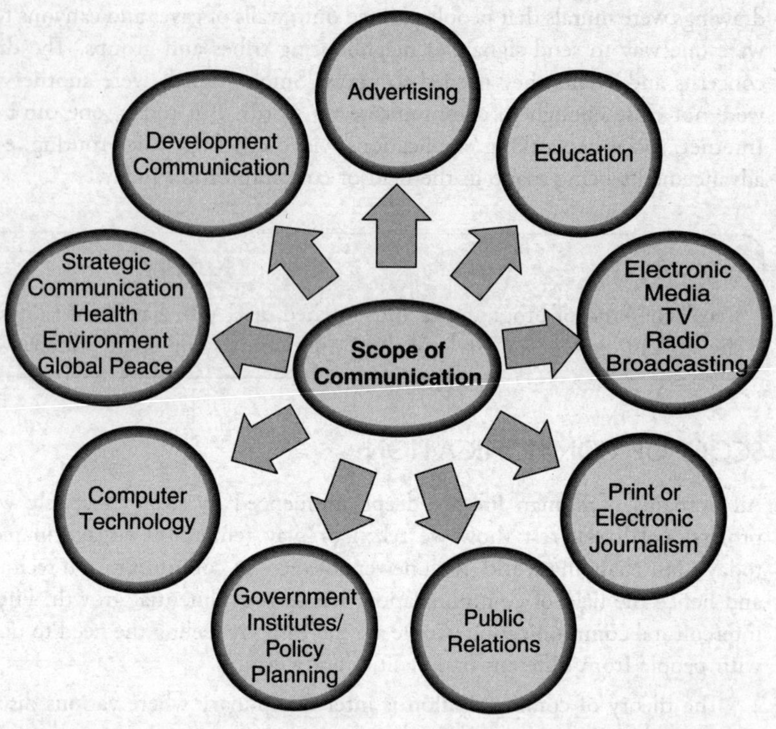

Source: Created by the authors.

Thus, it can be inferred that communication as a discipline is not only limited to its traditional or core theory but also linked with many allied fields. Its basic knowledge and practical application is needed in every profession today. Communication not only leads to self development, but also to the development of the society as a whole, by providing and grooming development professionals who are trained to bring the desired behaviour change for the betterment of the community and address many a issues of concern.

PRINCIPLES OF HUMAN COMMUNICATION

Human communication is based on certain foundational principles. The central postulates of communication (universally-accepted truths) are explained below.

Communication is transactional: Communication is a transactional process. It means that our communication with others progresses on the basis of responses produced to the original communication. The other implication is that each person is seen both as a speaker and as a listener and is therefore simultaneously sending and receiving messages, e.g. communication between a husband and a wife perpetuates through each second of their lives, whether they are discussing about their children, managing household chores, at work, talking or fighting. They constantly keep swapping their roles as speaker and listener. Any communication in this relationship is a result of the previous communication between them and will result in another event of communication.

Communication is a process of adjustment and is punctuated: Every time we interact, we adjust; we try to interpret and decode the symbols we receive, learn it and then understand it. Because not each and every individual involved in the communication sends or receives identical signals. To better understand adjustment, let us look at a few examples. In the case of communication within a family, if one of the members is unwell, all other members may feel low and sad. Similarly, in an educational institution if the laboratory staff goes on strike, neither will teachers be able to demonstrate nor will students be able to perform experiments. The overall goal of the institute to impart knowledge through practical learning will not be fulfilled.

The communication process is a continuous transaction. Communication flows in a systemic and organised process. For communication to occur, first there has to be (*a*) a sender, who sends the message and encodes it, then there has to be (*b*) a message appropriately designed, which flows through (*c*) a channel to (*d*) a receiver who decodes the message and interprets it. As the number of elements increase, the communication process becomes more complex. All these elements of communication must be organised to make the message interpretation effective. And for the conversation to be perceived better it is punctuated by the sender/receiver. Punctuation is the tendency to divide a continuous stream of communication into smaller sequences of stimuli and responses. Every participant in the communication process divides the communication into causes and effects to better understand what goes on.

1. Communication is transactional
2. Communication is process of adjustment and is punctuated
3. Communication involves content and relationship dimension
4. Communication is a package of signals
5. Communication involves symmetrical and complementary interactions
6. Communication is inevitable, irreversible and unrepeatable
7. Communication is multi-purposeful

Communication involves content and the dimension of relationship: Most communication interactions involve some degree of content. This content may be known to both the parties, or known by either of them or by none. For example, a teacher lecturing a diverse group of students shares content with them which she is well versed with but the students aren't. Further, communication also indicates the relationship between the two parties; the kind of dynamics that exists between them. For example, when a student enters late into a classroom, the teacher may get angry and say, 'Make sure you see me after the class.' This simple statement clearly indicates that the teacher is at a position of authority and expects her student to report to her after the class. On the other hand, if the teacher would have said, 'Please make sure you are on time next time'; this would have indicated that the teacher has empathised with the student and must have understood that the student's delay would have been due to some problem. Thus communication carries along with the content a relationship dimension as well.

Communication is a package of signals: Communication occurs not only through words, but also through gestures, body language and other non-verbal symbols. Usually, verbal and non-verbal symbols reinforce or support each other (DeVito 2006). As a result we convey our messages and feelings most effectively when our verbal and non-verbal symbols are aligned. One cannot claim to be excited about opening a gift box, if one continues to lie down on the bed. On the other hand, we may express dual feelings through the package of these verbal and non-verbal signals while communicating. For example, if a guest suddenly arrives at your house when you are very tired, out of formality you would indeed say, 'Welcome home, so glad to receive you'; but accompany it with a blank and unsmiling face and a cold hug, indicating the other half of your feelings—that you are not too pleased with receiving this uninvited guest. Thus, communication is a package of signals.

Communication involves symmetrical and complementary interactions: The interactions during communication are primarily of two types: symmetrical and complementary. In symmetrical relationships, both the members behave in a similar manner. In fact, what one does is reflected by the other. If one gets aggressive, the other gets aggressive too; if one gets excited, the other gets excited too. In symmetrical relationship, there is equality with minimal difference. Although this is good, an adverse effect of this type of relationship is when both individuals are negative in their behaviour; there is a likelihood of potential conflict that may worsen the situation to a great extent. Consider an example of two teenaged siblings fighting over an issue; one gets aggressive, the other gets aggressive, and consequently the situation spirals out of control. The other type of interaction is complementary interaction, in which two individuals indulge in different behaviours. Behaviour of one acts as a stimulus for the other to engage in a complementary behaviour. In this type of interaction maximisation of differences is observed. For example, in a family—if one partner acts in an authoritative way, the other may want to be democratic; if one acts superior, the other inferior and so on. As you know, culture often dictates such relationships. For example, the relationship between men and women tend to be asymmetrical across cultures but the degree of equality in a relationship may vary. In developed countries like Sweden, the difference may be minimal, in the US the difference may be moderate but in countries like India the difference may be high and in countries like Afghanistan the difference may be very high with restrictions even on mobility of women outside the house.

Communication is inevitable, irreversible and unrepeatable: Communication is inevitable. We human beings have an innate instinct to communicate, to talk, to ask, to tell others. The history of communication can be traced to story of human civilisation; it has been inevitable for human life to flourish. Once a message has been communicated it cannot be taken back. Another important factor to be noted is that the communication process cannot be reversed. You may have experienced situations where you may have used foul language and later on regretted it. Those words cannot be taken back. Even if you apologise, the damage done cannot be fully reversed. And, communication is unrepeatable. You can't exactly repeat a communication situation as it occurred, as contextual and personal factors cannot exactly help replicate a communication encounter that occurred previously. For example, a teacher usually repeats the same lesson across various sections. It would not be the same interaction across the various sections as the individual student composition varies. The context, physiological and psychological states of the students' and her/his mind operate differently and will make a difference in the way (s)he will transact this repeat class.

Communication has many purposes: Communication as a process not only helps us share our feelings, thoughts and actions, it also helps us change our beliefs and adapt to change that the other communicator intends for us. As a process, communication has many such purposes that help us deal and interact with the elements of our social system.

FUNCTIONS OF COMMUNICATION

As an all-pervasive phenomenon, communication performs many functions, some of which you learnt about in the previous section. However, specifically, communication is functional in the following ways:

1. *Information and understanding function*: One of the primary functions of communication is that it helps us in sending and receiving information; and based on how we interpret the message, affects our understanding of the message. Even to develop an understanding of a concept, the exchange of information is required. Similarly, repetitive reinforcing through communication only strengthens the efficacy of our understanding of the concept.
2. *Affinity function*: Another important function of communication is to create, initiate, maintain and sustain human relationships. This function of communication involves messages that articulate one's feelings towards the other and helps in establishing relationships. A boy and a girl who have feelings for each other need to express it in order to move ahead in a relationship. Often communication gap is cited as one of the major reasons by family counsellors for marriages falling apart. Effective communication in a relationship can increase affinity within members of that relation; similarly,

ineffective communication may decrease affinity and weaken a social relationship.

3. *Influence function*: Communication is a powerful tool and can bring about social change at the local and global levels. Through communication we can influence others and get influenced and even adapt to the influences of others. An advertisement commercial on TV is a communication attempt to influence its audience to buy a product. Similarly social movements of change may be influenced by an individual's or social group's act of communication through campaigns or speeches.

4. *Decision function*: Communication serves as an important decision making tool. Be it small or big, any decision requires us to think and communicate our concerns about the outcomes with ourselves and with others. We talk, we discuss, we evaluate before we arrive at taking a final call. All through this process of introspection and discussion we have been communicating to arrive at a decision we want to take.

5. *Confirmation function*: Perhaps, an important function of communication is that it lets us associate and disassociate with a practice, belief or change. Communication helps us in giving the nod and adhering to the decision we have taken and adapt to the change accordingly. For example, a proposal presented in front of the finance committee by the accountant of the company needs an approval or disapproval. The committee's decision so communicated will guide her/him to proceed in the same direction or change and enhance the proposed plan of action.

Figure 1.3: Functions of Communication

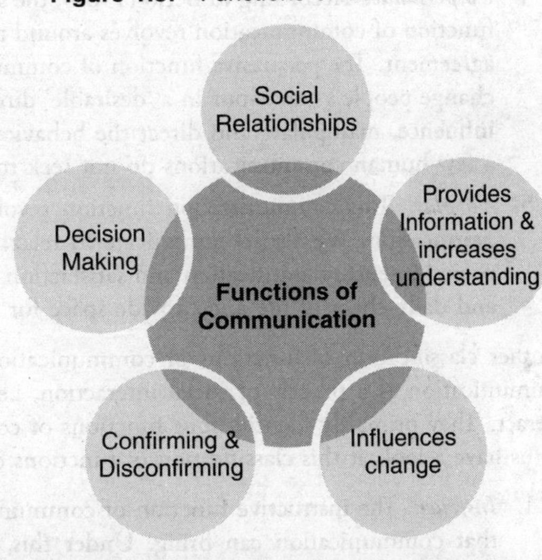

Source: Created by the authors.

Functions can also be understood as an interrelation between communication and inherent motivation. DeVito (2006) explains that the functions of communication are related to the satisfaction of our various needs and purposes. He identified five purposes of communication and these are explained here:

1. *To discover*: The purpose of discovering revolves around the need to know, acquire knowledge and learn; every individual needs to acquire knowledge about what is going on in the environment which concerns their lives. One also needs to know about one's own self and learn skills to adapt and adjust oneself to the environment. Hence communication helps us in providing an interface to create and access this knowledge and apply it for our personal and professional growth.

2. *To relate*: This function of communication revolves around the need to form relationships, relate to others and interact. It helps us interact and relate to others in various settings—be it in the family, or with friends, peers or colleagues. This further helps in maintaining individual, societal or organisational stability and identity.

3. *To help*: This function of communication revolves around the need to console, help, befriend, feel needed and gain satisfaction. Communication enables us to cater to the needs of the self and others. We guide, direct and instruct others and ourselves through our communications. We criticise, express empathy, support and even advise people. In fact, those who are hierarchically superior in the family, society or organisation, often initiate communication either for the purpose of informing their subordinates or for the purpose of telling them, what to do, how to do, when to do, etc.

4. *To persuade*: According to Berlo (1960), the sole purpose of communication is to influence people. This function of communication revolves around the need to control, influence, gain compliance and secure agreement. The persuasive function of communication, i.e. to induce people, is extremely important to change people's behaviour in a 'desirable' direction. Communication can be used effectively to control, influence, manipulate and direct the behaviour and attitude of others. However, it is noteworthy that a few human communications do not seek to influence change.
5. *To play*: This communication function revolves around the need for diversion, pleasure and sensory gratification. We also communicate to relax, enjoy, laugh and have fun. Leisure/play communication provides sensory gratification and satisfaction. This also helps us to distract ourselves from the pressures and daily chaos of life and provide space for self rejuvenation and contentment.

Another classification of functions of communication is given by Dahama and Bhatnagar (2003) who view communication as a process of social interaction, i.e. in a communication situation two or more individuals interact. They primarily identify four functions of communication—instruct, inform, influence and integrate. Let us have a look at this classification of functions of communication now.

1. *Instruct*: The instructive function of communication deals with the commanding nature and authority that communication can bring. Under this, the communicator transmits instruction with necessary directives and guidance to the next level, so as to enable them to accomplish their particular tasks. This function of communication is most prevalent in organisations. In this, instructions basically flow from top to the lower level.
2. *Inform*: This function of communication reflects the potential of communication to inform and create awareness. It is used to inform an individual or a group about a particular task or certain policies and procedures, or more simply even the weather forecast. Information passes from one level to another via a channel. Information can flow vertically, horizontally and diagonally across the organisation. Becoming informed, or informing others, is the main purpose of communication.
3. *Influence*: Another important function of communication is to influence. A complete communication process is necessary in influencing others or being influenced. An individual who has the potential to influence others can easily convince others to adapt or change certain behaviours. Hence, this particular function of communication implies the provision of feedback which reflects the effect of communication.
4. *Integrate*: Last but not least communication performs the function of integration. Integration happens at all levels, at interpersonal relationship level, at a family/organisational level, at the national and international levels. At all levels the purpose to integrate may be a common goal, such as peace, conflict resolution, achievement of harmony, etc. The integration function of communication mainly focuses on building cohesiveness within a setting, be it a family or a class or different departments within a large organisation. It helps in the unification of different management and group functions. It could relate to building bilateral relationships between two nations or a consensus on any international treaty.

The various functions involve changes that result from communication. Thus, they may be viewed as the outcomes or effects of communication. They may also be considered as the reasons why we communicate. Thus, if communication produces the desired change or adaptation to change, then it is functional or effective; if it is not then it is ineffective or dysfunctional.

SUMMARY

- Communication is a process involving sending and sharing of messages and information. It forms an indispensable part of human existence.

- Communication is the mode of transmitting information, culture, mode, emotions, thoughts, reactions as well as data in the form of symbols, figures and diagrams. Good communication reduces friction and promotes positivity.
- Communication is of many types. It happens at various levels and these are known as the levels of communication transactions.
- The key elements of the communication process are sender, message, channel, receiver and feedback.
- Communication is both an art and a science. While there is a scientific body of knowledge and set of principles that guide the communication process, each individual has a unique way of his own to practice communication.
- Communication has a wide scope and can be applied in diverse fields. Appropriate communication skills are essential for career development in almost each and every field.
- Communication is historical, in that it has evolved from age-old methods of communication. From the Classical Period to contemporary times, communication over the ages has progressed and made commendable advancements. Technology today has made communication much simpler and accessible to the common man.
- Communication is intertwined with culture. Culture and communication are interrelated. Communicating between different cultures may give rise to conflicts and requires essential communication skills.
- Human communication is based on a set of principles which are called the central postulates of human communication. These form the foundation for all interactive communication among human beings.
- Communication performs many functions—it builds and sustains our relations, it helps us in taking decisions, it is able to influence others and provides us information and improves our understanding of the concepts.

KEY WORDS

Communication: A process of sharing experiences till it becomes a common possession. It modifies the disposition of both the communicator and the receiver interacting in communication.

Levels of communication: Messages can be transacted at different levels depending on the number of people involved in communication or on the basis of context. These are known as the different levels of communication.

Rhetoric: Refers to the focus on persuasion and argumentation as skills. Aristotle examined the underlying elements of persuasion through public speaking through his work *Rhetoric*. He identified five canons of public speaking which were invention, arrangement, style, memory and delivery.

Classical period: This period spanned between the 5th century BC and the 4th century AD. Speech or oral communication was a dominant form of communication in this period.

Medieval and Renaissance period: The medieval period lasted from 400 AD to 1400 AD, while the Renaissance Period spanned from 1400 AD to 1600 AD. The particular highlight of these periods was that communication was no more limited to rhetoric, but extended to preaching and teaching.

Modern period: This period spanned between 1600 AD and 1900 AD and constituted the modern era of communication. It saw the advent of democratic and other political reforms and many powerful politicians emerged. This period gave importance to public speaking and mass communication.

Contemporary period: This period started in the 20th century AD and continues till date. It thrives on the development of new-age technology. It is during this period that computer technology has made inroads into lives of people across the globe.

Culture: Refers to the pattern of shared assumptions that have been invented, discovered or developed by a given group and are taught to new members as the correct way to think, perceive and behave.

EXERCISES

1. Define 'Communication' and briefly discuss the nature of communication.
2. Enlist and discuss the principles of human communication.
3. Go back to the first few days of your life in college, and examine what the different types of communication you indulged in. What has been the impact of those communications in your present academic and personal life?
4. Enlist the elements of the communication process. Illustrate and delineate the process of communication.
5. Discuss the scope of communication in contemporary society.
6. Briefly discuss the Classical Period in the history of human communication.
7. What role does communication play in your life?
8. What are your views on communication being a science and an art? Justify your answer with suitable examples.
9. Delineate the various types of communication interactions and levels of transactions.

REFERENCES

Barker, L. L., *Communication*, New Jersey: Prentice-Hall, 1981.

Barker, L. L. and R. G. Deborah, *Communication*, eighth edition, Boston, MA: Pearson, 2001,

Berlo, D., *Process of Communication: An Introduction to Theory and Practice*, New York: Holt, Rinehart and Winston, 1960.

Chhibber, Narinder K., 'Fast Growth of Mobile Communications in India: Lessons for Emerging Markets', available at http://classic.marshall.usc.edu/assets/006/5576.pdf (accessed 15 July 2014).

Dahama, O. P. and O. P. Bhatnagar, *Education and Communication for Development*, New Delhi: Oxford and IBH Publishing House, 2003.

DeVito, A. J., *Introduction to Human Communication*, New Jersey: Pearson Education, 2006.

Dewey, John, *Democracy and Education*, available at http://genius.com/albums/John-dewey/Democracy-and-education (accessed 31 March 2016), 2014.

Jandt, Fred E., *An Introduction to Intercultural Communication: Identities in a Global Community*, Seventh edition, California: SAGE Publications, 2013.

Lunenburg, Fred C., 'Communication: The Process, Barriers, and Improving Effectiveness', *Schooling* 1.1 (2010).

Leagans, J. Paul, 'Extension Programme Building' in *Extension Education in Community Development*, New Delhi: Directorate of Extension, Government of India, 1961.

McQuail, D., *Mass Communication Theory: An Introduction*, sixth edition, California: SAGE Publications, 2010.

Patri, V. R. and N. Patri, *Essentials of Effective Communication*, New Delhi: Greenspan, 2002.

Mcintosh, Perry and Richard A. Luecke, *Interpersonal Communication Skills in the Workplace*, New York: American Management Association, 2008.

Schramm, Wilbur, 'How Communication Works' in *The Process and Effects of Mass Communication*, edited by Wilbur Schramm, 3–10, Urbana, IL: University of Illinois Press, 1954.

Zeuschner, R., *Communicating Today: The Essentials*, Boston: Allyn & Bacon, 2003.

ONLINE SOURCES

http://www.jblearning.com/samples/0763755575/55577_CH02.pdf (accessed 20 May 2014)

http://www.academia.edu/4358901/managerial-skill-development.pdf (accessed 15 May 2014)

http://webcache.googleusercontent.com/search?q=cache:http://localcircles.org/2012/10/04/how-to-have-a-one-to-one-conversation/ (accessed 21 September 2015)

http://anugrahillahi.wordpress.com/2012/10/05/komunikasi-intrapribadi-intrapersonal-communication/ (accessed 12 August 2015)

http://h2oforlife.files.wordpress.com/2011/01/c11.jpg (accessed 25 February 2016)

http://webcache.googleusercontent.com/search?q=cache:http://www.unescocat.org/en/news/2011/07/15/diversity-for-dialogue-and-intercultural-communication (accessed 13 February 2016)

http://clas.uiowa.edu/sjmc/ (accessed 21 September 2015)

http://educators.medievaltimes.com/1-2-communication.html (accessed 31 March 2016)

2

TYPES OF COMMUNICATION

HIGHLIGHTS

- Levels of communication transactions
  - Intrapersonal communication
  - Interpersonal communication
  - Small group communication
  - Large group communication
  - Public communication
  - Mass communication
  - Intercultural communication
- Verbal and non-verbal communication
- Interpersonal and mass communication
- Mediated and unmediated communication
- Synchronous and asynchronous communication
- Formal and informal communication

A woman at the bus stop constantly looking towards one direction as she waits for her bus to arrive, a man in a bus constantly staring at a young girl sitting next to him, a small girl crying in the market with her hand pointed at her favourite toy, a teacher in a classroom stopping in between her lecture and looking at a bunch of boys seated at the back making noise. Have you have witnessed any of the situations above? If yes, do you think they communicate something? Yes, all these situations are communicative in nature. We might often think that communication is all about saying things aloud or writing thoughts down; however many a time our actions, body language, gestures and clothes can communicate way more than the words.

This chapter will unfold various systems of classifying communication. In later chapters you will study about each one of these types in much more detail. Also, we will discuss the various levels of communication transactions we participate in everyday.

The classification of the types of communication interactions is given below:

1. Based on levels of communication transactions
   a. Intrapersonal communication
   b. Interpersonal communication
   c. Small group communication

d. Large group communication
e. Public communication
f. Mass communication
g. Intercultural communication

2. Based on signs, symbols and language systems
   a. Verbal communication
      i. Oral
      ii. Written
   b. Non-verbal communication
      i. Kinesics (Movement)
      ii. Proxemics (Space)
      iii. Para language
      iv. Seating arrangements
      v. Clothing
      vi. Touch
      vii. Smell and Taste
      viii. Artifacts (Objects)
      ix. Colours
      x. Time
3. Based on the number of people involved
   a. Interpersonal communication
   b. Mass communication
4. Based on the participation level of the communicators
   a. Mediated communication
   b. Unmediated communication
5. Based on the time period involved
   a. Synchronous communication
   b. Asynchronous communication
6. Based on the organisational structures in which communication takes place
   a. Formal communication
      i. Downward
      ii. Upward
   b. Informal communication (Grapevine)

Now, let us discuss these classifications in detail.

BASED ON LEVELS OF COMMUNICATION TRANSACTIONS

In this section understanding will be built around the levels of communication transactions. These transactions differ from each other in terms of the number of people involved, type of channel used, kind of message disseminated—all of it depending on the prime objective of communication. It starts from the individual level and slowly grows beyond and involves many people forming a pyramid-like structure. Let us imagine a few situations—a group of friends interacting in the canteen, an interview being telecast on TV, a conversation with a friend over the phone. All of these have something in common. In all the three instances, an idea/message/perspective is exchanged via different mediums among varied numbers of people involved in the process of communication. A message can be communicated through many ways to a range of people.

Figure 2.1: Levels of Communication Transactions

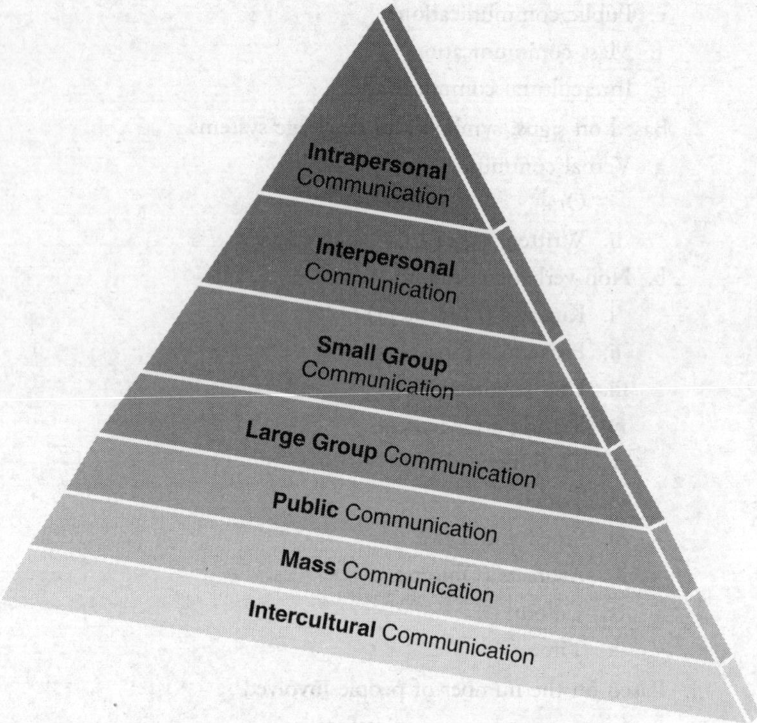

Source: Created by the authors.

Intrapersonal Communication

How often have you found yourself day-dreaming, introspecting about an issue that is of concern. You may not have uttered a word but your mind communicated with your heart. Intrapersonal communication is simply defined as communication with oneself, i.e. the receiver and the sender is the same individual. You learn to evaluate and persuade yourself, give reasons to make decisions. In all communication transactions the self/individual is very important. Intrapersonal communication helps form the 'self' which includes many dimensions like the physical self, the emotional self and habits. It also leaves an impact on personal orientation (value, belief and attitude) in all the whole personality is reflective of intrapersonal communication. Our sex, race, stature, abilities, disabilities, personality, intelligence and variables affect how we respond to messages of other people and also how we create messages for other people.

Interpersonal Communication

Interaction between two or more people is called interpersonal communication. In this form, you learn about others and reveal yourself to others. This type of interaction can take place between new acquaintances, old friends, colleagues, or family members anywhere through any channel. Through interpersonal communication we establish, maintain, and sometimes destroy (and even repair) relationships. The source and receiver in this form of communication are within each other's physical presence. The source in this communication setting can be one or more individuals, as can be the receiver(s). A variety of channels are available for use.

Image 2.1: Intrapersonal Communication

Source: Authors.

The receiver can see, hear, and perhaps even smell and touch the source. In addition, interpersonal messages can be private or public in nature. Feedback is immediate and makes use of visual and auditory channels. Interpersonal communication is far from simple, but it represents the least complicated setting.

Image 2.2: Interpersonal Communication

Source: Authors.

Image 2.3: Dyadic Communication

Source: Authors.

When communication is shared between two people it is called a dyad. Dyadic communication is one of the most common forms of interpersonal communication. The sender and the receiver both share responsibility to generate and share feedback for the process to be ongoing.

Small Group Communication

A group can be defined as a number of people who come together with a common goal and act together to accomplish it. These groups are formed to satisfy important social needs, provide information and knowledge and security (personal, social, professional) and boost self-concept. Groups are made to solve problems, develop new ideas, share knowledge and experiences. Small group communication is face-to-face interaction among 3–15 people who share a common goal or purpose. There are many types of small groups, which fulfill different purpose in an individual's life.

Image 2.4: Small Group Communication

Source: Authors.

For example, social groups (such as the family) that take care of our social needs like safety and solidarity, self esteem; work groups (such as the classroom) which are task oriented, resourceful, gives feedback; and decision making groups (such as students union) which solve problems and take decisions.

Some important characteristics of small group communication are:

- *Interdependence*: Group members influence each other's values, goals and attitudes. As groups become closer, members build trust, depend more on each other for advice, favours, tasks, etc.
- *Common perceptions*: They must share their views, discuss concerning matters and present their decisions and themselves as a group to others.
- *Motivation*: Group members must have some reason for belonging to the group. There must be some need that is met through membership.
- *Goals*: All groups should have a goal in mind and all the members should focus towards that goal.
- *Systematic*: Groups have a system. They have communication networks and patterns within to avoid confusion.
- *Complex*: The interaction within groups is extremely complicated. Group members deal with each other on at least three levels—with each other as individuals (different personalities), according to their roles in the group (distribution of tasks), and according to their roles in society and/or the larger organisation that the small group is part of.
- *Dynamic*: Group members get to know each other better, both as individuals and according to the way they function in the group. Conflicts also arise over time, and this influences group interaction.

Large Group Communication

This type of communication generally takes place in an organisational set up. Such a system may be of any size. For example, a number of people gather at a place for an exhibition or a conference. Also, institutions are run by a large group of people who work together for a common goal, for example, the administration and faculty members of a college, the management and employees of a restaurant are all members of a large group. Organisations develop their specific system (model) of communication that determines the norms (who and how) for individuals to interact with each other.

Image 2.5: Large Group Communication

Source: Department of DCE, Lady Irwin College.

Some of the characteristics of large group communication are:

- Hierarchical systems that are not fully interactive, and communication within them flows primarily in one direction and not always reciprocal.
- Direct links do not exist amongst many of the people within the system
- Long-lasting system
- Change is not inherent in hierarchical systems, i.e. influence of external and internal communications may not be uniform or may not have any effect at all.
- Can act as source, receiver or channel of communication when interacting with other systems.

Public Communication

A political leader's speech after a rally, prime minister's address to the citizens on Independence Day, a trade union member's address to other members in the event of a strike or a principal's speech to her/his students and teachers on the occasion of the founder's day, all of these are examples of public communication. In all the cases one dominant person talks to several others. This type of communication is referred to as public communication. Here the number of members of the audience is not important; it could vary from tens to hundreds to thousands. The most important

Image 2.6: Public Communication

Source: 'Rajagopal speaking to 25,000 people, Janadesh 2007' by Ekta Parishad (Wikimedia Commons; CC BY-SA 3.0).

identification is that, there is only one sender and several receivers. It could be used to inform, persuade and motivate people, in one go. Large numbers are targeted, the message is sent from a source with an intention to influence people's attitudes, behaviour or practices.

Image 2.7: Mass Communication

Source: 'The BBC newsroom at Broadcasting House in London' by Deskana (Wikimedia Commons; CC BY-SA 3.0).

Mass Communication

When a message has to be transmitted from its source/sender/encoder to its destination/audience, the role of mass communication comes into play. Mass communication involves spreading of message to the masses through rapid means of distribution at a relatively inexpensive cost to the consumer. Generally, two types of channels are used: (*a*) print media, which includes newspapers, magazines and books; and (*b*) electronic media which includes TV, internet, radio and films. Through both of these channels, the message is transported from its original source to a widespread audience. Through mass communication, audiences are entertained, informed and persuaded by the media. Mass communication systems lack the full potential for interaction. These systems are primarily linear, i.e. there is a one-way communication with little or no opportunity for receivers to have an impact on the sources.

Mass communication performs many functions. It gives information about everything under the sun. It is a versatile source of entertainment. It also plays a critical role in forming opinions among people about various issues; it helps in propaganda and agenda setting. All these have a great impact on our everyday lives. We will discuss these functions in further detail in Chapter Fourteen.

Activity

Who is your favourite public speaker or writer (either national, international, political or social)? Identify one speech or write up of their's and critically analyse and evaluate it. Write a brief note with your observations and critical comments. (100 words)

(Take the following questions into consideration while you evaluate: What was the main issue? Does it flow well? Were you able to understand? How informative was it? Did it persuade you enough to take action? Was it entertaining? Did it create an urge within you to read/hear more about it? Do you feel that any other aspect could be incorporated?)

Intercultural Communication

Intercultural communication is the interaction among people belonging to different cultures—different religious, social, ethnic and educational backgrounds. It aims to share information across different cultures and social groups. Through intercultural communication, you come to understand new ways of behaving and begin to see the tremendous variety in human thought and experience. Intercultural communication is sometimes used synonymously with cross-cultural communication. When the receiver of the message is a person from a different culture, the receiver uses information from his or her culture to interpret the message. The message that the receiver interprets may be very different from what the speaker intended. Even non-verbal expressions vary across cultures and can also hinder smooth communication process. Intercultural communication can be improved by keeping an open mind, and by being empathetic, self-aware, tolerant, sensitive and flexible towards others.

Image 2.8: Intercultural Communication

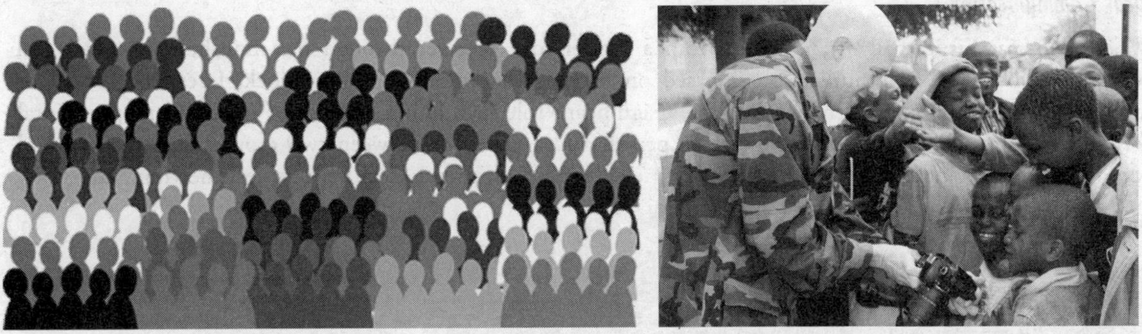

Source: pixabay (CC0 Public Domain); '090207-N-3875H-051 DAKAR, Senegal (Feb. 7, 2009)' US Navy photo by Lt. Dough High (Wikimedia Commons; CC0 Public Domain).

Except for intrapersonal communication all other levels of communication can be intercultural. Intercultural communication is very helpful in building cultural understanding and cross-cultural communication, cross-cultural negotiation, multicultural conflict resolution, customer service, business and organisational communication.

We will discuss this further in Chapter Five.

VERBAL AND NON-VERBAL COMMUNICATION

In communication two major forms are widely used—verbal and non-verbal communication. Both are distinct in nature and form but are mostly used simultaneously for sending and receiving messages. Let us study about them in detail.

Verbal Communication

The use of words in the form of speaking or writing is referred to as verbal communication. The human species is fortunate enough to have evolved language through which verbal communication has become possible. Humans have the ability to give their reactions meaning by converting them into symbols which are understood by others. Human beings listen, think, process and learn language, which in itself is quite a complex process. Humans slowly, understand and adopt effective use of language.

Image 2.9: Verbal Communication

Source: Authors.

While growing up, a child is exposed to different type of sounds and voices, as a part of learning behaviour they begin to imitate voices, they learn sounds, words, formation and gradually process meaning and acquire the skill of language eventually. Language is the most important tool of communication. Though most of the time is spent in listening to others and thinking, most critical interactions are based on verbal communication.

Types of Verbal Communication

Verbal communication can be further subdivided into two parts:

Oral Communication

When a message is verbally transmitted from a sender to a receiver through the mouth, it is called oral communication. Oral communication is based on language as a main building block. It can be formal or informal in its nature of occurrence. It plays a significant role in building a sense of trust and rapport. Oral communication can be between two persons, person and a group or between two groups. Examples of oral communication include face-to-face interaction, telephonic chat, speech, lecture, business meetings, etc.

Advantages of oral communication are:

- It is time saving.
- It is spontaneous.
- Useful in solving disagreements.
- It has high persuasive power.
- The speaker can mould the conversation according to the audience's reaction to make them comfortable.
- It enables quick decision making.
- Can be used to transfer private and confidential information.

Limitations of oral communication include:

- Lengthy conversations are a hassle.
- Non-verbal expressions (audience) can influence the chain of thought and the message to be disseminated.
- It is not sufficient especially in work-related formal communication.
- Lacks organisation.
- Can lead to misunderstanding.

Written Communication

Any form of communication that entails written words is referred to as written communication. Written communication is more formal, serious, and is based on certain rules of grammar which are specific to various/ different languages. It is a professional way of communication. In today's world communication through writing is the need of the hour. It is the most common form of communication in the professional world. Hence, these days it is essential for all professionals to develop effective written communication skills and to encourage the same in all employees. The information age has changed the way in which we communicate, and has placed an increasing emphasis on written communication.Written communication includes emails, letters, reports, advertisements, news releases, instant messages, etc.

Advantages of written communication include:

- Serves as evidence of an event, i.e. written proof
- Ambiguities are reduced which leaves minimum scope for misunderstanding

Image 2.10: Written Communication

Source: Authors.

- Written messages are easy to transmit
- Can be disseminated to a large number of people
- Memory retention is greater

Limitations of written communication are:

- It is very time consuming, can delay the process of communication
- The art of right expression is important
- Requires precision and correct grammar
- Immediate feedback and clarification is not possible
- Lacks secrecy

For effective written communication one should be clear, accurate, concise and polite while conveying.

Variations in Verbal Communication

Communication is a quintessential part of our everyday lives that we do not realise how big a difference it makes. Verbal and non-verbal communications are based on certain principles of communication. When these principles are common to the people involved in the process of communication they help in making inferences about the speaker's feelings, perceptions and attitude in a much better way. Over the years experts have recognised various components of non-verbal communication like gestures, postures, eye movement and have identified that these play a critical role in communication. However not much attention has been focused on the variations in the use of words and their psychological significance in verbal communication. The same words said with a few other words can make a lot of difference. For instance, when a teacher asks a student 'Why can't you focus in the class?' (s)he depicts anger. On the other hand if (s)he conveys the same message but gently as, 'Child, what is wrong? Why are you not able to focus in class?' then probably the child will try to mend her/his behaviour and feel sorry for her/his conduct.

If you notice carefully, just by adding a few more words the latter sentence has become more suggestive, polite and open in nature. Thus it's not only our tone and pitch which makes a difference but also the way we place words in verbal communication. The placement of words are not only indicative of a speaker's feelings for the listener but also make a difference in receiving a reply, as the listener might reply in the same way as the speaker. The variations in verbal communication include some linguistic components such as pronouns, tenses, words used to refer to a particular object. Object here refers to the main area/subject/theme around which communication is built. It could be a person, an event, experience or work. Through verbalised communication, words perform certain functions like:

- Assign the object being communicated about
- Establish the relationship among objects being communicated about
- Specify the relationship of the communicator to the objects
- Implicitly establish relationship of the communicator to the entire communication or parts of it

Verbal communication is very dynamic in nature, even for a fixed condition there can be many kinds of possible patterns. All these variations can be also served as a basis for making inferences about the communicator's experience of an event, the communicator's relationship to the addressee and the communicator's relationship to the communication process.

Non-verbal Communication

Many a time we do not communicate through spoken or written words, but through our body language and eye contact. Our gestures say a lot more than words could. This is regarded as non-verbal communication. It involves the use of symbols—such as gestures, facial expressions, eye contact, tone of voice, use of space and touch—to communicate information. There are times when we try to hide our true feelings, emotions or expressions but end up expressing them through non-verbal communication. Humans use non-verbal communication to supplement verbal communication. Let us discuss some of its important functions.

Functions of Non-verbal Communication

Everyday, consciously or unconsciously we give a lot of non-verbal signals. Non-verbal communication is dynamic in nature; on the one hand it helps control the flow of verbal messages, it helps lay emphasis on the point being communicated, and on the other it helps contradict verbal messages (if the sender wants to), for instance winking of the eye indicates pun. Some important functions performed by non-verbal communication are:

1. *Repeating*: Repeating refers to a non-verbal message which reinforces a verbal message that has already been communicated. For instance, if a teacher asks you a question, you give your answer verbally and simultaneously also nod your head in a 'yes' or a 'no'. This function is referred to as repeating as you repeat and reinforce your answer. In such a case either an oral answer or a simple nod would have solved the purpose; however many times this function is not performed without a thought or intent, and we perform it unconsciously.
2. *Substituting*: This function comes into play when it is difficult to use words to communicate. There are times when we want to speak a lot, or on the contrary when we are short of words, we substitute our feelings and emotions through non-verbal signals. When signs and symbols substitute words it's referred to as substituting. For instance, when we feel demeaned or when we feel ecstatic, we might not express through words but through gestures. Some non-verbal signs are universally popular and accepted (for example, 'thumbs up') and some are culture-specific (for example, 'namaste' in India).

3. *Complementing*: This function of non-verbal communication is noticed in two kinds of situations. First, there are many processes and techniques which require complementary non-verbal signals along with verbal messages. For instance, demonstration of anything like a cooking recipe, craft activity, dance, form of exercises. Second, in situations where one goes through complementary emotions or feelings. For example, getting emotional while winning or losing an award. If we lose, we feel happy and applaud for the winner, but at the same time we might also get emotional about our own loss.
4. *Deceiving/Revealing*: This function is performed when we don't want to hurt feelings or unnecessarily deceive people especially those who are dear to us. For instance, you may not like your friend's new dress, just to avoid hurting his/her emotions you might lie and praise the dress. If the person on the other side is sensitive to communication they may be able to pick the contrary behaviour. Our face may lie but other body parts do not lie as much. If much attention is paid to the other body parts one might be able to catch the contrary expressions, as our other body parts (hands, legs, eye contact) unconsciously behave differently due to nervousness and leave clues of our lack of confidence.
5. *Regulating*: Since childhood we are trained to not to interrupt elders in a conversation and many more such behaviours. When we are in a conversation we receive and give non-verbal signals which convey our agreement, disagreement, our urge to speak or need to stop, etc. Common signs include a nod, proper eye contact, movement of lips, etc. Through these signs a flow, a rhythm is maintained in a conversation.
6. *Accenting*: This includes a mix of nods, shrugs, blinks, etc. by emphasising a few words in a sentence, and enabling a change in the way the information is interpreted by the receiver. Words are referred to as accented when a particular word or phrase in a sentence is said in a varied pitch or stress. This changes the whole meaning, for instance: 'I will *study* tomorrow positively'; 'I will study tomorrow *positively*' and '*I* will study tomorrow positively'.

Types of Non-verbal Communication

Non-verbal communication is probably most easily explained by identifying the various features which the body uses for passing any message. They are as follows:

1. *Kinesics (Movement)*: Kinesics refers to the interpretation and understanding of body expression, language, and posture movement of either a part of the body or the body as a whole. The human body is versatile and expressive. It communicates a lot through its various parts. Our body sends across non-verbal messages to others, through body movements, facial expressions, eye contact, etc. Kinesics can be understood under two major heads as below:
   a. *Body expressions*: As our body is unique and every person has her/his own individualism, intentionally or unintentionally we send many non-verbal messages. They have been categorised and understood in terms of eye contact, facial expressions, hand gestures, movements, etc. Specialists like Paul Ekman and Wallace Friesen have given a classification of particular body expressions based on the functions of non-verbal communication discussed above. Let us now discuss the five body expressions given by Ekman and Friesen (2013).
      i. *Emblems*: These are the signs that communicate a message other than the topic of the current conversation. For instance, if someone is giving a speech and you are sitting in the last row. Suppose the person is not audible to you. You send out a signal which lets her/him know that they need to raise their voice. This signal sent by you is absolutely unrelated to the topic of the discussion but is able to convey your message.
      ii. *Illustrators*: These are non-verbal signs which add and complement the verbal communication. These may include pointing towards an object or a place, showing direction, a specific hand gesture of numbers or any other body expression.

iii. *Regulators*: These are signs used to regulate and maintain the flow of non-verbal communication. Signs such as eye gazes, nods, the smile, the frown, raised eyebrows, etc. assist participants to engage in a healthy conversation and smooth transitions.

iv. *Affect displays*: You must have heard of the situation, 'Smiling on the outside but crying on the inside'. Affect displays are referred to those signs which convey our internal emotional state. These are not always related to the current conversation. These are depicted through facial expressions, the eyes and other body parts.

v. *Adaptors*: Scratching the ears, holding the forehead or rubbing the eyes are a few movements which have now come to be recognised independently of bodily needs, they convey a meaning. These are adaptors that help us relieve tension or stress. People have distinct ways to use adaptors, as you may have noticed—some people twist or curl their hair, shake their legs while being seated, scratch their head, and so on. Adaptors are used at times of nervousness and as involuntary ticks. People who are in the habit of using a particular adaptor may not even realise how frequently they repeat that action, and that they are noticeable to others observing them.

b. *Body language*: Have you ever noticed the way you walk when you are feeling happy and joyous as compared to the time when you are sad or depressed? Our body is a true reflection of our state of mind. When a person is sad, (s)he walks with the head down and low energy, on the other hand if the person is happy (s)he walks with the chin up, head held high and with high energy and a smile. Similarly, body language also conveys about a person's openness and closed behaviour. Sitting cross-legged with arms tightly packed to the chest suggests a closed behaviour, vis-à-vis open arms and free body language which is indicative of an open personality. Body language can be understood with the help of following categorisation.

c. *Facial expression*: Face is the major source of communicating for non-verbal messages. In face-to-face interaction, the facial expressions play a critical role in transmission of messages. Many emotions like joy, sorrow, anger, fear and surprise are very easily and deeply depicted on the face. Actors and dancers use their face skilfully to display emotions.

Eye contact: The eyes are capable of revealing a lot about a person and their feelings. Eye movements are a natural and essential part of the communication process as they have the power to convey depth. Eye contact involves eye gaze, blink and movement. Eyes also communicate a lot of messages. Eye contact can serve different purposes at different times. When contact is properly maintained or a person tries to maintain it, it signifies interest in the information being shared or initiates a beginning of a new relationship. However, prolonged eye contact can arouse the feeling of discomfort. When it

Image 2.11: Types of Facial Expressions

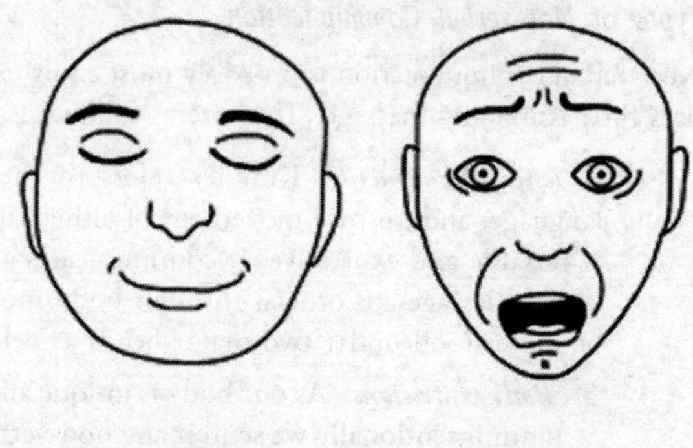

Source: 'Line drawings of faces as per emotion' by Barry Langdon-Lassagne (Wikimedia Commons; CC BY-SA 3.0).

is not maintained during a conversation, it could signify shame or a feeling of guilt. People often blink more rapidly when they feel distressed or uncomfortable. Normally we maintain eye contact with someone who is known or someone we intend to know. It is normal to gaze and maintain eye contact when both the individuals like each other's company and share things, while it is generally avoided with strangers.

Eye gazing also serves the function for feedback. Gazing at times signifies approval and acceptance, on the other hand it could also hamper the feeling of friendliness and convey a sense of disapproval depending upon the situation. For instance, a student gazing at her/his teacher's face after showing a wonderfully-made model expects approval and praise. A stranger gazing at a young girl in a public place could invoke disapproval. Through eye contact people are able to express their sentiments. The duration of a gaze depicts our mind more effectively than words could. In general, it is noticed that people establish more eye contact while listening and in situations of approval.

d. *Posture*: Our bodily posture also serves as an important part of body language. Posture refers to how we hold our body. Posture has the power to depict how a person is feeling, their state of mind, personality characteristics like confidence or docility, and even power structures especially where power and status differentials are large and understood by all. Sitting up straight, for example, may indicate that a person is focused and paying attention to what's going on.

2. *Proxemics (Space)*: The study of the cultural, behavioural, and sociological aspects of spatial distances between individuals is called proxemics. It involves personal space and territoriality as ways of communicating.

   a. *Personal space*: Humans are social animals and like to be in other people's company to gain a sense of belongingness and reassurance from them. On the other hand, we also like to maintain some physical distance between ourselves and others. Personal space distances vary according to the relationship involved. For instance, with friends we stand or sit close together but with strangers—especially of different sex—we try and maintain a distance. This distance also depends on cultures that people belong to.

   b. *Territoriality*: Territoriality refers to a pattern of behaviour wherein people mark a certain area against intrusion, from others. For instance, the office of the college's director is exclusive in nature and design; one cannot walk in without prior permission or an appointment.

3. *Para-language*: The use of volume, tone, rate, pitch, voice, etc. used to add and convey meaning to your words is referred to as para-language. It deals with 'how' a message is conveyed, rather than 'what' is being said. Emphasising some words through variations in the tone and the pitch used makes a lot of difference. You must have noticed that the meaning of a sentence changes the way it is said. The alterations made by the speaker in the pitch, rhythm, speed and volume results in a different meaning altogether. So while the content remains the same, the meaning would become different. An example can be a simple sentence like, 'Oh! You are not back yet,' which could show concern if spoken softly, however, if words are emphasised and said in a loud manner, they may sound aggressive and demanding a justification.

   The following are some components which affect para-language:

   a. *Pitch*: This refers to the frequency of the sound. Pitches are mostly categorised as low and high pitches. A higher pitch is usually associated with tension or disturbance whereas lower pitch signifies softness and control.

   b. *Rate*: This refers to the speed of words spoken per minute. A speed of about 90–120 words per minute is considered ideal, but there are cultural and sub-cultural variations in rates. Variations in rate at which words are spoken help create and maintain interest, while a constant rate creates boredom.

c. *Volume*: This refers to the loudness of speech. Besides the individual's voice quality, volume indicates power in communication. For instance, if youngsters speak with their elders in a high volume it conveys disrespect towards them.

4. *Seating arrangements*: We sit differently in diverse situations, depending on the seating arrangement. Seating arrangement encourages or discourages communication pattern between individuals. For instance some spatial arrangements like a round table conference and a family seated on a dining table for a meal encourages conversation as all the members face each other. Some seating arrangements like those in a classroom force people to sit in a manner in which they face away from each other, thereby obstructing communication between students and encouraging only communication between the teacher and each student.

5. *Touch*: This is one of the most elementary forms of communication. When a baby is born, the only form of communication experienced and understood by it is the power of touch much before other forms of non-verbal communication are learnt. A touch can communicate different feelings and emotions, for example a sudden touch of grasping someone's hand could communicate fear or high anxiety. A type of touch depicts different meanings in different relationships. Majorly, three kinds of touch have been identified:

Image 2.12: Touch

Source: Authors.

    a. *Professional touch*: This is associated with one's profession. For example, the touch of a life guard, spa therapists, physiotherapist, etc.
    b. *Social/polite touch*: These are social and personal in nature, and can be done to greet, welcome, bid goodbye, etc. For example, the handshake.
    c. *Personal-intimate touch*: These symbolise close levels of intimacy. For example, handholding, hugging, etc.

6. *Clothing*: Though clothes fulfill the function of protecting us from the weather, they also help in acceptance in social groups, ensure group identification, self-assertion, and more importantly also convey a lot about our personality, choices, tastes and interests. Clothes contribute to the first impression a person makes, and which in turn influences later interactions. For instance, one consciously dresses well for a job interview. A certain type of clothing also gives signals about one's profession—for example, in college, students dress up differently from teachers so that their identity gets established and people recognise them as who they are.

7. *Smell and taste*: Do you have any favourite smell? Or is there any smell which makes you feel sad or low? Do you associate a smell with a specific feeling or emotion? Smells too, like other forms of communication, convey different messages for different emotions. For example, the smell of frying sweets in the market reminds us of festive season, or the stench from an open drain reminds us of filth and may make us leave the place as early as possible. The same applies to taste. We immediately react through non-verbal expressions when we taste something very sour, spicy or bitter. Thus our sense of smell and taste plays a role in communication.

8. *Artifacts*: These include objects, jewellery, automobile, gadgets a person owns. They also communicate about one's personality, economic status, profession and self-concept. As soon as we learn to associate

material things with humans, places, time period they disclose a lot about associated habits, lifestyle, characteristics and experiences.

9. *Colours*: You must have observed that colour signifies specific signals, for instance red may signify celebration and warmth while green is associated with environment and so on. You may have noticed many times when a group of people go on strike they wear black. Why do you think this is done? Black is the colour of revolt. Some colours have universal synonyms attached to them and some are culture-specific. Red in India is considered auspicious and is worn for occasions like weddings, festivals and other celebrations whereas white is synonymised with mourning. On the other hand white in western countries is considered to be pure and serene and is worn at weddings. Sometimes colours also reinforce stereotypes.
10. *Time or chronemics*: Time or chronemics communicates attitude and status. For instance, subordinates arriving on time for an official meeting, or a person reaching at his own leisure for a job interview conveys about their status/hierarchy (in the former), attitude (in the latter) and overall seriousness towards their work.

Activity

Divide yourself into groups of four. Perform a small role play within your group on any of the following social situations. After performing the role play, write down those non-verbal behaviours you believe would have helped you emerge successful in the selected situation.

1. Appear in a job interview
2. Tell an interesting story or a joke
3. Desire to leave a conversation when the other person keeps talking
4. Leadership role in a class

INTERPERSONAL AND MASS COMMUNICATION

At times you are alone with yourself and at other times you go out for a movie with family. Communication is an integral part in all these situations. It makes life lively, informative and entertaining. However, what is different is the social setting which includes the number of people present and the medium through which communication is done. Let us now look at interpersonal and mass communication in some detail.

Interpersonal Communication

As already studied, interaction between two or more people is called interpersonal communication. In this form, you learn about others and reveal yourself to others. This type of interaction can take place between new acquaintances, old friends, colleagues or family members anywhere through any channel. Through interpersonal communication we establish, maintain, destroy (and sometimes repair) relationships. Some of the basic skills required to pull off a communication to reach close to perfection in interpersonal communication are:

- *Self-disclosure*: This is the ability to disclose oneself to others. This helps people understand you in a better way. People disclose their feelings, emotions, perspectives, intentions, beliefs, etc. Though it is not easy to disclose unless one shares a comfort zone, self-disclosure lies at the crux of interpersonal communication.
- *Context and timing*: Context is referred to as the surroundings or environment which gives meaning to the statements given. As one becomes careful to the context and timing, communication becomes more accurate.

- *Clarity*: Clarity is the art of saying things clearly, crisply and with precision. This helps the decoder understand the message without doubt or confusion, and keeps misunderstandings away.
- *Open listening*: Open listening is giving attention to the speaker's words. It is one step ahead than just hearing things. Skilful, attentive focused listening is important to interpersonal communication.
- *Feedback and feedforward*: Feedback helps maintain a communication flow, it regulates it and keeps it running. A proper feedback mechanism clears doubts, keeps listeners engaged with the communicator and helps give appropriate cues to people involved in the process. Feedforward, on the other hand, is anticipated feedback. For instance you have given a presentation and are waiting for the results. At this time you could think about positive and negative consequences of the judges' opinion and prepare your justifications.
- *Non-verbal behaviour*: Non-verbal behaviour is the behaviour exhibited through non-verbal communication, like facial expression, body language, eye movement, touch, clothes, etc.
- *Interpersonal attraction*: Interpersonal attraction is very individual in nature. You could be attracted to individuals for several reasons—same ideologies, thought process, values, attitude, same territory, interests, etc. Generally, we are attracted to people who are like us, and who accept us the way we are. One feels comfortable in a company where (s)he is accepted and is not the odd one out. When people receive a positive reaction about themselves, their attitude and personality traits, it boosts their confidence.

Mass Communication

This form of communication is highly accessible and most popular now. The early morning newspaper at your doorstep, TV in your bedroom, hoardings on the bus stops, magazines for your leisure, radio while you drive are all examples of mass communication. When a message has to be transmitted from the source/sender/encoder to its destination/audiences the role of mass communication comes into play.

Three kinds of systems prevail in mass communication:

- *One to many systems*: This is one of the most common forms of mass communication. Here there is one source (individual, small group, large group) and many receivers. The prime minister addressing the nation on Independence Day is a form of this communication. Any form of public speaking falls under this category.
- *Many to one systems*: This mass communication operates in a manner exactly opposite to the one to many system described above. Here, there are many sources and one receiver. The receiver can be an individual, a small group or a large group. For instance, people revolting against a government action, or demanding government's attention to any problem they are facing (price hike, etc.).
- *Many to many systems*: In this form of mass communication, there are many senders and many receivers. Mass media is an example of this system, if we pick a specific media like TV, under this if we choose news channels, there are many sources generating the same or similar news in different ways and languages for a large number of receivers.

Mass communication is characterised by:

- *Delayed feedback*: In mass communication, feedback gets delayed. Audiences' reaction reaches late or sometimes do not even reach the source at all.
- *Gatekeepers and opinion leaders*: Gatekeepers are individuals or a group of people who control/check/select the content that reaches the audience. Gatekeepers influence the communication process and restrict absolute free flow of information. They could be politicians, religious leaders, entrepreneurs or a group

of people who hold a set of opinions or views about things around them. They can take advantage of mass media and mould reality as they wish to. If they are a part of any mass media venture they can turn things their way and not let reality come through properly.

MEDIATED AND UNMEDIATED COMMUNICATION

The word mediated is derived from the Latin word *medius*, meaning middle. This form of communication is classified on the basis of whether a message is being transmitted with the help of some medium or not. Let us understand what this means.

Mediated Communication

The number of people who can take part in face-to-face communication is limited to one or a few who are within the communicator's visual field, and interaction is limited to those who have the opportunity to meet. In mediated communication the number and opportunity of people interacting can be virtually unlimited. Moreover, messages are not temporary and can be retrieved and repeated with complete accuracy to others (i.e. forwarded precisely to anyone). In face-to-face communication, the sender and receiver essentially occupy the same physical space, all their senses are involved in sending and receiving messages, personal characteristics are open to visual inspection, concealing anything is difficult and impressions are largely based on the verbal and non-verbal cues that are perceived by them. In mediated communication, the sender and receiver could occupy the same space or could be separated by hundreds of kilometers, personal characteristics are revealed to each other when you want to reveal them; concealing is easy and impressions are based on words, photos, videos and audio messages exchanged.

In mediated communication the person participates in the process of communication through a passive form (not active response). Mediated communication refers to generation of messages through the electronic medium. Simply put, it refers to communication that uses technology for message transmission. All of us in some way or the other participate in mediated communication. This type of communication, informs us, entertains us, persuades us and provides us with means of connecting with other people. An example of mediated communication includes use of TV, radio and newspaper to reach out to the masses.

Unmediated Communication

Also referred as face-to-face communication, in this type people involved are active participants of the conversation. This form of communication emerges when the parties involved are present in a way that enables them to capture the essence of communication through the use of all their senses.

SYNCHRONOUS AND ASYNCHRONOUS COMMUNICATION

Yet another classification of communication is related to the time period involved in the process of communication, i.e. time involved to receive and respond to the message. There are two forms—synchronous and asynchronous.

Synchronous Communication

In a synchronous communication, when the sender stops sending the message to the receiver, the communication remains in waiting mode until there is a response from the receiver. Only once a response message is received, will the communication continue. Your phone call to a friend is a form of synchronous communication.

A prerequisite for this type of communication is that whenever the message is initiated or sent, the receiving system or the receiver must remain active to accept the call and further process it if necessary. The tools used for this type of communication enable real-time communication—i.e. instantaneous communication—in a 'same time-different place' mode. This communication allows people to connect at the same time. A drawback of synchronous communication is that, by definition, it requires same-time participation—different time zones and conflicting schedules can create challenges. Also, we may require significant bandwidth for the communication to be efficient which makes this communication costly. However, technically speaking, due to the latency on digital networks, no communication is truly synchronous, there will always be a small delay of at least a few milliseconds or more between parties.

Asynchronous Communication

In an asynchronous communication, the sender sends the message and does not wait for a response from the receiver in the conversation. For instance, writing blogs, sharing a status update on facebook, text messages are all a part of asynchronous communication. In many cases, there is no response that is sent back to the sender. The receiver may receive and process the message later on. It allows people to connect at each person's own convenience. The advantage is that the receiver does not have to be available at the time the information is sent. For messages that require an immediate response to the sender, this type of communication becomes a barrier.

FORMAL AND INFORMAL COMMUNICATION

This type of communication is based on the flow of the information given. They are seen in organisations and play an important role in the smooth functioning of individuals and groups involved.

Image 2.13: Formal Communication

Source: 'The ministers of foreign affairs and other officials from the P5+1 countries, the European Union and Iran meeting for a Comprehensive agreement on the Iranian nuclear programme . . .' photograph by United States Department of State (Wikimedia Commons; CC0 Public Domain).

Formal Communication

Formal communication refers to a communication in which the content is directly or indirectly related to the professional work of the people involved in the communication. For instance, classroom lecture given by a teacher, students giving presentations to other classmates, communication taking place in an organisation are all examples of formal communication. Formal communication can include written, oral or non-verbal form of communication. Formal communication does not have a personal motive but an organisational goal behind it. The language used is precise, and careful attention is paid to grammar. People are conscious with non-verbal elements such as dress, posture and eye contact. The formal communication network is formed out of formal channels, created by setting a formal system of responsibilities according to the hierarchical structure of the organisation. Generally, formal communications are recorded for further reference and to maintain transparency.

This type of communication serves some other important functions as well:

1. Defines a channel through which important information will be sent.
2. Forms a transmission mechanism for the people involved in the communication.
3. Clearly states the objectives and expectations.

Types of Formal Communication

1. *Downward communication*: Communication from a higher level personnel to a lower level subordinate is called downward communication. It can also be referred to as top–down communication. This form is very common in organisations. Through this form of communication, roles and responsibilities are clearly laid out for subordinates. It helps in giving specific job descriptions, instructions, provide information about the company, and share ideas and strategies. Downward pattern is based on structure and control. However, managers should be positive in their communication. Too much control or criticism can affect the employees, hence judgment of a personal nature should be controlled. If carried out properly it can result in an efficient work environment.
2. *Upward communication*: Unlike downward communication, upward communication is non-directive in nature. It is the communication which takes place from bottom-up, i.e. from subordinates to managers, from students to teachers. For upward communication to take place successfully it is important to create a democratic and free environment where employees feel the freedom to express themselves. In places where there is a rigid hierarchical structure, this form of communication will not prevail due to fear.

Informal Communication (Grapevine)

Informal communication is not based on any lines of authority as is the case in formal communication. It arises out of all those channels that fall outside the formal channels and is also known as the grapevine. Informal communication takes place due to the needs of individuals. Normally, such communication is oral and may be expressed through non-verbal means such as the simple glance, sign or silence. For instance, a boss interacting with her/his subordinates over lunch about last night's cricket match would fall under the category of informal communication. Though the relationship between the employees is formal, the subject of the conversation and the environment are informal in nature. It helps build a conducive atmosphere for work. Despite such advantages, informal communication has certain disadvantages as well. Informal communication may contain facts, rumours and ambiguous data. At times it may create opportunities for gossip which may harm people or organisations involved. However, for the efficient working of any organisation both formal and informal communications are required.

Activity

Have a look at the following situations. Mark against each the most relevant type of communication applicable and discuss your answers with your classmates:

1. Farmers attending a meeting of a farmers' cooperative.
2. Friends gossiping in a group.
3. Meeting of the board of trustees of a private college.
4. Social message disseminated through a TV serial on a national channel.
5. A school principal addressing teachers during a staff council meeting.
6. A letter written to the municipal head regarding the problem of open sewage line in a colony.

SUMMARY

- The various levels of communication transactions are intrapersonal, interpersonal, small group, large group, public, mass and intercultural communication.
- Communication can be classified
  - On the basis of signs, symbols and language systems (verbal and non-verbal communication)
  - On the basis of level of communication (interpersonal and mass communication)
  - On the basis of participation level of the communicators (mediated and unmediated communication).
  - On the basis of time period involved (synchronous and asynchronous communication).
  - On the basis of organisational structures (formal and informal communication).
- Verbal communication involves the use of symbols that generally have universal meanings (language) but might be encoded and decoded differently according to one's environment, culture and past experiences. Verbal communication may be oral or written.
- The use of symbols, such as gestures, facial expressions, eye contact, tone of voice, body language, use of space and touch to convey feeling are all non-verbal communication. It is used to emphasise, contradict, complement, regulate and repeat a verbal message.
- In mediated communication the person participates in the process of communication through a passive form. It refers to the generation of messages through electronic medium.
- In unmediated communication the parties involved are present in a way that enables them to capture the essence of communication through the use of all their senses without an electronic medium.
- In synchronous communication the sender stops sending the message to the receiver and the message goes into waiting mode. It will remain in that waiting mode until it receives a response back from the receiver.
- In asynchronous communication the sender sends the message and does not wait for any response from the receiver in the conversation. In many cases, no response is sent back to the sender.
- Formal communication refers to a communication in which the content is directly or indirectly related to the professional work of the people involved in the communication. It may include written, oral or non-verbal form of communication. Formal communication does not have a personal motive but an organisational goal behind it.
- Informal communication, or grapevine, takes place due to the needs of individuals. It is not based on any line of authority as in the case of formal communication.

KEY WORDS

Proxemics: It is the study of the cultural, behavioural and sociological aspects of spatial distances between individuals participating in a communication situation.

Kinesics: It is the interpretation and understanding of body language, posture movement of either a part of the body or body as a whole.

Para-language: It is the use of volume, tone, rate, pitch, voice to add and convey meaning to one's words.

Gatekeepers and opinion leaders: They are individuals or a group of people who control/check/select the content that reaches the audience.

Intercultural communication: It is the interaction among people belonging to different cultures. It aims to share information across different cultures and social groups.

EXERCISES

1. Discuss the various levels of communication transactions.
2. What are the functions of non-verbal communication?
3. Explain types of non-verbal communication. How does non-verbal communication affect message? Explain with examples.
4. Discuss the various classifications of the types of communication with relevant examples.
5. Write a short note on the following:
   a. Body language
   b. Verbal communication

REFERENCES

Barker, L. L., *Communication*, eighth edition, New Jersey: Prentice-Hall, 2002.

Barker, L. L. and A. G. Deborah, *Communication*, Boston: Pearson, 2001.

DeVito, A. J., *Introduction to Human Communication*, New Jersey: Pearson Education, 2006.

Dominick, J. R., *Dynamics of Mass Communication: Media in the Digital Age*, New York: McGraw-Hill, 2005.

Ekman, P. and F. Wallace, 'The Repertoire of Nonverbal Behaviour: Categories, Origins, Usage and Coding', *Semiotics* 1 (1969): 63–92.

Ekman, P., W. V. Friesen and P. Ellsworth, *Emotion in the Human Face: Guidelines for Research and an Integration of Findings*, Amsterdam: Elsevier, 2013.

McQuail, D., *Mass Communication Theory: An Introduction*, sixth edition, London: SAGE Publications, 2010.

Patri, V. R. and N. Patri, *Essentials of Effective Communication*, New Delhi: Greenspan, 2002.

Thurlow, C., L. Lengel and A. Tomic, *Computer Mediated Communication: Social Interaction and the Internet*, California: Sage, 2004.

Zeuschner, R., *Communicating Today: The Essentials*, Boston: Allyn & Bacon, 2003.

3

PROCESS OF COMMUNICATION

HIGHLIGHTS

- Models of Communication
  - Linear, interactive and transactional models
  - Aristotle model of communication
  - Lasswell's model (1948)
  - Shannon and Weaver model (1949)
  - Wilbur Schramm's model (1954)
  - Berlo's–SMCR model (1960)
  - Osgood and Schramm's circular model (1954)
- Elements of Communication
  - Source/sender/communicator: Characteristics and influence on the process of communication
  - Message dimensions: Code, content and treatment and criteria of a good message
  - Channels of communication: Types, specific features and appropriate selection
  - Audience: Significance of audience characteristics
  - Feedback: Role and functions of feedback on the communication process, types of feedback, feed forward, barriers in getting feedback

We have seen about communication and its types in Chapters One and Two. We also discussed about the key aspects of the communication process. This chapter focuses on the models of communication suggested by various theorists and the various elements of communication.

MODELS OF COMMUNICATION

Models are simplified graphical representations of objects or processes and their operating principles. Models help us understand the components of an entire process and the relationship between them. Just as we have models in science and mathematics, we have models in communication. Proposed by communication theorists, these models position the core elements of communication in the process.

Classification of Models

Models can be classified under three broad categories: linear models, interactive models and transactional models.

Linear Models

Linear models of communication were the initial models of communication when communication was considered to be chiefly governed by the communicator and hence depicted only one-way communication, i.e. the prime purpose of communication focused on sending the message to the audience and persuading them. The key elements in these models are source, message, channel and receiver. There is no feedback mechanism in these models and that is why they are called linear models. These models are speaker-centric as the speaker decides what is to be sent, to whom and how. The receiver is in a passive role.

Interactive Models

Interactive models are a step forward as the receiver is also given importance, they portray an interaction between the sender and receiver. These models of communication depict two-way communication where feedback mechanism exists but only towards the end. Once the message is sent, the feedback received from the receiver can be communicated in spoken or written form or it can be through non-verbal communication such as gestures, body language, etc. The importance of a common field of experience between the communicator and the receiver in terms of culture, knowledge, background, language, etc. is also raised in these models.

Transactional Models

Transactional models are a further advanced version and emphasise on the need for spontaneous feedback. These models demonstrate that the elements in communication are interdependent. Both the speaker and the listener keep changing their roles simultaneously and can send and receive messages at the same time. Thus, here communication is an ongoing and continuously changing process. The new generation transactional models of communication consider communication as a dynamic process where the receiver is no longer the end point in the communication process but an integral part of the entire process. Both the sender and the receiver keep swapping their roles. The sender sending the message becomes the receiver when receiver starts responding.

THE EVOLUTION OF COMMUNICATION MODELS

Let us now discuss some specific models of communication given by communication experts.

Aristotle Model

Image 3.1: Aristotle

Source: 'Aristotle: Acryl Painting on Wood' by Jules Grandgagnage (Wikimedia Commons; CC0 Public Domain).

Aristotle gave the first model of communication about 2500 years ago, around 300 BC. It is one of the oldest models of communication that is linear in nature and is widely accepted even today. During his time the major form of communication was oral or spoken words. He was himself a great orator and called his study of communication as 'Rhetoric'.

According to Aristotle, the ultimate goal of communication was to discover the truth, not merely to win an argument. As we have already discussed in Chapter One, communication was oral at during the Classical Period, and Aristotle suggested five canons (principles) of public speaking—invention (identification of the subject, content and knowledge), style (the expression of the speech), arrangement or the flow of speech content, memory (since speeches were oral, the role of good memory was very important) and delivery (both verbal and non-verbal skills were given importance). He suggested three styles to persuade the audience—ethos, logos and pathos. Ethos is related to ethics, the speaker or the originator of the communication must have a good moral character. Logos is related to the logic, the use of logic and good reasoning and sound argument to convince the audience (the receiver of the communication). Pathos is the use of emotions to influence the audience. Using these three tenets, speakers can influence the minds of their listeners.

Figure 3.1: Speaker's Persuasion Styles given by Aristotle

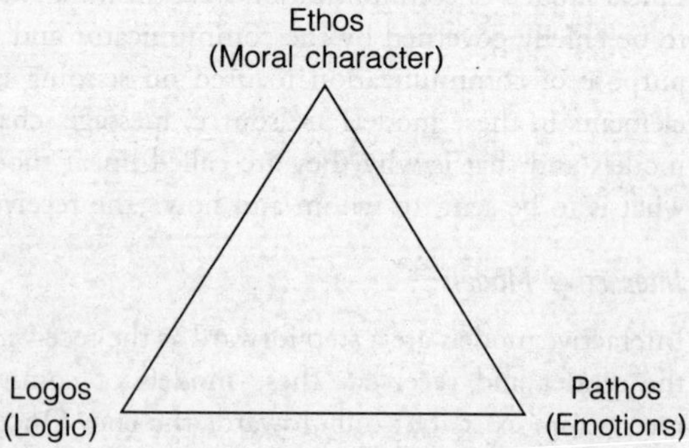

Source: Adapted by the authors from https://www.kibin.com/essay-w-riting-blog/ethos-pathos-logos/ (accessed 31 March 2016).

Aristotle's model, the first of its kind, reflects the dominant form of communication at that time, i.e. oral communication, and is most suited for public speaking even today. It has three main elements in speech-making—the speaker, the message and the audience. The speaker is considered as the centre of any communication process. The speaker is responsible to discover the ideas of speech, generate content, arrange them in a systematic order, stylise it and then deliver using both verbal and non-verbal communication skills. The message is intended to have an influence and effect on the audience. The audience was given a passive role of receptor. It is unidirectional but very simple, basic and easy to understand, and is thus the most widely-accepted model.

Strengths of Aristotle's Model

- It is simple and easy to understand.
- It provides the key elements of communication.
- It is the oldest model and still appropriate to today's world.

Figure 3.2: Aristotle's Model of Communication

Source: Adapted by the authors from http://communicationtheory.org/aristotle%E2%80%99s-communication-model/ (accessed 25 January 2016).

Limitations of Aristotle's Model

- It is a linear model, i.e. one-way, and speaker-centric, i.e. the speaker decides what to speak, how and to whom.
- There is no scope for feedback.
- The listener or the audience and their past experiences, willingness, etc. are not given importance and the listeners are considered to be always ready to get influenced by the speaker.

Lasswell's Model

In 1948, Harold D. Lasswell, an American sociologist and political scientist, gave a communication model which was primarily concerned with mass communication and political propaganda. The five key elements in Laswell's linear model of communication were communicator, message, channel, receiver and effect. The three main functions for communication according to this model were examining the environment, associating the components of society and understanding the cultural transmission between generations. Being a sociologist, the main focus of his model was to create an understanding of the behaviour aspect of communication, i.e. how each element in the process of communication affects the entire communication. Laswell's model is interesting as it tries to understand the entire process of communication by looking into each element in detail and studying its potential to influence the communication. His model raised the importance of research at various levels in the communication process.

Let us now study each of the elements of this model in detail.

- *Who says? | Communicator | Control research*: The communicator is someone who communicates messages or initiates the message. Since the communicator is the initiator and the key source of the message, (s)he is called the source. Sometimes in intrapersonal communication (s)he is called transmitter as (s)he transmits or sends the message across. Since the communicator is the originator of the message (s)he may have her/his own personal biases, preferences and motivation in the selection and treatment of message while communicating. Lasswell focused on understanding these motivations and biases as he believed that these will affect the entire process of communication.
- *Says what? | Message | Content research*: The communicator has great influence on what is to be said and how it is to be said. Since Lasswell was primarily concerned with mass communication and political propaganda, his key interests were: How is the message showcased in the media? How is it treated and presented in media? How close is it to the reality? The study related to these questions is called 'content' research. Content research may be in terms of the representation of individuals or in terms of social-cultural representation.

Figure 3.3: Lasswell's Model of Communication

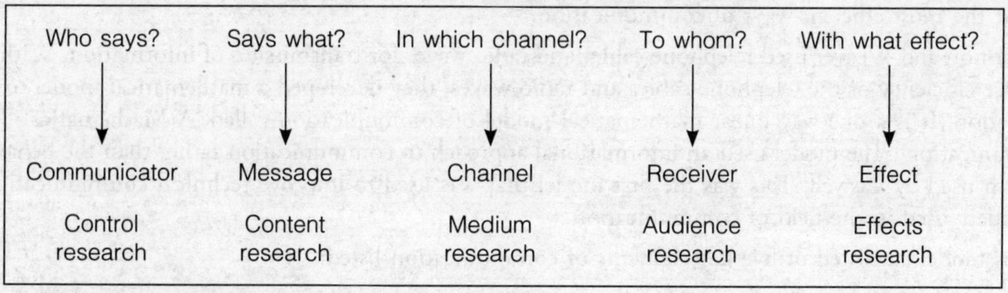

Source: Adapted by the authors from http://communicationtheory.org/lasswells-model/ (accessed 25 January 2016).

- *In which channel? | Channel | Medium research*: Channel is the medium through which message travels, like words are carried by sound waves, radio news are carried by both air and radio waves. Selecting the best channel to send the message is of utmost importance and it may vary from message to message and audience to audience. The study to identify an appropriate channel to deliver message is called 'medium' or 'media' research. This kind of research tries to find answers to questions like: Which media to choose? Is it appropriate to the audience? Will it appeal to them? Is the sender able to afford it? Is it worth sending the message? How should the message be designed?
- *To whom? | Receiver | Audience research*: Audience or receiver is very important for successful communication. It is essential to know your audience well in order to have effective communication. The research carried out to understand the audience—their likes, dislikes, their socio-cultural background, knowledge levels, and interests—is called 'audience' research. Nowadays lot of audience research happens in mass communication. It may be in the field of cinema or in TV or print media. Lasswell's model of communication does not directly talk of feedback as one of the elements of communication but assumes that communication must influence the receiver.
- *With what effect? | Effect | Effect research*: Lasswell was especially concerned with the consequences of mass communication on the masses, so one of his major contributions was the concept of 'effect'. Through the 'effect analysis', Lasswell aimed to know how certain messages affect receivers.

Strengths of Lasswell's Model

- It is simple and easy.
- It helps study the behaviour of the sender and the biases of the source. The emphasis is on the sender's bias in designing the messages and receiver's bias in perceiving them.
- It introduced the concept of media research. Media communicate to people and have some defined function to perform. This model led to developments in testing to see if the communication was effective or successful in clearly transmitting the message.

Limitations of Lasswell's Model

- Although Lasswell's model emphasised the need for media effect the model does not suggest a feedback mechanism.
- Noise as a barrier in communication is not discussed.

Shannon and Weaver's Model

This well-known model was developed in 1949 by the mathematician Claude Shannon and the scientist Warren Weaver. Both of them worked for Bell Telephone labs in the US. USA's prime concern at that time was to find out the most efficient ways of communication.

Shannon and Weaver used telephone cables and radio waves for transmission of information. With the goal to ensure efficiency of the telephone cables and radio waves, they developed a mathematical model to transmit information. It is a one-way linear mathematical model of communication called 'A Mathematical Theory of Communication'. The model used an informational approach to communication rather than the behaviouristic approach used by Laswell. This was the first model that was used to improve technical communication and is now widely used in the field of communication.

This model consisted of five key elements of communication listed:

1. An *information source* that generates a message
2. A *transmitter* that encodes the message into signals
3. A *channel* through which these signals were transmitted
4. A *receiver* which decodes these signals into original message
5. A final *destination* to which message has to ultimately arrive

Noise is a dysfunctional factor in the model. It is like any disturbance caused in the channel which may interfere with the message leading to some kind of miscommunication.

Figure 3.4: Shannon and Weaver's Model of Communication

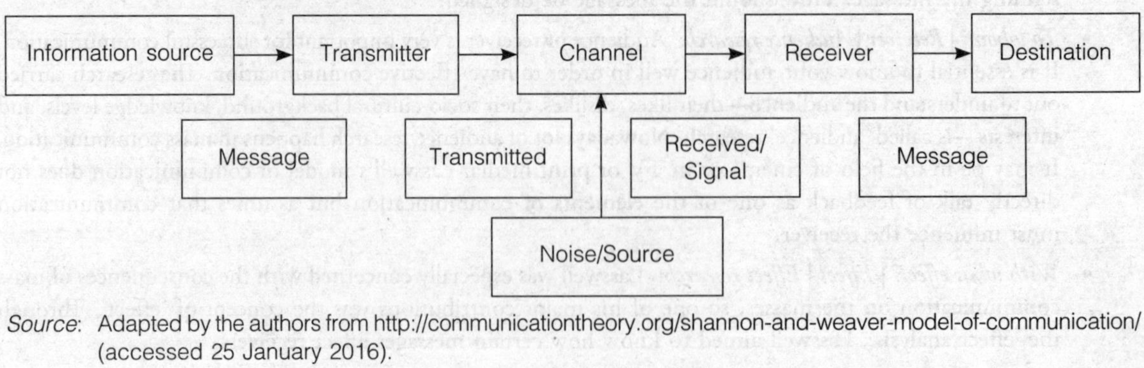

Source: Adapted by the authors from http://communicationtheory.org/shannon-and-weaver-model-of-communication/ (accessed 25 January 2016).

Let us try to understand these elements using the telephone. The caller is the information source, the transmitter is the telephone handset which codes the message into signals (i.e. the sound waves), telephone wires are the channels which carry the sound waves to the receiver (i.e. the receiver's handset) which decodes the message and helps it reach the call receiver. Noise can be any interference or disturbance caused in the telephone line. Shannon and Weaver's model has been highly criticised as a mechanistic model of communication as it discusses communication as a mechanical process of message generation and delivery. It is too message-centric in terms of sending it from a sender to the receiver. The complete focus of the model is on accuracy and efficiency of the delivery of message rather than on the intent of the sender and receiver.

Shannon and Weaver focused on three levels of problems in the process of communication:

- *Technical* problems, which are the problems that refer to the accuracy in transferring the message.
- *Semantic* problems, which refer to how precisely the message is being conveyed.
- *Effectiveness* problem, which refers to how effectively the received messages affect the behaviour of the receiver.

They suggest that if the technical problems are addressed then semantic and effectiveness problems can be taken care of.

Strengths of Shannon and Weaver's Model

- The model is simple to understand and is apt for application in all forms of communication technology.
- They introduced noise as a barrier or distraction in the entire communication process.

Limitations of Shannon and Weaver's Model

Application of Shannon and Weaver's model of communication to all kinds of communication processes may pose several limitations:

- It only deals with a mechanistic representation of communication. The entire focus of the communication process is on accuracy and efficiency in delivering the message from the sender to receiver. Thus, it reduces the potential of human communication to a process of merely transmitting information.
- There is no relationship between the sender and receiver. They are treated as instruments.
- The sender is an active decision maker. And the receiver has the passive role of merely absorbing information.
- No importance is given to the message and its treatment. It does not deal with meaning, content and quality of the message.
- Message is considered context-free. Context and meaning are treated equally. Both the sender and receiver are considered to share the same background and roles—social, economic, cultural. One's situation and political and cultural conditions of the environment may influence the communication process. One cannot separate a message from its context and time as with changing time and context the entire meaning of message may change.
- Decoding of a message is shown as a mirror image of encoding which is not how it actually is. Decoding is the interpretation of the receiver which may get affected by some biases at the receiver's end. This model leaves no space for receiver's interpretation.
- The model is a linear model of communication and there is no provision of feedback.

Berlo's–SMCR Model

The model was developed in 1960 by the communication theorist David K. Berlo. He raised the importance of the psychological view in understanding communication processes in his book *The Process of Communication*.

The six basic elements in the process of communication as per Berlo's model are source, encoder, message, channel, decoder and receiver. He also introduced the concept of fidelity (accuracy) and expanded the concept of noise. He discussed that eliminating noise enhances fidelity and vice-versa. According to him, the meaning of noise can be broadened to include factors in each of the elements of communication that reduce the effectiveness of communication.

Berlo's model is an SMCR (Sender-Message-Channel-Receiver) model and is linear in nature, not specific to any particular communication.

Figure 3.5: Berlo's–SMCR Model of Communication

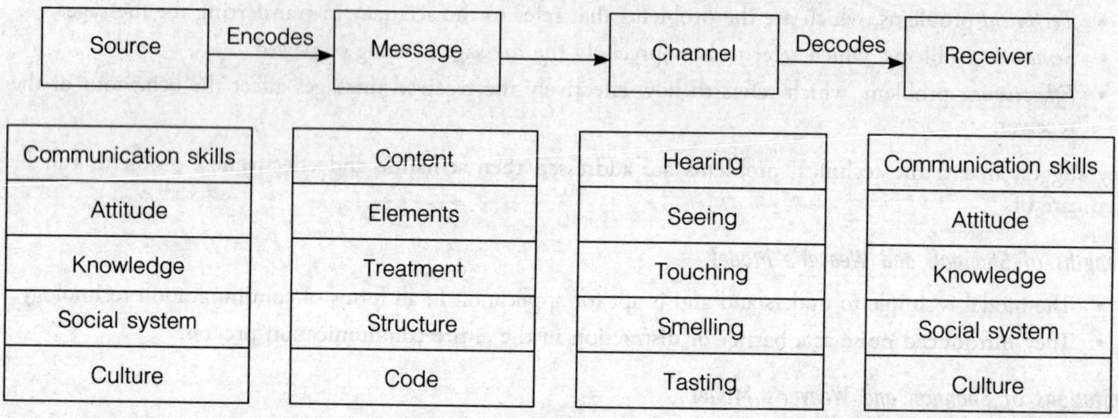

Source: Adapted by the authors from http://communicationtheory.org/berlos-smcr-model-of-communication/ (accessed 25 January 2016).

In interpersonal communication, the source and encoder can be clubbed together because the sender himself/herself encodes the message to be sent. Also, the receiver decodes the message himself/herself, and thus, can also be called as decoder.

1. *Source-Encoder*: The source can be a person, a group of people, an organisation, a company or an institution which generates the message. Source determines what message is to be sent to the receiver and in what way so that it has the desired impact and response from the receiver. (S)he encodes the message but there are certain factors which may affect the fidelity of the communication process.

   With its focus on the psychological aspect of communication, Berlo's model suggests that the following points influence the sender:

   - *Communication skills*: The individual's communication skill has a great influence on the process of communication. There are five major communication skills that are required by a communicator: two of them are related to encoding—writing and speaking; two are related to decoding—listening and reading; and one is related to decoding and encoding—reasoning. If the sender has good communication skills (s)he will be able to design and deliver the message in an effective manner.
   - *Attitudes*: The attitude of the sender towards own self, subject and their audience play an important role. A positive attitude towards oneself helps boost interest to grow, learn more, take initiative, look for timely feedback to enhance her/his skills. Further, a positive attitude towards the subject keeps the communicator updated on the subject. It is also essential to have a positive feedback towards the audience, welcome their queries and comments and use them for further improvement in communication.

- *Knowledge*: The knowledge of the subject, audience, situation and process of communication is very important for the communicator to make the communication effective.
- *Social-cultural system*: Social-cultural systems vary from one community to another, from one set of people to another. It is important to know and understand the audiences' social-cultural aspects like values, beliefs, religion, taboos and general understanding of society.

2. *Encoder*: The sender or communicator of the message is referred as encoder as (s)he encodes the message. For mass communication, the encoder and sender may be different whereas in the case of interpersonal communication the encoder and sender can be clubbed together. For instance, the encoder codes the sender's message before transmitting it through the TV, whereas in a personal face-to-face conversation the act of encoding is part of the sender's delivery itself.
3. *Message*: It is the actual product of the communication process. The factors which are important and must be considered in generating the message are:
   - *Content of the message*: The content of the message should be complete, accurate, updated, suitable to the audience and of their level of understanding.
   - *Code*: The code of the message refers to the form in which it should be sent, i.e. the language in which it should be developed, if it should be written, spoken or oral, what type of music is to be used, etc. It has to be very carefully chosen as a wrong selection can make the communication weak and ineffective.
   - *Treatment*: Treatment of the message refers to the way it is designed and packaged for delivery. It must take into account the audience's knowledge level and background and also follow a structure.
4. *Channel*: Channel is also referred as the medium through which a message is sent. These can be magazine, films, radio and for all of these, we may use one or more of our senses to receive the message. A variety of channels are available today. The communication source is supposed to select an appropriate channel for effective communication. The factors that may influence this selection of channel are: availability of channel, channel outreach potential, source preference, impact of channel, purpose of the message and money one can spend on the channel. These will be discussed in detail later in this chapter.
5. *Decoder*: The receiver of the message is also called the decoder. In the case of interpersonal communication decoder and receiver will be the same and will be the final link in the whole communication process.
6. *Decoder-Receiver*: This is the final connection in the communication process. The receiver is the person for whom the message is being sent by the source. Factors influencing the source of the communication are applicable to the receiver too. For example, communication skills of the receiver—that is, how well the receiver can listen, read—and his command on the language, may affect the decoding or interpretation process. The attitude of the receiver towards the source, herself/himself and the message may affect the communication process. It may be possible for the receiver to have better knowledge than the source on some particular issue. The socio-cultural context could be different in many ways from that of the source, and this may influence a different interpretation of the message. There is a possibility that these biases may change the entire meaning of the message. Thus, it is essential for the source to be aware of the receivers' potential and how they view things beforehand.

Strengths of Berlo's Model

- Expanded the concept of noise as introduced by Shannon and Weaver.
- Described the importance of treatment of message in order to fit it to a certain channel.

Limitations of Berlo's Model

- It is a linear model of communication although a complex one.

- Needs the receiver to be on the same level as the communicator for effective communication, which is not feasible in real-life situation.

Wilbur Schramm's Models

In 1954, Wilbur Schramm, a well-known communication expert, gave his first model of communication and adapted it from Shannon and Weaver's Model. Schramm recognised the communication process as a purposeful exercise to establish common understanding between the source and the receiver. According to his first model, the source encodes the message and sends it to the receiver who decodes the message. He replaced the transmitter with the encoder and the receiver with decoder. The final destination is the receiver. This model is interactional in nature.

He placed noise as a barrier in the entire communication process. As a communication expert, he realised the importance of content, thus encoding of the message is given importance over just transmission of information as was done by Shannon and Weaver.

Figure 3.6: Schramm's First Model of Communication

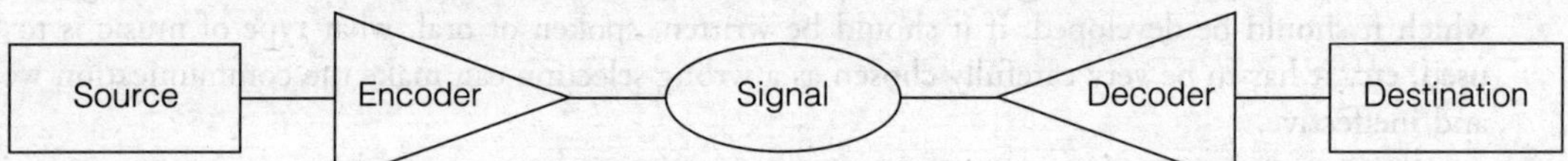

Source: Adapted by the authors from https://commtheories.wikispaces.com/Wilbur+Schramm (accessed 25 January 2016).

Schramm pointed out that to achieve commonness in understanding of the message, both the sender and receiver must have certain things in common—like socio-cultural backgrounds—and named it as 'field of experience'. In his second model, he introduced this concept of field of experience. As we see in Figure 3.7, the two rectangles indicate two individuals trying to communicate. The source encodes the message, sends it via a signal, the receiver decodes and the message reaches the ultimate destination, i.e. the receiver. His second model is another example of the interactive model. This communication will happen only when both the individuals share a common field of experience. These are represented by two big circles in the figure. The bigger the overlap between the fields of experience the more effective the communication will be.

Figure 3.7: Schramm Second Model of Communication

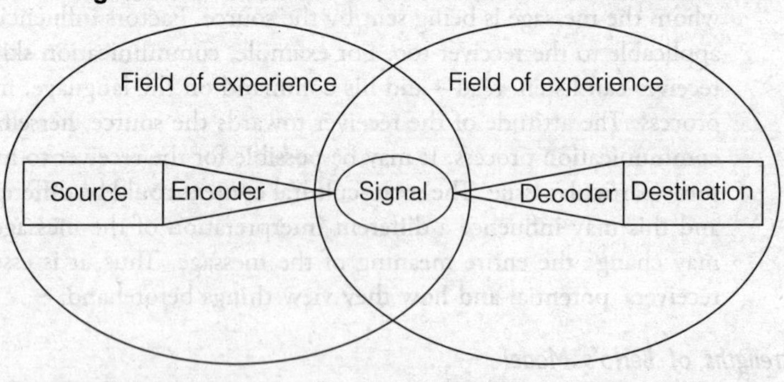

Source: Adapted by the authors from https://commtheories.wikispaces.com/Wilbur+Schramm (accessed 25 January 2016).

Strength of Wilbur Schramm's Models

Introduced the concept of field of experience to both the receiver and the sender as their own experiences greatly influence encoding and decoding the message. Both the sender and receiver encode and decode the message in light of their past experiences and exposure in the particular subject area.

Limitations of Wilbur Schramm's Models

- Does not talk about any of the barriers to communication, like noise.

- Feedback is not discussed in a greater detail in the model.
- The roles of sender and receiver are clearly distinguished. The role of the sender is to only encode the message and that of the receiver is to only decode the message.

Osgood and Schramm's Circular Model

Schramm further refined his model with Charles Osgood and stated that communication cannot start at a point and end at a point; it is dynamic and a never-ending process. They gave the circular model of communication where the participants of any communication process swap their roles of being sender and receiver. A sender can simultaneously be a receiver and vice-versa. This is an example of transactional model of communication.

Osgood and Schramm's circular model shows that the source is not always the encoder and the receiver is not always the decoder, they keep swapping their roles. When the sender is sending message (s)he is encoding it and the receiver is decoding it. Once the message reaches the receiver, the receiver decodes and interprets it; and raises questions or gives feedback. At that particular time, the receiver is performing the role of the encoder as (s)he is encoding the question/query or feedback for the sender and the sender becomes the decoder as (s)he is trying to understand the query and take feedback. Thus, communication is a dynamic and an ever-changing process. An experienced communicator always considers the importance of feedback in communication and tries to make communication a two-way process. (S)he decodes the feedback, interprets it, encodes and sends the message in such a way that the communication effort becomes more effective. This model particularly raised the importance of feedback along with the encoding and decoding processes in the field of communication.

Figure 3.8: Osgood and Schramm's Model of Communication

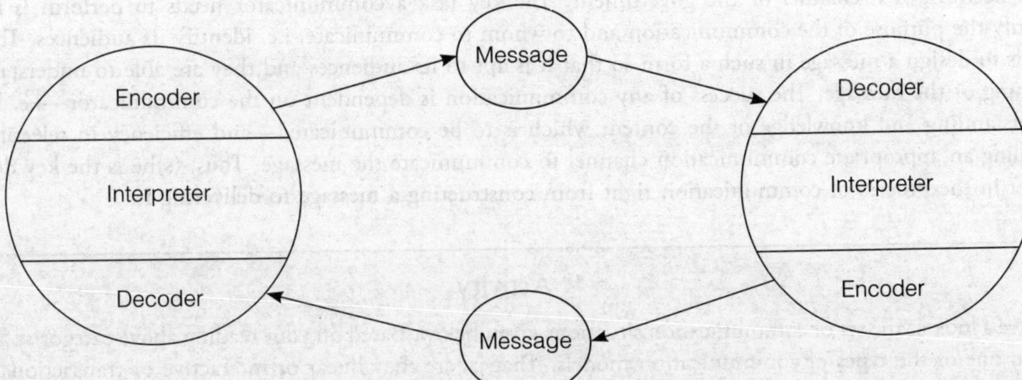

Source: Adapted by the authors from http://communicationtheory.org/osgood-schramm-model-of-communication/ (accessed 25 January 2016).

Strengths of Osgood and Schramm's Model

- The model presents communication as a two-way process.
- It is a dynamic model, circular in nature suggesting that there is no separate sender or receiver. They keep swapping their roles to make communication more effective and meaningful.
- Feedback is given prime importance.
- Reduction in physical noise in the process of communication can increase the fidelity of communication.

- This model raised the important factor that communication is not only the process of coding and decoding of messages but also the interpretation of messages.

Limitations of Osgood and Schramm Model

- This model does not talk about semantic noise.
- This model does not distinguish between the transmitter and the source, and the receiver and the destination.
- It is not very suitable for communication situations without feedback or with very limited feedback.

Now we have examined the various models of communication and observed that different communication theorists have used various elements to depict their perception of the communication process. The sender and receiver have been recognised by all theorists. Some of them considered communication as a one-way process whereas others depicted communication as a two-way process where feedback plays an essential role. Let us now understand each of the element of communication in details and their role in making communication more effective.

ELEMENTS OF COMMUNICATION

The basic elements of communication process are the sender, message, channel, receiver and feedback.

Source/Sender/Communicator

The communicator is the originator who decides what message is to be sent, to whom, how and when? So, (s)he is the initiator of the communication process. It can be an individual, a group of people, organisation, cable network, TV channel or the government. The key task a communicator needs to perform is to first identify the purpose of the communication and to whom to communicate, i.e. identify its audiences. The next task is to design a message in such a form so that it is apt to its audiences and they are able to understand the meaning of the message. The success of any communication is dependent on the communicator—i.e. her/his understanding and knowledge of the content which is to be communicated—and efficiency in selecting and handling an appropriate communication channel to communicate the message. Thus, (s)he is the key decision maker in the process of communication right from constructing a message to delivering it.

Activity

Have a look at the set of communication situations given below. Based on your reading above categorise them into one of the types of communication models. That is, are they linear or interactive or transactional?

1. Two friends discussing their experience of the first day in college.
2. A young girl watching a show on Channel V on the TV.
3. A young boy chatting on WhatsApp.
4. Parents discussing the poor performance of their son with his teacher.

Encoding is the process of putting the idea or message in codes, i.e. we either speak or write our message. In interpersonal communication the communicator encodes the message to express it and is called the encoder, and the receiver decodes the message to comprehend it and is called the decoder. Otherwise, especially in mass communication, the encoder is different from the sender. The role of the communicator is very essential to the whole process of communication since (s)he is the person who gives expression to the whole message by selecting an appropriate message relevant to the audience, treating it in a manner that it remains simple but retains the essence. The sender has to identify an appropriate channel which is accessible and is appreciated by the audience.

Senders should possess the following characteristics to facilitate the communication process:

- *Knowledgeable*: The sender should be knowledgeable about why communication is needed, what has to be communicated and who is seeking that communication. Therefore, a communicator needs to be knowledgeable about (*a*) subject, (*b*) audience and (*c*) objectives of communication. (S)he should have good command over the subject and be updated about it. A person who has a good understanding of the subject will be confident and be able to make it simpler for others to understand. Further, the communicator must know the art of getting familiar with her/his audiences. A good knowledge of the audience helps in effective designing and transmission of the message. The communicator must have a clear understanding about the prime purpose behind the communication effort being made, only then can the message be effectively designed and sent through an appropriate channel.
- *Communication skills*: According to Berlo (1960), a communicator must be well versed in five important communication skills—writing, speaking, reading, listening and reasoning. Out of the five skills good writing and speaking are crucial for encoding the message correctly, and these affect the fidelity of the communication process. Command over the language is an important factor in developing good writing and speaking skills. With good language, i.e. a sound vocabulary and good grammar, one is not only able to communicate well but also think clearly. For effective speaking accurate pronunciation and knowledge of complementary gestures is essential. Reading and listening are decoding skills. (S)he must also have good reading and listening skills as that contributes to widening the horizon of knowledge and creating a better understanding of the underlying linkages among various aspects of the message. (S)he must also be able to analyse the audiences' feedback. A good communicator, apart from being an encoder and decoder, must also have good reasoning skills—i.e. the ability to comprehend new learning. For that one needs to be knowledgeable enough to establish linkages between old and new knowledge, think logically and relate them to real-life situations.
- *Attitude*: The communicator must have a positive attitude towards (*a*) himself, (*b*) the content and (*c*) the receiver. A communicator must have a positive attitude towards herself/himself because the positive attitude helps in building confidence for delivering her/his ideas. To make the audience believe in the message, it is essential to support it with logical reasoning. A communicator has to show a positive attitude towards audience ideas, enquiries and feedback for improving future communication. This enhances audience bonding with the communicator. For instance, while attending a lecture, you do not agree with some points your teacher is discussing and your teacher does not allow you to state your view and discuss it. Will you be participating in the class with the same enthusiasm the next time? So, a positive attitude of the communicator which allows the audience to participate in the discussion for further clarification on the subject matter or to provide feedback enhances audience participation and interest, and respect for communicator. The communicator must have a positive attitude towards the content or subject. If the sender is interested and values the subject or an issue, (s)he will try to take out time to read, talk or inquire about it and update and feel confident to talk to the audience about it.
- *Organised*: (S)he should be well organised in the mind and must have the ability to think clearly, organise her/his thoughts properly, be sure of the objective behind sending the message and the audience. A communicator who is not very clear and organised cannot provide clarity to someone else.
- *Socio-cultural systems*: Socio-cultural systems affect the communication process. People in different social classes communicate differently. Similarly, people with different cultures behave and communicate in

different ways. Socio-cultural systems may partly affect the selection of words, meanings attached to those words, even the purpose of communication, the choice of receiver or the choice of channel, etc. Sometimes mere translation of message into a local language is ineffective as the real essence of the message is lost in translation. Similarly, some things which are casual in a culture may be taboo in another. The lifestyles of people vary from one culture to another and the regional variations in India is a great example for this. Thus, knowing socio-cultural systems of audience increases the acceptability of the communicator and also reduces the errors.

- *Credibility and attractiveness for the audience*: The audience must have faith in the sender only then will the message have an impact on the audience. The credibility of the speaker is decided by its audience. The speaker or the communicator may think that (s)he has a good hold on the subject and has great skills to pursuade her/his audience but it is the audience's acceptability that ultimately decides the credibility of the speaker. Aristotle mentioned that speaker's credibility before the audience decides her/his potential to persuade the audience. Apart from credibility and appearance, status also has a great influence on the audience.
- *Homophily and heterophily*: Communication is most cherished when both the sender and the receiver have certain similar traits such as beliefs, educational/cultural/social backgrounds, gender, religion, etc. Homophily refers to some kind of similarity between the two communicators. Similarly, hetrophily—the dissimilarities between the two communicating individuals—may be a hindrance in the communication process. This has been addressed by Schramm in his second model of communication where he emphasises the need for common field of experience between the two people who try to communicate with each other. The more common the field of experience shared by them the more effective the communication will be.

Message

The message is the idea or information which a communicator wants to convey to their audience. A good message is valid, unambiguous, comprehensive and useful to its audience. It is the actual product of the communication process. It may be spoken words, written words, paintings, photographs, animation, films, etc.

Criteria of a Good Message

A good communicator always tries to make a message clear, unambiguous, easy to communicate and unbiased. Some points which the communicator must keep in mind while designing a good message are:

1. *Simple and clear*: A good message, especially in a mass communication context must be simple so that it is easily understood by the audience. It should not be very technical as the audience are generally common people who may not be familiar with technical terms and jargon. Also it should not have any words with dual meanings as it can lead to miscommunication.
2. *Use of correct codes*: The treatment of message should be done very carefully in terms of selection of words, phrases, visuals and emotions so that it conveys the correct feeling and creates a common platform of understanding among the audience and its communicator.
3. *Easy to understand*: The communicator's potential to make the subject simple at the beginning and slowly raising the level of discussion, develops audience's interest and involvement as they are able to build on the issue along with the communicator.
4. *Lesser socio-cultural biases*: As much as possible the message should be free from any cultural biases. The communicator must have a good knowledge of the socio-cultural background of the audience before designing the message.

5. *Divisibility*: The communicator must be able to divide the message in parts if the message is too long. The division must be done in a manner such that it does not lead to dissemination of incomplete information. Rather, one part should become the building block for the next part of the message. It should be decided based on the total information to be dispersed and the audiences' capacity to comprehend and follow it.

The following are three essential components of a message:

1. *Code*: It is a group of symbols that can be structured in a way so that the message is meaningful to the receiver. Language, light signals, notes for a musical composition are all codes—for example, ships communicate through light codes. All codes have a vocabulary, a structure, so that they are recognisable. According to Berlo, when a communicator is encoding a message, (s)he must keep three things in mind—which code? What are the elements of the code? What structure of the code is to be selected? For example, if English language is the code, sounds, letters and words are its elements and arrangement of these in a sentence is the structure of the code. So, encoding is a process of careful selection of codes, its elements and putting them together as a structure in a way that makes perfect sense to the decoder.
2. *Content*: Content refers to the material in the message, selected by the source to express her/his purpose. It is also the information or the inference which the receiver will draw from the message. If one has to present information in parts, then they should be presented in an order so that can be understood by the receiver clearly.
3. *Treatment of message*: The treatment of a message means the way in which message is to be handled so that the receiver gets it easily and interprets it in the way intended by the sender. Treatment can make a message interesting or dull. The first step is to decide that—how should a message be delivered? For example, if we want to create awareness among urban young girls about their safety using TV snippets, we need to be very careful while selecting the appropriate situation when such incidents may happen, their attire, possible responses to the situation, etc. so they are able to connect with it and are able to learn that if something like this happens to them, their immediate action should be such and such. Murphy and Hilderbrandt (1991) give 7Cs for correct message treatment:
   a. *Completeness*: The message should contain all the necessary information. It should have answers to most of the questions which may arise in the mind of audience after receiving it.
   b. *Conciseness*: The message should be brief, crisp and short, duplication or repetition of information should be avoided.
   c. *Credibility*: The message should be authentic and from a verified and dependable source. Facts and figures which are accurate only should be used.
   d. *Consideration*: The speaker should focus on the audience and must show interest in them.
   e. *Clarity*: The words selected to deliver the message should be simple, and the audience must be familiar with them.
   f. *Courtesy*: A communicator has to be tactful, thoughtful and appreciative of her/his audience and always use expression to show respect towards them.
   g. *Correctness*: A communicator should always use correct language, facts and figures and be sure of the accuracy of the message and maintain acceptable writing mechanics.

Channel

The channel is the medium through which information flows. A channel is a vehicle, a pathway or a device through which message gets transmitted. For example, the TV, telephone, cell phones, SMS, radio, books, bulletins, newspapers, magazines, journals, the internet, websites, emails, blogs, meetings, protests and demonstrations are all channels. According to Berlo, in communication, there are three major meanings of the word 'channel'—modes of encoding and decoding a message, message vehicle and vehicle carrier. To understand this, let us consider a situation where a person is singing and you are listening to her/his song. How does this happen? The various channels here are (*a*) the words in the song, written in a language and the music are modes of encoding, (*b*) her/his voice that is the sound waves produced is the message vehicle, and (c) the air through which these sound waves travel is the vehicle carrier.

Types of Channels

Channels can be classified into the following five types:

1. *Verbal and non-verbal channels*: It is not necessary for a channel to always be verbal, it can also be non-verbal. For example, when you are talking to another person, you are using language as the verbal channel for communicating your message but at the same time your gestures are also communicating your message using non-verbal channels.
2. *Formal channels or informal channels*: Formal channels are pre-determined, there are specific routes through which they pass and they follow a hierarchy, i.e. upwards, downwards or lateral. On the other hand, informal channels are free to move in any direction, skip authority levels and operate where people get together as a group. These are generally oral and information is passed by word of mouth and hence runs the risk of getting distorted and being inaccurate.
3. *Private and public channels*: Private channels are those where the communicator or the sender sends message to another person or a small group in an informal set up, as in having a face-to-face conversation with a friend or speaking over the telephone, or a group of friends in a face-to-face conversation or a group chat. Public channels are those where the sender is sending a message to a large group or the masses in a formal set up which may be a face-to-face situation (as in public forums, rallies or speeches) or assembled audience (in a movie hall) or unassembled audience (on TV).
4. *Interpersonal and mass communication channels*: Interpersonal channels are generally used in face-to-face communication with two or more people whereas mass communication channels are mechanical devices through which an individual or a group reaches out to a larger audience which may be physically separated. The direction of flow of message in an interpersonal communication is two-way whereas in mass communication it is generally one-way. The speed of reaching out to large audiences is high in mass media channels as compared to interpersonal channels. The possible effect of an interpersonal communication can be behavioural change in the audience, whereas in the case of mass media channels the effect is mostly limited to creating awareness and increasing knowledge.
5. *Localite and cosmopolite channels*: Localite channels refer to the channels within the same social-cultural systems whereas cosmopolite channels refer to communication between many social-cultural systems. The origin of the localite channels is always from within the social system of the receiver whereas cosmopolite channels originate from outside the social systems of the receiver. Interpersonal channels may be localite as well as cosmopolite depending on the size of the audience but mass media channels are always cosmopolite. For example, your local cable TV operator advertises products/shops/services available in a smaller geographic area close to your residence of use to the local residents. A newspaper on a Sunday morning may carry tens of pamphlets announcing tuition classes, hobby classes, repair and maintenance services available in your colony but the main newspaper contains advertisements of big brands available at large stores in the city where people from the entire city may go. Thus, a cable TV and a pamphlet are examples of localite channels whereas the main newspaper is an example of cosmopolite channel.

Selection of a Channel

Some of the important points that a communicator must keep in mind while selecting a channel are:

- *Know the audience well*: Spreading the message to the audience is much easier when you know your audience. You know their likes, dislikes, knowledge and awareness levels, culture, taboos, so it becomes quite easy to select a channel for them. But for an unknown audience the task is much more complicated.
- *Availability*: The communicator must select a channel which is locally available, known and well-accepted by the receivers.
- *Cost*: The communicator must identify a channel which is cheap but most widely available with the audience. It must be easy to obtain and be handled by the communicator.
- *Preference of the communicator*: The communicator must select a channel (s)he is familiar with and feels comfortable to handle.
- *Suitability to the content and the receiver*: The communicator must select a channel which is available to the audience and is suitable and convenient to the receivers. For example, a teacher sending readings by email to the students may be the most suitable for students studying in colleges in cities with larger penetration of computers and internet facilities but the same may not be so appropriate in a smaller town or village where students may have limited access to computers, internet and electricity.
- *Effectiveness*: A channel must be effective in terms of bringing together the sender and the receiver to a common platform of understanding.
- *Use multiple channels (if required)*: Sometimes one channel is sufficient to communicate the message but at other times one may have to use a combination of channels depending on the audience. The Pulse Polio campaign—which was aimed at achieving the national health goal of eradicating polio from India—tried to use all possible channels of mass media and interpersonal communication to motivate and mobilise parents of young children to ensure all children under the age of five are vaccinated.
- *Frequency of use*: Repetition enhances acceptability. This is the reason behind the use of jingles in advertisements to sell products, as they are repeatedly played to the audience, several times over during a programme so they remain always in the eyes and ears of the people. The communicator must keep in mind the objective of the message, nature of the message, degree of directness versus abstractness, level of difficulty, scope, time, the audience (their size, knowledge and interests). (S)he must be skilled enough to use appropriate parallel channels to strengthen the chances of reception and absorption by the audience.

Receiver/Decoder/Audience

The receiver is a person or an instrument that receives message from the sender. (S)he obtains message from the source using her/his senses and decodes or interprets it using her/his past knowledge, experiences, perceptions, thoughts, believes, values and feelings. The receiver is also called as decoder since (s)he decodes the message sent to her/him.

At times we may think that the decoder only decodes our words or the verbal message we have sent. But we should remember that our non-verbal cues like gestures are also taken into account by the audience or the listener, as the decoder decodes the message using all of her/his senses. Thus, based on the present verbal message, non-verbal cues received and past experiences, (s)he deduces one final message. This amazing process that happens in a fraction of second is called decoding.

According to Berlo (1960), audience characteristics have a huge influence on the entire process of communication. The entire communication is designed in such a way that it is well received by its audience. The audience should possess characteristics:

- *Good listening abilities*: The audience is also the receiver and decoder of the message sent. If (s)he has a good listening capacity, (s)he will be able to listen, try to comprehend and understand the real meaning of the message. In case (s)he is a bad listener, less attention will be paid to the message and much of the information will be lost, thus making the communication process ineffective.
- *Positive self-image, attitude and willingness*: A positive self-image leads to generate willingness in our own selves. We feel like growing, have confidence in us. A positive self-image in audience will allow them to participate, brainstorm on the issue and critically analyse it. It will lead to generation of feedback from the audience in the whole communication process. They would like to ask questions and justifications to clarify their doubts which will actually lead to effective communication. Also, if they are willing and open to learn new concepts, it enhances their participation and makes the whole communication process more engaging.
- *Previous knowledge*: Prior knowledge on the subject gives a platform to the communicator to address the issue more critically with the audience. If prior knowledge exists on the subject, the audience will have a certain viewpoint on the issue. The communicator can use it as a platform to further build upon it.
- *Interest*: If the audience is interested in the issue or the communicator their attention will be sustained. It will also increase their attention span, generate further interest and debates.
- *Socio-cultural system*: It is essential to know the socio-cultural systems of the receiver beforehand as previous knowledge about the socio-cultural systems of the receiver will help remove any social or cultural biases from the communication process.

Feedback

Audience response to a message is called feedback. It can be positive or negative. It is a very essential component of any communication process as it helps the communicator understand how well a message is received by its audience and whether or not it has led to a common understanding between the source and the audience. It also helps the source know about the scope for improvement in the communication process.

Feedback is also like an action–reaction process, wherein the audience responds to a message sent by the communicator. A positive feedback suggests that the receiver was able to understand and interpret the message sent and a negative feedback conveys the lack of understanding on the part of receiver. The feedback acts as a check or measures the effectiveness of the message or the entire communication process and also guides future action. It is an error-correcting mechanism. A good communicator always seeks timely feedback for further enhancement of the fidelity of the communication process. An effective feedback should have a specific purpose—whether we want to assess the communicator, the message, the audience, the channel or the entire process itself. It should also be descriptive as it will help the communicator identify and rectify the pitfalls in the communication process. It is important that the feedback reaches the communicator in time so that required improvement can be made, else the purpose of the feedback will be defeated.

Types of Feedback

We can classify feedback as follows:

1. *Self and listener feedback*: When the communicator is able to assess herself/himself while communicating whether the audience is able to understand and connect with the message it is called self feedback. When listeners or the receivers of the message give feedback to the communicator on various aspects of the process, it is called listener feedback. It can be through verbal, non-verbal or written communication.
2. *Positive and negative feedback*: This can be observed by the communicator herself/himself while communicating. If the audience is listening attentively and taking interest, it is a positive feedback. Let us take an example from a classroom situation. The teacher is able to assess her/his class by analysing

students' attentiveness and participation. If the students are listening to the teacher, asking questions, clarifying doubts and are able to relate the discussion to their real life and respond with examples from their lives, then it is a positive feedback. But if the students are not attentive, are busy talking or surfing mobiles, a teacher may get a negative feedback from the class. (S)he would decide to stop or alter the presentation style or seek student's opinion so as to bring them back into the class with attention so that they are benefitted by the class discussion.

3. *Person-focused and message-focused feedback*: A teacher's feedback on a student's performance in an exam is an example of person-focused feedback. A message-focused feedback, such as the feedback of an audience to a public speech with loud claps or hooting, is message-centric.
4. *Immediate feedback*: This feedback is received as soon as the message is received. It is generally part of interpersonal communication whereas in mass communication feedback gets delayed. However, with available technology, this problem has been overcome to some extent. Today listeners are able to participate in discussions from their home while the programme is being telecast on TV or on the radio. In case of newspapers too, readers can reach out to the editor/author of an article through emails and social media which connects them much faster.
5. *Low- and high-monitoring feedback*: Low-monitoring feedback is generally an informal, spontaneous and honest reaction of the receiver, whereas, high-monitoring feedback may be given by the audience in consideration of the situation, source and the relationship between them and the source. An example of the low-monitoring feedback is the visitor's book maintained by hotels and restaurants. The book records feedback about their experiences of using their services and products and people are spontaneous in giving their comments or suggestions. From this type of feedback, the managers and owners of the hotel or restaurant learn about what needs to be improved. They may not be so concerned with who wrote these comments but most certainly with the content of the feedback. Also, not every customer may accept or like to leave comments or suggestions even if requested. On the other hand, high monitoring feedback is when the audience or participants are being observed for their willingness to give feedback and the comments being made. For instance, when all the participants in a training workshop are expected to give responses on a feedback sheet. The participants may be guarded in their response about the 'usefulness' of the training or about the 'skills' of the trainer or any other aspects, as they may not like to leave a negative feedback. At times, they may even be conscious of disclosing their identity with their comments in order to avoid any negative repercussions.
6. *Supportive and critical feedback*: Supportive feedback is given to support, encourage, and console a person whereas a critical feedback is to be given during the critical evaluation of the performance of an individual. An example of supportive feedback is the feedback given while coaching someone to acquire a new skill set, the coach ensures that so that the new learner does not lose confidence. On the other hand, an example of critical feedback would be the case of a guru teaching a classical dance form to a student who has been with her/him for a long time, the guru will be critical of even small mistakes because the expectations are high.

Feedforward Messages

Feedback is given once the message is delivered whereas a feedforward is the information which is provided to the audience before the message is delivered. For example, the content page or preface of a textbook gives a glimpse of what is inside the book or a movie preview gives an idea about the film. According to DeVito, feedforward has four major functions to perform:

1. To open channels of communication. For example, while we say to someone we don't know 'Haven't we met before?' we may actually open up a channel of communication.
2. To preview the future message.

3. To altercast, i.e. the process of putting a receiver in a specific role and responding in terms of the role assigned. For example, while practicing for an interview with a friend and giving the role of the interviewer to that friend and getting feedback on your performance is feedforward before an actual interview.
4. To disclaim, i.e. to basically persuade the audience to pay attention to the speaker.

Role and Function of Feedback in the Communication Process

Feedback plays a very important role in making communication a two-way process. It is also known as return process. Feedback returns the listeners' response, impressions, expressions, agreement or disagreement with the communicator and thus helps make the communication process cyclic. Osgood and Schramm's communication model also suggested the importance of feedback in making communication a dynamic process.

Let us now try to understand various roles and functions of feedback in the communication process:

1. *Creates understanding, goes beyond knowledge giving*: The prime purpose of communication is not information giving but rather information sharing. If the audience is unable to provide feedback it means (s)he lagged somewhere in understanding the complete message. It may be because of the communicator's incompetence in sharing the knowledge or the audience inattention. Feedback helps us understand where we have lagged behind. Further, feedback provides an opportunity for the audience to raise questions for further clarification.
2. *Acts as an alert*: Feedback acts as an alert for the communicator. A positive feedback by the audience reflects acceptance of the message whereas a negative feedback shows rejection. This helps the communicator assess her/his communication skills, aptness of the issue discussed, knowledge of the content and willingness of the audience to communicate further on that particular issue. Herein the self-feedback of the communicator is also of critical value. The communicator generally gets a very good idea of her/his effectiveness in the process of delivery of messages in face-to-face situations. Some time spent in reflecting after the end of a communication is a good way to strengthen the positives and overcome negatives. But since not all communication situations are face-to-face, the audience or reader's feedback becomes a very important tool to improve future communication.
3. *Understand the areas that need to be reworked for content*: A general feedback will be ineffective. Specific feedback helps understand major pitfalls. One can actually analyse the possible reasons for those mistakes and try to find ways to overcome them in the future. The intention of feedback is to improve the quality of the message conveyed by the communicator and hence feedback provides a mechanism to understand and critically look at the areas of the message that need to be reworked in terms of content.
4. *Suggestive feedback helps pinpoint mistakes in presenting ideas*: A descriptive feedback is suggestive in nature and very specific comments are given indicating ways by which improvements can be brought about in the style of presentation to make communication more smooth and effective. Thus, it helps in pinpointing mistakes and adds value to the process of communication.

Barriers in Getting Feedback

Taking feedback makes communication an effective process but sometimes we face problems in getting feedback. These barriers can be any of the following:

- *Limitation of the channel*: Sometimes the channel itself acts as a barrier in getting feedback, or it is time consuming. For example, getting a direct feedback from audiences in mass communication is a difficult task.

- *Shyness of the receiver*: The receiver feels hesitant or shy to give feedback. It is the responsibility of the communicator to create a comfortable environment for the audience to respond and give feedback.
- *Discouragement by the communicator*: Sometimes communicators may not allow sufficient space for the audience to respond and give feedback.
- *Socio-economic barriers*: Audience may themselves feel unworthy of commenting on a speaker who is very high in the hierarchy. The communicator should be humble and create a feeling of equality among the audience.
- *Untimely message*: Feedback may be delayed, especially in mass communication, due to the nature of the channel.
- *Language barriers*: Language may act as a barrier in communicating feedback. Sometimes, the audience is not able to package the feedback in the correct form due to poor articulation.

An effective communicator must use feedback in a constructive way to make communication more effective. (S)he must:

- Take criticism as advice
- Be precise and focused in taking feedback
- Be curious to learn about opportunities for self-improvement through other's feedback
- Use feedback in a problem-solving manner
- Take suggestions for self-development
- Express gratitude to the audience for both positive and negative feedback
- Take steps towards self-improvement

Activity

Identify the various elements of communication processes (sender, message, channel, receiver, feedback, feedforward, noise) discussed above in the communication situations described below:

1. A teacher teaching a group of seventy students using the lecture method.
2. A project leader making a presentation on a new project and assigning tasks to a group of juniors using a PowerPoint presentation.
3. A student reading a textbook.
4. Two friends talking to each other over the telephone. One of the friends is attending a wedding reception and other one is at home.
5. A film director screening his documentary film to his friends before its release.

SUMMARY

In this chapter, we have tried to understand the major elements of communication and various models suggested by communication experts to establish the relationship between them.

- The basic elements of communication are source/sender/communicator, message, channel, audience/receiver, feedback and noise.

- The models are summarised in the table below:

Model	*Type*	*Elements*	*Special Feature*
Aristotle	Linear	Sender Message Receiver	• First attempt to explain the process of communication. Simplest and widely acceptable
Shannon and Weaver	Linear mathematical model	Source Message Transmitter Channel Receiver Message Destination Noise	• Talks about the process of communication in terms of transmission of information • Introduced noise as dysfunctional factor • Distinguished between the transmitter and source, and receiver and destination
Lasswell	Linear, transmission model of communication, primarily concerned with mass media	Communicator Message Channel Receiver Effect	Introduced the concept of effect
Berlo's SMCR	Linear	Source Encoder Message Channel Decoder Receiver	Introduced the concept of fidelity and noise, and established the inverse relationship between noise and fidelity in the process of communication
Schramm	Interactive	Source Encoder Signal Decoder Destination Field of experience	• Established the concept of commonness among the sender and the receiver through field of experience • Suggested that the more common the field of experience is between a sender and a receiver, the more effective will the communication be • Both the source and receiver perform functions of encoder and receiver • Does not distinguish between the transmitter and source, and receiver and destination
Osgood and Schramm	Transactional	Encoder Interpreter Decoder Message Receiver	• Communication is a two-way process • Introduced the concept of feedback emphatically • Encoder and decoder keep swapping their roles.

KEY WORDS

Source/sender/communicator/transmitter/encoder: A person who designs and sends the message across.

Channels of communication: Medium through which a message is sent across its its audience.

Audience/receiver: An individual or a group of people or mass population for whom a message is designed and sent.

Feedback: Audience response to the message sent. It can be positive or negative.

Noise: Any kind of hindrance or interference which interrupts the entire process of communication and makes it less effective.

EXERCISES

1. Identify the basic elements of communication. Discuss them in detail with examples.
2. State the various characteristics of a communicator and its influence on the process of communication.
3. Discuss the criteria of a good message.
4. What are the points a communicator must have in her/his mind while selecting an appropriate channel?
5. What is the significance of audience characteristics?
6. Elaborate the role and functions of feedback on the communication process.
7. List the various models of communication, both linear and cyclic. Discuss any two of them in detail.

REFERENCES

Barker, L. L., *Communication*, eighth edition, New Jersey: Prentice-Hall, 2002.

Berlo, D. K., *The Process of Communication*, New York: Holt, Rinehart & Winston, 1960.

De, Dipak and Basavaprabhu Jirli, *A Handbook of Extension Education*, Jodhpur: Agrobiotic India, 2010.

DeVito, J., *Human Communication: The Basic Course*, Eighth edition, London and New York: Longman, 2000.

Dahama, O. P. and O. P. Bhatnagar, *Education and Communication for Development*, New Delhi: Oxford and IBH Publishing House, 2003.

Murphy, Herta A. and Herbert W. Hildebrandt, *Effective Business Communications*, sixth edition, New York: McGraw-Hill, 1991.

Patel D. A., A. M. Dher and C. S. B. Pawar, *Communication and Development in India*, New Delhi: Rajat Publications, 1998.

Rayudu, C. S., *Communication*, Mumbai: Himalaya Publishing House, 2003.

Singh, R., *Teaching and Communication in Extension Education*, New Delhi: Sahitya Kala Prakashan, 1987.

ONLINE SOURCES

http://communicationtheory.org/category/communication-models/ (accessed 26 January 2016)

http://www.oxfordreference.com/view/10.1093/oi/authority.20110803100459436 (accessed 5 July 2013)

http://itc-maribor.blogspot.in/2012/01/harold-lasswell.html (accessed 5 July 2013)

http://pegasus.cc.ucf.edu/~rbrokaw/commtheory.html (accessed 5 July 2013)

http://grammar.about.com/od/rs/g/Sender.htm (accessed 5 July 2013)

www.aber.ac.uk/media/Documents/short/trans.html (accessed 5 July 2013)

http://journal.fibreculture.org/issue12_maras_print.html (accessed 5 July 2013)

4

BARRIERS TO EFFECTIVE COMMUNICATION

HIGHLIGHTS

- Types of barriers
- Classification on the basis of nature of problems
  - Physical and mechanical
  - Language and semantic
  - Socio-psychological
  - Organisational
  - Personal
- Classification on the basis of phases of communication
  - Relating to the communication
  - Relating to transmission of message
  - Relating to the receiver
- Ways to overcome barriers and achieve effective communication

Have you ever been in a situation, where you wanted to convey a message but were unable to do so? Try and remember those times. What were some possible reasons behind message failure? Was your message unclear or did you end up saying something else? There could be many reasons why any communication may fail. When a message is not received in the way it was intended, the disruption is referred to as a barrier in communication. Many a time a breakdown in communication can be the reason for problems in our professional and personal lives. Also, due to a communication gap between the sender and the receiver incomplete and inadequate communication can lead to the message being misunderstood or misinterpreted. These hindrances or obstacles which distort the process of communication are barriers to communication.

In this chapter, we will try to understand the various types of barriers in detail, how they hamper the process of communication and how they can be eliminated. In the first part of the chapter we will discuss classification of barriers and in the second part about the ways to overcome these barriers. We start by first understanding different types of classification of barriers given by different communication specialists.

TYPES OF BARRIERS

A number of communication specialists have classified barriers under various categories. A few ways of classifying barriers are:

- On the basis of the people involved in the process of communication (their socio-psychological background, educational level, differences in perceptions, emotions, attitudes, environment, etc.)
- On the basis of the medium/channel through which communication is carried out (noise, distance, technical, semantic, wrong handling)
- On the basis of message (language, symbols, out of context)
- On the basis of phases of communication
- On the basis of organisational structure (inflexible structure, one-way flow of communication)
- On the basis of personal factors (lack of confidence, knowledge level, offensive style)

Let us now focus on the barriers on the basis of two criteria which provide a holistic view of all the barriers in the communication process:

1. On the basis of nature of problem/barrier
2. On the basis of phases of communication

While the nature of a problem could be related to physical and mechanical, language and semantic, socio-psychological, organisational or personal hindrances; barriers on the basis of phases of communication are most likely linked with the communicator, the transmission of message and the receiver. Let us now discuss the possible barriers on the basis of the above two criteria in detail.

CLASSIFICATION ON THE BASIS OF NATURE OF PROBLEM

Physical and Mechanical Barriers

The physical and mechanical barriers may be caused by noise, distance, time and information overload and these are discussed below.

Noise

Noise refers to any obstruction or interference which is external in nature in the process of communication.

What happens when you receive a phone call regarding work while you are on a shopping spree with a friend in a flea market where all the shopkeepers are shouting to sell their products or when there is a party next door and loud music is being played? Are you able to hear or convey your message effectively? Communication in such scenarios becomes very stressful. You might miss out on some important detail or you might not be able to convey your message properly. Noise refers to those features that interfere in the process of effective communication. Some common forms of noise may include noise of vehicles honking and construction work, disturbance in the telephone line, machinery, loud music, human sounds, etc. Sometimes bad weather conditions may cause network-related problems which may lead to bad connectivity.

Image 4.1: Noise

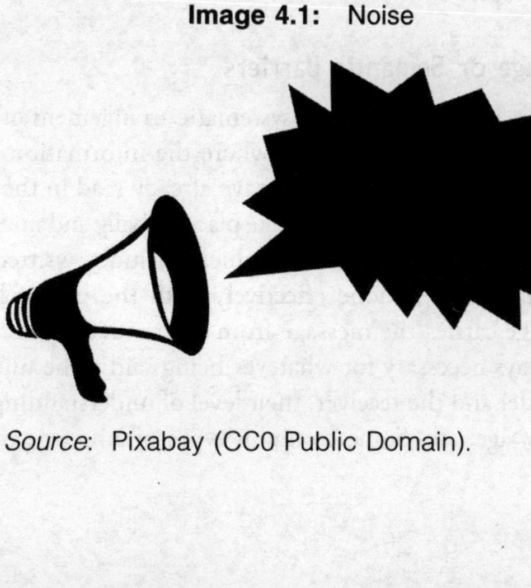

Source: Pixabay (CC0 Public Domain).

In the above-mentioned situations, the receiver's attention is distracted due to physical noise which in turn disturbs communication. Noise can also be psychological in nature. When a person is stressed, anxious or preoccupied with thoughts it leads to mental disturbance. In such a scenario the receiver might not be able to comprehend the conveyed information correctly. For instance, while you are preparing for an examination, if you have a tough subject coming up the next day and your friend calls up to discuss a personal problem. What will happen? There is a chance that you might not be able to listen or guide her/him the way you would have if you were free of stress. However, it has to be noted that communication can never take place in an absolutely noise-free environment; the amount of noise may differ.

Distance

Long distance becomes a barrier especially if you have to make a telephonic call. What happens when you have to communicate with your family through the telephone in some other continent? Generally, you would look at their time to see if they would be awake and then make a call. In such cases, if there is a connection problem or disturbance in the line then the communication is difficult and can often result in miscommunication or incomplete communication.

Time

At times messages have to be delivered with a timeline in mind. If a message gets delayed it may lose its purpose altogether; the celebration of an important event on a specific day and time, for example. You may have observed the importance of wishing good luck before an examination or sending good wishes for birthdays and anniversaries in maintaining warmth in our personal relationships. They make a person feel 'good' about us being with her/him during such important moments. Similarly, warning of a rough sea in weather forecast must reach the coastal fishing communities well in time so that they may be better prepared to meet the situation. If such a message gets delayed, it loses its purpose. The same might happen if the information is given out too early, as it may get lost and forgotten by time the event actually happens.

Information Overload

What will happen if you were taught five lessons of a subject in a day? Will you be able to grasp all the topics covered? Will you understand all the things said by the teacher? You might not. The receiver cannot understand or comprehend messages if they are overloaded with information beyond a point. They might be passive listeners to what is being said, but may be subjected to unnecessary pressure, confusion and distortions. In such situations the receiver may not act upon as expected, may make mistakes or may delay actions and decisions. Thus, information overload may lead to losing on most of the messages communicated or may lead to loss of interest of the listener. Information provided in a single session must be comprehensive and focus on one topic.

Language or Semantic Barriers

Language can be defined as a systematic arrangement of symbols, signs and words in a manner where the information could be encoded and decoded. As you have already read in the previous chapters, communication can take place verbally and non-verbally, hence verbal communication which includes written or oral communication is done effectively with the use of language.

> **Semantic:** This barrier is based on 'mis' interpretation of messages. Due to linguistic error, sometimes an easy communication may not get interpreted in the same manner as it is supposed to be.

Language carries the message from the sender to the receiver. However, as discussed in the above section, it is not always necessary for whatever being said to be understood in the same manner. Understanding depends on the sender and the receiver, their level of understanding, various socio-cultural and economic factors, educational statuses, age, etc. Some common types of language or semantic barriers are as follows:

No Clarity in Message

A message is said to be unclear, when it is incomplete or abrupt in its formation. Loosely assembled words, usage of wrong words not aligned with the context, poorly organised information, lack of proper expression, use of jargon, slang and inadequate vocabulary are some cases which make the message unclear.

Damaged Translation

Have you ever been in a situation where you acted as a channel where you were given a job to take a message from the source to the receiver who belonged to different backgrounds? If yes, while transferring the information did you make some alterations in the language, sentence formation, choice of appropriate words keeping the receiver of the information in mind? Translation is not just mere conversion of a message from one language to another, it is an expert linguistic task wherein the person carrying the information skilfully translates the message according to the receiver's profile without changing the actual meaning of the message. For example, when a legal advisor explains law terminology to a layperson.

Image 4.2: Damaged Translation

Source: 'A warning sign in Guilin states in Chinese' by Kelisi at the English language Wikipedia (Wikimedia Commons; CC BY-SA 3.0).

Specialist's Language

It is common practice for people who belong to the same professional or technical group to talk using some typical words or 'jargon'. This use of language which is only understood by the people belonging to that group distances them from other people. This acts as a barrier. Very often people come from different professional backgrounds and will be unable to understand leading to miscommunication. For instance, a group of doctors discussing about a patient, the use of terminologies and jargon might not be understood by people from a non-medical background.

Underlying Assumption

Messages may have some underlying assumptions which might not be communicated. Even though a message appears to be clear and straightforward, the assumption behind it might not be apparent. This is a barrier in communication. For instance, when future plans regarding a product are discussed with an employee it is an underlying un-communicated assumption that the employee will keep the information confidential.

Use of Words with Different Meanings

There are many words in the English language which have various meanings depending on the situation. And sometimes these words can lead to miscommunication. For example, let's take the word 'bash'. It has various meanings—to harm someone physically, to attack or to have a party. Also, people from different cultures may interpret the same word differently due to differences in their socio-cultural backgrounds. For example, the word 'auto' in India generally refers to the three-wheeler auto-rickshaw, whereas in the West 'auto' is synonymous to automobiles (mostly cars). Similarly, there are certain slangs which are commonly used in western cultures and which may not mean the same in other cultures. For example, the word 'cheers' is commonly said while sharing a drink; it is also commonly taken as a sign of acknowledgement and appreciation in western countries but not so in India. These ambiguous words with different meanings must be avoided.

Denotations and Connotations

The literal or the actual meaning of the word is known by its denotative meaning. For example, names of objects and places usually have a denotative meaning; i.e. they mean the same across cultures—fan, phone, etc. They do not have any emotions or qualities attached to them. On the other hand, connotations are subjective, they are words that may carry different meaning for different people; i.e. words that are descriptive in nature, for example, beautiful, smart, cunning and talkative. As you can make out, some of them are positive in nature like beautiful and smart (positive connotations), while some are towards the negative side like cunning and talkative (negative connotation). Some words have both positive and negative connotations. The right meaning will be extracted according to the context they are used in. For example, when a teacher says to a parent 'She is very talkative in the class', she means, the child disturbs other students, with a negative connotation. However, when the same thing is said by a friend to another friend 'She is very talkative in the class, I don't get bored at all' it is with a positive connotation. One should thus try to make balanced use of denotations and connotations, specifically keeping in mind the target audience. Judicious and precise use of these words can help make the communication effective.

Socio-psychological Barriers

Do you think your present state of mind has any effect on the process of communication? And, on the way you receive/decode or encode a message? Do you communicate in the same way, when you are under stress and when you feel excited or ecstatic? Do you feel any social pressure while you choose to communicate? The process of communication (many times unconsciously) is affected by an individual's state of mind. Some of the psychological barriers can be described as follows:

Differences in Perception

It is understandable that individuals perceive, organise and understand their environments differently. However, it has to be noted that this difference leads to formation of certain perceptual barriers. These barriers may be due to different occupations or socio-economic status or ethnicity. The thoughts, vocabulary, expression are all influenced by the experiences we have had.

Differences in Attitudes

People have different opinions and thereby have different attitudes which decide the reception of any message communicated to them. If some news is going along with one's beliefs their attitude towards the message will be favourable. If, however, the opposite is the case, that is if the news is going to be against one's belief the response may not be an approving one. For example, if you have prepared very hard for a test you expect a good result. However, if you get marks below your expectation you will be disappointed and your attitude changes. Hence expectation and perception can change attitude which can become a barrier.

Emotions

The current emotional state of an individual also determines how (s)he would receive and interpret any message. For example, when someone is in jubilation, the individual is likely to miss out certain information because they may give less attention to the message. Under various emotional states interpretation of the message may also be different.

Inattention

Inattention—intentional or otherwise—acts as a great hindrance to effective communication. Communication has no impact on those who are unable or unwilling to listen. Difficulty in reception of message may be a reason for inattention. Hindrance can also take place when the receiver responds quickly to the message without listening to it properly. In such times the sender should act maturely and creatively, and adapt to handle such quick conclusions.

Closed Minds

It is important to have an open mind during interpersonal communication, so that all the contexts—explicit or implicit in the words—are taken note of. People who communicate with a closed mind are likely to ignore certain contents which are not of their concern as they keep their attention only to specific topics. This leads to inefficient communication resulting in further inefficient response.

Premature Evaluation

Sometimes, we meet people and form a perception about them in our minds which unconsciously affects our behaviour and interaction with them. When we get to know them better, our initial judgment may change. The same happens in the process of communication. Premature evaluation of an individual is dangerous, be it consciously or otherwise. Arriving at a conclusion without grasping the full information is not only incorrect but also risky. Once a conclusion is set on one's mind, we become closed to further information. Such premature evaluations therefore prevent effective communication and should be avoided.

Distrust

Distrust is not an implicit state in a receiver's mind. It arises out of repeatedly incoherent sets of communicated messages from the message sender. Incoherent communication may involve ill-considered judgment or illogical decisions or frequent changes in the original communication by the communicator. Because of distrust, the receiver cannot decide if the message has to be agreed to and accepted or not. Hence even when the communication is apparently delivered, it still remains incomplete, rendering it ineffective. In such cases, if openness in relationship is established, the receiver will be able to accept anything that is communicated without much discord.

Resistance to Change

People are generally resistant to change. Change of any sort brings a difference in one's life, it could affect their routine, lifestyle, working pattern and so on. Unless and until change is not desired by people themselves, they remain resistant to new thoughts, ideas or information. Thus when new information that can cause change is filtered and rejected easily, the resistance acts as a psychological barrier.

Image 4.3: Cultural Differences

Source: 'Harmony Day' by Magnus Manske, DIAC Images (Wikimedia Commons; CC By 2.0).

Cultural Differences

Norms, language, gestures, values, attitude and perceptions are an integral part of culture. Cultures vary from one place to another.

When people from different cultures meet and interact with each other a cultural exchange takes place. The difference in culture may act as a barrier if people are closed in nature. Lack of acceptance and lack of ability to appreciate other cultures may result in ineffective communication. Thus, one should try and be culturally sensitive while communicating. For instance, if someone visits a village in India, wearing clothes that the villagers are not used to or speaking a language which is new to them may create a cultural barrier and hamper the process of effective communication.

Organisational Barriers

Organisation is a collection of individuals who work towards a common goal or an objective. Legal organisations are categorised into various types—government, non-governmental, international, partnerships, cooperatives, etc. Effective communication is essential for the smooth functioning of an organisation but a lot of times an organisational structure can create barriers. Some such organisational barriers are:

One-way Flow

Communication is a two-way process, in which feedback plays a very important role in completing the process of communication cycle. One-way traffic is very common in organisations with strict hierarchical structures. Flow of information is generally from the top to bottom and subordinates do not get a chance to give their feedback because of the lack of feedback mechanisms in the system. Without feedback from the receiver the message runs the risk of lack of understanding or even total misunderstanding. For instance, if a principal of a school issues a notice for students, the orders have to be followed by the students. Even if there is a resistance due to a genuine problem they don't have much of an option to oppose the orders.

Organisational Structure

At times organisations consist of many levels of hierarchies. Such a structure creates gap between various levels of employees. Several layers of authority, strict status relationships and a number of communication procedures to navigate through these layers create a barrier to communicate not only from bottom to top but also from top to bottom. It may result in filtering of information by the time it reaches the last person and the message may have lost its purpose or essential aspects.

Rules and Regulations

When we channelise the free flow of thought, the message is bound to be filtered and some information is lost. This channelising is due to rules and regulations of an organisation. Though rules are important in extracting information necessary for the functioning of an organisation, it may end up discarding some useful chunk which may add value to the organisation.

Distance Barriers

As discussed earlier, communication is weakened by the distance between two individuals. The related explanation for an opinion or a message may be wrongly or incompletely conveyed to the receiver.

Image 4.4: Organisational Structure

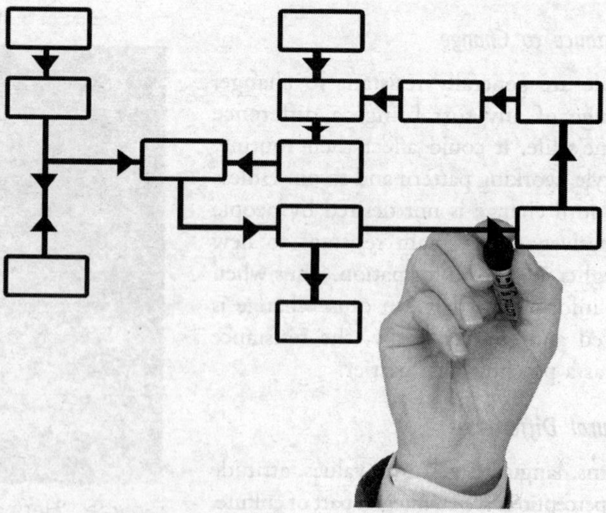

Source: Pixabay (CC0 Public Domain).

Physical Barriers

Physical barriers like noise and malfunctioning modes of communication may lead to loss of information between the sender and receiver.

Mechanical Barriers

Mechanical barriers include malfunctioning equipments, distorted wires, low voltage, volume, etc. If the tools and machines are not working properly, then communication will not be propagated from the sender, causing a loss in the overall process. 'Server down' is a common message received when the internet connection fails and as a result the entire communication process comes to a standstill.

Personal Barriers

We have discussed about the many barriers which hamper the process of communication. However there are some factors which are internal and personal to the individuals involved in the process of communication. These intrapersonal barriers, related to an individual's personality, attitude, interest and capacity to handle situations may also affect the message which is to be delivered or received.

Lack of Confidence

Have you ever found yourself in a situation where you are unsure about an answer in the exam and are not confident enough to answer it. But then, later, once the exam is over, you realise that what you were thinking was right! You just wish you could go back and redo the answer, this time certainly with a lot more confidence. Lack of confidence may result in incorrect message delivery. Confidence in a person reflects her/his understanding of the issue and even portrays a positive image to the receiver.

Ignoring Communication

Sometimes some messages may be ignored right away just by looking at who the sender is. You have a fair idea of what the message is by knowing who the sender is. Due to this some messages are ignored or not reacted to. For instance, you may receive a lot of text messages in a day. You may receive some on buying and selling property, on new plans or schemes in the market, new products, etc. Do you read all those messages carefully? Do you save all the messages or do you delete some of them even without looking at them? Many a time, taking a hint from its sender or the issue flagged in the message, we simply delete the message and do not let it register in our mind.

Filtering of Information

Withholding of some information and not forwarding or receiving parts of the message is referred to as filtering of information. From the sender's perspective certain details may be perceived as not important to be communicated or shared with others. From the receiver's perspective there may be deliberate or accidental missing or inattention to some aspects of the communication. These are filtering processes at work. These two phases in the communication process could result in loss of information and ultimate breakdown of communication. For example, what was said in a class by the teacher may not be communicated in the same way to your classmate who was absent.

Message Overload

If message overload is a routine occurrence, there is a grave danger to the orderly and smooth flow of communication. The effect of overload may be omission of message, errors, delay, filtering and approximation. Again, these are barriers to communication.

Perceptual Barriers

These relate to the process by which we receive and interpret messages. Different people interpret the same message differently, leading to lowering of communication effectiveness. For instance, stereotype is one perceptual barrier. Here interpretations of messages are infused with biases. We have a preconceived notion about a person, about a brand, about an institute; while some may be on our preference list, others are rejected for no other reason but, the perception we have about them.

Offensive or Abrasive Style

Often communication fails not because of 'what' is said but 'how' it is said. Confrontational or hurtful style of communication leads to negative interpersonal interactions and thereby communication breakdown. A teenager who is being objected on a daily basis by his/her parents for extravagant lifestyle habits and rude behaviour could resort to breaking of glass or furniture to express anger and distress. This would only deter effective communication between the parents and the teenager.

CLASSIFICATION ON THE BASIS OF PHASES OF COMMUNICATION

Relating to the Communicator

Ineffective Environment

Communication gets affected by the environment in which it is carried out. Let us understand this with a simple example. Imagine a situation when your friends have come to meet you at your home. You are sitting in a room and talking just about anything, all of you are totally relaxed. Suddenly, your parents come into the room and sit with you. What happens? Are you able to communicate in the same way as before? Does your tone, pitch and subject matter change? Yes, they do. Suddenly your parents' presence brings a difference in your conversation. Why does this happen? Out of respect, fear or shyness you and your friends stop conversing in the same way or change the topic. A similar situation occurs when a teacher suddenly walks into the class during break time to make an important announcement. In such situations, the environment becomes ineffective for a casual conversation to take place.

As we already know different environments cause different types of communication. Communication will be formal in nature when interacting with seniors in the office or in an educational institution. It will be informal when we are with friends, in the canteen or in restaurants. Formal or not certain things remain constant: respect for the opinions of others, openness in the process of communication, equality and right to speak up, strong rapport and responsiveness. If these are missing in the communication, they create an ineffective environment.

Disorganised Efforts to Communicate

Communication needs to follow a rhythm or a pattern. For example, if a teacher starts explaining the result of a chemical reaction before explaining the process, most students will not be able to understand the concept. It is critical to organise communication and plan the message in such a way that it is easily understood by the receivers.

Standard of Correctness

It is better to not give any information than give the wrong information. It is important for the sender to be sure of the facts while communicating, and ensure a standard of correctness is maintained.

Standard of Social Responsibilities

A sender has to keep in mind her/his social responsibilities towards the society. Sometimes, some loose communication may wreck havoc in the society, though the intention behind that could be something innocuous as an attempt to elicit laughter. An insensitive joke might affect some people or sections of the society. For instance, if someone spreads a rumour about a bomb in a particular area, the scare could have been intended as a joke, but when it spreads it won't remain the same for others.

Cultural Values and Social Organisations

A communicator should respect, and be aware and sensitive towards the cultural values of their audience. For instance, if some young students who live in a metropolitan city are made to visit a rural interior village, what will happen? Their presence itself can create a barrier in the process of communication and not let people open up. If the same batch of youngsters, dress in a manner more acceptable in that scenario, learn some basic local words, try and follow some cultural norms of the local people, it will help them form a rapport and get closer to the community.

Inaccurate Symbols

Symbols and signs must be used carefully; they can serve as a barrier in effective communication if not understood properly. There are certain symbols which are universally accepted and some whose meaning and understanding are restricted to a particular culture. For example, a hug or handshake can be taken differently across different cultures.

Relating to Transmission of Message

Wrong Handling of the Channel

Lack of understanding about proper handling of the channel can become a barrier in transmission of the message. For instance, if you handover a mobile phone with new features to a person who has never used it before and ask her/him to send an SMS, the person may not be able to transmit the message immediately or may face difficulties in performing this task or may not be able to do it at all.

Wrong Selection of Channels

Suppose you have to transmit a message in a village where there is no electricity. What channel will you select? TV, radio or a puppet show? Definitely, you will pick a channel which does not depend on electric power. Out of the given options, radio or a puppet show will be best suited. If the same message is to be disseminated among school children in a city then you may chose some other channel for the same message. Thus, selection of channel greatly depends upon the general conditions of the place and on the type of audience.

Physical Distraction

Anything which distracts the sender or the receiver and obstructs transmission of message is referred to as physical distraction and this can be an obstruction in the transmission of message. A student attending a lecture in the classroom could be distracted if an adjoining lawn is being mowed at the same time.

Use of Inadequate Channels in Parallel

At times the same message can be delivered through a number of channels. However, when these parallel channels are inadequate and are not in sync with the target audience, environment, usage, etc. they fail to communicate the message. For example, in a village where the literacy rates are low, posters with written text and leaflets without any pictures will not serve the purpose of communicating the message behind a campaign.

Relating to the Receiver

Attention of the Listeners

Have you ever been caught in a class day-dreaming? Or have you ever felt out of place when you are in a group. In such situations, generally, the receiver's attention span is low and this becomes a barrier to the process of communication. The intended message is delivered yet it is not decoded by the receiver as it should have been due to loss of attention.

Problem of Cooperation, Participation and Involvement

Equal involvement of both receivers and senders results in successful completion of communication process. Though it is the sender who initiates the communication process, the desired result is achieved only when both the parties take equal initiative. The receiver's job is to listen and grasp information, however proper comprehension of information and decoding will take place only when the listener listens attentively and actively. This is especially important at the grassroots level where participation of the community people ensures effective transmission of message because they have been involved in the process and the message is being framed as per their needs. On the other hand if the community has not participated during the generation of the message, a worse case where non-acceptance and aversion for the message could arise. So, unless the respondents are on the same frequency, messages will be transferred but may not be accepted.

Homogeneity of the Audience

A communicator should understand the nature of their audience. Homogeneity of the audience refers to the similarity in the audience's socio-cultural habits, language and literacy levels. Lack of homogeneity acts as a crucial barrier to communication. Having a sound grasp of the homogeneity in the demographic profile well in advance helps in crafting the message and selecting suitable channels. The communicator can wield a stronger influence and ensure better delivery of message to a highly homogenous audience. That is, the more homogeneous the audience the greater the chances of successful communication.

Attitude of Audience towards the Communicator

Imagine a conversation with a friend and one with a stranger at the door. Do you have the same attitude while receiving information? No. The attitude of the receiver is critical in communication since it determines the degree of sincerity within the communication. A communicator should always try and make the audiences maintain a positive attitude towards her/him.

WAYS TO OVERCOME BARRIERS AND ACHIEVE EFFECTIVE COMMUNICATION

As you know, the process of communication does not end with just the transmission of message. Information delivery from the sender to the audience does not ensure that the process of communication is complete and will result in the desired action. Communication is said to be complete once the receiver reciprocates to the message received. Unless and until, feedback is received and ideas are exchanged, it remains one-sided and the cycle remains incomplete. Communication is said to be effective only when it comprises of the following characteristics:

Two-way Channel

As discussed earlier, no communication is complete unless two-way communication is established. It is imperative that a channel be kept open for feedback in any form of communication. Exchange of information is important for the communication to be a meaningful.

Mutual Trust

For communication to be effective and ideal, mutual trust between the sender/transmitter and receiver must be established. This ensures proper delivery of messages, openness in feedback and two-sided communication. Absence of mutual trust may result in gaps and misunderstanding.

Clarity of Message

To a large extent decoding of a message depends upon its encoding. If the message is unclear, not organised properly and is ambiguous, it will be tougher to comprehend. Hence a message should be clearly framed and it should not confuse the receiver.

Timely Message

Communication loses its value when it becomes old. Timeliness is a very critical factor which ensures effective communication. To achieve desirable results/actions it is essential that the message is communicated on time.

Consistency of Message

The message which is communicated should be in sync with previous and future communications. The aim of communication is to make things clear for the audience, thus conflicting messages, would make communication inconsistent and can thereby lead to confusion in the audience. If there is an important notification or a major change which might be conflicting with previous communication it should be clearly mentioned and communicated to the receiver.

Good Relations

People involved in communication should be sensitive to the values and feelings of others and make sure they don't hurt them. Understanding each other's perspectives and respecting them is critical to not only maintain a good relationship for the future but also for effective communication in the present.

Feedback

Any communication is complete only when proper feedback is received. Improper feedback creates ambiguity in the sender's as well as in the receiver's minds. However, it has to be remembered that feedback is not possible in all the types of communications very easily.

Empathetic Listening

One should always listen patiently to what is been said before making any judgments or interrupting the speaker. Empathetic listening ensures free flow of thoughts and perceptions which are very important for meaningful communication to take place.

Flexibility

Flexibility is required in the communication systems and acceptance of others perspectives. Rigid and closed systems and process become a hindrance and do not ensure free flow of thoughts.Thus flexibility is essential to ensure effective communication. Flexibility in terms of message flow, channels, feedback, etc. is important.

SUMMARY

In this chapter, we introduced the various barriers in process of communication transactions.

- When a message is not received in the same way it was intended, that disruption is referred as a barrier in communication.

- Breakdown in communication is a reason for professional, business and personal problems. Incomplete and inadequate communication causes misunderstanding and misinterpretation, resulting in difficulties.
- Noise barriers are any external factors that interfere with effective communication.
- The classification of barriers is summarised in Table 4.1 below.

Table 4.1: Classification of Barriers

Classification on the Basis of Nature of Problem

Physical and Mechanical Barriers	*Language or Semantic Barriers*	*Socio-Psychological Barriers*	*Organisational Barriers*	*Personal Barriers*
• Noise • Distance • Time • Information overload • Use of words with different meanings • Connotations and denotations	• No clarity in message • Damaged translation • Specialist's language • Underlying assumption	• Differences in perception • Differences in attitude • Emotions • Inattention • Closed minds • Premature evaluation • Distrust • Resistance to change • Cultural differences	• One-way flow • Organisational structure • Rules and regulations • Distance barrier • Physical barriers • Mechanical barriers	• Lack of confidence • Ignoring communication • Filtering of information • Message overload • Perceptual barriers • Offensive or abrasive style

Classification on the Basis of Phases of Communication

Relating to the Communicator	*Relating to Transmission of Message*	*Relating to the Receiver*
• Ineffective environment • Disorganised efforts to communication • Standard of correctness • Cultural values and social organisations • Inaccurate symbols • Wrong concept of the communication process	• Wrong handling of channel • Wrong selection of channels • Physical distractions • Use of inadequate channels in parallel • Channel's capacity	• Attention of the listeners • Problem of cooperation, participation and involvement • Problem of homogeneity • Attitude of the audience towards the communicator

KEY WORDS

Physical and mechanical barriers: The physical and mechanical barriers may be caused by noise, distance, time and information overload.

Technical barrier: Any physical hindrance in transfer of message which is not intended by the sender or receiver is considered as a technical problem. For example, disturbance in the connection, channel failure, etc.

Semantic barrier: This barrier is based on misinterpretation of messages due to linguistic errors.

Influential barrier: This barrier is concerned with lack of effectiveness or influence with which the meaning of the message is conveyed and when the desired results are not achieved.

Noise: Refers to any obstruction or interference which is external in nature in the process of communication.

EXERCISES

1. Discuss noise and interpersonal barriers?
2. Discuss various barriers on the basis of stages of communication?
3. Discuss the concept of barriers in the process of communication? How can one overcome these barriers?
4. How is language a barrier? Explain with examples.
5. What are the common barriers experienced by individuals in the process of communication in day-to-day life.
6. Illustrate with examples possible barriers that may arise when a development intervention is targeted to a group of community people at the grassroots. What steps can be taken to eliminate these barriers?
7. Write short notes on the following:
   a. Organisational barriers
   b. Socio-psychological barriers
   c. Barriers relating to the receiver
   d. Barriers relating to the transmission of message

REFERENCES

Barker, L. L., *Communication*, New Jersey: Prentice-Hall, 1981.

Barker, L. L. and R. G. Deborah, *Communication*, eighth edition, Boston, MA: Pearson, 2001,

DeVito, A. J., *Introduction to Human Communication*, Boston, MA: Pearson Education, 2006.

Dominick, J. R., *Dynamics of Mass Communication: Media in the Digital Age*, New York: McGraw-Hill, 2005.

Ekman, P. and F. Wallace, 'The Repertoire of Nonverbal Behaviour: Categories, Origins, Usage and Coding', *Semiotics* 1 (1969): 63–92.

McQuail, D., *Mass Communication Theory: An Introduction*, sixth edition, California: SAGE Publications, 2010.

Patri, V. R. and N. Patri, *Essentials of Effective Communication*, New Delhi: Greenspan, 2002.

Thurlow, C., L. Lengel and A. Tomic, *Computer Mediated Communication: Social Interaction and the Internet*, California: Sage, 2004.

Zeuschner, R., *Communicating Today: The Essentials*, Boston: Allyn & Bacon, 2003.

ONLINE SOURCE

http://www.liberatingstructures.com (accessed 20 September 2015)

UNIT II

CRITICAL FACTORS IN HUMAN COMMUNICATION

Having dealt with the basics of human communication, let us now step into understanding how cultures impact communication. What is the relationship between culture, perception, the process of listening and communication? Culture, the complex set of beliefs, value systems, attitudes and rituals, provides a unique identity to a group of people. Chapter Five helps us understand how intercultural communication can be made effective by mastering the art of decoding to derive appropriate meanings and overcoming barriers. How we behave in our day to day life with people of the same or different cultures, is majorly based on how we perceive stimulus around us. Any situation can be analysed in terms of its perceptual connotations. We will then proceed to understand the process of forming perceptions in Chapter Six. What are the factors affecting perception? How can we become more perceptive without being judgmental?

One of the barriers in communication, and specifically in intercultural communication, is poor listening. Chapter Seven elaborates on how listening is the pivot of the communication process. In order to empathise with someone we need to first listen to that person carefully. Following listening is the process of learning. In the last chapter of this unit we will learn how various audio-visual aids can be used to communicate. This unit attempts at weaving the concepts of culture, message decoding, meaning formation, skills and tools that can help individuals interact effectively.

5

CULTURE AND COMMUNICATION

HIGHLIGHTS

- Relationship between communication and culture
- Characteristics of culture
- Understanding cultural meanings
- Intercultural communication
- Importance of intercultural communication
- Barriers in intercultural communication
- Overcoming intercultural barriers

The world around us is rapidly changing. These changes are taking place across societies and cultures. People are constantly striving and aspiring for a better life marked not only be advances in food, clothing and shelter but also in things beyond—like interconnectedness, comradeship and entertainment. The process of globalisation has led to intra- and inter-country mobility and migration, and has thereby encouraged widespread use of communication technologies. People today are increasingly communicating across cultures for reasons such as business, socialisation and politics.

Today, our TV sets beam programmes from different countries, exposing us to a whole new set of ideas and behaviours. Most of the business and information sharing happens in an intercultural environment. In a multinational organisation, a manager or a boss may be required to appoint leaders from very different ethnic backgrounds and work cultures. Here a person sensitive to the intercultural aspects of relationship-building is likely to be more successful. Thus to avail the opportunities that come our way and for bettering their prospects, people are leaving their native communities and increasingly interacting with those who are from socio-economic and cultural backgrounds not similar to theirs. However, in such situations most people do not feel comfortable and confident in their communication. Cultural variations in communication styles, verbal and non-verbal cues, display of emotions, beliefs and attitudes explicitly influence communication and, consequently, people's ability to communicate their ideas confidently. Thus, understanding cultural differences and the role of culture in influencing communication has become a critical concern and there is a need to develop what is known as 'intercultural competence' for communication.

In Unit I we have understood that the term 'culture' refers to the complex collection of knowledge, folklore, language, rules, rituals, habits, lifestyles, attitudes, beliefs and customs that link and give a common identity to a particular group of people at a specific point in time and influence our ways of behaving and communicating. Culture needs to be understood not only as something synonymous with race and nationality but also as the set of shared beliefs, attitudes and practices across the society. Cultural diversity today has become a key dimension of most societies. Cultural differences can exist not only among people of different countries races and places of origin, but even among individuals from the same country, who speak the same language and have had similar education.

Cultural diversity presents a tremendous challenge because it forces us to pay attention to our communicative behaviour and to give up preconceived stereotypes. Today, understanding cultural diversity and its role in communication is central to realising social and organisational goals successfully.

RELATIONSHIP BETWEEN COMMUNICATION AND CULTURE

The relationship between communication and culture is a complex and intimate one. Cultures are created through communication; that is, communication is the means of human interaction through which cultural characteristics—customs, roles, rules, rituals, laws or other patterns—are created and shared. It is not so much that individuals set out to create a culture when they interact—in relationships, groups, organisations or societies, but rather cultures are a natural by-product of social interactions. In a sense, cultures are the 'residue' of communication. Without communication and communication media, it would be impossible to preserve and pass along cultural characteristics from one place and time to another. Thus we can safely say that culture is created, shaped, transmitted and learned through communication. The reverse is also true; that is, communication practices are largely created, shaped and transmitted by culture. Organisations also have cultures, often apparent in particular patterns of dress, layout of workspaces, meeting styles and functions, ways of thinking about and talking about the nature and directions of the organisation, leadership styles and so on. Where a group traditionally meets, whether meetings begin on time or not, what topics are discussed, how decisions are made and how the group socialises are all elements of what become defining and differentiating elements of its culture over time. An often-observed difference is in workplace relationships—in some organisations people may call their boss by their first name and may be casual in their attire and communication with each other, while in some other organisations formal communication and formal attire is the work culture.

Image 5.1: Cultural Diversity

Source: 'IMG_1505.jpg' by AFS-USA Intercultural Programs (flickr; CCA By 2.0).

The culture in which a person is raised profoundly affects every aspect of that person's communication behaviour and interpretation of messages. Communication among people of diverse backgrounds (and, therefore, with diverse communication patterns) is challenging.

It is observed that on many occasions people become ethnocentric, i.e. they believe their personal native culture is superior and judge everyone else's behaviour by the norms of their own culture. But successful communication among culturally diverse individuals requires them to give up their ethnocentricity.

To fully understand the deep relationship between communication and culture, it is necessary to think in terms of ongoing communication processes rather than a single communication event. For example, when a group of people meet for the first time, the members bring with them their individual thoughts and behaviour patterns from previous communication experiences and from other cultures of which they are, or have been, a part. As individuals start to engage in communication with other members of this new group, they begin to create a set of shared experiences and ways of talking about them. If the group continues to interact, a set of distinguishing history, patterns, customs and rituals will evolve with time. Some of these cultural characteristics would be quite obvious and tangible, such that a new person joining the group would encounter ongoing cultural 'rules' through which they would learn to conform to communication. New members would in turn influence the group culture in small—and sometimes, large—ways as they become a part of it. In a reciprocal fashion, this reshaped culture shapes the communication practices of current and future group members. This is true with any culture. Communication shapes culture and culture shapes communication.

Activity

Have a conversation with one of your classmates, ideally one who belongs to a different cultural background. Make a list of rituals performed by different family members, when a new baby is born. Then tell her/him about yours. Discuss the similarities and differences.

What is Culture?

The cultures of groups are relatively simple compared to those of organisations and, especially, societies. Let us see some definitions which talk about different aspects of culture.

> Culture . . . is that complex whole which includes knowledge, belief, art, morals, law, custom, and any other capabilities and habits acquired by man as a member of society.
>
> —Edward Tylor, *Primitive Culture* (1871)

> A collective name for all behavior patterns socially acquired and socially communicated by means of symbols.
>
> —Raymond Zeuschner, *Communicating Today* (2002)

> Culture is man's medium; there is not one aspect of human life that is not touched and altered by culture. This means personalities, how people express themselves (including show of emotion), way they think, how they move, how problems are solved, how their cities are planned and laid out, how economics and government systems are put together and function.
>
> —Edward Hall, *Beyond Culture* (2008)

> Culture refers to the relatively specialized lifestyle of a group or community consisting of their values, belief, artifacts, ways of behaving and ways of communicating. Culture includes all that members of a social group have produced and developed—their language, modes of thinking, art, laws and religion.
>
> —Joseph A. DeVito, *Human Communication* (2011)

Culture thus refers to the pattern of values, beliefs, symbols (including language), norms and behaviours shared by an identifiable group of individuals.

In the process of 'enculturation', i.e. becoming part of a culture, you are taught how to perceive the world, to think, to communicate and to behave. Teaching is done both formally and informally as you learn the lifestyle of the family and community you are born in. Small primary groups, like the family, are vital to this process and are the chief way individuals become 'enculturated'. This process happens so gradually and automatically that, unless something happens to make us question our behaviour, we are rarely aware of how culture affects us. Our own culture's effect on us is invisible unless we make it a point to look for it.

Similarly 'acculturation' is the process of adopting cultural traits and social patterns of another group. As individuals, groups, organisations and nations are exposed to new ideas and behaviours, these start penetrating and mixing with existing practices. Thus new norms emerge, shifting and changing the old ones. Sometimes the process of acculturation is slow and gradual but when aided by dictatorial forces it may be sharper and faster. The effects of acculturation can be seen at multiple levels in both interacting cultures. At the group level, acculturation often results in changes in customs and social institutions. Noticeable effects of acculturation could be changes in food, clothing and language.

> As enculturation is used to describe the process of first-culture learning, acculturation can be thought of as second-culture learning.

'Cultural identity' refers to the degree to which a person learns, accepts and identifies with the symbols, meanings and standards of behaviour common to a particular group. Individuals are taught such things as language, how and when to speak, how to perceive the world, and 'what is' and 'what is not' appropriate behaviour. Cultural identity influences our communications and the interpretation of the communication and behaviour of others as well.

Culture thus refers to any group of people with a shared identity. For example, a cultural grouping can refer to ethnicity (Punjabi, Marathi, American, Italian, Brown, White), a professional grouping (college students, school teachers, doctors, accountants), an interest grouping (choir group, theatre group), or even a socio-economic class (labourers, daily-wage earners, service class, middle class). All social units, be it a relationship, group, organisation or a society, have a distinct culture. As different social units are formed and interact over time they develop their own distinct culture. Groups also develop cultures which are composed of the rules, rituals, customs and other characteristics that give an identity to their social unit.

The most rich and complex cultures are those that are associated with a society or a nation. A societal or national culture also includes such elements as significant historical events and characters, philosophies of government, social customs, family practices, religion, economic philosophies and practices, beliefs and value system, and concepts and systems of law.

Within most complex cultures, groups that see themselves as distinct, but are part of a larger culture, emerge and are termed as subcultures or co-cultures. The concept of co-culture, highlights the fact that in most cultures, many cultures exist simultaneously within, as well as apart from other cultures and no one culture is inherently superior over co-existing cultures, although one culture may dominate others. Co-cultural groupings can be formed on the basis of any shared interest and usually display characteristic symbolism that enables them to have a distinct identity.

Activity

Talk to your grandparents/elders in the family about their daily routine when they were young. Then make a similar list while talking to your parents. Finally make another list of practices that you follow every day. Compare the three lists. Observe intergenerational changes.

Characteristics of Culture

While the defining characteristics or a combination of characteristics of each culture are unique, all cultures share certain common functions. Some important characteristics of culture are as follows.

Cultures are Learnt

Communication helps in transmitting ideas from one person to another and from one generation to the next. An individual learns about one's own culture through her/his family, peers, educational institutions and organisations through the process of 'enculturation'. For example, family rituals for childbirth, death or weddings are something one learns through enculturation throughout while one grows up. But it is not necessary for a person to always carry forward the family culture or the community's culture that (s)he was born in. For example, when a person goes out of her/his city to work or to study (s)he learns about rules, rituals, customs and other characteristics of the culture of that city through the process of acculturation. Progressively, those 'rules' and 'values' become an integral part of the 'host' culture. How easily one adopts a new culture depends on similarities between the two cultures, familiarity, age, education and an individual's personality.

Cultures are Dynamic

In fact, cultures are constantly changing, though the change is sometimes very slow and imperceptible. Many forces influence cultural change. As discussed, cultures are created through communication and it is also through communication between individuals that cultures change over time. Each person involved in a communication encounter brings the sum of her/his own experiences from other (past or present) cultural memberships. In one sense, any encounter between individuals in new relationships, groups, organisations or societies is an intercultural communication event, and these varying cultural encounters influence the individual and the cultures over time. Travel and communication technologies greatly accelerate the movement of messages from one cultural context to another, and in small and large ways, cultures come to influence one another through communication. Phrases such as 'melting pot', 'world community' and 'global village' speak to the inevitability of intercultural influence and change.

Cultures are Subjective

There is a tendency to assume that the elements of one's own cultures are logical and make good sense. This idea follows that if in other cultures, relationships, groups or organisations seem different, those differences are negative, illogical and sometimes nonsensical. If, for example, an individual happens to be in a romantic relationship in a culture that is characterised by public display of affection, (s)he may perceive behaviours of other people who come from some reserved relational culture as strange. An individual might even be tempted to conclude that a 'reserved' relationship lacks depth and intensity. This phenomenon is true in a variety of situations. With regard to culture, the tendency for many people is to equate 'different' with 'wrong', even though all cultural elements come about through essentially identical communication processes.

Cultures are Largely Invisible

Much of what characterises cultures of relationships, groups, organisations or societies is invisible to its members, much as the air is invisible to those who breathe it. Language, of course, is visible, as are greeting conventions, special symbols, places and spaces. However, the special and defining meanings that these symbols, greetings, places and spaces have for individuals in a culture are far less visible. For example, one can observe individuals kissing when they greet, but unless one has a good deal of cultural knowledge, it is difficult to determine what the behaviour means in the context of the culture of their relationship, group, organisation or society. In other words, it is difficult to tell, without adequate cultural knowledge, if the kiss is a customary greeting among casual acquaintances or if such a greeting would be reserved only for family members and lovers.

UNDERSTANDING CULTURAL MEANINGS

Culture is transmitted from one generation, country and community, individual to another through signs. The meanings of these signs are socially acquired. It is a collective process that occurs with a specific context. A sign is an entity that indicates the presence of something else. For example, touching the feet of an elderly person is a 'sign' of respect in many Indian cultures. During any communication process individuals constantly interpret these signs which can be presented in the form of language, gestures, movements or visuals. These interpretations of signs may differ for each individual due to various cultural influences and past experiences. Therefore, it is important to understand how these meanings are formed and what their role in communication is.

As we have studied in Chapter One, communication is an ongoing process. Individuals are constantly engaged in communicating with each other. During these interactions one tends to focus more on explicitly-used verbal and non-verbal signs. The ability of a good communicator lies in the ability to understand the more subtle and implicit meaning of signs in the process. If one misses the actual meaning then it may cause misunderstanding between the source and receiver. The system that helps in understanding the meanings of signs is known as Semiotics. This theory was proposed by the French linguist Ferdinand de Saussure. It is an interdisciplinary approach that helps in understanding the relationship between culture and communication. According to this theory a 'sign' is a union of the 'signifier' and the 'signified'. For example, when someone says 'apple' an image of an apple comes to our mind based on certain physical properties of an apple (round shape, red

Figure 5.1: Relationship between 'Sign', 'Signifier' and 'Signified'

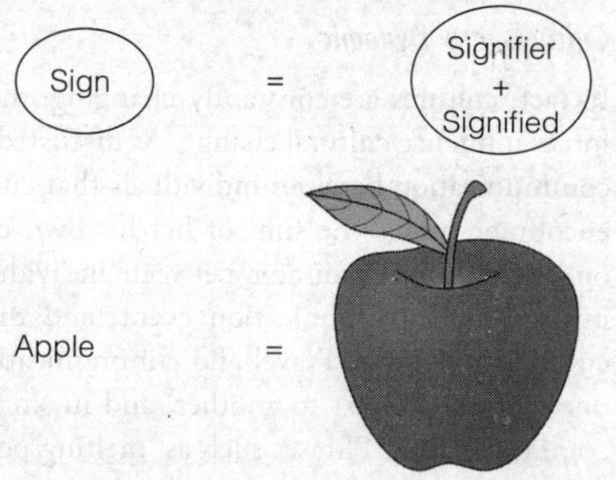

Source: Adapted by the author with inputs from the internet.

Image 5.2a: One Image of Cow

Source: 'Cow, Uttarakhand, India' by Yann (Wikimedia Commons; CC By 3.0).

Image 5.2b: Another Image of Cow

Source: 'Cow on Delhi Street' by John Hill (Wikimedia Commons; CC By 3.0).

colour, etc.). One does not think in terms of separate alphabets, i.e. a-p-p-l-e. The relationship between the 'signifier' and the 'signified' can be arbitrary or conventional but none can exist without each other.

It is easier to understand the assigned meaning which is socially accepted by almost every culture. But sometimes the meaning differs for people of different cultures. Speakers of the same language can associate different meanings with words which may or may not be in sync with their own experienced reality. For example, when someone says the word 'cow' what sort of images come to our mind?

> Semantics is a branch of semiotics. It is the study of meaning. Semantics tells the way meanings are attached to words or images by people who use them. These are not literal meanings suggested by a dictionary. These are the meanings acquired and accepted in a particular cultural context and hence come across differently for different people.

Text, images and gestures carry cultural and ideological meanings with them and are extremely crucial for the process of human communication. The theory of semiotics helps us understand the meaning of these texts, images and gestures to be able to communicate more effectively.

Meanings can be broadly divided into two categories—denotative and connotative. Denotative meaning is the first level of meaning. It is the literal meaning of a word, text, image or a gesture. For instance, when one says the word 'rose' the image of rose as a flower may come to our mind. It does not have any meaning or interpretation other than that. On the other hand, the connotative meaning suggests a second level of meaning of the same thing. So, if someone uses the word 'rose' on Valentine's Day, the meaning of the same word changes. It is the cultural or emotional meaning that a word or phrase carries, in addition to a word's or phrase's literal meaning. As DeVito (2011) explains, that connotative meaning adds value that is culturally encoded to that of first order (denotative) of meaning. It is described as either positive or negative, with regards to its pleasing or displeasing emotional connection. Understanding the theories behind signs and their meanings helps in creating and interpreting while communicating interpersonally especially in intercultural situations.

> **Activity**
>
> Identify twenty words with their denotative and connotative meaning. Discuss them in class with others and find out which could be easily misunderstood or misinterpreted.

INTERCULTURAL COMMUNICATION

In today's multicultural world, intercultural interactions cannot be avoided. The function of communication is not just to satisfy the need to socialise with others but also to record, preserve and share the existing knowledge of the present times for future generations. As discussed earlier, terms like 'global village' clearly underline the unavoidability of intercultural interactions. In a world that has become a global village, as McLuhan (2011) says, with new communication technologies geographical boundaries get smaller and prospects for cross-culture communication increase. In that case the need for understanding, appreciation and tolerance of other cultural systems has to increase.

> Intercultural communication, to put it simply, takes place when two or more people from different cultures or subcultures communicate with each other. While interaction between and among individuals from the same culture or subculture are called intracultural communication.

During communication among individuals from the same culture or co-culture, much of the communication behaviour can be taken for granted. But while communicating with individuals from different cultures, one must be alert to the added potential for misunderstanding. It is important that intercultural interactions begin without any bias. Often such communications are backed by one's identity and cultural values that the person acquired while growing up. Therefore, denial of the existence of cultural differences cannot help build bridges among communities. Rather, it is important to acknowledge these differences and find solutions to get maximum benefit during communication and cultivate better understanding and tolerance. Keeping all of this in mind, in this section, we will try to understand the relationship between culture and communication and some parameters that may govern effective intercultural situations.

Importance of Intercultural Communication Competence

The concept of intercultural communication emerged during post–World War II period. After the War, the US government started to set up businesses and soon realised the need for training to prepare their officials to face intercultural communication scenarios. Later it became an interdisciplinary field studying language, history, semantic and the social sciences to make participants understand cultural issues from diverse perspectives. One of the most important things in intercultural communication is to understand these diverse perspectives. According to one theory cultural differences are only superficial and there is no right and wrong culture. On the other hand some others propose that cultural behaviours can only be judged within the culture it exists and that outsiders cannot be judges of this.

A person with intercultural competence will choose a middle path and try to understand why people from a certain culture, with a specific value system and background, behave the way they do. In contemporary societies—where social pressures push human beings to take extreme positions vis-à-vis ethics—understanding the importance of intercultural interactions become imperative. These interactions help raise questions and develop a better understanding of class, race, socio-economic divides and religious diversity in the society while communicating with others.

Therefore, intercultural competence enables one to:

- *Bring awareness about one's own personal privileges or deprivations*: Intercultural communication makes us aware of other cultures and also helps us recognise and underline the privileges and/or deprivations that one faces because of a particular socio-cultural background. For example, imagine the communication transaction when an individual who lives in a cosmopolitan city meets and interacts with an agricultural labour from a remote village with meagre means in life. In this case, learning for the city-dweller may not just mean understanding the hardships of an agricultural labourer's life but it may also be becoming aware of her/his own privileges as a city dweller. Understanding other cultures makes a person realise her/his position in the society.
- *Helps understand demographic diversity*: Often one hears that India's strength lies in unity in diversity. But does it only refer to cultural diversity? India's demography is extremely diverse not only in terms of culture and ethnicity but also in terms of the social and economic status of its people. One may say that demographically India is one of the most diverse countries in the world. Intercultural competence helps us understand this diversity better.
- *Prepares to deal with economic interconnections*: In the globalised world where people work in multi- and transnational corporations and organisations, economic integration and new communication technologies have broken down geographical boundaries. People are not apprehensive to leave their country to earn their bread and butter. Often, people have to work in organisations where they interact with people from diverse linguistic backgrounds, opinions and interpretations of life. In order to make the best out of these intercultural interactions, a number of organisations conduct training sessions to help their employees to develop skills for better communication. It helps them interpret verbal and non-verbal gestures of clients as well as their own team members and subordinates.

Barriers in Intercultural Communication

Intercultural communication is characterised by cultural dissimilarities among people and their communication style, values, beliefs and perceptions. But sometimes individuals fail to perceive these dissimilarities and create barriers. Some of the barriers which need to be taken care of are as follows.

Ethnocentric Behaviour

The interactions with people of a culture different from ours can easily go haywire if the intercultural contexts are not taken seriously and understood properly. One of the most common challenges that need to be overcome in intercultural contexts is 'ethnocentrism'—i.e. the belief that her/his culture is superior to other cultures. Communities take great pride in their cultural values and belief systems but immediately assuming that other cultures are inferior creates a gap and can lead to intercultural conflicts. For example, in India, dog meat is eaten in Nagaland. Now, for a person who lives in North India this might sound shocking and unbelievable but this is part of cultural identity of the Nagas.

Stereotyping

It hinders the growth of intercultural relationships. Sometimes stereotyping helps in knowing what to expect from others. Stereotypes can be positive or negative. For example Asian-Americans have often been regarded as a 'good minority'. Another example would be that girls with blonde hair are considered 'stupid'. This sort of negative stereotype is harmful because several researches show that, once they are adopted, stereotypes are difficult to get rid of. Stereotypes are formed through family, peers, media and personal experiences as well. If a person has a stereotypical image about a particular culture it becomes difficult to even break the ice while having intercultural interactions. Stereotyping can lead to discrimination against individuals and communities based on gender, race, class or caste. One has to understand that stereotyping occurs at the subconscious level and therefore has to be abandoned consciously to enhance intercultural competence.

Culture Shock

Culture shock means the impact one might feel while entering a different culture. Culture shock is common among migrants and tourists. It occurs during the first phase of the acculturation process. Even when one goes fully prepared to another state or country, one can never predict the unexpected. Differences in non-verbal communication and unwritten rules play a crucial role. Cultural shock occurs when one is unable to deal with: (*a*) unfamiliar characteristics of other's culture, (*b*) unfriendly, hostile atmosphere of the new culture, and (*c*) unfamiliarity with the new language. Zeuschner (2002) has described four stages of culture shock.

1. *Honeymoon stage*: This is also known as anticipation or excitement phase. It occurs when a person goes to a new cultural environment and is excited to be in a new situation.
2. *Crisis stage*: Soon, when the honeymoon stage is over, the crisis stage begins. It occurs when the person begins to see the difference between her/his own culture and the new culture one has to adapt to. This is the time of coming out of one's comfort zone and seeing the reality and feeling disoriented due to the unfamiliarity of the new cultural atmosphere.
3. *Recovery stage*: If one makes an effort to understand the new culture and its beliefs, values and language systems then it becomes easier to communicate with others. In this phase one starts making sense of the new cultural context and experiences.
4. *Adjustment stage*: This phase begins with learning and adjusting to the rules and customs of the new cultural context.

Failure to Perceive Difference

Finally, it is important to recognise the fact that cultural contexts of people are different. If these differences are not recognised and respected, and if unconsciously it gets conveyed that one's culture is better than other, it may lead to confusion and meaningless interaction. These differences do not exist only in value systems but also in the meaning of words, sign and symbols. Perceiving differences in connotative meanings is crucial for a successful intercultural interaction. One has to keep reminding oneself that it is important to empathise with people while communicating to them in intercultural contexts. One needs to discover new ways of dealing with differences, find similarities and move beyond stereotypes.

Activity

Discuss the intercultural experiences of your classmate who has come to live in the city from somewhere else. Enquire, if (s)he faced ethnocentric behaviour? Was she typecast because of her race or caste or class? How did she deal with it?

Overcoming Intercultural Barriers

Rather than avoiding intercultural interactions one needs to face them with confidence which can be developed in various ways.

Building Knowledge

Here knowledge has two components: knowledge of the self and of the other. Knowledge of the self helps in understanding how one's own culture is perceived by others, whereas prior knowledge about other cultures helps to know how people think and behave. Often knowledge helps in packaging the message to be communicated.

Keeping the Attitude Right

It has many components: respecting other cultures, tolerance for ambiguity and being nonjudgemental.

Empathy

It plays a very important role in intercultural communication. One cannot really put oneself into another person's shoes until knowing something about her/his past experiences and the context of her/his cultural identity.

Building Dialogue

It is important to engage in a dialogue. One has to become a better intercultural listener to exchange stories of collective histories, expression, celebrations and mourning. This helps lay down the foundation for openness, curiosity and empathy.

SUMMARY

- In today's rapidly changing world understanding about cultural differences and the role of culture in influencing variations in communications has become a critical concern for all of us.
- In a world that has become a 'global village', new communication technologies emerge, geographical boundaries get smaller and prospects for cross-culture communication increase.

- Each culture is unique but also shares some common characteristics. It is learnt, dynamic, subjective and largely invisible.
- Culture is created, shaped, transmitted and learned through communication. On the other hand, communication practices are largely created, shaped and transmitted by culture.
- Culture is transmitted through the social processes like enculturation and acculturation.
- During the communication process cultural signs and symbols presented in the form of language, gestures, movements or visuals are constantly interpreted by individuals. Since these interpretations of signs may differ for each individual, understanding how these meanings are formed and their role in communication in imperative.
- Theories of semiotics and semantics help us understand the meaning of cultural signs and symbols.
- Intercultural interactions help develop a better understanding one's privileges, demographic and socio-economic, religious diversity in the contemporary social milieu.
- Ethnocentric behaviour, stereotyping and culture shock are some of the barriers that need to be overcome during cross-cultural communication.
- Building dialogue, knowledge and empathy for other cures help overcome barriers in intercultural communication.

KEY WORDS

Culture: It refers to the pattern of values, beliefs, symbols (including language), norms and behaviours shared by an identifiable group of individuals.

Enculturation: It is the gradual process of becoming part of a culture by learning the lifestyle of the family and community.

Acculturation: The process of adopting cultural traits and social patterns of another group.

Cultural identity: It refers to the degree to which a person learns, accepts and identifies with the symbols, meanings and standards of behaviour common to a particular group.

Semiotics: The system of deconstructing meanings of signs proposed by the French linguist Ferdinand de Saussure.

Denotative meaning: It is the literal meaning of a word, text, image or a gesture. It does not have any meaning or interpretation other than that.

Connotative meaning: It suggests a second level of meaning of the same thing.

EXERCISES

1. Intercultural communication competence is important in a world which has become a 'global village'. Discuss in detail.
2. Discuss any two definitions of culture given by eminent scholars of cultural studies.
3. What are the different characteristics of culture?
4. What is intercultural communication?
5. Explain the barriers in intercultural communication. What are the possible ways to overcome these barriers?

REFERENCES

DeVito, Joseph A., *Human Communication: The Basic Course*, twelfth edition, New York: Pearson, 2011.

Hall, Edward H., *Beyond Culture*, Garden City, NY: Anchor Press/Doubleday, 2008.

Martin, Judith M. and Thomas K. Nakayama, *Intercultural Communication in Contexts*, sixth edition, New York: The McGraw-Hill Higher ED, 2012.

McLuhan, Marshall, *The Gutenberg Galaxy*, Toronto: University of Toronto Press, 2011.

Rogers, Everett M., *A History of Communication Study: A Biographical Approaches*, York: Free Press, 1997.

Tylor, Edward, *Primitive Culture: Researches into the Development of Mythology, Philosophy, Religion, Language, Art and Custom*, available at https://archive.org/stream/primitiveculture01tylouoft/primitiveculture01tylouoft_djvu.txt (accessed 15 April 2016).

Zeuschner, Raymond, *Communicating Today: The Essentials*, New York: Pearson, 2002.

6

PERCEPTION

HIGHLIGHTS

- Concept of perception
- Perception and communication
- The process of perception formation
- Occurrence of stimulation
- Organisation of stimulations
- Evaluation/Interpretation of stimulation
- Perceptual filters
- Adjusting to avoid perceptual filters

We are all unique. Even with the similarities in physical attributes, ideas and behaviours between siblings, twins, family members and friends, we are all markedly different. We all have our own 'world', our own way of looking at and understanding our environment and the people within it. A situation may be the same but the interpretation of that situation by two individuals may be vastly different. For instance, watching a TV programme may be riveting to one person but to another it may be a boring way to spend time. One person may see a product as useful and practical but another may feel that it is inefficient and impractical. The physical attributes of two objects or individuals may be identical, but they are perceived quite differently because each individual has imposed upon the object/person their own interpretations, judgment and evaluation.

We all see things in different ways. We all have our unique picture of the 'real' world and this is a complex and dynamic process. We do not passively receive information from the world; we analyse and judge it. We may place significance on some information and regard other information as worthless; and we may be influenced by our expectations so that we 'see' what we expect to see or 'hear' what we expect to hear. This process by which individuals make sense of things is called perception.

Perception involves the organisation, identification and interpretation of sensory information in order to represent and understand the environment. It is a process by which one becomes aware of the many physical and chemical stimuli working on the senses. For example, vision involves light striking the retina of the eye, smell is mediated by the odour molecules, and hearing involves pressure waves.

Perception has been defined as the process by which we interpret sensory data (Lahlry 1991/2001). It is the ability to see, hear or become aware of something through the senses; a neuro-physiological process, including memory, by which individuals becomes aware of and interpret external stimuli. Perception is the root of all behaviours. Any situation can be analysed in terms of its perceptual connotations.

Look at Image 6.1. What do you see? Do you see a young, attractive, well-dressed woman? Or do you see an older, poor woman? Or can you now see both? And who can say with certainty that there is just one 'correct' answer? Despite the fact that we all are 'physically seeing' the same thing, each one of us may have our own version of what we are seeing—our own perceived view of reality.

Thus, understanding the perceptual process is of great significance today. In this chapter, we will learn about why perception is important in communication. We will discuss the process through which our perceptions are formed, the factors affecting perception and how we can become more perceptive without being judgmental.

Image 6.1: What Do You See in this Image? An Old or a Young Woman?

Source: '*My Wife and My Mother-In-Law*, by the cartoonist W. E. Hill, 1915 (adapted from a picture going back at least to a 1888 German postcard)' (Wikimedia Commons; CC0 Public Domain).

CONCEPT OF PERCEPTION

Several scholars consider perception to be an 'information processing' process that involves not only the recognition of various stimuli in a message but also coherently organising and deriving meaning from them. The 'information' is not implicit in a message and emerges through our perceptual processing of it. Individuals receive, screen and process message stimuli differently. This 'Information Processing' that each individual engages in helps form one's perceptions.

Perception is shaped by learning, prior knowledge, memory, past experiences, psychological state and expectation. Our concept of the self influences how we see ourselves, perception is how we see and perceive others. According to McCroskey (2005) perception is formed in three stages. First, by observing 'properties' of people that are most visible—age, weight, length of hair, skin colour and clothing. Second, by observing their social behaviour—angry outbursts, smiles, frowns and verbal statements. This second level of observation will strengthen or change perceptions. Finally, judgments are made based on these observations.

Often impressions about others are created with a little carelessness. People pay attention to those who they think are important, such as family, friends and colleagues. Other impressions about unknown people or those one meets for the first time are created without much thought and are sometimes inaccurate. Thus awareness and evaluation based on perception is subjective and is largely based on expectations, attitudes and other psychological factors. In other words, perception by its very nature is always selective.

The way a person views the other person will have an impact on their interactions. As a source, the way one perceives the receiver will have an impact on the way (s)he attempts to communicate with her/him. Similarly, the receiver's response will be based on her/his perception of the source. In either case the communication process will be affected.

PERCEPTION AND COMMUNICATION

As discussed in the previous chapters, communication is a process of exchange of ideas. The main purpose of communication is sorting, selecting and sending of messages in such a way that when listeners receive it, they can fully understand the meaning of that message. But how these messages will actually be understood and perceived depends on the perception of individuals engaged in communication. Because of perceptual differences, the meaning of messages may be totally distorted and the intended meaning may get lost. People's perception depends largely on their past experiences, socio-cultural background and the way they are taught to observe people and objects around them. Our perceptions shape our reality and determine how we communicate with others as well as how we perceive other's communicating with us. Thus, perceptions about a situation may vary since everyone perceives situations differently. However, variations in perception do not imply that one person is right and the other is wrong.

One of the key aspects in developing communication competence is being able to distinguish between a fact, opinion and judgment. Incorrect perception may lead to breakdown of communication process, whereas correct perception can help build long-standing relationships. Perception effects our communication with others and communication too effects our perception. Therefore perception and communication form a cyclic and continuous process.

The following are some aspects of communication transactions and perceptions of persons involved in the communication process.

Figure 6.1: Perception Pyramid

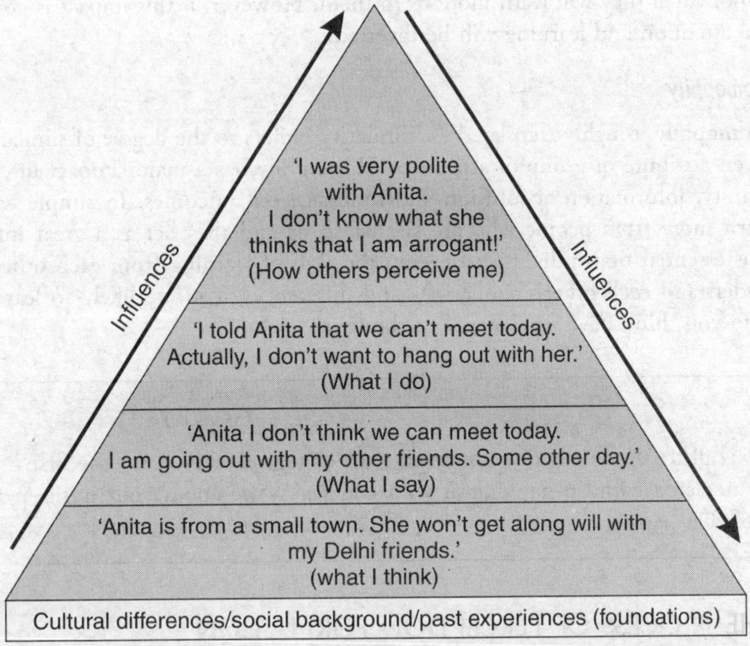

Source: Based on a concept by David Armano; adapted by the authors with inputs from http://www.bellartefutsal.com/site/index.php?option=com_content&view=article&id=394:the-pyramid-of-perception&catid=49&Itemid=236&lang=en (accessed December 2015).

Acceptance and Denial

Our acceptance and denial of a situation as well as our communication is governed to a great extent by our past experiences with someone or something. For example, we tend to listen to the lecturer or presenter we like the most; we talk to our friends and listen to their discussions very carefully as compared to others; we generally opt for restaurants based on our previous experience or on reviews of our friends. Since exposure is necessary for any communication outcome to be possible, these attitudes towards others can obviously affect all outcomes. If we have a positive attitude towards a situation then we are more likely to accept that situation or person and expose ourselves to the situation or the person. However, a negative attitude towards someone can limit this exposure and create denial in the process of communication. Denial, a term in psychology, is one of the primitive self-defense mechanisms that we use if we do not want to accept reality around us. When any stimulus is not in accordance to our existing belief and values we tend to deny it. It is important to understand that unlike acceptance, denial is the work of our unconscious mind. It may happen due to an inability to accept the reality; for example, the news of the death of a loved one in an accident may evoke this kind of response.

Attitudes and Beliefs

Our attitude towards the other communicator will have an impact both on the way we perceive messages of that person and on the way in which we expect our messages to be understood by that person. For example, if we believe that there is no truth in what the person says, we would simply disregard their talk and would not believe what has been said. Similarly, if we perceive that a person has a strong attitude towards an issue or a topic, we may interpret what the person says in light of that attitude rather than specifically on the basis of the message itself. Messages are therefore mediated by our attitude towards a person in the communication. The credibility of a message is based on our perception about the source and the degree of credibility we accord to it.

Attention and Learning

Our attention and learning during the communication process are a result of our attitude towards the communicator. This governs how much we learn from them and, in turn, how much they learn from us. When we pay more attention to a few messages, we learn more from them. This is particularly important in the academic and work environment. If a student or an employee has a positive attitude towards a teacher or a senior, then they will learn more from them. However, if this impact is governed by negative experiences then the attention and learning will be diverted.

Homophily

Homophily, roughly translated as 'similarity', refers to the degree of similarity between communicators on any given attribute or group of attributes. Homophily has a major impact in communication, and particularly on affinity, information acquisition and influence on outcomes. In simple words, we tend to get attracted and learn more from people who are similar to us and they act as a great influence. In almost all organisations it is essential that individuals develop the skill of learning from each other to the extent that the individuals understand each other's similarities and differences. You are likely to learn from your friends and colleagues who you think have similar way of thought.

> **Activity**
>
> Recall the scene when you entered your college classroom for the first time. Think of the person that you interacted with on day one of your college. Write about your initial perception and changed impression of that person.

THE PROCESS OF PERCEPTION FORMATION

Perception is a complex process and involves the processing of information. The perception formation process takes place in three basic stages: (*a*) occurrence of sensory stimulation, (*b*) organisation of sensory stimulation, and (*c*) interpretation-evaluation of sensory stimulation. It is important to understand these stages.

Figure 6.2: Perception Process

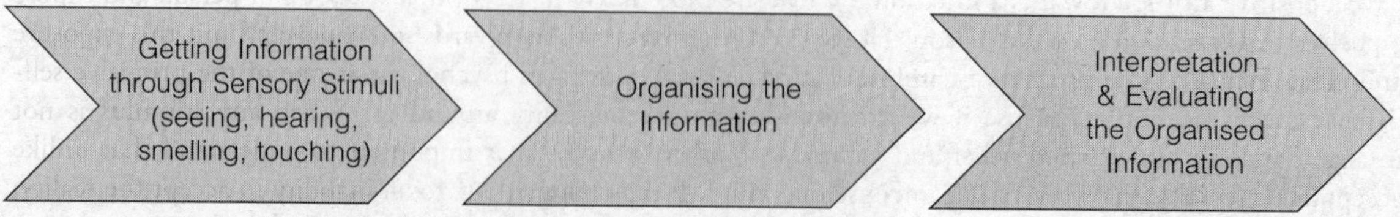

Source: Based on a concept by Joseph DeVito; adapted by author.

Occurrence of Sensory Stimulation

At the first stage of occurrence of sensory stimulation, the person gets information through the sensory organs. Once a person receives the information the 'processing' of that information begins. The process of selection of information is a multi-layered and complex process. We are bombarded with so much information every day that it is impossible for our brains to process and make sense of it all. In order to deal with this our brain automatically leaves out some of the information coming in through our senses. This process of focusing and selecting incoming information through our sensory system is the first part of the perception process.

Just think about the many possible stimuli you may pay attention to while walking in the park. You may hear a familiar voice, the chatter of a flock of birds; see a jogger wearing a pair of shoes you really like, bright flowers blooming, a dilapidated garden bench, a ferocious dog and his master; the smell of burning leaves, someone's fragrant perfume that you wear too; the stimuli are endless. So, how do we decide what to select and what to leave out?

According to Fiske and Taylor (1991) the human brain pays attention to a stimulus which is, (*a*) visually and aurally attractive, (*b*) meets our needs and interests, and (*c*) fulfills our expectations. For example, people watch only those TV serials they find visually and aurally interesting. Human beings selectively expose themselves to certain content, pay attention to and 'retain' only that information which is in sync with their expectations. This entire process of selection of information ultimately leads to selective perception which, in most cases, is subjective. Several factors influence this first step of the perceptual process and what we select and give attention to. These factors are:

Sensory Capacities and Preferences

People differ in their sensory limits, sensory preferences, as well as in their ability to discern between stimuli. These differences consequently influence their ability to receive and process information and their variations in perceptions. For instance, some people need not wear woollen on a cold winter day while others might find the weather intolerable despite several layers of woollen. Some people can differentiate between similar-looking herbs and spices by smelling, or can notice the slightest of variations which others might be totally oblivious of. Further, people not only differ in their sensory capacities but also in their preferences for sensory stimulations. For instance, while most youngsters usually like listening to loud rock music, older persons may prefer classical melodies.

Needs and Interests

Needs and interests have a central role in guiding the information we seek and the stimuli we respond to. We tend to pay greater attention to information we perceive will fulfill our needs and interests. For example, when you are deeply engrossed in completing a crucial report or an assignment, you may screen out ringing telephones, the sound of a TV programme, the horns of cars in the street or your parents talking. Similarly when your vehicle is low on fuel and you are looking for a petrol pump the sign of a station would be your most important concern and you may be totally oblivious to other signage's or hoardings. Thus, the most desirable and the urgent needs most certainly affect your perceptual process. Of course, at times we also find things interesting that don't necessarily meet our needs. We all get engrossed in a TV show, video game or a random project and pay close attention to it even at the expense of something that actually meets our needs like studying or doing some pressing tasks.

Expectations

Our expectations also influence the information and stimuli we give salience to. Interestingly both expected as well as unexpected information can ascribe salience to any situation. Hence when we expect something to happen we pay attention to the slightest of cues and stimuli. So when you are eagerly waiting for someone to arrive, you may look out for any cues signalling their arrival, like their car stopping outside your house or their footsteps on their way to ring the doorbell. Similarly, when something unexpected or out of the ordinary happens it also attracts our attention. Strong or rigid expectations from another person may limit one's understanding and perception in some cases.

Psychological Factors

Psychological factors also affect what is perceived. These include factors such as personality, mental states and motives that influence our inclination to perceive certain stimuli and readiness to respond in certain ways. Psychological factors influence individual differences in the type of information individuals need as well as how they acquire and use information from the environment to make sense of their world. When a person strongly desires to fulfill her/his social and psychological needs the perceptual ability is affected. For example, an individual's need to be socially affiliated or accepted by a group or a community will draw her/him to perceive things from that group's perspective. Many a time, a person's anxiety and mental stress weaken her/his perceptual capabilities.

Cultural Aspects

Perceptual tendencies depend a lot on a person's cultural beliefs and values. The ability to perceive something depends on the socio-cultural environment in which one is born and brought up. Edgar Schein (1992) argued that culture is 'a pattern of basic assumptions—invented, discovered or developed by a given group as it learns to cope with its problems of external adaptation and internal integration—that has worked well enough to be considered valuable and therefore to be taught to new members as the correct way to perceive, think and feel in relation to these problems.' Words used and the meaning ascribed to them by people, their gestures and movements, actions and behaviours, the artefacts and symbols used by them are all a reflection of their culture. Further, cultural differences lead to generation of stereotypes that act as important perceptual filters.

Extrinsic Factors

Extrinsic factors refer to the nature and characteristics of stimuli. There is usually a tendency to give more attention to stimuli which are in strong contrast to their background; for example, brightness, movement, intensity, repetition or loudness. Any number of these factors may be present at a given time or in a given situation. It is the total pattern of the stimuli together with the context in which these occur that influence perception. This is why when we see hoardings on the road side we are attracted to some of them instantly.

Image 6.2: In this Photo which Visual Caught your Attention First? Why do you think you were Attracted to it first?

Source: 'Pvr Saket' by rohtak8 (Wikimedia Commons; CC By 3.0).

Organisation of Sensory Stimulation

The next stage in the formation of perception is the organisation of sensory stimulation. Organising information can be understood by drawing an analogy of organising one's bookshelf. When books pile up, we organise them according to the theme or according to the author. We group them according to their similarities and dissimilarities. It helps us to arrange this way so we may easily refer to any book in the future. Similarly, sensory stimuli are also organised in our brain. According to researchers at the Gestalt School of Psychology the process of perception is innately organised and patterned by our brain. They identified some principles that help us understand how the brain organises stimuli. These are based on the aspects of proximity, similarities, dissimilarities and closure of stimuli.

Proximity

This principle refers to the tendency to organise shapes and patterns instantly into meaningful groupings or patterns on the basis of their proximity or similarity. This allows for the grouping together of elements to be perceived as a larger group. The brain groups together the elements instead of processing a large number of smaller stimuli and allows us to understand and conceptualise. Observe Figure 6.3. The proximity of the dots have enabled us to group them together making them one whole figure.

Figure 6.3: Parts Closer to Each Other in Time or Space tend to be Perceived Together

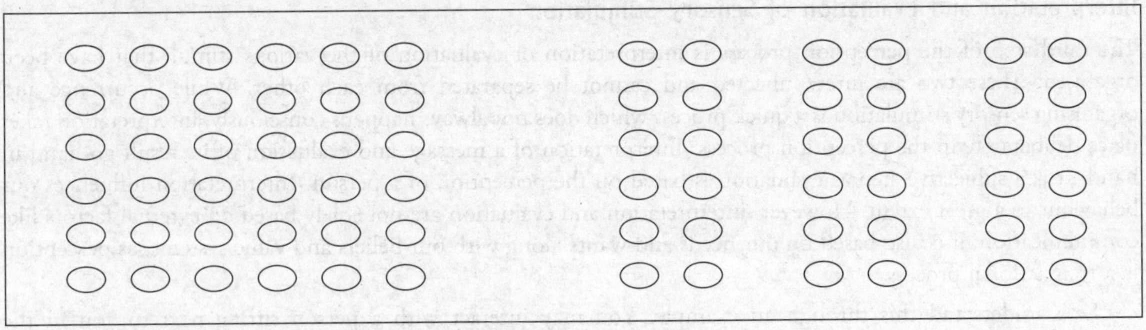

Source: 'Gestalt proximity.svg' by Eumedemito (Wikimedia Commons; CC0 Public Domain).

Similarity

Perception is also formed based on similarities and dissimilarities. According to this principle, stimuli that physically resemble each other in various aspects such as colours, texture, sound, taste, etc. are perceived as one whole part. This allows for people to distinguish between adjacent and overlapping objects based on their resemblance. Thus our brain uses similarity to distinguish between objects.

Image 6.3: Similarity in Colour Enable the Grouping of the Football Players for the Audience

Source: 'Chelsea's Eden Hazard takes on Norwich City's Jonny Howson' by Ben Sutherland (flickr; CC By-SA 2.0).

Closure

The principle of closure refers to the brain's tendency to complete figures or forms even if they are incomplete, partially hidden, or if part of the information needed to make a complete picture is missing. Look at Figure 6.4.

Perception goes beyond the sensory information and converts patterns to a three-dimensional reality that we understand. However this conversion process, as we can see, can be very tricky. We may not be aware of the inferences we are making and they may at times be incorrect. Thus, we go beyond what is given and make assumptions about the world. Grouping information and looking for patterns is a natural thing to do. If patterns are always associated with stereotypes and prejudgments then they become barriers in the process of perception formation and hence hinder the communication process.

Figure 6.4: What do You See? Circle or a Broken Circle? Rectangle or a Broken Rectangle?

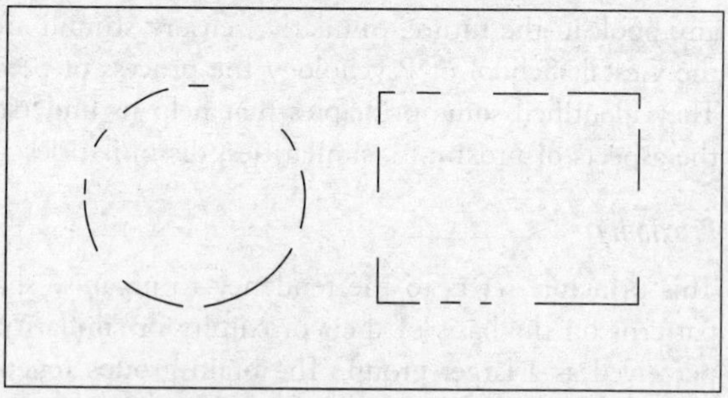

Source: 'Gestalt closure.svg' by Eumedemito (Wikimedia Commons; CC0 Public Domain).

Interpretation and Evaluation of Sensory Stimulation

The third step of the perception process is interpretation or evaluation of the various stimuli that have been organised. These two are interconnected and cannot be separated from each other. While occurrence and organising sensory stimulation is a quick process which does not always happens consciously, interpretation takes place deliberately in the perception process. Interpretation of a message and evaluation of its result go hand in hand. It is a subjective step as evaluation is based on the perception of a person. Interpretation influences our behaviour to a great extent. However, interpretation and evaluation are not solely based on external factors like communication; it is also based on our needs and wants along with our beliefs and value systems, as perception is a transactional process.

Let's understand this through an example. You may interact with a person sitting next to you in the train or during a bus journey for some time and may forget about it in a few hours. However, if during this interaction, you find some desirable traits, it would make you think about the interaction and the memory of that interaction lingers in your mind and you wish to communicate with the person again; and the feeling may be reciprocal. It would be transactional as it brings the two participants in the communication situation in unison. There is always a transactional relationship between the 'perceiver' and the 'perceived'. It means how we perceive a new situation or an individual depends not only on how they look but also on our innate desire to associate with that situation or an individual at that point of time. The following are some of the key processes that have been found to influence our perceptions.

Implicit Personality Theory

There is a set of beliefs and assumptions that we have about how certain traits are linked to other characteristics and behaviours. It describes the specific patterns and biases an individual uses when forming impressions about people, situations, objects, etc. Once we know a trait, we assume that the person also exhibits other traits that are commonly linked to that key characteristic; this is also called the 'halo effect'. We have a natural tendency to view a number of characteristics and link them together in a person both positively or negatively. These implicit rules regarding characteristics of a person can prevent us from perceiving a person or a situation realistically.

Perceptual Accentuation

Sometimes we highlight the fact that we expect and want to see. Perceptual accentuation, can distort your perceptions of reality and you may perceive what you need to or want to perceive; you magnify that symbol which will satisfy your needs and wants. For example, an alcoholic may easily spot a bar at the corner of a crowded street. Sometimes, we also do not see our own delimiting patterns of behaviour and but perceive negative qualities in others that we have ourselves projected on them. For example, persons with an inflated sense of ego do not recognise their own limitations nor accept corrections, but may point out others' limitations or correct them.

Primacy–Recency

It focuses on the individual's tendency to be influenced by whatever occurs first or comes last. The adage, 'First impression is the best impression' aptly focuses on the influence of primacy of effect on our perceptions. Primacy and recency can limit individuals' understanding of situations and persons since first impressions need not always provide a holistic picture. An adverse side of this is that individuals may try to deceive others by putting forth early impressions that may be totally incorrect.

Stereotyping

Stereotyping refers to having a fixed impression about a group of people. It influences how we meet and interact with any person belonging to that group. We apply to that person all characteristics we assign to that group. Interestingly, when individuals do not know that the person belonged to that group they would behave very differently. Stereotypes distort accurate perception. Because of our stereotypes we may fail to see many other dimensions of individuals and only attribute those qualities that we believe is typical of her/his group.

Attribution

Attribution theory explains the process you go though in trying to understand about your own and/or others' behaviours, particularly the reasons or motivations of these behaviours. Attribution helps you to make sense of what you perceive. It helps you to give order and logic to the perceived stimuli and better understand the possible causes of the behaviours you observe. Attribution also helps make predictions about what will happen and what others are likely to do.

Activity

Match the following. Discuss your choice of answers.

Stereotyping	'My wife is perfect. She never argues with me.'
Primacy-recency	'Blondes have no brains.'
Perceptual accentuation	'The minute I met her and she opened her mouth I knew she is from a small town.'
Implicit personality	'He doesn't drink alcohol. He must be a man of high morals.'

PERCEPTUAL FILTERS

In the three stages of perception formation, the stimuli go through the processes of deletion, distortion and generalisation. Deletion leads to omission of extra information and occurs because there is a limit to how much information we can receive every day. Along with deletion, we also distort information. Distortion of information occurs largely because we observe only a small part of our environment. After deletion and distortion we start to see patterns which lead to generalisation. Generalisations enable us to make conclusions based on what we know and we think are 'facts'. Sometimes these generalisations help us understand and expect the obvious. But, in an intercultural context, generalisations can also prove to be incorrect and at times even dangerous.

For example, if we continuously have an unpleasant experience in a different culture we may tend to 'generalise' that all members of that culture are bad.

Since there are so many influences, and because these influences are likely to combine in unknown ways and even have some cumulative effect, our perceptions are affected in diverse and multifarious ways. These factors together form our 'perceptual filters', which form the lens through which we view the world. The filters once formed cannot be changed very quickly. However, it is important to be aware of our perceptual filters so that deletion, distortion and generalisations can be minimised.

Figure 6.5: Several Factors Influence Human Perception

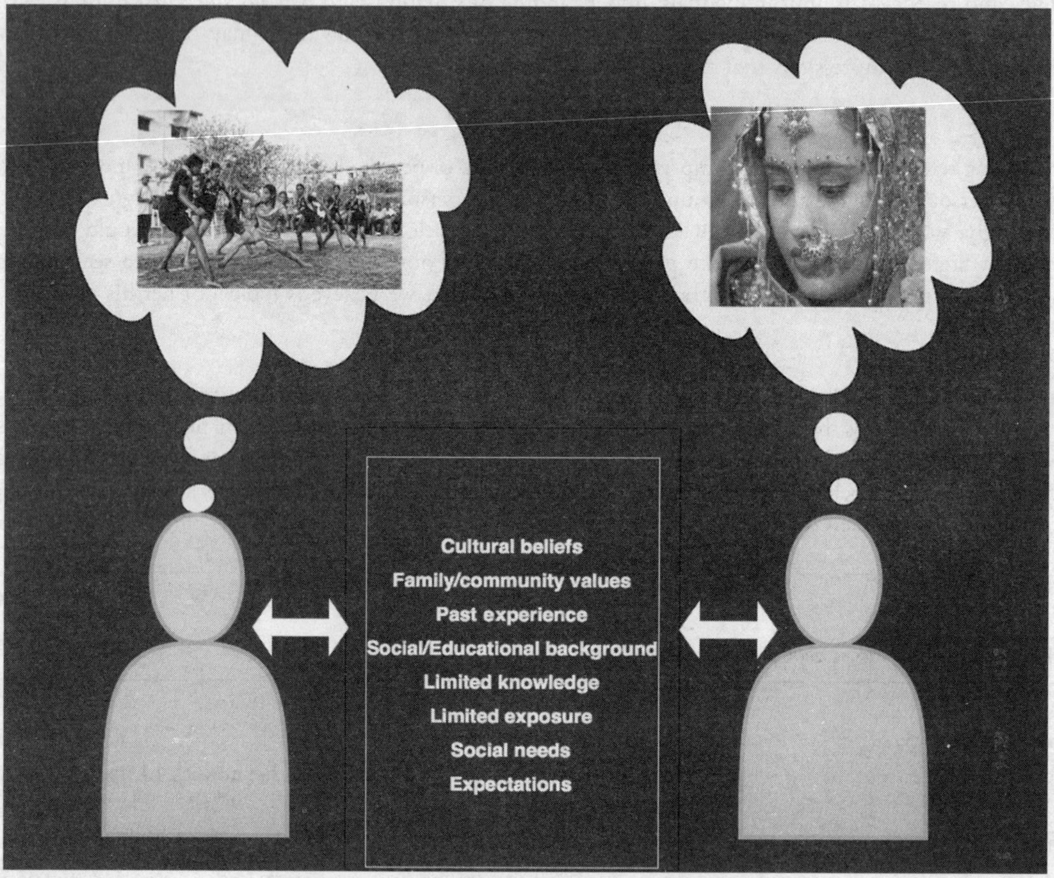

Source: Created by authors based on inputs from the internet.

Adjusting Our Perceptual Filters

We can take the following steps to be able to form a more accurate and dependable perception about the world around us. These steps may help us reduce the effect of perceptual influences on us and hence increase the probability of having a better environment for human interactions.

- *Take time to conclude*: Time helps us think about our observations and arrive at a conclusion. Forming perceptions about someone in haste may create problems. The first impression may or may not always be correct and accurate. We should try to find out more about the person you interact with.

- *Be a good listener*: Being a good listener helps us become physically and psychologically more available for the person we are interacting with. It is important to know her/his perception to be able to respond and formulate our perception.
- *Seek more information*: If you do not know enough about the person/subject, first accept your ignorance. There is nothing wrong in it. The next step will be to seek more information about the person/subject. Additional information helps us make better judgments about people. It is likely to produce alternative and additional perspective.
- *Be prepared to adjust*: Hasty conclusions often lead to errors in judgments. They prevent us to think about alternative perspectives. But even if an error of judgment occurs and one realises it, then there should always be readiness to change the perspective.

SUMMARY

- Perception is the awareness or comprehension or understanding of something. It involves the organisation, identification and interpretation of sensory information in order to represent and understand the environment.
- Perception is highly subjective and based on expectations, attitudes and other psychological factors.
- It is a cyclic and a continuous process. It effects our communication with others and communication too effects our perception which in turn again effects the communication.
- There are three stages of perception formation process—occurrence of sensory stimulation, organisation of sensory stimulation and interpretation-evaluation of sensory stimulation.
- The first stage is based on various aspects such as sensory stimulation, needs, interests, psychological factors and cultural factors.
- The stage of the process is dependent on aspects like proximity, similarity and closure.
- The key processes that influence our perceptions are perceptual accentuation, primacy-recency, consistency, stereotyping and attribution.

KEY WORDS

Homophily: It refers to the degree of similarity between the communicators on any given attribute or group of attributes.

Proximity: This principle refers to the tendency to organise shapes and patterns instantly into meaningful groupings or patterns on the basis of their proximity or similarity.

Similarity: Perception is also formed based on similarities and dissimilarities. According to this principle, stimuli that physically resemble each other in various aspects such as colours, texture, sound, taste, etc. are perceived as one whole part.

Closure: The principle of closure refers to the brain's tendency to complete figures or forms even if they are incomplete, partially hidden, or if part of the information needed to make a complete picture in our minds is missing.

Implicit personality theory: It proposes the specific patterns and biases an individual uses when forming impressions about people, situations, objects, etc.

Perceptual accentuation: It highlights the fact what you expect and want to see. It can distort your perceptions of reality and you may perceive what you need to or want to perceive.

Primacy-recency: It focuses on individual's tendency to be influenced by whatever occurs first or by what comes last.

Consistency: It is the tendency to maintain balance among our perceptions or attitudes.

Stereotyping: It refers to a fixed impression about a group of people. Stereotypes may distort accurate perception.

Attribution: This theory explains the process you go though in trying to understand about your own and or other's behaviours, particularly the reasons or motivations of these behaviours.

EXERCISES

1. What is Perception? Do you see any relationship between perception and opinion?
2. Explain the process of perception formation through its three stages.
3. How does understanding the process of perception formation help in effective communication among individuals?
4. What are the different types of perception filters? How do they hinder communication process?
5. What are the steps that may help to reduce the effect of perceptual filters on us?

REFERENCES

DeVito, Joseph A., *Human Communication: The Basic Course*, twelfth edition, New York: Pearson, 2011.

Dhama, O. P., and O. P. Bhatnagar, *Education and Communication for Development*, second edition, New Delhi: Oxford and IBH Publishing Company, 2005.

Fiske, Susan T. and Shelley E. Taylor, *Social Cognition*, second edition, New York: McGraw-Hill, 1991.

Lahlry, S., 'A Blueprint for Perception Training' in *Communication Theories: Origins, Methods, Uses*, edited by W. J. Severin and J. W. Tankard, fourth edition, New York: Longman, 1991 [2001], available at http://uts.cc.utexas.edu/~tecas/syllabi2/adv382jfall2002/readings/sev4c.pdf (accessed April 2016).

McCroskey, James, *An Introduction to Rhetorical Communication*, ninth edition, New York: Routledge, 2005.

McCroskey, James and Virginia Richmond, 'Willingness to Communicate: Differing Cultural Perspectives', *The Southern Communication Journal* 56 (1998): 1.

McCroskey, James. C. and Lawrence Wheeless, *An Introduction to Human Communication*, Boston: Allyn and Bacon, 1976.

Sarvaes, Jan, *Approaches to Development Communication*, Paris: UNESCO, 2003.

Schein, E., *Organizational Culture and Leadership: A Dynamic View*, second edition, San Francisco: Jossey-Bass, 1992.

Smith Karen, Communication: The gateway to Online Instructional Environments, Gratto, USA, 2005, available at http://www.itdl.org/Journal/Dec_06/article05.htm (accessed April 2016).

ONLINE SOURCES

http://education.purduecal.edu/Vockell/EdPsyBook/Edpsy5/Edpsy5_needs.htm (accessed April 2016)

http://www.slideshare.net/JagannathPadhy/motivation-and-communicationppt-14270929 (accessed April 2016)

http://writingcommons.org/genres/public-speaking/speak-confident/coping-with-the-unexpected (accessed April 2016)

http://www.jamescmccroskey.com/publications/060.pdf (accessed April 2016)

7

LISTENING

HIGHLIGHTS

- Hearing vs listening
- Defining listening
- Listening and empathy
- Purpose of listening
- Process of listening
- Listening differentials
- Types of listening
- Developing listening competency

Listening is a very important communication skill. Listening is the first step through which human beings learn about their surroundings. A few researches suggest that the foetus in the womb reacts to external sounds. After birth, listening becomes the primary means by which children learn to speak. They hear sounds, pay attention, remember and recognise, and finally try to imitate them. According to Adler, Rosenfeld and Proctor (2012), we spend a significant amount of our lifetime listening. Of the time spent on communicating each day, 45 per cent is devoted to listening.

Figure 7.1: Time Spent on Communicating and Listening

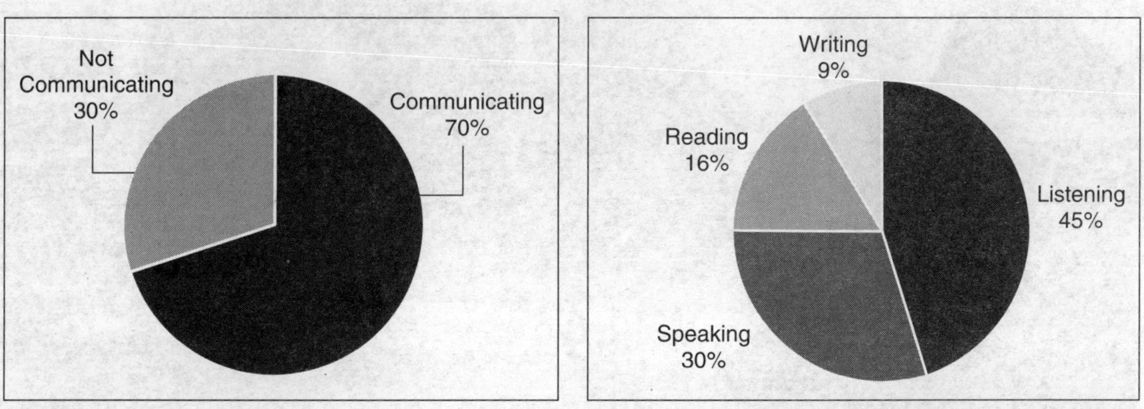

Source: Adapted from the research by Adler, Rosenfeld and Proctor (2012) with inputs from http://www.skillsyouneed.com/ips/listening-skills.html (7 December 2015).

Ancient Indian scriptures emphasise the primacy of listening and consider *shruti*—that which is 'heard'—as a transcending process that leads us to revelation and unquestionable truth which is considered eternal. In the same vein researchers and communication scholars also reiterate the critical significance of listening skills in all aspects of our lives. Effective listening provides us with a variety of benefits like learning, relating to others, building relationships, influencing and helping others. It is a process which begins with receiving, captures our attention and continues through understanding, remembering, evaluating and responding. Conversational listening implies a constant exchange in the roles of speaker and listener. The process of listening is affected by many variables like environmental setting, message source, message and the listener which function differently in different communication interactions.

In the communication process listening is as important as speaking. A good communicator has to be a good listener first. How we listen deeply impacts our communications and the meaning we derive from others communications. But even before that we need to understand the difference between hearing and listening.

HEARING VS LISTENING

Hearing and listening are terms that are usually used synonymously. Most people assume that listening is the same activity as hearing. People perceive their hearing ability to be the same as their listening skills. We often think we are listening when we are only hearing. There is a world of difference between hearing and listening. Hearing is a physiological function that occurs by default while listening involves a deliberate act of paying attention in order to understand what the other person is saying.

Hearing, one of the five senses, is the ability to perceive sound by detecting vibrations through the ear. According to the Merriam-Webster dictionary, hearing is 'the process, function, or power of perceiving sound; specifically the special sense by which noises and tones are received as stimuli.' During hearing, vibrations are detected by the ear and then converted into nerve impulses and sent to the brain. Thus it involves only the physical reception of sound waves by auditory mechanisms. The process of hearing takes place even when we are asleep. Most people are quite capable of receiving sounds but that does not mean they are listening.

Image 7.1: Listening is about Paying Attention and Deriving Meaning

Source: Authors.

Actually, hearing is the first step in listening. Once the sound waves are received, we pay attention to those sounds which are then organised in a meaningful pattern and deciphered, leading to the beginning of the process of understanding. Listening requires concentration, deriving meaning from the sound that is heard and reacting to it. Listening is a process of communication, where if the person is not listening it can cause a break in communication. Listening is defined by Merriam-Webster dictionary as follows: 'to hear something with thoughtful attention: give consideration.' One might think that understanding comes automatically from paying attention, but it is not so. Sometimes we pay attention to the sound but are unable to organise the sounds into meaningful patterns or form associations to understand and comprehend the meaning.

Cultural differences lead to differences in how people communicate and listen. Understanding the variations in styles of expressing themselves, the use of symbols, metaphors even silences deeply impact the communicative process. Lack of sensitivity could lead to errors in our understanding about what the other person is saying and the meaning we derive from their communications.

DEFINING LISTENING

At times people appear to be listening but they may be attending to some internal dialogue or concerns. This type of listening is called pseudo-listening. In pseudo-listening listeners do not focus or pay attention to what the speaker is actually saying, they just pretend to be listening. A highly ineffective way to communicate, pseudo-listening occurs largely because of some personal need of the listener. There are several reasons why pseudo-listening occurs among listeners. These range from listening for seeking attention and signs of potential rejection by the speaker, listening for specific information only, focusing on one's own rebuttal or on what one is going to say rather than what the speaker is saying, pretending to listen so the listener would listen later, listening to find weaknesses or vulnerabilities so that one can gain an advantage and argue against the speaker. People also do 'half listening' because they think it is a polite thing to do and fake listening because they are afraid of hurting the speaker's feelings or offending her/him, or when the listener is not interested in the conversation or does not know how to get out of the conversation.

Let us now look at some definitions of listening to arrive at the holistic perspective.

> The process of listening can be described as a series of five steps: receiving, understanding, remembering, evaluating and responding.
>
> —Joseph DeVito, *Human Communication* (2011)

> Listening is the process of receiving, constructing meaning from and responding to the spoken or non verbal messages.
>
> —P. Emmert (quoted in Brownell 2012)

Following these definitions, we can draw out certain characteristics which differentiate listening from hearing and understand its features.

Listening Involves Multiple Cues

Listening is not just about the transmission and reception of sound and verbal expressions. Integral to listening are both verbal and non-verbal message exchanges between the speaker and the listener.

Listening is a Mental Process

During listening the listener is actively engaged in the process of constructing meaning from the messages. It involves listeners going through various stages through which they comprehend, evaluate and interpret the various verbal and non-verbal cues and derive their own meaning through them.

Listening is an Active Process

Listening involves gaining clarity about both the content and the emotion of the messages. Both the speaker and the listener need to engage in an active exchange to clarify their perspectives and understanding of the situation, ideas and their feelings.

Listening is Contextual

The context plays an important role in creating an environment in which the speaker feels free and safe to talk and the listener to listen.

Listening is Purposeful

Listening is a skill of critical significance that influences all aspects of our lives. How the receiver assesses, makes sense of what they hear influences their actions and behaviours and, consequently, their ability to realise their goals.

LISTENING AND EMPATHY

A key aspect influencing the process of effective listening is empathy. Understanding another person's viewpoint, especially one that is the opposite to yours, needs empathy and is central to having good listening skills.

Activity

Make a group of 10–15 people stand in circle. One participant will tell a known story/folklore. After the story finishes another person repeats the story in exactly the same manner. While (s)he speaks, the group leader says 'stop' and asks the person next to her/him to continue where the first person left off. Continue to do this. After sometime go in an unexpected order and pick a random person from the circle and ask them to continue the discussion. Discuss the process of 'hearing' and 'listening'.

Listening is often characterised as the ability to 'put oneself into another's shoes'. So empathy is a deeper emotional experience and it goes beyond sympathy, which is a feeling of care and understanding for the suffering of others. Sympathy essentially implies a feeling of recognition of another's sufferings and emotions while empathy is actually sharing another's sufferings and emotions. In empathy you try to understand someone's point of view by placing yourself in that situation. It is a deeper emotional experience.

Though both sympathy and empathy are used interchangeably they differ in their emotional meaning.

Image 7.2: Empathy is Deeper than Sympathy

Source: Image by eliola (Pixabay; CC0 Public Domain).

Empathy enables us to understand emotionally and intellectually what another person is experiencing. Empathising does not mean you need to agree with the other person. While empathising with others, we never lose out on our own identity or ideas and beliefs. We can be critical and empathetic at the same time. Critical aspects of empathy include awareness of the state of being of another, understanding their condition, a personal identification with the situation and appropriate emotional response.

Empathy allows the communicator to sense the emotions of an audience and is the key for mutual understanding and inspiration communicated to the audience from a communicator. Lack of empathy involves a poor sense of communication that fails to understand the perspective of the audience. Verbal and non-verbal messages help contribute to building empathy with the audience. A simple nod or 'I understand' can go a long way in helping another person feel that (s)he is being listened to and not chastised for how they might be feeling. Empathy helps people open up without hesitation and to feel that they are not alone and that someone is truly concerned about how they feel.

Many researchers have indicated that people find it easier to be empathetic for positive responses with those who belong to the same culture. But this is a contested position. An empathetic listener can connect to anyone. It may take time to relate to someone who belongs to a different culture but it is achievable. Being able to practice empathy is one of the biggest skills one can learn. In a world that spends so much time picking at flaws and igniting fear and anger in people, empathy can be a soothing balm. It can help us lead a more fulfilling and healthier life.

Image 7.3: Listening for Comprehension, Empathy, Appreciation and Criticism

Source: Authors.

PURPOSE OF LISTENING

According to Zeuschner (2004) there are four basic purposes of listening in the process of communication. Understanding these four purposes makes us a better communicator.

1. *Comprehension*: One of the key goals of listening is to comprehend and respond. For example, in a discussion we first need to listen and understand what the other person is saying. Even if we agree or disagree, we need to listen first as it help us to respond correctly.
2. *Appreciation*: One of the key purposes of listening is to enjoy something. For example, going to a music concert and engaging in appreciative listening.
3. *Empathy*: Empathy is the ability to put in self into another's shoes. It is deeper emotional experience. When we listen to a friend or a person in need, we engage in empathetic listening in order to give our attention and care to the person. Here empathetic listening also means listening with open mind and without judging the other person.
4. *Criticism*: Critical thinking means comprehending and analysing the information carefully to be able to make an informed decision. Critically thinking helps us filter out information and forms an important part of our evaluation of the messages.

PROCESS OF LISTENING

As already mentioned the process of listening involves a series of five phases—receiving, understanding, remembering, evaluating and responding. All the five phases occur in sequence but are performed with little awareness and often in rapid succession.

Figure 7.2: Stages of Listening

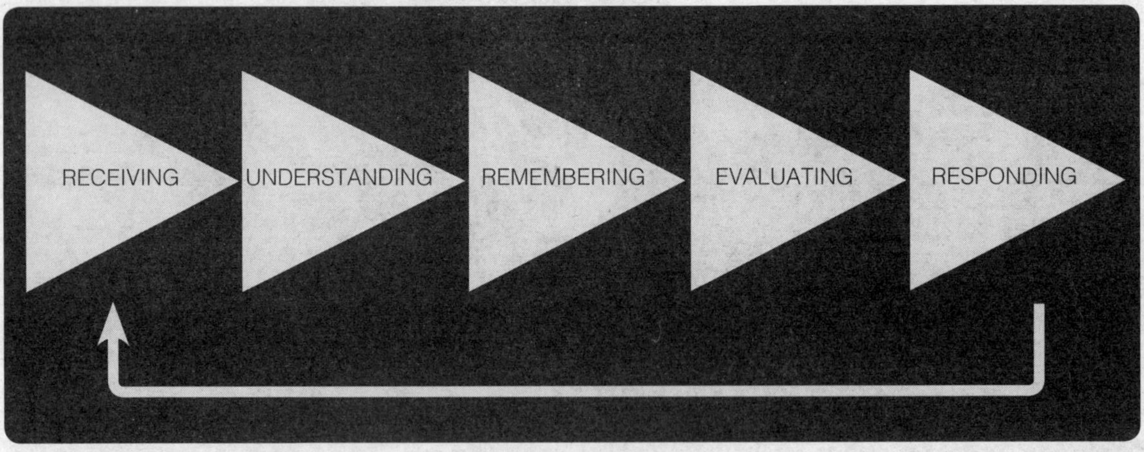

Sources: Adapted from Joseph DeVito (2011) by the authors.

Phase I: Receiving

Hearing is the first step towards the complex process of listening. Hearing is a physical response. In other words, you must hear to listen, but you need not listen to hear. The perception necessary for listening depends on how much attention we pay. We are bombarded with information from the world around us. Sometimes our mind becomes overloaded with the stream of everyday stimuli—loud voices, smells, lights and so on.

But our brain screens these stimuli and permits only a select few to come into focus. This selective perception is called attention which is an important requirement for effective listening. This stage of listening can be made more effective by:

- focusing your attention on the speaker's verbal and non-verbal messages
- avoiding distractions in the environment
- focusing your attention on the speaker's messages
- avoiding interrupting the speaker until (s)he is finished

Phase II: Understanding

In order to receive meaningful messages, hearing and perceiving sounds is not enough. We also need to understand symbols. For this we need to understand the meaning of the stimuli we have perceived. The symbolic stimuli include not only words but also other sounds like applause, siren, horn, and sights like a white uniform. The meanings attached to these symbols are a function of our past associations and of the context in which the symbol exists. It is at this stage that parents are able to tell whether a child is babbling or attempting at meaningful speech. The listener must understand the intended meaning and context assumed by the sender for achieving successful communication.

The understanding phase of listening can be made more effective by:

- relating the speaker's new information to what you already know
- seeing the speaker's messages from the speaker's point of view
- avoiding to judge the message until it's fully understood as the speaker intended it
- asking questions for clarification, if necessary
- asking for additional details or examples if needed and rephrasing/paraphrasing the speaker's ideas.

Phase III: Remembering

When an individual receives a message (s)he interprets it and also adds it to her/his memory bank. This addition is termed as remembering and it is not considered important by some communication analysts. Anyone listening to the court testimony of eyewitnesses about a murder will immediately realise that what is remembered may be different from what was originally seen or heard. It is because our attention and memory are selective.

We can make this remembering phase of listening more effective by:

- taking notes or by recording the messages
- identifying the central ideas
- summarising the message in an easier-to-retain form, but without ignoring crucial details or qualifications
- repeating names and key concepts to yourself
- identifying the pattern and using it to organise what the speaker is saying

Phase IV: Evaluating

We evaluate to judge or weigh the evidence, to sort out facts from opinion and to determine the presence or absence of bias or prejudice in a message. During this stage the listeners render judgment as a function of this criterion. For an effective listener it is important that (s)he does not begin this activity too soon. Beginning this stage of the process before a message is completed requires that we no longer hear and attend to the incoming message. As a result the listening process ceases and so does our chance to participate as active listeners. This evaluation stage of listening can be made more effective by resisting evaluation until you fully understand the speaker's point of view, distinguishing what is factual from what is opinion or personal interpretation by the speaker and identifying any biases, self-interests or prejudices that may lead the speaker to present it unfairly.

Phase V: Responding

Responding is the final stage of the listening process. Responding occurs in two phases. The first phase comprises of the responses you make while the speaker is talking and the second phase comprises responses you make after the speaker has stopped talking. Responding is the only way by which the sender determines the degree of success in transmitting the message. The feedback during listening may range from silence to smiling or frowning, to requesting clarification. Responses after the speaker has stopped talking are generally more elaborate and might include empathy ('I know how you feel'), asking for clarification ('Do you mean this new plan will replace the old one?'), challenging ('I think your evidence is weak') and agreeing ('You're absolutely right; I'll support your proposal when it comes up for a vote').

LISTENING DIFFERENTIALS

There are many factors which have an impact on what we listen and how we listen. Understanding these factors helps us to listen better and prepares us for any unanticipated situation as a listener or a speaker.

Culture

When the speaker and the listener come from different cultures, the differences and their effects are naturally much greater. As discussed earlier, culture deeply impacts the communication process and hence also the way we listen. The culture in which you were raised will influence your listening habits in variety of ways.

Language and Speech

A key cultural aspect influencing listening is language and speech. No two speakers speak exactly the same language. Every speaker speaks an idiolect, a term in linguistics which refers to a person's unique and particular way of way of speaking. Therefore, while adjusting your listening understand that the speaker's meanings may be different from yours even though you both know the same language. Another aspect of speech is that of accents. Those whose native language is a tonal one such as Chinese (where differences in pitch signal important meaning differences), may speak English with variations in pitch that may seem puzzling to others.

Non-behavioural Differences

Speakers from different cultures have different display rules, cultural rules that govern which non-verbal behaviours are appropriate and which are inappropriate in a public setting.

Feedback

Members of some cultures give very direct and honest feedback. For example, speakers from the US expect feedback to be an honest reflection of what their listeners are feeling. In other cultures such as in Japan and Korea, it is more important to give feedback in a positive way.

Credibility

What makes speakers credible or believable will vary from one culture to another. Credibility in this context has to do with 'who' is saying. For example, in a class, a teacher's response to a query raised by a student will be perceived to be more credible than an answer by another student. This is because the teacher is perceived as an authority in the subject.

Gender

According to Larry Barker and Kittie Watson (2000), men and women typically employ different listening styles. Men are more likely to be action-oriented listeners which means they focus on listening to information pertinent to the task at hand. Action-oriented listeners have little patience for speakers who ramble off topic or include unnecessary details. Women are more likely to be people-oriented listeners. They connect with the emotional message and undertones of a conversation and are more concerned with the occurrence of the conversation than with the information discussed. Women often interject with small acknowledging remarks such as 'Yes', 'I see' and 'mm-hmm' to show the speaker that they are actively listening and processing the contents of the conversation. The difference in response style can cause women to assume that men aren't actively listening to them in conversations, while men tend to think that women 'over listen'. These differences in listening are largely the result of the way in which men and women have been socialised.

TYPES OF LISTENING

Because one listens for different reasons and for different end results, the key aspects of listening vary according to situation and circumstances. There are five dimensions of listening that illustrate the appropriateness of different modes that contribute to effective listening in different communication situations (DeVito 2011).

Active and Passive Listening

Active listening is not merely to be able to repeat what the speaker has said but also to be able to understand the speaker's message. Active listening serves three very important functions: First, it helps check if the listener has understood what the speaker said and more importantly what (s)he meant. Reflecting back the perceived meanings gives the speaker an opportunity to offer clarification. Second, through active listening the speaker gets to know that her/his feelings are acknowledged and accepted. Third, active listening stimulates the speaker to explore feelings and thoughts of the listener.

Passive listening, however, is listening without talking and without directing the speaker in any non-verbal way. It shows acceptance of message without any visible disagreement. Passive listening allows the speaker to develop her/his thoughts and ideas in the presence of another person who accepts but does not evaluate. By listening passively you provide a supportive and receptive environment. Another form of passive listening is just to sit back, relax and let the auditory stimulation massage you without exerting any significant energy or effort, and especially, without directing the stimuli in any way.

Empathetic and Objective Listening

Empathic listening is a means of both increasing understanding and enhancing a relationship. Although empathetic listening is the preferred mode of responding, there are times when you need to go beyond it to measure the meanings and feelings against an objective reality. At times one has to put her/his empathic responses aside and listen with objectivity and detachment.

Non-judgmental and Critical Listening

Effective listening includes both non-judgmental and critical responses. For non-judgmental listening one needs to listen with an open mind. We need to listen critically with a view toward making some kind of evaluation and judgment. It is important to listen first and then evaluate the message. Listening with an open mind will help supplement critical listening.

Surface and Deep Listening

In listening, you have to be particularly sensitive to different levels of meaning. If you respond only to the surface level communication (i.e. the literal meaning), you miss the opportunity to make meaningful contact with the other person's feelings and real needs.

DEVELOPING LISTENING COMPETENCY

The process of listening is affected by many variables which function differently in different communication interactions. It is to be noted that each of these variables can act either as barriers or as aids in the listening process and influence the process of effective listening.

The Listener

No matter how excellent the speaker is or how important the message is communication cannot occur unless a listener is present. The physical state of the listener can affect the listening situation. The attitude of the listener can become a barrier to effective listening. This is more of a psychological factor. If you see yourself superior to others with nothing to gain from listening to them, you have created self-imposed barrier to communication. Also, if you feel a speaker is superior you may be so willing to accept whatever is said that critical learning cannot take place. Habits influence our listening and hence can influence the process of communication too. If we learn to fake attention in school in order to please our teachers the habit may carry over to work situations too. Listening only for facts is another poor listening habit. This makes the conversation ineffective as the focus is only on facts and some meanings and attitudes of the speaker may go unnoticed.

Environmental Setting

The physical environment is important. For instance, noise is both distracting to your attention and damaging to your ability to hear. Similar interference can be caused by crowding or by heat, cold or rainfall. A physical condition that affects listening behaviour in groups and over which the listener may have little control is the seating arrangement of people involved. A round table helps in free-flowing communication and effective listening over other seating arrangements which may create barriers.

Activity

Identify the type of listening by reading the following response statements. Discuss what could have been the possible impact on the speaker after hearing the following responses.

'Excuse me, can you please clarify the second point you mentioned in your speech?'

'I was listening to you carefully so that I don't miss any factual information in your statement.'

'What you did is not right. But I am sure you have a reason for that.'

'I don't agree with you. You are wrong.'

'Yeah, yeah … I get that. Now move on!'

The Message Source and the Message

It is known that we all listen closely to people we respect or admire whereas we pay less attention to those we feel are our inferiors. For example, research suggests that women are at a disadvantage when they are a message source as they are perceived to be more submissive, less assertive and less willing to take a stand than their male counterparts; they are viewed as less believable, and hence are listened to less carefully (Liska and Watson 1983). In addition to this, speakers themselves determine how easy or difficult the listening situation will be for the listeners. The factor of novelty and significance of message applies to all messages. It is noted that unusual signs catch our eye on the highway. In the same way intense, emotion-filled messages also capture our attention.

Listener's Responsibilities

In a communication process a listener has specific responsibilities, the most important of which is not only to pay attention as we have just mentioned but also to show active signs of effectiveness. A speaker can usually judge the listener's level of attention by facial expressions, gestures and nods that express listening activity. A smile or nod can indicate support while a frown or head shake suggests disapproval.

There are specific actions we can take to improve listening attentiveness. During the course of communication, the active listener might choose to reflect the message back to the speaker by periodically interjecting comments. Sometimes comments help clarify doubts and aid in understanding. The listener should also try to recognise the speaker's intent or purpose. Always use all your powers of concentration to the greatest extent. You already know many ways to be a better listener, but it is also important to actually behave that way during a real listening situation.

STEPS FOR EFFECTIVE LISTENING

In today's high-tech, high-speed, high-stress world, communication is more important than ever, yet we seem to devote less and less time to really listen to one another. Genuine listening has become a rare gift, because it involves gifting someone our precious time. Listening helps build relationships, solve problems, ensure understanding, resolve conflicts and improve accuracy. At work, effective listening means fewer errors and less wasted time. Here are ten steps to help you develop effective listening skills as given by Dianne Schilling (2012).

Step 1: Establish Eye Contact with Your Audience/Receiver.

As soon as you enter the venue, have a quick glance at the setting. After that look at the person and try to gauge her/his attention level. In some conversations the speaker is in a position to demand eye contact; for example, while one is talking to a junior subordinate. If the receiver is not looking into your eyes due to shyness, uncertainty, guilt or any other emotion, don't force but try to make eye contact as and when possible.

Step 2: Remain Observant.

Once eye contact is established, don't keep staring at the other person. Pay attention to the verbal and non-verbal feedback you are getting from your receiver. Remain observant throughout the conversation.

Step 3: Be Open-minded.

Never pre-judge the person who is speaking. Her/his context may be different. Try to keep all your pre-conceived notions aside and pay attention to the person speaking.

Step 4: Create a Mental Picture of What the Speaker is Saying.

Creating visual imagery of what has been spoken may help you receive and remember more. Make written and visual notes. Don't be in a rush to respond to information. If your thoughts start to wander, immediately force yourself to refocus.

Step 5: Don't Respond in Haste.

Even if you are a quick thinker, let the other person finish what (s)he is saying. Do not jump the gun. It may also be considered rude if you keep interrupting the speaker. Moreover, you may miss out on certain important points while creating your response in anticipation.

Step 6: Be Patient. Wait for Your Turn.

There may be instances when you don't fully understand what has been said and why. Again, don't interrupt; wait for your turn. When the speaker stops ask for clarification.

Step 7: Don't Ask Questions to Grab Attention.

Without listening or paying attention to the entire information presented, people sometimes ask questions just for the sake of it. Try to be a patient listener.

Step 8: Empathising Helps.

Try to feel what the speaker is feeling at that point of time. (S)he may be going through certain emotions. Ensure that you're listening by communicating that you understand. It takes energy and concentration. But it is a generous and helpful thing to do, and it facilitates communication like nothing else does.

Step 9: Give Genuine Feedback.

Give verbal and non-verbal feedback. Sometimes, saying 'oh, really' or 'hmm' or nodding helps the speaker.

Step 10: Non-verbal Vocabulary is Equally Important.

Don't just listen to the words. Remember that words convey only a fraction of the message. Listen to the gestures as well. Non-verbal gestures and the body language of the speaker compliments the information that reaches you. These are cues you can't ignore.

SUMMARY

- Effective listening provides us with a variety of benefits like learning, relating to others, building relationships, influencing and helping others.
- Hearing is the first step in listening. It is a physiological function that occurs by default.
- Listening involves a deliberate act of paying attention in order to understand what the other person is saying. Therefore, it requires concentration, deriving meaning from the sound that is heard and reacting to it.
- Characteristically, listening is a mental and active process that involves multiple cues. It is contextual and purposeful.
- Empathy is a fundamental communication skill for effective listening and communication.

- Empathy includes awareness of the state of being of another, understanding of this condition, a personal identification with the situation and appropriate response.
- Main purposes of listening are to comprehend, appreciate, empathise and criticise.
- The process of listening has five stages—receiving, understanding, remembering, evaluating and responding. All the stages occur in a sequence with little awareness and in a rapid succession.
- There are many factors like culture, language and speech, feedback and credibility of the speaker and gender that influence audience's listening habits.
- Depending upon the context, listening can be active or passive, empathetic or objective, non-judgemental or critical and surgical or in depth.

KEY WORDS

Hearing: It is one of the five senses of a person and it is the ability to perceive sound by detecting vibrations through the ear. It is a physical response to the stimuli.

Empathy: It is defined as the ability to mutually experience thoughts, emotions and direct experience of others.

Active listening: It involves hearing carefully, to be able to repeat and reflect upon what had been said by the speaker.

Passive listening: It is listening without talking and without directing the speaker in any non-verbal way. In most cases it means acceptance of message without any visible disagreement.

Empathetic listening: It is a type of listening which involves hearing and responding to increase understanding.

EXERCISES

1. How is the process of listening different from hearing?
2. 'An empathetic person is always a good listener.' Discuss the relationship between empathy and listening.
3. What are the factors that impact the process of listening?
4. How can non-judgmental listening be distinguished from critical listening?
5. Discuss the reasons behind why paying attention to non-verbal cues is imperative in the process of listening.

REFERENCES

Adler, R., L. Rosenfeld and R. Proctor, *Interplay: The Process of Interpersonal Communication*, twelfth edition, New York: Oxford University Press, 2012.

Aggarwal, Ravi, *Communication: Today and Tomorrow*, Jaipur: Sublime Publications, 2008.

Barker, Larry, *Communication*, eighth edition. New York: Pearson, 2001.

Barker, Larry and K. Watson, *Listen UP*, New York: St. Martin's Press, 2000.

Brownell, J., *Listening: Attitudes, Principles, and Skills*, fifth edition, New York: Pearson, 2012.

DeVito, Joseph A., *Human Communication: The Basic Course*, twelfth edition, New York: Pearson, 2011.

DeVito, Joseph A., *Interpersonal Communication*, New York: Pearson Higher Ed, 2012.

Gupta, C. B., *Basic Business Communication*, New Delhi: Sultan Chand & Sons, 2011.

Liska, Mechling E. and K. Watson, *Effective Listening: Key to Your Success*, New York: Random House, 1983.

Peters, Tom, *Thriving on Chaos: Handbook for a Management Revolution*, New York: Harper Perennial, 1991.

Schilling, Dianne, *Effective Listening Skills in a nutshell*, available at http://o.b5z.net/i/u/8001286/f/TLI/How_To_Develop_Effective_Listing_Skills.pdf (accessed 6 April 2016), 2012.

Zeuschner, Raymond, *Communicating Today*, Luis Obispo: California Polytechnic State University, 2004.

8

LEARNING AND COMMUNICATION

HIGHLIGHTS

- Learning as a communication process
- Characteristics of learning
- Domains of learning
- Adult learning
- Communication aids and learning

The 21st century is considered to be a 'knowledge-based society'. An individual's ability to generate and use varied forms of knowledge is of vital importance. In the knowledge economy change is so rapid that people constantly need to acquire new skills and must learn to adapt to the changing environment. The process of individual's need to learn, relearn and continuously adapt is simply known as 'lifelong learning'. Learning is generally associated with classrooms, courses, assignments and exams. However, these perceptions reflect a limited view and most of us understand that apart from schools, colleges and university we learn a lot from our family, peers and our everyday experiences.

Learning is said to be the change in behaviour resulting from the interaction between a person and a stimulus. According to Hill (cited in Woolfolk 2009: 232) learning has happened when an experience causes a relatively permanent change in an individual's knowledge or behaviour. The change may be deliberate or unintentional, for better or for worse, correct or incorrect and conscious or unconscious. One of the key aspects emerging from these definitions is that learning is a process through which we acquire new knowledge, thus modifying and reinforcing our existing knowledge, behaviours, skills, values or preferences. It involves individuals amalgamating different types of information to find new meaning and perspectives.

LEARNING AS A COMMUNICATION PROCESS

Human learning takes place through communication. As discussed in the earlier chapters that information is passed from one individual to another through the process of communication. A child learns the culture of her/his family through transference of ideas, gestures, information from parents and other family members. Therefore, we say that the mother is the first teacher of a child since the mother and her child usually spend a lot of time together, especially during infancy and early childhood, leaving an indelible mark in the child's mind and helping her/him adapt to the family environment. Now, when the child learns from the mother not only does she learn what her/his mother 'says' but also what she 'does'. So, we all learn about new things and situations not only by what we are told but also by what we observe. Thus, both verbal and non-verbal communication form the basis of learning.

The learning grows with expansion in the environments in which we move. A young child learns so much and very fast through friends, neighbours, teachers and others in the near environment and begins to interpret the shared meanings. In formal settings, such as schools and colleges, people learn not only through what they read but also through the interpersonal communication between students and teachers and among students. In formal settings, such as schools and colleges, people learn not only through what they read but also through the interpersonal communication between students and teachers and among students. The transition from information to knowledge is most often done by interpersonal communication even if it could be argued that intrapersonal communication is the main characteristic of learning. For this, we need access to both the written and spoken language (Wigforss 1999). In college you may attend your theory class with a big group of 100–130 students. You may follow what the teacher teaches. However, if this is followed by a tutorial in a group of 15–20 students with the teacher, the intensity of interaction, the frequent flow of messages between the student and the teacher helps clarify and makes learning more permanent.

An interesting humanistic perspective on the learning process is offered by American educational theorist David Kolb (1984). His model illustrates how individuals learn from the variety of material and experiences offered to them. The theory offers a cyclic understanding of learning consisting of four stages. Learners can begin at any stage but must follow the stages in a sequence. These are:

Figure 8.1: David A. Kolb's Model of Experiential Learning

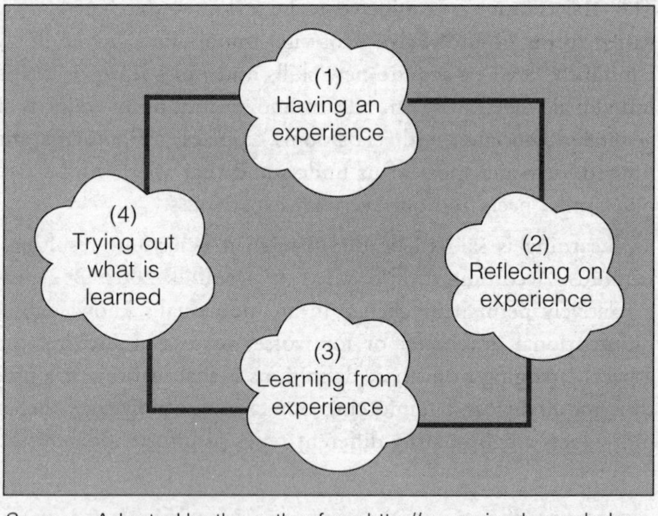

Source: Adapted by the author from http://www.simplypsychology.org/learning-kolb.html (accessed 28 December 2015).

- At this stage concrete experience is learning through experiential learning. Here learners learn best by active involvement in good examples and through discussion with others. They often have difficulties with generalisation in the sense that every learning experience is perceived as unique.
- In the reflective observation stage learning is through looking and listening. Here learners tend to prefer lectures and they are not too fond of discussions with others. This group generally profits from a variety of subject area settings and a variety of teachers from different disciplines.
- In the abstract conceptualisation stage learning is through thinking and analysing. Here learners tend to be more interested in 'theories' than people and prefer learning situations where theories and systematic analyses are emphasised.
- In the active experimentation stage learning is through experimenting and testing. Here learners tend to learn best from experimental activities in a small group setting and believe lectures are too passive settings for learning.

Each of Kolb's stages suggests how experience is translated through reflection into concepts, which in turn are used as guides for active experimentation and the choice of new experiences. Each stage in the learning process is necessary for proper achievement of learning.

Kolb further identified four learning styles which correspond to these stages. Each of the four learning styles represents an ability which a learner may possess to a greater or lesser extent. These are (*a*) assimilators, who learn better when presented with logical theories, (*b*) convergers, who learn better when provided with practical applications of concepts, (*c*) accommodators, who learn best when provided with 'hands-on' experiences, and (*d*) divergers, who learn better when are allowed to collect and observe a range of information. A well-organised learning programme should take into account these aspects when offering individuals learning opportunities.

CHARACTERISTICS OF LEARNING

Learning is a gradual process that happens over time and it is shaped by our past learning and knowledge. Most importantly, learning leaves imprints on individuals consequently impacting their ideas, skills and behaviours. The following are some characteristics of learning.

Learning is a Lifelong Process

Learning can take place at any stage of life as it is a lifelong process. Learning starts the moment we are born and continues throughout our whole life. Learning is a constant in every person's life. In general, people's learning capacity remains significantly high throughout the life, though the rate or speed of learning tends to decline with age. Thus, whatever our age be we continue to learn individually or in groups, in various environments and settings.

Learning Can be Formal, Non-formal or Informal

Formal learning refers to hierarchically structured systems of learning. These include recognised institutions having definite curricula. In the Indian context, not all people get exposed to formal education through primary school or higher education due their economic and social status. Non-formal learning opportunities include vocational training. Informal education is unorganised and unstructured learning in people's day-to-day life. People are oblivious of their informal learnings. When a person becomes aware of the purpose of the informal learning, it becomes non-formal learning. If this learning later becomes institutionalised then we call this as formal learning.

Figure 8.2: Differences between Formal, Non-formal and Informal Learning

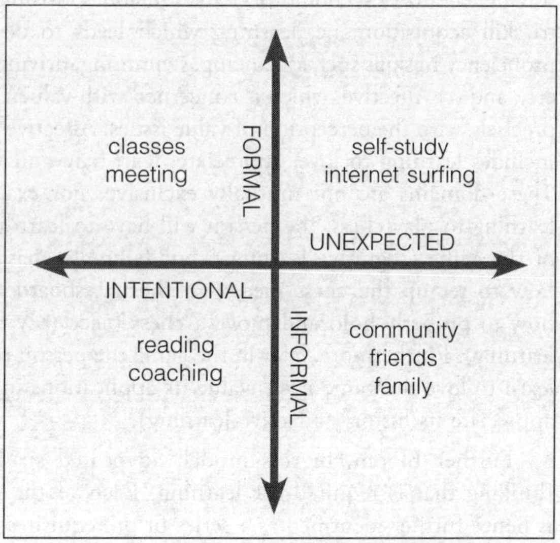

Source: Based on a concept by Marcia Conner, adapted by the authors with inputs from http://edutechwiki.unige.ch/en/File:Mlc-iifu-04.gif#filelinks (accessed 28 December 2015).

Learning May be Intentional or Unintentional

When learning has specific objectives, and there exists a clear focus on the systematic transfer of knowledge, it is said to be intentional. Unintentional or incidental learning is unplanned learning that happens due to a situation or environment. Like informal learning, this is also unorganised and unstructured and is considered by many as the 'natural way of learning'. Unintentional learning can happen through observation, interactions and reflections. Mostly, people are unaware of their unintentional learnings.

Learning is Highly Contextual

The social process of learning is influenced by the learner's interactions with her/his environment, both physical and cultural. And, the macro and micro environment of learning has a direct influence on the goals of learning and realisation of these goals. Thus understanding the learners and their socio-cultural circumstances and socio-economic environments is important.

DOMAINS OF LEARNING

Learning is maximised if the communicator is able to understand the needs and interests of the person on the receiving end, i.e. the learner. If (s)he knows about the factors that can stimulate and accelerate the learning process, better results can be achieved. For the last several years, scholars have worked through two strands: subject matter and psychology of learning. Most theories about the process of learning are based on these two strands. In this chapter we will discuss only two theories to examine how to plan appropriate learning experiences for the learners to achieve different objectives of the teaching learning process.

Bloom's Taxonomy

'Bloom's Taxonomy', a popular framework proposed by Benjamin S. Bloom, was initially developed as a tool to measure educational objectives. It elaborates on creating a common framework for learning processes and also expanding the range of educational possibilities beyond specific subject matter.

'Blooms Taxonomy', a popular theory proposed by Benjamin Bloom, elaborates on the forms and levels of learning. This theory suggests three domains of learning: (*a*) Cognitive, which refers to knowledge structures and includes learning aspects related to recall, analysis, problem solving, etc.; (*b*) Psychomotor, which includes learning related to skill acquisition, i.e. learning which leads to developing proficiency in skills such as dancing, swimming, driving, riding, etc.; and (*c*) Affective, which is concerned with values, or more precisely with the perception of value issues. Affective learning includes learning to love, appreciate, fear, hate and worship. These domains are not mutually exclusive. For example, in learning to play chess, the person will have to learn the rules of the game (cognitive learning); but (s)he also has to learn how to set up the chess pieces on the chessboard and also how to properly hold and move a chess piece (psychomotor learning). Furthermore, later in the game the person may even learn to love the game itself, value its applications in life and appreciate its history (affective learning).

Figure 8.3: Bloom's Taxonomy

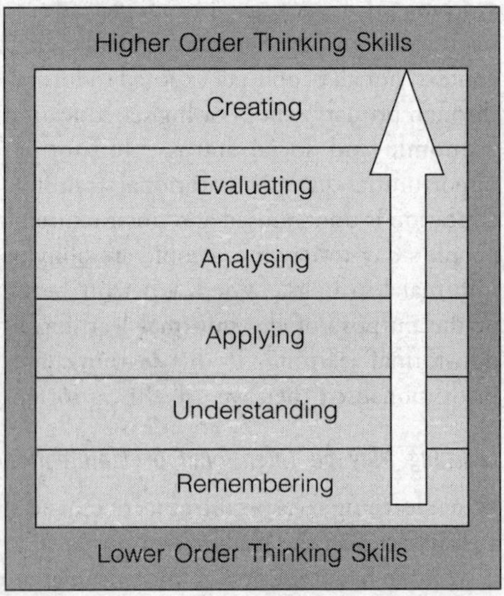

Source: 'Bloom's Taxonomy' by Xristina la (Wikimedia Commons; CC BY-SA 3.0).

Further Bloom, in this model, advocated six levels of thinking that is required for learning. Each of the domains is hence further identified as a series of prerequisites or levels that need to be addressed for complete learning in a particular domain. Bloom identified three basic lower levels of thinking, viz. knowledge, comprehension and application, and three higher levels of thinking, viz. analysis, synthesis and evaluation.

Several scholars think of the levels as stairways in which learners are encouraged to achieve a higher level of thinking. If a learner has mastered a higher level, then (s)he would have automatically mastered the lower levels. Thus within the cognitive domain, from the simple recall or recognition of facts, forms the lowest level, through increasingly more complex and abstract mental levels, to the highest order which is evaluation.

In the recent past, the taxonomy has been revised to include new terms such as: (*a*) Remembering, which involves retrieving, recognising and recalling relevant knowledge from long-term memory; (*b*) Understanding, which involves constructing meaning from oral, written and graphic messages through interpreting, exemplifying, classifying, summarising, inferring, comparing and explaining; (*c*) Applying, which is carrying out or using a procedure through executing or implementing; (*d*) Analysing, which is breaking material into constituent parts, determining how the parts relate to one another and to an overall structure or purpose through differentiating, organising and attributing; (*e*) Evaluating, which is making judgments based on criteria and standards through checking and critiquing; and (*f*) Creating which involves putting elements together to form a coherent or functional whole, reorganising elements into a new pattern or structure through generating, planning or producing (Krathwohl 2002: 215).

Edgar Dale's Cone of Experience

Another model that can be helpful in understanding how effective learning takes place by providing the learner various mediated experience is Edgar Dale's Cone of Experience. This model has been used by many to select appropriate medium for the maximum learning to take place. It offers a chance to recognise the role of experience in developing understanding, building concepts and remembering.

Figure 8.4: Edgar Dale's Cone of Experience

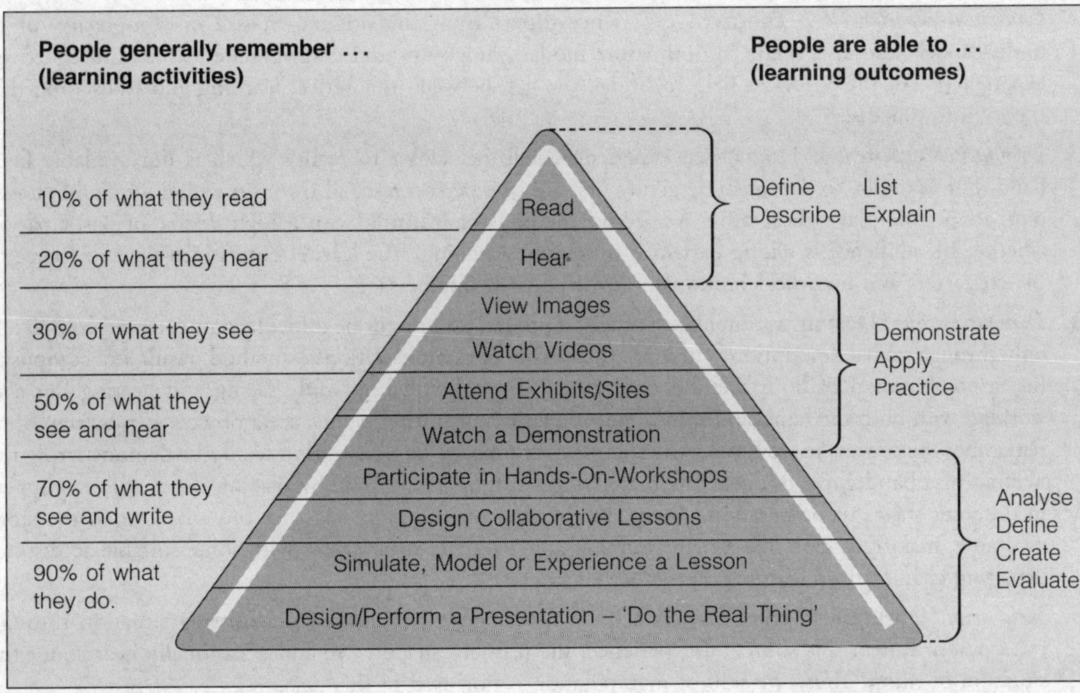

Source: 'Edgar Dale's cone of learning' by Jeffrey Andersen (Wikimedia Commons; CC By-SA 3.0).

A representation of Edgar Dale's cone is shown in Figure 8.4. We see that the range of experience starts from being direct at the top and becomes abstract towards the bottom. At the bottom of the cone, the source of experience is most effective in producing the desired quality and quantity of learning. As one moves up from the bottom of the cone, the number of sensory organs involved decrease. Thus, the bottom most and the top most sources show two extremes for involvement of sensory organs. People generally remember 10 per cent of what they read, 20 per cent of what they hear, 30 per cent of what they see, 50 per cent of what they hear and see (video, for instance), 70 per cent of what they say or write and 90 per cent of what they say as they do something.

Thus, as per the figure, what learners will be able to do at each level of the cone (the learning outcomes they will be able to achieve) is relative to the type of activity they are doing (reading, hearing, viewing images, etc.). The numerical figures on the left side of the image indicate that practical, hands-on experience in a real-life context will allow learners to remember best what they do. However, it is important to remember that this doesn't mean reading and listening are not valuable learning experiences, but that 'doing the real thing' can lead to the retention of the largest amount of information. This is in part because those experiences near the bottom of the cone are closer to and include real-world experiences, and thereby make use of all our senses; it is believed that the more the senses that are used, the greater our ability to learn from and remember an event.

Different levels in Dale's cone show how different types and methods help for learning to take place. of learning experience takes place.

1. *Direct, purposeful experiences*: Direct purposeful experience of concepts, ideas or generalisations rests upon a broad base of experiences and these experiences range from direct, sensory experiences (at the base of the cone) to direct verbal participation (at the top of the cone). The word 'purposeful' denotes that the experiences are meaningful and active rather than passive.
2. *Contrived experiences*: A contrived experience differs from the original in size or complexity, or in both. Models, diorama (i.e. a 3D miniature model), mock-ups and cutaways are included in contrived experiences. All these devices help to bridge the gap between theoretical learning and translating that theory into practice.
3. *Dramatised experiences*: Dramatised experiences help get closer to reality which is not available first-hand. For example, to demonstrate giving first aid to a person rescued from drowning we could choose puppets or role play. These are a few active methods of learning with a high degree of participation whether the audience is taking part in it or simply watching. The learner enters into the experience of the characters and becomes emotionally involved with the message.
4. *Demonstrations*: Demonstration helps visualise a process that might be difficult to understand completely only through verbal description. There are three types of demonstrations—method, result and composite (i.e. a combination of both method and result). These involve not only seeing and hearing but also working with both the hand and mind. Since in a demonstration people see a process step by step, they remember the process more easily. An example of composite demonstration would be demonstrating the making of a hand/glove puppet. The major stages can be first shown by placing three or four puppets in different stages of preparation. Then, the dressing up the puppet as per the character in the story or drama, making it look like a man, woman, and a teacher or a farmer with some suitable accessories depicting characteristic features can be demonstrated.
5. *Field trips*: During field trips learners acquire first-hand experience of the existing situation through observation. But in this source of experience, the learner can only see and occasionally hear about the situation or thing. Thus, the skill of manipulation is not used in this case.
6. *Exhibits*: Exhibits are systematic representations of reality. These can only be seen, and are therefore less effective in the cone of experience.

7. *Motion pictures*: Motion pictures or films involve sound and moving pictures. That is why they are placed above in the cone of experience. However, motion pictures are not as popular as TV.
8. *Visual symbols*: These consists of devices used to assist in communicating by visible means in order to create an impression of reality in the audiences' mind; for example, posters, charts, flannel graphs, leaflets, etc.
9. *Verbal symbols*: Verbal symbols are spoken or written words. They bear no physical resemblance to the object or ideas they represent. That is, the word 'iron' does not look like a piece of iron or like the iron used to press clothes. However, it is a word that has more or less the same meaning for all of us. Although words are abstract symbols, they are indispensable for interpreting every other audio-visual material on the cone.

ADULT LEARNING

Understanding the various theories provide insights about the structuring of learning and factors that could influence the process. However scholars have differentiated between learning among children and adults. Malcolm Knowles is regarded as the father of adult learning. As stated in Merriam (2001), Knowles coined the popular term 'Andragogy', the art and science of helping adults learn, which he felt required a different approach from pedagogy or children's learning. Andragogy is a theory that holds a set of assumptions about how adults learn and emphasises the value of the process of learning. Knowles identified the following as six principles of adult learning.

1. Adults are internally motivated and self-directed
2. Adults bring life experiences and knowledge to learning experiences
3. Adults are goal oriented
4. Adults are relevancy oriented
5. Adults are practical
6. Adult learners like to be respected

Through practical fieldwork experiences, interacting with real clients and their real-life situations, adult learners move from classroom and textbook mode to hands-on problem solving where they can recognise firsthand how what they are learning applies to life and the work context. The following principles provide valuable guidelines for structuring learning for adults.

- *Problem-centred learning*: Adults learn better when the learning process is directed towards solving problems. Problems motivate adults to acquire new information. Adult students become ready to learn when they experience a need to learn it in order to cope with real-life tasks or problems.
- *Meaningful learning*: Adult learning must be designed in accordance to the learner's interest, age, readiness and capacity to understand. Further, adult learners want to know the relevance of what they are learning to see if it maps to what they want to achieve.
- *Experience-centred learning*: It is very important to provide or create an environment which allows the learner to accept the learning experience. Adults like to be given opportunities to use their existing foundation of knowledge and experience that has been gained over the years and apply them to their new learning experiences.
- *Participatory goal setting*: Adult learners resist learning when they feel others are imposing information, ideas or actions on them. If the goals are forcefully imposed on learners, they feel uninterested, and

consequently poor learning takes place. Therefore, involving learners in setting some learning goals can enhance their learning experience.

- *Feedback learning*: Feedback to adults about their progress helps sustain learners' motivations. Providing timely constructive feedback based on evaluations and appraisals acts as a definitive motivator for adults to continue to learn.
- *Respecting learners*: Respecting the learners is crucial for keeping them interested and motivated. Respect can be demonstrated by taking interest, acknowledging the value of their past experiences, regarding them as equals in life experience and encouraging expression of ideas at every opportunity.

In India, like in any other developing nation, a number of out-of-school adolescents, young adults and many other people employed in semi-skilled jobs need to be exposed to the benefits of education and skills training. Their economic compulsions limit their formal educational opportunities. Therefore, a number of adult literacy programmes aimed at functional literacy are run by government and non-governmental organisations. These programmes are planned on the basis of the principles of adult learning to make their learning experiences more meaningful and useful for people participating in such programmes to improve their livelihood opportunities and quality of life.

COMMUNICATION AIDS AND LEARNING

A communication aid is anything that helps an individual communicate more effectively with those around them. This could range from a simple blackboard to any electronic equipment like a LCD screen. Communication aids make the process of learning more effective. In a developing country like India where the literacy rate is so low, communication aids have special significance. They can help the facilitators cross the barrier of illiteracy and reach out to people. Communication aids help to catch the attention of the audience from various socio-cultural backgrounds and enable them to focus on the core of the message content. They create an active learning atmosphere especially in situations where the audience is heterogeneous.

Image 8.1: Interactive Aids Facilitate the Learning Process

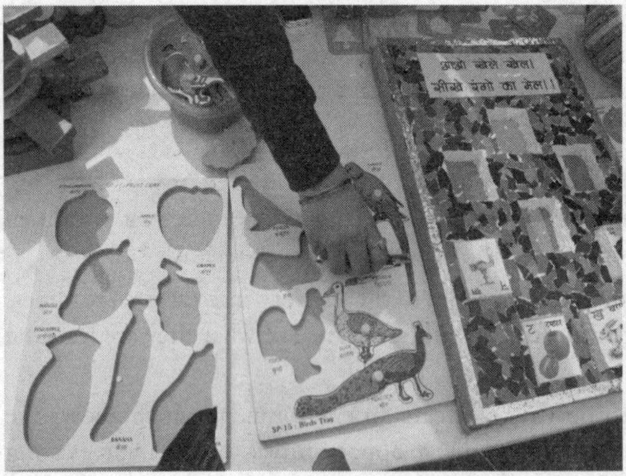

Source: Department of DCE, Lady Irwin College.

The various definitions of communication aids focus on their advantages in the learning process, nature of learning as well as the learning process.

Anything used in an instructional situation to help us reach the instructional objectives through coordinated involvement of both sight and hearing are commonly referred to as 'AV' materials. Burton says, Audio-Visual aids are sensory objects or images which initiate or stimulate and reinforce learning (as cited in Aggarwal 2007: 296), are those sensory objects or images which initiate or stimulate and reinforce learning. According to Kinder (ibid.), AV aids are any device which can be used to make the learning experience more concrete, more realistic and more dynamic.

Thus, communication aids are helpful in providing many direct, indirect and vivid experiences and resolving the problems of forgetting, verbalism and individual differences among the audience (Chandra, Shah and Joshi 1989). Sometimes new concepts are easily forgotten and research has proved that AV methods and tools help retain learning for longer periods. Verbalism becomes a barrier if the audience is not literate. It is a barrier even for a literate audience since sometimes the use of words takes place without understanding the meaning.

Role of Audio-Visual Aids in Learning

- *Crossing the barrier of time and space*: Various AV aids can be used to explain concepts which are not part of the learner's experiences.
- *Overcoming inadequacy of the language*: AV aids cross the language barrier between the facilitator and the audience. They help create meaningful vocabulary and maintain continuity of thought.
- *Sharing of experiences*: If the audience belongs to urban/rural background or to a different socio-cultural background, AV aids may help in sharing and bringing out the commonality even in the heterogeneity.
- *Understanding abstract and complex ideas*: It is easier to discuss abstract ideas by showing more concrete material.
- *Gaining better sensory experiences*: They help in developing understanding and retaining knowledge for a longer time.
- *Organising ideas*: They help the audience organise concepts and ideas that have been presented.
- *Increasing motivation*: AV aids increase active participation of the audience and help ensure maximum involvement.

Classification of Audio-Visual Aids

AV methods and tools create opportunities in which people gain the abilities and stimulations necessary for effective and long-term learning. But the person using the AV aids should be able to differentiate between a method and a tool based on its utility for a specific target community or group of people.

Communication methods and aids can be classified in different ways. Some of these are discussed below.

According to Evolution

- *First-generation media*: Handmade charts, graphs, exhibits, models, hand-written materials.
- *Second-generation media*: Printed/illustrated text, printed graphics, workbooks.
- *Third-generation media*: Photographs, slides, film-strips, films, recording, radio, tele-lectures.
- *Fourth-generation media*: TV, programmed instruction, language laboratories, electronic digital computers.

According to the Senses Involved

- *Audio aids*: Radio talks, tape recordings, disc recording, telephone.

- *Visual aids*: Slides, OHP (Over-Head Projector).
- *Audio-visual aids*: Motion picture, TV telecast, sound-synchronised slides, radio, computer and other digital aids.

According to the Use of Projection Facility

Visual aids can be further classified as projected and non-projected aids based on whether these involve projection. In some cases the projected aids come with a fixed commentary—i.e. voice is included with the motion or vision, as in the case of TV and cinema. In the case of variable commentary projected aids, commentary is provided by the communicator—as in the case of film-strips, slides, OHP. Non-projected aids include presentations like flash cards, charts, flip books and displays like maps, posters, photographs, bulletin boards.

Two / Three-Dimensional

Further visual aids can be two-dimensional like posters, charts and maps or three-dimensional like puppets, specimens, samples, real objects and 3D films.

Interpersonal Communication Methods and AV Aids

Interpersonal communication methods are the processes through which information, ideas and concepts are disseminated for the target groups. These methods structure the learning process. They are selected as per the need of the target group and are modified and improvised depending upon the situations. Availability of appropriate skilled facilitators is imperative to bring about a desired learning outcome for the target audiences. Some of the interpersonal communication methods are as follows.

Demonstrations

A demonstration is a visualised explanation of an important fact, idea or process. It is an effective way for showing how certain things work. In demonstration one can use different material to mix and match to create something new or talk about an existing technique. For example, practical lessons such as applying a bandage, using a stove, making a low-cost sanitary napkin or preparing a nutritious dish.

Demonstrations can be of three types:

1. Method demonstrations explain a process in a step-by-step manner. It is time consuming and requires careful planning. It provides the audience an opportunity to 'learn by doing' through direct personal experiences.
2. Result demonstrations are useful to show the results of demonstrated practices in comparison to existing practices or control. For example, increased productivity of a farm by sowing high-yielding variety of wheat as compared to the traditional variety.

Image 8.2: Demonstrating a Process (Puppet Making)

Source: Department of DCE, Lady Irwin College.

3. Composite demonstration uses a mixed method. It shows the process partially followed by showing end product depending upon the amount of time and resources available.

Advantages

- It is an audience-friendly participatory method.
- It creates interest among the audience about the topic.
- It can be used to explain complex ideas in an easy and safe manner.
- It is a cost-effective method.
- It can be used successfully for all types of audience.
- Experiments which are difficult for students to perform can be demonstrated.

Disadvantages

- It is a time-consuming method.
- All the audience may not be able to keep pace with the demonstrators instructions, as different people have different speeds of learning.
- Giving a good demonstration requires high level of planning, preparation and practice on the part of the demonstrator.

Field Trips

Field trips are undertaken to help audience understand real-life situations observing people, places and programmes themselves. For example, the audience may be taken to a community radio station to see how radio programmes are made and broadcasted.

Advantages

- Field trips give wide-experiences that are rich and meaningful and most often find favour with the audience. They reinforce the principle of 'seeing is believing'.
- They always lead the audience to have a total experience. Thereby, the communicator can influence their ideas, attitudes and values effectively.

Disadvantages

- Field trips require time and money along with careful planning to ensure a meaningful experience for the audience.
- Field trips often depend on timing and organising of the visit and events or programmes and therefore involves a lot of external factors too.

Home and Farm Visits

Home and farm visits face-to-face communications for special purposes by

Image 8.3: Home Visits

Source: Department of DCE, Lady Irwin College.

visiting people's homes. They are an essential part of the learning process. Home visits enable the communicator to gain the confidence of families and secure their friendship and cooperation. The communicator can convey her/his message in person clearly. (S)he can also address any doubts or queries of the persons being visited.

Advantages

- This method helps the communicator locate leaders and co-operators in the community.
- This method ensures that the percentage of adoption (acceptance) to exposure (efforts) is high.
- It helps the communicator understand information gaps, analyse problems and enable them to take their own decision.
- First-hand information is given to people as there is a direct contact between the people and the communicator.

Disadvantages

- It is hugely time consuming as the communicator individually meets a lot of people.
- Neighbours not visited may be disappointed and accuse the communicator of favouritism.
- It is a costly method.
- The timing of the visit is crucial, as the communicator can only visit at a time convenient for each family.

Discussion

Group discussion is a problem-solving approach where two or more people talk and think together in a group. Here, there will be face-to-face mutual interchange of ideas, facts and opinions between members of a relatively small group having a common concern or working towards the development of a programme of action relating to the problem. It is not just casual conversation. This kind of discussion clarifies and enriches members' thinking and develops an attitude of objectivity. It enables the group to understand every members' point of view and come to a common understanding of problems and build consensus towards solutions.

Image 8.4: Group Discussion

Source: Department of DCE, Lady Irwin College.

Advantages

- It is scientific method which employs the reflective thinking pattern—a scientific method which leads the reflective thought (Dewey 1933).
- It is primarily a problem-solving experience.
- It creates a high degree of interest to entertain the participants.
- Continued experience with such group discussion improves capacity for critical and analytical thinking and also makes members improve their speaking and listening powers.

- Experience with such group discussions improves the capacity of decision-making in individuals.

Disadvantages

- As it is slow process, it is not effective in taking decision during an emergency.
- To some extent in small groups and most certainly in large groups, it is difficult to establish unity and togetherness to have a discussion. Factions amongst the audience in the village may hinder successful implementation of this method.
- The size of the group has to be limited, because everyone should be able to hear each other. The effectiveness of the method is best realised with limited size of the group.

Image 8.5: Meeting to Pass on Information

Source: Department of DCE, Lady Irwin College.

Meeting

A meeting can be organised for various target groups depending upon the need and objectives of learning. For example, youth groups or mahila mandals (women's groups) or leadership training meetings. Meetings are used to pass on certain information for considerat`ion and future action of the participants, and also used as an opportunity to share new information or news and publicise new programmes.

Advantages

- A lot of people can be reached.
- It can be used to introduce all kinds of subjects.
- It can boost the urge of individuals for social contacts.
- Group psychology can be used to promote or develop the programme.
- The desired change can be accomplished at a low cost.
- Reactions of the people to a new programme can be assessed.

Disadvantages

- Suitable meeting place and facilities may not always be adequate.
- Circumstances beyond control, unfavourable weather, etc. might reduce the attendance.
- Scope of discussion is limited except for a few questions and answers.

As explained above, Audio-visual aids are tools or materials used to facilitate the methods described above. If these aids are selected carefully on the basis of social-cultural and economic background of the target audience, they can provide a holistic learning experience. Some of these aids are used for interpersonal processes and some are used for group processes. Some of these aids can be categorised as following:

Displays

These include flat maps, diagrams, posters, pictures, flannelgraphs, flipbooks and charts. These usually include a thought-through attractive arrangement of material. Displays can be used for (*a*) stimulation of a new idea, (*b*) publicising an idea, (*c*) explaining concepts attractively, and (*d*) bringing in various dispersed ideas together.

Image 8.6: Flannelgraph

Source: 'Flanell-Noa1a' by Knut (Wikimedia Commons; CC0 Public Domain).

Flannelgraph is storytelling system that uses a board covered with a fabric (usually flannel, but khadi and markin could also be used) and mounted on a stand. The story to be communicated is depicted on the flannelgraph. They are useful to build a story or demonstrate a progression. It is an inexpensive aid that can be used for demonstration purposes. They are effective in promoting audience participation.

Exhibits are used to display a variety of materials coherently arranged pertaining to a theme. They stimulate pupils to question or consolidate what is already learnt. Exhibits planned and prepared by pupils with the guidance of the teacher should be encouraged and preferred. Exhibiting the pupil's accomplishments will stimulate attention and appreciation among the pupils.

Bulletin board is a wall-mounted board which is used to showcase leaflets, pictures, posters, charts, sketches, etc.

Image 8.7: Bulletin Board

Source: DCE Department, Lady Irwin College.

Advantages

- AV aids make communication process more stimulating and dynamic, because of step-by-step presentation which results in developing a topic.
- They can be adopted for various topics and for various types of audiences.
- Using simple, low-cost materials such as magazine clippings and coloured paper, the communicator can prepare interesting illustrative talks.
- No electricity is required, thus, it can be used in areas where other visuals cannot be employed.
- They are portable and easy to use.

- They can be prepared locally and well in advance.
- They can be used for a more vivid explanation of an idea.
- They are usually low cost and can be put to repeated use.

Disadvantages

- AV aids cannot be used in front of a large audience.
- These cannot be used in illustrations of complex ideas.
- Corrections or changes are difficult to make.
- There is a tendency to use material which is too small or too detailed.
- AV aids may be a possible distraction if they are put up for the entire session and are not used throughout.

Projected Aids

There are two types of projected aids: (*a*) those which have motion along with visual and audio, i.e. motion pictures or films, and (*b*) those where commentary is added from outside by the facilitator, i.e. filmstrips, slides and transparencies.

Motion pictures or films can reconstruct a period with dramatic intensity and realism and help relive a past event. They facilitate understanding of other people, their land, and culture and values as well as history and science. Films bind the interest of the audience, presenting systematic information and in arriving at generalisations. They help bring the world and experts in a particular field into the community, which is ordinarily not possible. Films help visualise information on entire processes such as manufacturing woollen cloth from the shearing of sheep, shipment of fleece, carding of wool to weaving of yarn into fabric. Films are useful also in introducing or summarising discussions. Films show continuity of events, and cause and effect in a short period of time.

Image 8.8: Filmstrip

Source: 'Film strip' by Bart Everson (Wikimedia Commons; CC By 2.0).

Filmstrip is a series of individual pictures appearing in a pre-decided sequence.

Slide is a single-mounted transparency or a clear glass. It is usually 2 × 2 inches photographic or hand-drawn. A variety of printed materials like pictures, graphs, cartoons, etc. can be put on the slides along with the text. These slides can be developed in a series and projected to tell an audio-visual story or convey facts and figures and complex processes. Unlike a filmstrip the sequence of slides can be changed.

Transparencies are plastic sheets of 10 × 10 inches used to write on with a felt pen and projected through an overhead projector. It can be viewed by a much bigger group.

Power-Point presentation is a computer-based AV aid that can be used as a tool. It is made using computer software and projected through an LCD projector.

Advantages

- A projection can be seen clearly by a large audience.
- The viewer's attention is attracted and held by a bright picture in a dark room.
- Details can be emphasised.
- Colour, motion and sound add realism and hold learner's interest.
- Films can allow learners to 'experience' things that would otherwise be impossible.
- Can be showed, stopped and/or reversed for analysis.

Image 8.9: Slides

Source: 'Negativ and Reversal 35mm Film' by Ivan2010 (Wikimedia Commons; CC By-SA 4.0).

Disadvantages

- Projected aids are expensive.
- Too many details can be overwhelming.
- Films slides get outdated and do not last long.
- Suitable projecting equipment and a power source are needed. This can lead to difficulties with setting up, maintenance and transport.
- Requires basic technical know-how.

Graphic Aids

These are two-dimensional materials which are used to convey an idea, fact or relationship between two elements. It helps present an abstract idea in a visual form and hence make it comprehensible.

Graphs are pictorial representations of numerical and statistical data. Graphs make the abstract statistical data easily comprehensible. They are very useful in presenting co-relationships and overall trends. Bar graphs, line graphs, pie charts, flowcharts and area graphs are most commonly used types of graphs.

Figure 8.5: Bar Graph

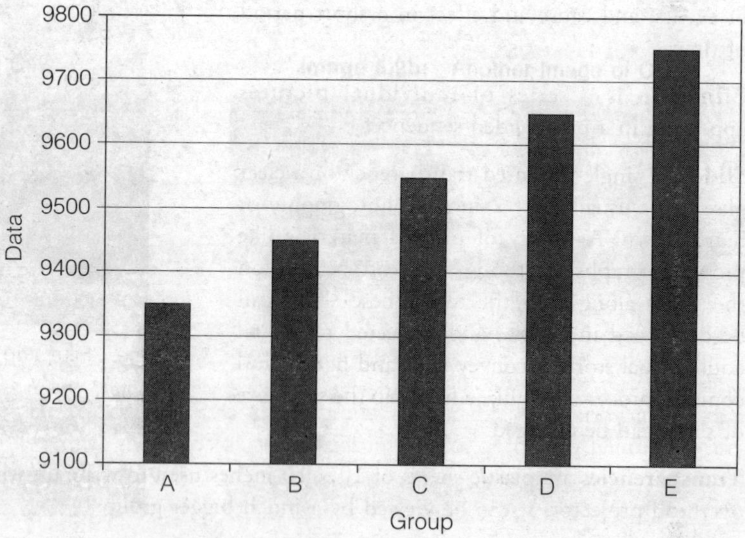

Source: 'Incarceration Rates Worldwide ZP' by XceptivZP (Wikimedia Commons; CC0 Public Domain).

Charts help present details in a concise and summarised manner. They can be used with other aids for clear thinking. They also help focus fact and figures to the essentials.

Posters compel attention and motivate action. They convey a message at a glance. They help to

Figure 8.6: Pie Chart

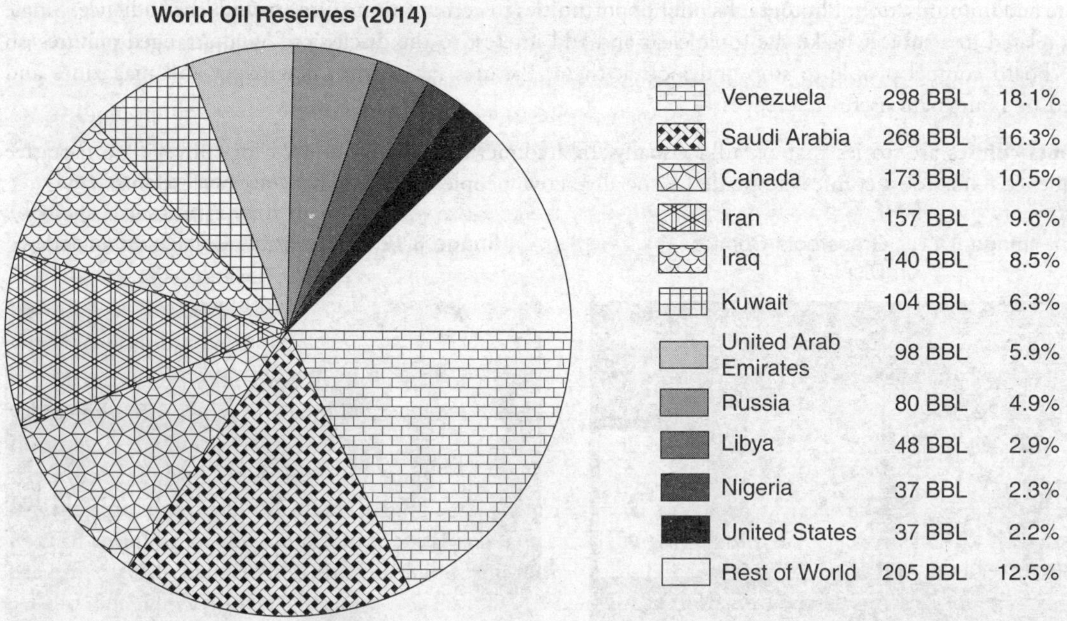

Source: 'World Oil Reserves by Country-pie chart' by Delphi234 (Wikimedia Commons; CC0 Public Domain).

drive home a single idea. They are effective both when used and when combined with other AV aids. They are often used in exhibits to highlight demonstrations. Posters can be locally produced. They may be drawings, pictures, photographs, paper-outs, silhouettes, cartoons or sample of fabrics. Posters can be used directly in training sessions, to remind the audience of a key message or advertise something they might forget.

Flip chart is an album of drawings, pictures, charts. This aid helps narrate a story. It is handy and can be easily carried and is easy to prepare. It can be prepared by the trainer/teacher or facilitator because it requires two pieces of cardboards, sheets of paper, colour pencils or ink and brush, a few pictures, etc.

Image 8.10: Use of Flip Charts

Source: 'community-midwife-in-badakhshan-uses-postpartum-family-planning-flip-card-during-her-counseling-session' by Hassan Zakizadeh (Public Domain Images; CC0 Public Domain).

Flash cards are a series of cards which are presented before the audience in a proper sequence to tell a complete story. When each card is flashed before the audience it is accompanied by a verbal commentary.

Pictures may be easily collected and classified, and used for innumerable purposes along with other aids. They are useful for showing comparisons and contrasts in topics such as family planning, flower arrangement, nutrition, child care and immunisation. Photographs offer opportunities to communicate directly with the audience. Single pictures related to a subject make the topic clear and add interest to the discussion. Well-arranged pictures on a notice board compel people to stop and look at them. Pictures taken from newspaper and magazines and compiled in albums are useful references.

Grassroots comics are stories that are told visually. In a comic, the visuals are used for conveying a narrative in a sequence. Grassroots comics are made by socially-active people, rather than by art professionals.

Image 8.11: Grassroots Comics on Display

Source: Department of DCE, Lady Irwin College.

Image 8.12: Grassroots Comics Explained by Artists

Source: Department of DCE, Lady Irwin College.

Three-Dimensional Aids

These aids help to provide contrived experiences to the audience.

Model is a three-dimensional imitation of a specific object. A model can be a shrinked or enlarged version of an object, or it can represent the object in its actual size. While making and presenting a model for the target group one must be accurate and the group must be aware of the scale of the model.

Puppetry can be used innovatively for telling stories in the community. A puppet is an inanimate object or representational figure that is made to move by human effort before an audience. Although an ancient form of entertainment, puppetry serves as an applied art to convey meaningful messages.

Different types of puppets are used in Indian puppetry. The differences exist not only in names, but also in form, structure, manipulation and presentation techniques.

Image 8.13: Glove Puppet

Source: Department of DCE, Lady Irwin College.

1. **Glove puppet** is like a three-fingered glove which fits in one hand. The first finger is inserted inside the head and moves it. The middle finger and thumb fit in the hands

and move them. These are very often used with young children and can be characterised for human or non human characters like fruits and vegetables.

2. **Rod puppet** is a puppet that is attached by rods to the necks and hands. In most cases, the control comes from below. Rod puppets may also be worked with rods from above or any other direction which can assure good movement and performance. These are popularly used in West Bengal.
3. **Shadow puppet** casts a shadow when the puppeteer manipulates them between a light source and a screen. A shadow puppeteer learns to move the puppet in and out of the light so its shadow grows and shrinks and goes in and out of sharp focus to narrate the story. These are popularly used in Andhra Pradesh, Karnataka and Odisha.
4. **String puppets** are one of the most difficult forms of puppetry to manipulate effectively, as these puppets hang on strings. Usually there are eight strings attached to these puppets. These are also called Marionettes. These are very popularly used in Rajasthan.

Image 8.14: Use of Scroll

Source: Department of DCE, Lady Irwin College.

Scroll or **Cantastoria** is an ancient performance form of picture-story recitation, which involves sung narration accompanied by reference to painted banners, scrolls or placards and music. The narrative image is central and the narration is built around it. In parts of India it is known as Patachitra. Traditional folk media forms are personal, familiar and credible.

The scroll is usually unrolled from side to side. The text in it is written in lines from the top to the bottom of the page. When unrolled one page of the scroll is exposed at a time with the remaining pages rolled up to the left and right of the visible page.

Role play is an activity in which one or more persons assume the role of a character in an imaginary situation, and narrate and/or act out that character's dialogue, responses and motivations. They break formal barriers and approach people directly. It is a form of theatrical performance and presentation in outdoor or indoor public spaces without a specific paying audience. These spaces can be anywhere—shopping centres, car parks, recreational reserves and street corners. It helps in group decision-making, interpersonal skills, positive behaviour change, developing insights and conflict resolution.

Image 8.15: Role Play

Source: Department of DCE, Lady Irwin College.

Selection of AV Aids

Learning experiences of adults must be put together into systematic units, series or programmes that reinforce each other. This is because organisation of learning is the key in communication. Organising learning deeply influences attitudes and behaviours of individuals because it directly impacts the efficiency of instruction and degree to which changes are brought about in the learners. Therefore, it is imperative that the communicator understands which methods and tools are to be used for targeted group of learners.

Figure 8.7: Process of Selection of Communication Media

Step 1
- Specification of learning objective

Step 2
- Organisation of Techniques

Step 3
- Organisation of Materials

Step 4 and 5
- Selection factors

Step 6
- Implementation

Step 7
- Evaluation

Source: Created by the authors with inputs from the internet.

The communication objective should be clear in the facilitator's mind. As soon as the learning objectives are laid down clearly the selection of AV aid becomes easier. One must know the scope and limitations of a particular AV aid or material vis-à-vis interpersonal and group communication. The criteria for selecting a particular AV aid will have two aspects which need to be co-related while taking the decision. First, effectiveness of materials and techniques in meeting learning objectives set by the selector; and second, advantage or disadvantages linked to that particular aid.

While selecting an AV aid the above factors need to be seen along with the criteria of objective fulfillment. It is to be noted that no AV aid will fulfill all these criteria fully. One needs to see the degree to which they fulfill. For example, in a role play the scope of learning factual information is low but it can help develop attitudes to some extent. It can help ensure active participation of the audience. Similarly, three-dimensional aids involve at least three senses—hearing, touch and sight—but the scope for learning principles and relationships is low.

Adults can learn and change their behaviour if they feel the need and interest in a given development concern, be it health, environment, gender or human rights. There are certain characteristic ways and principles of adult learning which every communicator should be aware of. This will help the communicator design a learning and behaviour change programme for groups. Audio-visual methods and tools help in making the communication process engaging and interactive for the audience.

SUMMARY

- Learning is generally associated with classrooms, courses, assignments and exams. However, learning is a life-long process.
- AV Aids help to initiate or stimulate and reinforce learning.
- An AV aid can help in crossing the barriers of time and space, overcoming inadequacy of language, sharing of experiences, understanding abstract and complex ideas, gaining better sensory experiences, organising ideas and increasing motivation of the learner.
- Edgar Dale's cone of experience explains the interrelationship of the various sources of experience as well as their individual positioning in the learning process.
- Some of the interpersonal communication methods are demonstration, field trips, meetings, group discussions and home/farm visits.
- AV aids can also be categorised as displays, projected aids, audio aids, graphic aids and three-dimensional aids.

KEY WORDS

Blooms taxonomy: It is the theory proposed by Benjamin Blooms to elaborate the forms and levels of learning. It suggests three domains of learning: cognitive, psychomotor and affective.

Andragogy: It is the art and science of helping adults learn. It assumes that adults focus more on the process of learning.

Communication aid: It is an aid that helps an individual communicate more effectively with those around them.

Audio-visual aids: Sensory objects or material which initiate or stimulate and reinforce learning.

Cone of Experience: It is a model proposed by the American educationist Edgar Dale in 1946. It includes various learning theories to describe learning experiences and assumes that tangible experiences remain with the audience for longer than the abstract experiences.

Demonstration: It is a method of visualised explanation of an important fact, idea or process happens.

Field trips: It a method of experiential learning that helps audience understand real-life situations by observing people, places and programmes themselves.

Grassroots comics: These are comics created to tell stories from the grassroots. The creators of these comics are socially-active people rather than art professionals.

EXERCISES

1. Explain the various characteristics of the learning process.
2. How does learning take place in adults? What are the possible guidelines for structuring learning process for adults?
3. Elaborate on the role of AV aids in learning for adults. How are these aids classified?
4. Explain the different levels of pyramid in Edgar Dale's Cone of Experience to illustrate the different types of learning experiences.
5. Enlist and elucidate the different interpersonal communication aids and their possible advantages and disadvantages.

REFERENCES

Aggarwal, J. C., *Essentials of Education Technology*, second edition, New Delhi: Vikas Publishing House Pvt. Ltd., 2007.

Chandra, A., A. Shah and A. Joshi, *Fundamental of Teaching Home Science*, New Delhi: Sterling Publishers Private Limited, 1989.

Dale, E., *Audio-Visual Methods in Teaching*, third edition, Illinois: The Dryden Press, 1969.

Dewey, J., *How We Think*, available at http://rci.rutgers.edu/~tripmcc/phil/dewey-hwt-pt1-selections.pdf (accessed 7 April 2016), 1933.

Dubey, V. and I. Bishnoi, *Extension Education and Communication*, New Delhi: New Age International Publishers, 2009.

Kolb, D., *Experiential Learning: Experience as the Source of Learning and Development*, first edition, New Jersey: Prentice Hall, 1984.

Krathwohl, D., *A Revision of Bloom's Taxonomy: An Overview*, first edition, Ohio: College of Education, 2002.

Merriam, S. B., 'Andragogy and Self Directed Learning: Pillars of Adult Learning Theory', *New Directions for Adult and Continuing Education* 89 (2001): 3–14.

Saunders, D., *Visual Communication Handbook*, Worcester: Ebenezer Baylis and Son Ltd. and London: The Trinity Press, 1979.

Sharma, S., *Modern Methods of Teaching Home Science*, New Delhi: Swarup & Sons, 2002.

Wigforss, E., 'The Role of Communication in Learning Technologies', Paper presented to 16th Annual Conference of the Australasian Society for Computers in Learning in Tertiary Education, Brisbane, 1999.

Woolfolk, A., *Educational Psychology*, ninth edition, New York: Pearson Higher Educationm 2009.

UNIT III

COMMUNICATION SYSTEM

How an individual communicates with the self is significantly different from the way the same person communicates in a dyadic situation or in a small or large group of audiences. There are different forms of communication that we use to convey messages to one another depending on the nature of message and the number of people involved in communication and the objective of communication. This process of communication in different situations depending on the size of the audience, the unique set of characteristics of the elements of communication for communicating with the self or others, is known as communication system. This unit is devoted to the various communication systems humans engage in.

In the first chapter, we look at intrapersonal communication—communication with the self. We will understand the various aspects of self such as, self-concept, self-awareness, self-disclosure and self-esteem and how these different selves of an individual facilitate or hamper his/her communication behaviour. The second chapter deals with interpersonal communication—the sharing of feelings and ideas with other people. We will study how communicating with others allows us to meet our basic needs of communicating and forming relationships as well as more abstract human needs for effective participation in a socially diverse world. The third chapter is on small group communication—communicating information that is of common interest to group members. We will understand the theories and stages of group formation here. The final chapter deals with organisational communication—communication within large organisations or businesses. Here, we will try to understand the characteristics of organisations, the difference between casual and organised groups and functions of communication in organisations which include but are not limited to keeping supervisors and subordinates informed, persuading the clients and others involved in organisational communication, regulating and exercising control and integrating the members of the organisations.

9

INTRAPERSONAL COMMUNICATION

HIGHLIGHTS

- Understanding the self
- Self-awareness
- Mapping the self: Johari Window
- Self-concept
- Self-esteem

Fundamentally all communications start and end with us. While communicating with others, our decisions about what to communicate, how to communicate, with whom to communicate as well as the meaning we derive from others' communications are defined by our 'self'. We have already been introduced to a type of communication that takes place within ourselves—intrapersonal communication. This form of communication is an intrinsic dimension of every person's self and takes place every moment we live. When we are observing, thinking, contemplating, choosing, deciding while doing activities and tasks, creating, studying, watching a film or even when we are day-dreaming, we constantly engage in intrapersonal communication.

Intrapersonal communication takes place whenever we evaluate and react to internal and external stimuli. It involves messages being sent and received within ourselves. We are both the source and destination in this type of communication. Our brain waves are the channel and they may result in a range of outcomes such as new ideas and thoughts emerging, firming up of decisions, and may lead to a range of actions or behaviour. So, when we walk in a garden full of flowers, or hear loud music, we evaluate the external stimuli and decide our reaction. We may like or dislike the walk or the music, and consequently this may influence our decision about how long we walk in that garden or whether we would enjoy or complain against the loud music.

However, intrapersonal communication goes beyond just 'talking to oneself'. It is influenced by a range of physical, social, cultural and emotional aspects that act as filters and consequently influence our interactions. Our physical characteristics, our emotional state, our intellectual capacity, our social position, our self-concept, our perceptions about social roles, and our habits, attitudes, values and beliefs together influence our intrapersonal communication. The self is the most important aspect in the communication process because who we are and how we perceive ourselves and others influences our communications with others.

In this chapter, we explore the various aspects of the self—self-concept, self-awareness and self-esteem and understand how our intrapersonal communications are largely guided by our self-concept and self-esteem.

They act as filters in every interaction with others and determine how we approach, respond to, and interpret messages.

Understanding the Self

The study of intrapersonal communication begins with knowing ourselves and understanding the 'self'. It seeks to understand the question 'who am I'? When asked to describe themselves, most people list characteristics, likes, dislikes, hobbies, preferences, groups they are part of, etc. The 'self' can be defined as a central inner force, common to all human beings and yet unique in each; it is the deep-set source of growth. The 'self' is a sum total of who we are.

Experiences, interactions, opportunities, perceptions, etc. come together to influence and contribute to shaping individuals and their 'self'. Our family, the school we attend, the groups and organisations we are part of, and the roles we assume at different stages of our lives define and shape us and make us the person we are. Hence, an individual person, through her/his daily interactions and from the messages received from others and sent to others, has a unique set of experiences. Consequently individuals and their 'self's are unique.

SELF-AWARENESS

One of the key aspects about understanding the self is developing our self-awareness. Let us look at this concept in some detail.

Many Selves

As soon as we begin to examine the self, we discover that the self has many aspects. In fact, each one of us has many selves. The fact we behave differently when we are with different people or environments or when we know we are being observed point to the fact that we have layers of multiple selves. William James (1890/2010) identified three components of the self—the material self, the social self and the spiritual self.

Material self is a total of all of the tangible things you own—your possessions, your home, your body or any other thing you own. The material self suggests that 'you are what you have.' The material self has acquired great importance in most cultures today. People spend huge amounts of money and resources trying to have the right look, appropriate clothes to wear, possess latest gadgets, etc.

Social self is the part of you that interacts with others. Each person has many social selves. You interact differently with your friends, family members, colleagues or with any acquaintances. For example, when you talk to your close friend about an issue, you may be willing to reveal more thoughts and feelings than you would in a conversation with your teacher or even your parents.

Spiritual self consists of an individual's internal thoughts about their values and moral standards. It does not depend on what you own or whom you talk with; it is the essence of who you think you are and of your feelings about yourself.

Body Image and Self-awareness

Body image is both the mental picture that we have of our body and how we perceive ourselves when we look at a mirror. Body image deeply influences the self. If you hate your body it's not easy to feel good about yourself. Social norms define body image and these norms are either rejected or reinforced by our family, friends and the larger socio-cultural system we are part of. Thus, body image refers to the way we perceive ourselves in relation to the social standards of our culture. This mental image each one of us possesses may influence our communication patterns. For instance, if we think we are too fat or thin, or not fair enough or have the hair of the right colour we may feel out of the crowd. We may become withdrawn which modifies our attempts to send messages to others and affects our interpretation of the messages we get from others. A major problem among young college girls of today is the feeling of not having the perfect body. This feeling may lead to eating disorders like anorexia or bulimia. Similarly, young men also feel they have to fit the stereotypes of strength, height and other physical attributes.

Self-disclosure and Self-awareness

A very important way people understand themselves better is by receiving other people's reactions to their self-disclosure. Self-disclosure occurs when you purposefully provide information to others about yourself. Self-disclosure ranges from revealing harmless information about who you are to admitting your deepest fears and most private fantasies. Disclosing personal information not only provides a basis for another person to understand you better, but also conveys your level of trust and acceptance of the other person. Because others self-disclose, you are able to learn about them and further deepen your interpersonal relationship with them. Understanding how self-disclosure occurs and the general characteristics of self-disclosure can provide insights into how individuals can become aware of 'who' they are.

Risks and Rewards of Self-disclosure

Sometimes our disclosure may lead to personal or social rejection. For example, parents who are the most supportive of all interpersonal relations may reject children who come out as gay/lesbian, i.e. self-disclose their sexuality. It may lead to intrapersonal difficulties and difficulties in adjustment with the self.

Self-disclosure has great rewards too. It may bring self-knowledge, increase our ability to cope, improve communication and increase the depth of a relationship. When we self-disclose we gain a new perspective about ourselves and a deeper understanding of our own behaviour. It may also help improve communication. For example, you can tell when someone is being sarcastic. It also helps in establishing a meaningful relationship between two people. By self-disclosing, we tell others that we trust, respect and care enough about them and the relationship to reveal information about ourselves. This in turn leads the other individual to self-disclose and forms the beginning of a meaningful relationship. This is referred to as 'dyadic effect'.

Figure 9.1: Dyadic Effect

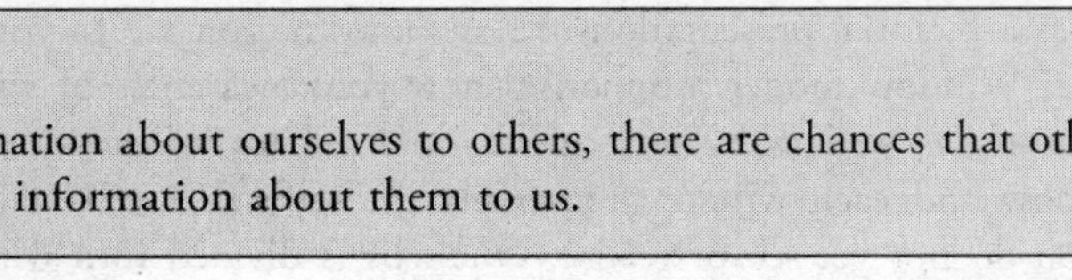

Source: Created by the authors.

> **Dyadic Effect**
>
> When we disclose information about ourselves to others, there are chances that others will also feel more comfortable in disclosing information about them to us.

Characteristics of Self-disclosure

Individuals tend to self-disclose more readily under certain circumstances. Some of these factors are discussed in Table 9.1.

Table 9.1: Characteristics of Self-disclosure and their Implications

Characteristics of Self-disclosure	*What does it Imply?*
Group size	Self-disclosure occurs more in small groups than in large groups. A dyad (group of two people) is the most comfortable setting for self-disclosure. For example, we may feel more comfortable in disclosing our personal problems with a friend rather than with a whole group of friends. With one listener, we can monitor our disclosures—i.e. continue if there is support from the listener and stop if not. With more than one listener, such monitoring becomes difficult, because the listeners' responses may vary.
Liking	We tend to disclose information about ourselves to people we like, love or trust and not to people we dislike. This is because the people we trust will be more supportive and positive.
Age	The chances for self-disclosure are greater when we talk with those who are approximately of our age group. It is seen that there is more intimacy in relationships of similar-age dyads. For example, self-disclosure occurs more in the same-age peer group.
Competence	Competent communicators self-disclose more than less competent ones. This may be because they have more positive things to say about themselves or they have more self-confidence which is necessary for taking risks associated with self-disclosure.
Personality	Extroverts and highly sociable people tend to self-disclose more than introverts and those who are less sociable. People who are apprehensive about talking in general self-disclose less than those who are comfortable in oral communication. Also, people with high self-esteem are more likely to engage in self-disclosure than those with low self-esteem.
Topics	We are more likely to disclose information about our job or hobbies than about our sex life or financial situation or some other confidential subject. Generally, the more personal the topic the less are the chances of self-disclosure. Also, we are more likely to disclose information that reveals positivity rather than negativity.

Source: Created by the authors.

There can be many more factors influencing self-disclosure including culture, gender and relationship that we share with the other individual. However, self-disclosure and its effects can be so significant that people think critically before deciding to disclose or not. Like any other communication, it is irreversible—i.e. once something is said, it cannot be taken back. We cannot erase the conclusions and inferences that listeners have made on the basis of our disclosures.

MAPPING THE SELF: JOHARI WINDOW

The Johari Window is a model used to examine the self-disclosure process. Developed by Joseph Luft and Harry Ingham, it provides a pictorial presentation of how 'known' you are to yourself and others (West and Turner 2011). The Johari Window model summarises how your awareness of who you are is influenced by your own level of disclosure, as well as by how much others share information about you with you. The model looks like a window and each window represents the self. The self includes everything about you, including things even you do not yet see or realise. One axis is divided into what you have come to know about yourself and what you do not yet know about yourself. The other axis represents what someone else may know about you and you do not know about yourself. The intersection of these categories creates a four-panel window. Each quadrant or window contains a different self. Let's see a representation of Johari's Window in Figure 9.1.

The Open Self

'Open self' represents all the information, behaviours, attitudes, feelings, desires, motivations and ideas that we know about ourselves and are also known to others. The information included here might vary from our name, skin colour, sex, age, political and religious affiliations and job title. For example, both you and your friend may know that you do not like to be near people who smoke cigarettes.

Figure 9.2: Johari's Window of Self-awareness

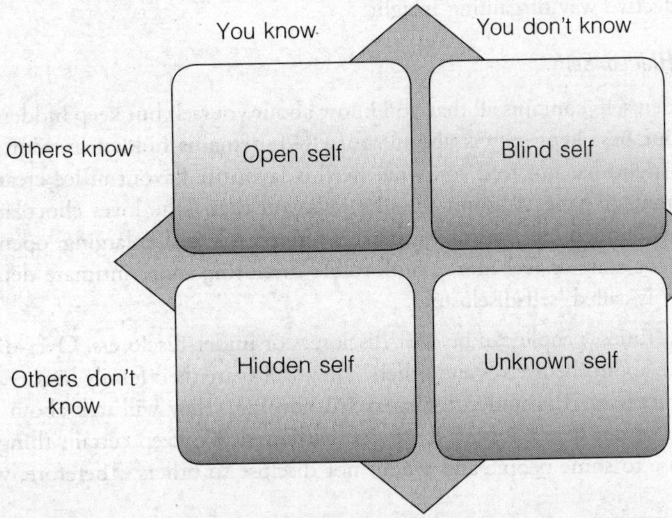

Source: Created by the authors, adapted from West and Turner (2011).

The size of the 'open self' quadrant will vary depending on the individuals with whom we are dealing. Some people probably make us feel comfortable and are supportive. To them we open ourselves more readily. To others we may prefer to leave most of our self closed. For example, when we meet a person for the first time, the size of 'open self' is not very large since there has been little time to exchange information. As the process of getting to know one another continues, the size of 'open self' may gradually increase. The size of 'open self' also varies from person to person. Some people tend to reveal their innermost desires and feelings. Others who are shy prefer to remain silent about both significant and insignificant details.

The Blind Self

'Blind self' represents information about ourselves that others know but we do not know. This may vary from relatively insignificant habits like using the expression 'you know', rubbing your nose when you get angry or having a strange body odour. For example, your friends might notice that you are embarrassed and nervous when you meet a new person, but you are unaware of this fact. Similarly, in an ongoing conversation between you and your friend, your friend may notice that you are not maintaining eye contact while you may not be consciously aware of it. Your friend may also not say anything to you, since (s)he may not want to embarrass you.

Communication depends on both parties having the same basic information about the other. If blind areas exist, communication will be difficult. We may be able to shrink our blind areas by communicating with others and getting feedback about ourselves.

The Unknown Self

'Unknown self' represents those parts of ourselves about which neither we nor others know. This is the information that is buried in our unconscious self or that has somehow escaped our notice. Examples of unknown areas could be a natural ability or aptitude that a person does not realise (s)he possesses, a fear or aversion that a person does not know or an illness that has not manifested itself.

We can gain insight into the unknown self from a number of sources. Sometimes this area can be revealed through temporary changes brought about by experiences with narcotics, special experimental conditions such as hypnosis or various projective tests or dream analysis. The exploration of the unknown self through open and honest interaction with trustworthy people like one's parents, friends, counsellors, children and lovers is an effective way of gaining insight.

The Hidden Self

'Hidden self' contains all that you know about yourself but keep hidden away from the others. This area includes all your best kept secrets about yourself. It remains hidden in your personality (Singh 2010). For example, your friend has not told you what her/his favourite flavour of ice cream. This information is in her/his hidden quadrant or pane. As soon as (s)he tells you that (s)he loves chocolate, (s)he discloses this information from her/his 'hidden self', shrinking her/his hidden self and enlarging 'open self'. As we get to know and trust each other we start to feel more comfortable disclosing more intimate details about ourselves. This process, as we know, is called 'self-disclosure'.

At times, people can be over-disclosers or under-disclosers. Over-disclosers tell everything, keeping nothing hidden about themselves and others. They will share their family history, sexual problems, financial status, failures and successes. The under-disclosers tell nothing. They will talk about you but not about themselves. Most of us fall somewhere between these two extremes. We keep certain things hidden and disclose other things. We disclose to some people and we do not disclose to others. Therefore, we are selective disclosers.

Activity

Think about the category that you fall under. Are you an over-discloser, under-discloser or selective discloser? Give reasons to support your answer.

Effective communication is said to occur when there is a good balance between disclosure and feedback (Wright 2009).

As you may have now realised, the Johari Window is a person-specific model. Your Johari Window for you and your best friend will differ from your Johari Window for you and an acquaintance or a stranger. The sizes of the panes/selves can change as your relationships evolve. For example, after you disclose something personal to a stranger, 'open self' increases and 'hidden self' shrinks.

Figure 9.3: Change in Johari Window

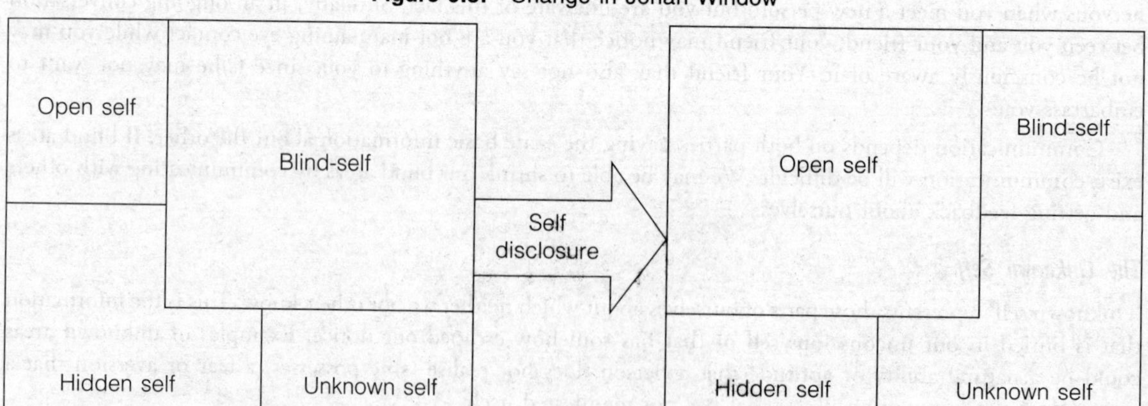

Source: Created by the authors.

The main objective of the Johari Window is to increase the size of the open self through disclosure so that both you and your partner can build a better relationship by reducing the hidden self. Also, it is important that disclosure is reciprocal. The other person should also reveal information about herself/himself as you reveal information about yourself. The open self also increases through feedback you get from others about your behaviour. This information helps you reduce your blind area, because others often see things in you that you do not see (Singh 2010).

The more information you can bring into the open from the hidden, blind and unknown selves, the better your intrapersonal and interpersonal communication will be.

Ways to Increase Our Self-awareness

As discussed above, the more aware we are about ourselves, the better we will be able to control our thoughts and behaviour. The following are certain ways through which we can increase awareness about ourselves.

Dialogue with Your Self

No one knows us better than we do, but the problem is that we seldom have conversation with ourselves. In order to know who we are it is very important to engage in dialogue with ourselves.

Listen

We can learn about ourselves by listening to what others have to say about us. People constantly give us feedback about ourselves which can help us increase our self-awareness. We can specially learn a lot about our blind self by listening to what others have to say about us. For example, your friend may tell you that you get very nervous while talking to strangers. By listening to her/him and by knowing about this aspect of your behaviour, you will decrease the area of your blind self and enhance your awareness about yourself.

See Our Different Selves

We are viewed differently by each of our friends and relatives. So it is a good idea to look at ourselves the way different people see us. For example, you may visualise how your mother, father, teacher, best friend and others see you because you are a blend of all these views.

Increase Our Open Self

When we reveal ourselves to others, we learn about ourselves at the same time. We bring into clear focus what we may have forgotten about ourselves. As we discuss ourselves, we may see connections that we had previously missed. And, in receiving feedback from others, we further gain insight into ourselves. Through these multiple ways, we increase our awareness and we further increase the likelihood that a meaningful and intimate dialogue will develop. It is through such interactions that we get to know ourselves best.

SELF-CONCEPT

Self-concept is a general term used to refer to how someone thinks about or perceives one's self. Self-concept is how we think about and evaluate ourselves. To be aware of oneself is to have a concept of oneself (McLeod 2008). While perception is our view of the outside world, self-concept is the way we view ourselves. The two are interrelated and constantly interact with each other. What we think about ourselves determines what we see around us. Also, the information we get from outside ourselves provides valuable feedback and helps us create an image of who we are. For example, if I think that I am a wonderful cook I would take every positive comment as a support of that notion and any discouraging remark from anyone as a sign of jealousy or humour.

In other words, our self-concept is an image of who we are. It is how we perceive ourselves—our feelings and thoughts about our strengths and weaknesses and our abilities and limitations. Self-concept develops from the image that others have of us and reveal to us, the comparisons that we make between ourselves and others, our cultural experiences in the realms of race, ethnicity, gender and gender roles and our evaluation of our own thoughts and behaviours.

Building Our Self-concept

There are several factors that influence the ways by which we develop our self-concept. These factors complement each other in developing a holistic view of our self-concept. Understanding these factors provides insight into how self-concept can be developed.

Table 9.2: Sources of Self-concept

Cultural traditions	Interactions and perceptions	Comparison with others	Social roles	Self-evaluations and reflections

Source: Created by the authors.

Cultural Traditions

Who we are is also reflected in the attitudes, beliefs and values that we learn through our culture. Values are broad, life-orienting, enduring concepts of good and bad, right and wrong. Values are central to who we are and are resistant to change. For instance, we are likely to value education if our family and close friends also value education.

Attitudes reflect our likes and dislikes. If I like my college, watching Hindi movies or eating chocolate ice cream, I hold positive attitudes towards these things. I was not born with a fondness for chocolate ice cream, I learned to like it. We constantly explore and alter our attitudes but they are always an expression of our basic value system.

Beliefs are ways in which we structure our understanding of reality—what is true and what is false. Most of our beliefs are based on previous experiences. Beliefs are constructs that lie between attitudes and values and are more likely to change than our core values but do not change as much as our attitudes (i.e. likes and dislikes). An individual may have many beliefs—for example, we may value education and may have a favourable attitude towards college education but believe that college X is better than college Y. Hence, the beliefs that we express are instances of the specific, case-by-case operation of our core values and long-term attitudes.

Through the various groups we are part of, we learn cultural norms, traditions and mores. These provide benchmarks against which we can measure ourselves. They instil in us a variety of beliefs, values and attitudes about various issues—for example, about success, how we define it and how we should achieve it; the relevance of our religion, race or nationality; the ethical principles we should follow in business and in our personal life. Hence our success in achieving what our culture defines as success—for example, scoring high marks in an exam or owning a large expensive house—may contribute to a positive self-concept. Our failure to achieve what our culture teaches—for example, not being married by the time you are 30—may contribute to a negative self-concept. When we demonstrate the qualities that our culture teaches, we see ourselves as a cultural success and are rewarded by other members of the cultural group. Seeing ourselves as culturally successful and being rewarded by others contributes positively to our self-concept. When we fail to demonstrate such qualities, we are more likely to see ourselves as a cultural failure and are ostracised and punished by other members of the culture group which may contribute to a more negative self-concept.

Interactions and Perceptions

If we wished to see the way our eyes looked, we would probably look in a mirror. But, what would we do if we wanted to really see the person we are? Cooley (1988) advanced the 'looking glass' concept that suggests you learn who you are based on your interactions with others which are reflected back to you. That is we learn who we are by interacting with others, much as we look into a mirror and see our reflection, only here the looking glass is figurative. We look at the image of ourselves that others reveal to us through their communications and especially through their behaviour and the way they treat us. This concept is also known as 'reflected appraisal'.

We do not rely on everyone's opinion to develop our self-concept. We usually seek opinion of those individuals who we think are competent and trustworthy and are most significant in our lives—our 'significant others'. As a child, you would look to your parents and your school teachers. As an adult you might look to your friends and romantic partners. If these significant others think positively about you, you will see a positive self-image reflected in their behaviours which will influence how you see yourself, i.e. your self-concept. For example, if a teacher appreciates a fifth-grade student for being good in public speaking, the child would see a positive self-image reflected through her/his teacher's words and start feeling positive and confident about her/his public speaking skills.

Thus the people you meet and the groups you are a part of deeply impact you and the shaping of yourself. That we cannot have a concept of our own self-identity without interactions with other people is a central belief in the work of George Herbert Mead. Mead is credited with the development of symbolic interaction theory while Herbert Blumer (1969) actually coined the term 'symbolic interaction'. The theory describes the process through which our interactions with others influence our thoughts about others, our life experiences and ourselves. Based on how other people react to our use of words and symbols we interpret what a word, symbol or experience means. Symbolic interaction theory has had a major influence on communication theory because of the pervasive way our communication with others influences our attitudes, beliefs, values and self-concept. (Turner 2013)

Comparison with Others: Social Comparisons

Another way we develop our self-concept is by comparing ourselves with others. Social comparison helps people measure how well they think they are doing. I'm good at playing a musical instrument (because I won a competition beating others); I can't cook (because others cook better than I do); I'm not good at socialising (most people I know seem to be more comfortable interacting with others). We judge about how well or badly we can perform certain tasks with implied references to how well others perform the same tasks. We compare ourselves not just with anyone but with members in our peer group.

When we want to gain insight into 'who am I' and how effective or competent we are, we look to our peers, generally to those who are similar to us or have the same abilities as we have. For example, after an examination, we want to know how we performed in relation to other students in our class. We compare our marks with other students to get a clear idea as to how well we performed. Similarly, the way we dress for occasions and celebrations might also be influenced by constant comparisons we make with our peer group. Parents and family members also make constant comparisons with siblings, cousins or friends in terms of grades, marks, discipline, dressing and general behaviour, all of which influence our self-concept.

Social Roles

We all play various roles in our lives. You may be a daughter, a sister, a friend, a student, a team captain and so on. Each of these is a real part of you. Our communication with the self and others is in the context of the above mentioned roles and how we perceive our roles. Our perception of ourselves and the social expectations of the roles we play throughout the day determine our communication patterns and behaviour.

> Cultural conventions and expectations play a major role in defining different social roles and hence shaping our self-concept and our behaviour. Although it is changing, culture is still male-dominated. What we consider appropriate and inappropriate behaviour is often different for men and women. For example, fathers who work 60 hours a week are said to be 'diligent and hard-working' but mothers who do the same are criticised as 'neglectful and self-centered'. Stereotypical role expectations require extensive discussion and negotiation. Although our culture defines certain roles as masculine or feminine, we can still exercise individual choices about our gender roles. For example, in some sections of society today, there is greater acceptance of men helping in household chores and taking care of children.

Self-evaluations and Reflections

Although our self-concept is deeply affected by others, our own descriptions and labelling of our own attitudes, beliefs, values and actions also play a role in shaping our self-concept. We constantly also evaluate, reflect upon, interpret and react to our own behaviour. This process is called self-reflexiveness; that is, the human ability to think about what we are doing while we are doing it. We talk to ourselves about ourselves. We are both participants and observers in all that we do. This dual role encourages us to use labels to describe who we are.

These self-reflexive evaluations contribute to our self-concept. For example, if we believe that lying is wrong and we lie, we will probably evaluate this behaviour in terms of our internalised beliefs about lying and will react negatively to our own behaviour. We might experience guilt as a result of our behaviour contradicting our beliefs. On the other hand, if we do something good which we evaluate as a positive behaviour (for example, a work of charity), we would feel good about this behaviour and, as a result, about ourselves. Hence, the more we understand why we view ourselves the way we do, the better we will understand who we are.

We can gain additional insight into ourselves by looking more closely at self-awareness using the Johari Window concept. This can also improve our communication with others since the more we know ourselves, the better we will be able to manage our thoughts and behaviour.

SELF-ESTEEM

Self-esteem is another important aspect of self. Self-esteem broadly refers to the feeling of self-worth people have. There are two types of self-esteem: personal and group self-esteem.

Personal self-esteem refers to the way you feel about yourself. How much do you like yourself? How valuable a person do you think you are? How competent do you think you are? The answers to these questions reflect the value that you place on yourself.

Group self-esteem refers to your evaluation of you being a member of a particular group. Those may be political, social, racial or ethnic groups based on your religion, nationality, gender, caste, or social or political affiliation.

Personal and group self-esteem are interrelated. Personal self-esteem is influenced by your group self-esteem. For example, if you feel positive and proud about being a member of the Fashion Society of your college, and you see yourself as a competent and valuable member of the society, you may develop a high positive self-esteem.

Now a question arises: Why is it important to develop a positive self-esteem? The major reason is when you feel good about yourself—about who you are and what you are capable of doing—you perform more effectively. When you think like a successful person, you are more likely to act like one. And, when you think you are a total failure, you are more likely to act like a failure. Increasing your self-esteem will help you function more effectively in college, in your career and in your interpersonal relationships.

Psychologist Eric Berne (1964) developed the concept of 'life position' to describe our overall sense of our own worth and that of others. He identified four life positions: (*a*) 'I'm OK, you're OK,' or positive regard for self and others; (*b*) 'I'm OK, you're not,' or positive regard for self and low regard for others; (*c*) 'I'm not OK, you're OK,' or low self-regard and positive regard for others; and (*d*) 'I'm not OK, you're not OK,' or low regard for both self and others. Your life position is a driving force in your relationships with others. People in the 'I'm OK, you're OK' position have the best chance for healthy relationships because they have discovered their own talents and also recognise that others have been given talents different from their own.

Another way researchers talk about being 'OK' is by referring to what is called 'face'. Face is a person's positive perception of himself or herself in interactions with others. 'Face' is the use of communication to maintain one's own positive self-perception (self-face) or to support, reinforce or even challenge someone else's self-perception (other-face). You are involved in face work, for example, when you announce to your parents that you made to the merit list during your most recent semester exam in college. By telling them about your academic success, you are using communication to maintain your parents' positive image of you and thus reinforce your own positive self-image. The effort you expend to save face (protect your positive image) reflects the kind of perception you want others to have of you.

Building Our Self-esteem

Low self-esteem can affect our own communications and interactions. It is believed that most of our societal problems stem from our collective feelings of low self-esteem. Our feelings of low self-worth may contribute to our making wrong choices or decisions that may impact and mar the quality of our lives. For instance, we may choose the wrong discipline of study, become dependent on alcohol or other substances, and experience problems with eating and other vital activities. Building and maintaining a healthy sense of self-esteem is a critical societal goal.

The following are some methods for building self-esteem.

Curbing Self-destructive Beliefs

Each individual has apprehensions, negative thoughts and beliefs that are usually unfounded. If these are not curbed, they can become self-destructive. These self-destructive beliefs can damage our self-esteem and prevent us from building meaningful and productive relationships. These negative and self-destructive beliefs may be about (*a*) us ('I am not creative' or 'I am not good enough'); (*b*) the world around us ('People are laughing at me'); or (*c*) our relationships ('If I become close to a person, I will get hurt or will be cheated by her/him'). Identifying these beliefs can help us to examine them critically and realise that they are illogical, unfounded and self defeating.

Self-affirmation

Engaging in a self-affirmation exercise can be invaluable for boosting our self-esteem. Self-affirmation exercises essentially remind us of our successes from time to time. It requires us to concentrate on our potentials and not our limitations. By focusing on our good deeds, strengths, positive qualities and good relationships we have with our friends and relatives, we can help ourselves boost our confidence and self-esteem.

Nurturing People

An effective way of building self-esteem is by being around positive people who are optimistic and make us feel good about ourselves. People who constantly find faults with just about everything are negative and discouraging and should be avoided as far as possible. Building a network of a few positive people can help us stay positive and keep our self-esteem intact through the highs and lows of life.

Short-term Goals

Setting short-term goals that can be successfully achieved in a short span of time can boost our self-esteem as success builds self-esteem. Each success makes achieving the next one a little easier. Remember that the failure of a project is not the failure of the self. Failure is something that happens outside of us, not inside. Successful people deal with setbacks by cultivating the attitude that distinguishes failures from successes.

Re-contextualising and redefining events and experiences from a different point of view can provide fresh perspectives. Just as reframing a work of art can give the painting a whole new look, reframing events that cause us to devalue our self-worth can change our perspective. If, for example, you get a report from your supervisor that says you should improve one area of your performance, instead of listening to the self-talk that says you are bad at your job, re-examine the event within a larger context—you need to tell yourself that one negative comment does not mean you are hopeless as a worker. Of course, all negative experiences should not be lightly discarded and left unexamined because you can learn from your mistakes. However, it is important to remember that our worth as human beings is not dependent on the result of a single exam, a response from a teacher or a prospective employer, or one defeat in a game.

Developing Honest Relationships

Having at least one person who can help you objectively and honestly reflect on your virtues and vices can be extremely beneficial in fostering a healthy, positive self-image. As we noted earlier, other people play a major role in shaping our self-concept and self-esteem. The more credible the source of information is, the more likely we are to believe it. Honest, positive support can provide encouragement for a lifetime.

Letting Go of the Past

Your self-concept is not a fixed construct. That is, it does not remain constant. As things and circumstances change, you and others around you also change. Individuals with low self-esteem may hold on to events and experiences that happened years ago and persistently refuse to let go of them. Constantly replaying negative experiences in our mind only serves to make it difficult for our sense of worth to change. Becoming aware of the changes that have occurred, and can occur, in your life can assist you in developing a more realistic assessment of your value.

Seeking Support

You provide social support when you express care and concern as well as listen and empathise with others. Having someone socially supportive is especially important to us when we experience stress and anxiety or are faced with a difficult personal problem. Social support from a friend or family member can be helpful, but some of the self-image problems may be so deep-rooted that you need professional help. A trained counsellor or therapist can help you. The technique of having a trained person listen as you verbalise your fears, hopes and concerns is called talk therapy. There is power in being able to put your thoughts—especially your negative thoughts and emotions—into words. By saying things out loud to an open, honest, empathetic listener, we gain insight and can sometimes figure out what we are experiencing.

SUMMARY

In this chapter, we looked at intrapersonal communication and the various aspects of self: self-concept, self-awareness, self-disclosure and self-esteem.

- Intrapersonal communication is a basic level of communication involving sending and receiving of messages within the communicating individual.

- There are many aspects like one's experiences, body image, values, attitudes, beliefs, interactions, opportunities and perceptions which constitute the self and consequently each individual.
- In the Johari Window model of self, there are four major areas—the open self, the hidden self, the blind self and the unknown self.
- To increase self-awareness, have dialogue with yourself, listen to others to reveal your blind self, see yourself from different perspectives and increase your open self.
- Self-disclosure refers to a form of communication in which information about the hidden self is communicated to another person.
- Self-disclosure is more likely to occur under certain circumstances like when the discloser likes the other person, both are approximately of the same age, when the discloser is an extrovert and highly sociable, and when the topic of disclosure is fairly impersonal and positive.
- The risks of self-disclosure include personal and social rejection, and intrapersonal difficulties.
- The rewards of self-disclosure include increased self-knowledge, a better ability to cope with difficult situations and guilt, efficient communication and a better chance for a meaningful relationship.
- Self-concept refers to the image you have of yourself. It's developed from the image others have of you and reveal, the comparisons you make between yourself and others, and the way you evaluate your own thoughts and behaviours.
- Self-esteem refers to the way you feel about yourself, the value that you place on yourself. It may be increased by attacking your self-destructive beliefs, engaging in self-affirmation, seeking our nurturing people, working on projects that will result in success and recognising that you don't have to be loved by everyone.

KEY WORDS

Intrapersonal communication: It takes place whenever we evaluate and react to internal and external stimuli. It involves messages being sent and received within ourselves.

Self-awareness: It is one of the key aspects about understanding the self. William James (1890) identified three components of the self—the material self, the social self and the spiritual self.

Body image: It is both the mental picture that we have of our body and how we perceive ourselves when we look at a mirror. It deeply influences the self.

Self-disclosure: It occurs when you purposefully provide information to others about yourself. It has both risks and rewards.

Johari Window: It is a model used to examine the self-disclosure process. Each quadrant of the window contains a different self. These are—open self, hidden self, blind self, unknown self.

Open self: It represents all the information that we know about ourselves and are also known to others.

Blind self: It represents information about ourselves that others know but we do not know.

Unknown self: It represents those parts of ourselves about which neither we nor others know.

Hidden self: It contains all that you know about yourself but keep hidden from others.

Dyadic effect: When we disclose information about ourselves to others, there are chances that others will also feel more comfortable in disclosing information about them to us. This is known as dyadic effect.

Self-concept: It is how someone thinks about or perceives one's self. We develop our self-concept through our cultural teachings, interactions with others, comparisons with others, social roles that we play and through our self evaluations and reflections.

- **Self-esteem:** It refers to the feeling of self-worth people have about themselves. There are two types of self-esteem—personal and group self-esteem.

EXERCISES

1. How would you draw the Johari Window for an intimate relationship and for an initial interaction with a stranger?
2. How are the processes of disclosure and feedback related to Johari's Window of self awareness? Explain with the help of a sketch.
3. Self-disclosure is more likely to occur under certain circumstances than others. Do you agree? Discuss.
4. What are the potential rewards and risks associated with self-disclosure?
5. Have you experienced negative results due to self-disclosure (as a sender or receiver)? If so, what could have been altered in the decisions of what, where, when or how to disclose that may have improved the situation?
6. What are the ways in which we develop our self-concept?
7. How does membership of a particular group affect our self-esteem? Explain with the help of an example of a group that you belong to.

REFERENCES

Barker, Larry L., *Communication*, fifth edition, New Jersey: Prentice-Hall, 1990.

Berne, Eric, *Games People Play: The Basic Hand Book of Transactional Analysis*, New York: Ballantine Books, 1964.

Blumer, H., *Symbolic Interactionism: Perspective and Method*, Englewood Cliffs, NJ: Prentice-Hall, 1969.

Cooley, Charles H., *On Self and Social Organization*, Chicago: University of Chicago Press, 1998.

DeVito, Joseph A., *Human Communication: The Basic Course*, eighth edition, New York: Longman, 2000.

James, William, 'The Self and Its Selves' in *Social Theory: The Multicultural Readings*, edited by C. Lemert, 161–66, Philadelphia: Westview Press, 1890 [2010].

Khanna, Sushama, *Training of Human Processes*, New Delhi: Abe Books Pvt. Ltd., 2009.

McLeod, S. A., *Self Concept: Simply Psychology* available at http://www.simplypsychology.org/self-concept.html (accessed 10 September 2015), 2008.

Singh, Kavita, *Organizational Behavior: Text and Cases*, New Delhi: Pearson Education Ltd, 2010.

Steinberg, Sheila, *An Introduction to Communication Studies*, Cape Town: Juta & Co. Ltd, 2007.

Turner, Jonathan H., 'Symbolic Interactionist Theories of Identity' in *Contemporary Sociological Theory* by Jonathan H. Turner, 331–55, Newbury Park, CA: Sage, 2013. Available at http://www.sagepub.com/sites/default/files/upm-binaries/50436_ch_16.pdf (accessed 15 April 2016).

West, Richard and Lynn H. Turner, *Understanding Interpersonal Communication: Making Choices in Changing Times*, second edition, Boston: Wadsworth Publishers, 2011.

Wright, Marc, *Gower Handbook of Internal Communication*, second edition, England: Gower Publishing Ltd, 2009.

Zeuschner, Raymond F., *Communicating Today*, Boston: Allyn & Bacon, 1997.

ONLINE SOURCE

http://www.cengagesites.com/academic/assets/sites/4713/Chapter%2015.pdf (accessed 15 July 2015)

10

INTERPERSONAL COMMUNICATION

HIGHLIGHTS

- Nature of interpersonal communication
- Motivations for interpersonal communication
- Interpersonal communication and relationship development
- Aspects influencing interpersonal communication
- Theories of interpersonal communication
- Interpersonal communication and conversation
- Interpersonal communication and conflict
- Building interpersonal competence

Interpersonal communication is central to our everyday lives. We constantly engage in communicating with family, friends and even strangers, we reach out to others to share our ideas and feelings. It occurs in different environments—formal or informal, direct face-to-face or mediated through technologies like telephone and the internet. For instance, interaction between the interviewer and interviewee is an example of formal interpersonal communication which can be face-to-face or through a web-based technology like skype. Friends chatting with each other in a party is an example of interpersonal communication in an informal setting. Most interpersonal messages are informal and arise from everyday face-to-face encounters. They are usually spontaneous, unplanned and loosely organised.

Through interpersonal communication we reach out to others and share our feelings and ideas. This sharing of experiences, both positive and negative, is the essence of interpersonal communication. Through our interpersonal interactions, we share our joys and sorrows, make others understand what is happening in our lives and seek help to sort out our problems and concerns. Close friendships, family ties and romantic relationships are made, maintained and sometimes destroyed largely through interpersonal interactions. In fact, the success of family and most relationships depend heavily on the interpersonal communication among members. For example, colleagues who give us advice and feedback help us increase our effectiveness on the job. Friends who believe in us often help us to come out of a problem and become the person we want to be. Also, sometimes we just want to be with the people we like and trust. Through our interpersonal communications we build connections and establish relationships that satisfy our social needs and help us realise our personal and professional goals. As we relate to others, the messages we send and receive shape us. In fact, there is a direct link between how good we are at communicating and how satisfying or fulfilling we find life.

Hence, effectiveness as an interpersonal communicator profoundly impacts our lives, directly influencing our personal success and happiness.

NATURE OF INTERPERSONAL COMMUNICATION

Interpersonal communication involves few people, often just two. According to this definition interactions between a customer and a sales attendant at a shop, a phone conversation between two friends, a meeting involving a few parents and a teacher are all examples of interpersonal communication. However, one must note that a useful distinction has to be made between the momentary communication transaction of the sales exchange and the personal relationship that are built over time in the conversation with parents. They involve thoughts and feelings beyond a superficial level. Interpersonal communication could also be defined as the verbal and non-verbal interaction between two or more interdependent people. That is, interpersonal communication takes place between people who are in some way connected. This definition not only emphasises the number of people taking part in the interaction but also on the interconnectedness and intimacy of the interactions.

Let us now understand the characteristics of interpersonal communication.

Involves Interdependent Individuals

As we saw interpersonal communication is the communication that takes place between people who are in some way linked to each other. However, in these linkages not only are the individuals simply 'connected' in a web of relationships they are also interdependent. The action of one person has consequences for the other person. For example, a child's trouble with the class teacher will affect the parents, other siblings and extended family members.

Inherently Relational

The interconnectedness of interpersonal communication makes it relational in nature. That is, interpersonal communication takes place in a relationship, affects the relationship and defines the relationship. The way you communicate is determined by the kind of relationship that exists between you and the other person. You interact in one way with your best friend or your sibling and in a very different way with a neighbour, a work colleague or a casual acquaintance.

Exists on a Continuum

Interpersonal communication exists along a continuum, ranging from relatively impersonal at one end to highly personal at the other. The impersonal end of the continuum includes simple conversations between people who don't really know each other; for example, a waiter and a customer dining at a restaurant or a conductor and a traveller. At the other end are highly personal communications that takes place between people who are intimately interconnected; for example, conversation between a father and son or between best friends. Several interactions lie in-between; for example, the person who delivers milk every day, the parent–teacher interactions that take place periodically.

Figure 10.1: Continuum of Interpersonal Relationships

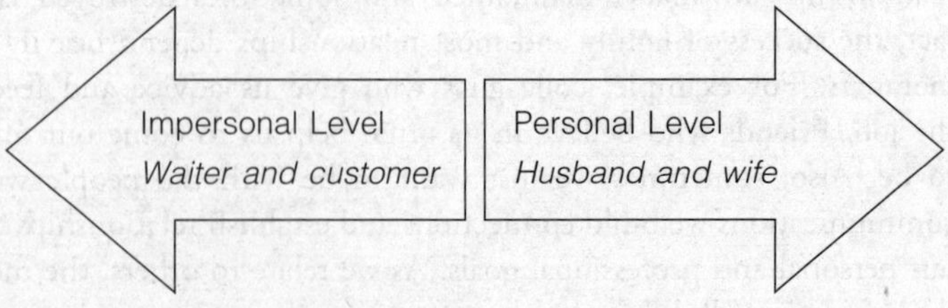

Source: Created by the authors.

In impersonal communication we interact largely on the basis of our social roles and exchange messages. In personal communications, on the other hand, we interact on a broad range of topics and largely on the basis of personal roles, according to the rules we have ourselves established rather than any societal rules. For example, a mother and daughter interaction is very personalised and everyone has their special way of greeting and interacting, and may cover any topic—it could be about clothes, a movie, a person, and some worries and concerns.

Involves Verbal and Non-verbal Messages

The words you use as well as your facial expressions, i.e. your eye contact and body posture, send messages. Likewise, you receive messages through your sense of hearing as well as through your other senses, especially visual and touch. The use of verbal and non-verbal messages is determined by the situation. You don't talk to your best friend in the same way you talk to your college professor or your parents. In some situations non-verbal signals convey more meaning while in others verbal signals communicate more information. Most often they work together and it's important to understand how they are occurring together.

Exists in Varied Forms

Mostly, interpersonal communication takes place in the form of face-to-face interaction. For many people, face-to-face remains the most powerful and intimate human interaction as face-to-face discussion facilitates immediate feedback, contains visual, audio and non-verbal cues, acts as a personal source and uses natural body languages. However in today's high-tech era, many interpersonal communications are mediated by technology.

One such form is Computer Mediated Communication (CMC) which uses computer and the internet to provide connectivity at the global level. Computer technology makes it possible for people to do their job without being physically present, allowing them to work from their home or from across the world.

Like direct communication, mediated communication may be formal or informal, personal or public. Some computer-mediated communication (for example an email, tweet or a post on Facebook) are asynchronous, meaning that these do not take place in real time, as discussed in Chapter Two of Unit II. You may send your message today, but the receiver may not read it for a week and may take another week to respond. Consequently, much of the spontaneity created by real-time communication is lost here. You may, for example, be very enthusiastic about a topic when you send your email but practically forget it by the time someone responds. Through instant messaging, you interact online in real time; the communication messages are synchronous—they occur at the same time and are similar to phone communication.

Involves Personalised Transactions

Figure 10.2: The Transactional View of Interpersonal Communication

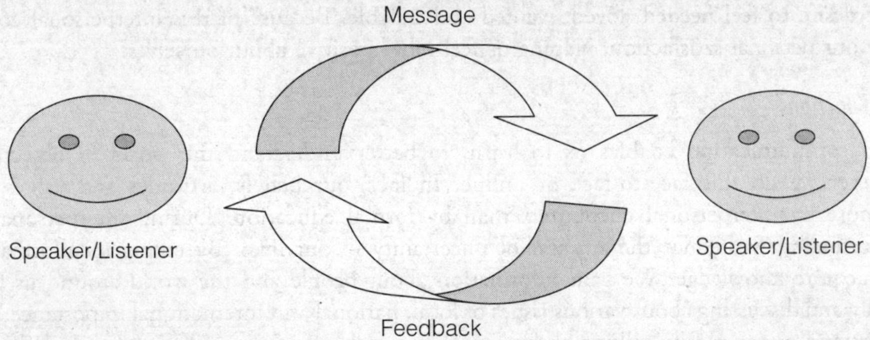

Source: Created by the authors.

Much interpersonal communication is dyadic in nature and involves people who are in close contact. During the conversation, the participants alternate from one role to the other—sometimes originating messages, at other times, responding to them. If one participant only listened and the other only spoke, communication would soon break down. This is represented as personalised transactional view, in which, as you send messages, you are simultaneously also receiving messages from your own communications and from the reactions of the other person.

How does Interpersonal Communication Enhance Our Lives?

Understanding the functions of interpersonal communication helps us accomplish a variety of purposes. Interpersonal communication helps us discover who we are, it fulfills our need for human contact and personal relationships, and can prompt us to change our attitudes and behaviour. In these ways interpersonal communication serves four kinds of functions: psychological, social, information and influence. Appreciating how interpersonal communication serves these varied functions can help us achieve our own interpersonal goals more effectively.

Psychological Functions

Interpersonal communication helps us relate to others and to form meaningful relationships whether it is face-to-face or online. Such relationships help alleviate loneliness and depression, enable us to share our joys and pleasures, and make us feel more positive about ourselves. We interact to support and help others in everyday life—online and offline, you console a friend who is upset, counsel a student about what career to choose or offer advice to a colleague at work. In fact, having good relationships are crucial for physical and psychological well-being.

Interpersonal communication also enhances our understanding of others. Through our interactions with others, we learn how different individuals affect us. In fact, we depend on interpersonal communication to develop our awareness and maintain our sense of self. Different contexts help us figure out who likes or dislikes us and why, when and why to trust or distrust someone, what behaviours bring out the strongest reactions, under what conditions we have the power to influence another person, and whether we have the ability to resolve conflict.

Social Functions

Our interpersonal contacts fulfill our social needs to varying degrees. Through interpersonal communication we are able to begin and sustain relationships. When we are in a relationship with someone whose needs complement or balance our own each of us is able to have our needs met. When our needs are not complementary we may experience relationship struggles or conflict. Interpersonal communication helps remove feelings of isolation, fulfilling our desire to feel needed, loved, wanted and capable. Because of this interpersonal communication may increase our personal satisfaction, helping us feel more positive about ourselves.

Information Functions

Interpersonal communication enables us to learn, to better understand the world of objects, events and people, whether we do this face-to-face or online. In fact, our beliefs, attitudes and values are probably influenced more by interpersonal encounters than by formal education. During interpersonal contacts, as we share information we reduce the amount of uncertainty in our lives. By taking in information we meet the need to acquire knowledge. We gain information about people and the world around us by interacting interpersonally and discussing about various issues of local, national and international importance. We are better able to understand our world by talking about a problem with a friend or family member. They can help us better understand the situation.

Sometimes we also gain information about ourselves—our strengths and weaknesses—in the conversations we have with our closed ones. They may give us feedback about our blind self and help us to increase our self-awareness. It helps us to think and evaluate more effectively. For example, we are able to make better decisions by seeking suggestions from our friends and family members.

Influence Functions

We use interpersonal communication to influence others, sometimes subtly and sometimes openly. Interpersonal communicators are both the users of and targets of persuasion. Interpersonal communication is often directed towards a goal, and even though we may not be conscious of it we often use strategic communication to achieve the goal. We methodically plan how to get what we want. We seek advice from others who we believe can help us. It is a mutually reinforcing activity we engage in together; we are both affected by what each of us does and says.

Sometimes, we also communicate interpersonally in order to change behaviour in some way, whether it is our own or someone else's. For example, parents may scold their child because they want to bring about a change in her/his behaviour. Similarly, a counsellor may communicate interpersonally with the client to bring about a change in her/his behaviour in some way.

MOTIVATIONS FOR INTERPERSONAL COMMUNICATION

Have you ever thought why we communicate with others? We communicate to develop identities, establish connections, coordinate with others, deepen relationships, and work out problems and possibilities. Interpersonal communication is central to our effectiveness in our everyday lives. It is the essence of meaningful relationships in personal, social and professional contexts.

Psychologist William Schutz (1966) developed the 'interpersonal needs' theory which emphasises that our tendency to create and sustain relationships depends on how well we meet three basic needs—inclusion, control and affection.

- **Need for affection** refers to the desire to give and receive love and liking. For example, we want people to act warmly towards us. We like it when people share their feelings with us and when they encourage us to do the same.
- **Need for inclusion** refers to the desire to be social and included in groups. For example, we want other people to include us in their activities.
- **Need for control** refers to the desire to influence the people and events in our lives. For example, we try to exert control and influence over things. We enjoy organising things and directing others.

Expanding Schutz's ideas, Abraham Maslow (1970) proposed that we communicate to meet a range of human needs. Maslow organised various needs into a hierarchy of five types of needs namely physiological, safety, belongingness, self-esteem and self-actualisation. According to Maslow, the basic needs must be satisfied before we can focus on those that are more abstract.

Physiological Needs

These are the most basic needs. Humans need to survive first and communication helps us meet this need. To survive, babies must alert others when they are hungry or in pain. And others must respond to these needs. Beyond survival, humans need to communicate if they are to thrive. For example, we discuss medical problems with doctors to stay healthy, and our effectiveness in communication affects what jobs we get and how much we earn to pay for medical care, food, leisure activities and housing.

Safety Needs

We also meet safety needs through communication. For example, if someone is threatening you, you need to seek help to protect yourself. Couples must talk with each other about safe sex. The ability to discuss private and difficult issues related to sex is essential to our safety.

Belongingness Needs

The third level in Maslow's hierarchy is belongingness or social needs. All of us need others to be happy, to enjoy life, to feel comfortable on the job and to fit into social groups. We want the company and acceptance of other people and we want to give company and acceptance to other people. We communicate to meet belongingness needs by talking with others, sharing thoughts and feelings, watching films together and working on projects together. Also, interpersonal communication introduces us to ideas that broaden our perspectives. For example, after talking with someone, you may gain a new perspective about the situation.

Self-esteem Needs

Moving up in Maslow's hierarchy we find self-esteem needs, which involve valuing and respecting ourselves and being valued and respected by others. Esteem is a desire for dignity, achievement, competence and status. Some people get graduate degrees, others master difficult skills in sports and others do even more to gain admiration and respect from their peers.

Self-actualisation Needs

Our last basic human need is for self-actualisation or striving for all that we are capable of being. Self-actualisation includes long-range goals for using our full potential and developing ourselves in all areas. Self-improvement is one form of self-actualisation. Throughout our lives, we meet small challenges such as winning a match or just competing in it or getting an A in a course. Our ultimate goal is being and doing all that we are capable of to achieve personal satisfaction.

Figure 10.3: An Interpretation of Maslow's Hierarchy of Needs

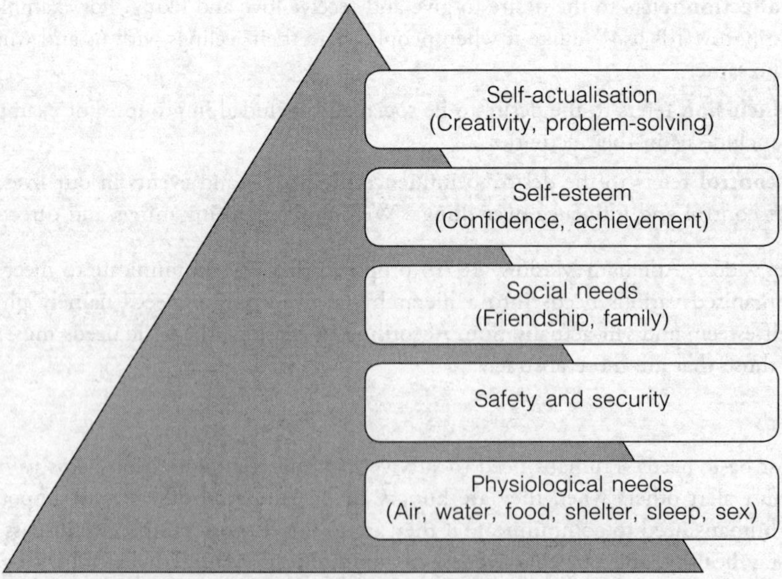

Source: Adapted by the authors from Steinberg (2007).

Maslow discussed that the likelihood of meeting these needs depends on our ability to effectively participate in this diverse social world. Each of these needs is part of the dynamics of interpersonal interaction since these needs drive us to engage in relationships in order to be fulfilled and satisfied.

INTERPERSONAL COMMUNICATION AND RELATIONSHIP DEVELOPMENT

Interpersonal communication is the primary way through which we build relationships with people around us. We are social beings; we exist partly in terms of our relationships with other social beings. Each person pursues a relationship for unique reasons. One reason we form relationships is because they help reduce the uncomfortable feeling of loneliness. For some of us, relationships provide intellectual stimulation when we talk about ideas or argue about different interpretations of a film. We also look at ourselves through the eyes of others so relationships help us to gain self-knowledge. The most general reason to establish relationships which can include all others is that we seek to maximise our pleasures and minimise our pains. This is evident from the fact that the first impulse on having something extreme happen (whether positive or negative) is to share it with someone.

Types of Relationships

In terms of the relational contexts of interaction and the types of expectations that communicators have of one another, there are a few categories of relationships.

Friendship

Friendship is an unconditional interpersonal relationship where individuals enter into by their own will and choice. Friendship is a relationship where there are no formalities and individuals enjoy each others' presence. Theories of friendship emphasise the concept of friendship as a freely-chosen association. The entire relationship of friendship revolves around trust and give-and-take.

Family

Individuals related by blood or marriage are said to form a family. Family communication patterns establish roles and identities. Family dysfunction may also be exhibited by communication patterns.

Romantic

An interpersonal relationship characterised by passion, intimacy, trust and respect is romantic. Individuals in a romantic relationship are deeply attached to each other and share a special bond. A sense of respect and mutual admiration is also essential. Partners must reciprocate each other's feelings for the charm to stay in the relationship for a longer period of time.

Professional Relationships

Individuals working together for the same organisation are said to share a professional relationship. Individuals sharing a professional relationship are called colleagues. Colleagues may or may not like each other.

Stages of Development and Disintegration of Relationships

The development of any relationship follows a typical pattern. Communication Scholar Mark Knapp (1984) studied these patterns and identified ten stages in the relationship development process for coming together and coming apart. The coming together stages are: initiating, experimenting, intensifying, integrating and bonding. When a relationship begins to fall apart, it goes through five stages: differentiating, circumscribing, stagnating, avoiding and terminating. All relationships may not follow the same pattern, but having this information may help us to understand what is happening in our relationships.

Table 10.1: Mark Knapp's Stages of Coming Together and Coming Apart

Coming Together	*Coming Apart*
Initiating	Differentiating
Experimenting	Circumscribing
Intensifying	Stagnating
Integrating	Avoiding
Bonding	Terminating

Source: Created by the authors.

Coming Together/Relationship Development

Initiating

During this first stage of relationship development, we make contact, greet the other person and engage in conversation about matters we have in common. It may last anything between a few minutes to a few weeks. During this time we make conscious and unconscious judgments and observations about the other person, because the first contact allows us to form an instant and lasting impression. We make an evaluation of a person's potential for future relationship. We also draw conclusions about her/his intelligence, interests, economic status and so on.

Experimenting

Also known as the 'Do you know?' period of interaction, during this stage we begin experimenting with the unknown. We make an effort to continue the interaction after initiation by including topics of a more specific and personal nature; for example, opinion on different types of food or movies. We begin expanding the open segment of the Johari Window by revealing a bit more from our hidden self in this stage. It is to be noted that a relationship moves from one stage to the next only if both parties continue the pattern. So, if the other person ignores you or focuses on weather and other impersonal topics, then you must realise that the relationship is still in its initiating stage.

Intensifying

This stage comes when both the parties are mutually interested in furthering the relationship on the basis of information received from the experimenting stage. One of the main indications that this stage has begun is the amount of time we spend in each other's company. We begin to disclose even more from the hidden self. We may even offer each other some feedback about each other's blind self. At this point, feedback regarding our blind self is likely to focus on the positive attributes we see in each other and less likely to involve any criticism. As the relationship develops, people start using slangs and develop a mutual code language that only they understand.

Integrating

If both parties find that their interpersonal needs are being met in a particular relationship, and if they feel comfortable enough, they may move on to the next stage, integrating. At this stage, they begin to share many commonalities such as interests, attitudes and friends. The two are now seen as a unit; mutual friends feel that they can inquire about one from the other. They start revealing more personal information to each other and develop a feeling of strong and mutual trust. They may freely use each other's personal items without seeking permission. For example, many hostellers and roommates may not feel the need to seek permission to use each other's personal items like phone or a book. They may also make social commitments on behalf of each other on the assumption that they know each other's schedules and likely response.

Bonding

In this final stage of relationship development, serious commitments and sacrifices are made. Marriage is the most accepted form of commitment and usually gains social and institutional support. At this stage, the open pane of the Johari Window will continue to grow and the other three will decrease in size. Mark Knapp indicates that each step follows and builds on the previous ones.

Coming Apart/Relationship Disintegration

Similar to relationship steadily developing, a relationship may reverse direction or terminate. This depends on several factors—the type of relationship (romantic or friendship) as well as the uniqueness and flexibility of the communication. For instance, when the pains begin to exceed the pleasures we begin to look for ways to exit the relationship. Having unrealistic expectations from each other may also ruin the relationship. Sometimes, dissatisfaction with money may lead to dissatisfaction with the relationship. This is true for married couples when they encounter financial difficulties. Unhappiness with work life may also lead to difficulties in relationships. Most people cannot separate problems related to work from their relationships.

The five levels through which a relationship disintegrates, as explained by Knapp, are as follows.

Differentiating

This stage is marked by a separation or split. Differences occur at every stage of relationship development, but at this stage, there is increased interpersonal distance. The partners begin to want freedom and individuality. They may begin discussing each other in front of a third person even when they are both still in the room, leading to a hostile and defensive behaviour. In the Johari's Window the open pane shrinks and the hidden pane expands.

Circumscribing (Restricting)

When the relationship begins to disintegrate, there is less communication. Topics of conversation are controlled to reduce conflict and tension. Everything appears to be fine externally but there are difficulties internally.

Stagnating

Here the interpersonal atmosphere is cold. Silence is the hallmark of this stage. Only brief verbal exchanges take place. It may seem like a short stage, but some couples stay in this pattern for years. The reason for staying together may be social pressures, housing needs, restrictions on finances, belief in the sanctity of marriage or the need to raise children.

Avoiding

At this stage, one or both parties act as though the other person does not exist. Each person tries to find ways to avoid interaction since it is annoying to be around each other.

Terminating

Termination refers to final ending of a relationship which may be immediate or delayed. For example, a marriage may terminate because of an extramarital affair. On the other hand, school friends may come to this stage later on in life by not being able to make plans to get together periodically.

As we conclude this section, it has to be noted that breaking up of a relationship is generally considered negative but it need not actually be negative always. Sometimes, a relationship may be unproductive for one or both the parties. Breaking of such relationships may be the best thing to happen. Ending a relationship provides a period for the individuals to regain their independence and self-reliance. It may help in learning that can be used later on.

Activity

Choose a relationship that has ended. Can you identify behaviours that fit the characteristics of each stage? For each stage, list some behaviours that 'prove' you were in that stage.

Initiating	Experimenting	Intensifying	Integrating
Bonding	Differentiating	Circumscribing	Stagnating
Avoiding	Terminating		

ASPECTS INFLUENCING INTERPERSONAL COMMUNICATION

Several people hesitate to engage in interpersonal communication. They feel shy, experience discomfort or inhibition in interpersonal situations that interferes with their communication goals. Communication apprehension, or the fear or anxiety associated with communication with other people, also influences people's willingness to communicate. Our success or failure in addressing certain aspects in our own interpersonal communication determines how satisfying our interpersonal relationships will be. Understanding the following aspects that affect interpersonal relationships can help us improve our interpersonal skills.

Self-concept and Self-esteem

In the previous chapter we learnt that self-concept and self-esteem act as critical filters affecting our interaction with others. They determine how we approach, respond to and interpret messages. Individuals whose sense of self-worth is high are better at solving problems, think highly of others, accept praise and accolades without feeling embarrassed, are confident in admitting their strengths and weaknesses, are comfortable when interacting with others who view themselves as highly competent, are more likely to seek opportunities to improve skills that need improving and will evaluate their overall behaviour more positively than people with lower self-esteem. Specifically, our self-concept and self-esteem affect our ability to be empathetic to others and interpret messages and also our style of communication.

Self-disclosure

Self-disclosure is the vehicle by which others know what is going on inside you, what you are thinking and feeling and what you care about. In addition, self-disclosure is a primary source of satisfaction in long-term interpersonal relationships. Self-disclosure may be difficult in the beginning of a relationship because of well-learned habits that help us avoid emotional pain. However, as the relationship progresses and trust is developed we usually begin to share information that is private and personal. Confiding in others and receiving their confidence thus becomes one of the most effective interpersonal communication skills.

Trust

One of the most fundamental expectations people have of their friends is that they will not reveal their secrets. When you say, 'Oh, I won't tell anyone, your secret is safe with me,' do you really mean it? The most intimate secrets are known by family members. Our parents and siblings know quite a few things about us that we would not want others to know. Trust plays an important role in these cases. Trust affects the quality of our interactions and interpersonal relationships. We feel secure knowing that we can trust a friend or family member. We also realise the importance of being trustworthy in return.

Feedback

We constantly seek feedback from others to shape our behaviour, in social situations especially, where our actions need to conform to the behaviour of the group. Feedback enables us to clearly convey the true meaning of our communications and helps remove any ambiguity. One should be careful while using abstractions, jargons, clichés or any other habitual use of language that can interfere with clear communication. Clarity in communication enhances interpersonal relationship development. We can provide feedback and gain clarity by paraphrasing (confirming or correcting your understanding of a message), by asking questions (demonstrating our interest and our desire for more information) or by responding with feeling statements (showing that we care about our partner).

Non-verbal Behaviour

Non-verbal behaviour plays a strong role in interpersonal relationships. A smile or hug can sometimes convey so much that words may not be needed. Behaviour associated with the eye is also important in interpersonal situations. Besides showing interest and care, eye contact can also express the desire for dominance. Touch is another non-verbal factor important in interpersonal relationships. Touching usually communicates intimacy—couples walk with their arms around each other, a child hugs her/his doll. It is also important to understand the cultural acceptance of non-verbal expression which we have already studied.

Listening and Empathy

We have already understood the importance of listening in communication transactions. We also looked at the concept of active listening. Active listening has a crucial role in building interpersonal relationships. While interacting with others, one should not only hear but also listen by focusing attention on what is being said and understanding its meaning fully. It involves not just focusing attention but also forgetting our own concerns and biases for some time and responding intelligently and empathically to what is being said. We should actively listen to both words and non-verbal messages so that our feedback is accurate and appropriate.

Crucial to active listening and interpersonal communication is developing empathy. When we empathise with someone, we are able to experience what the other person is experiencing from that person's point of view. Empathy does not mean that we agree with what the other person says. We never lose our own identity or our attitudes and beliefs. It makes us understand emotionally and intellectually what the other is experiencing. If we try to practice empathy, we will find ourselves becoming more aware of another individual's qualities. However, empathy is difficult to achieve with persons who are culturally different from one's own culture. While empathising it is important to use reinforcing statements which encourage the speaker to continue talking about the issue. For example, we may use comments like 'I see', 'I understand' and 'Yes'. Also, it is important to maintain eye contact and show interest and agreement with our facial expressions, nods and eye movements.

To sympathise, on the other hand, is to feel sorry for the other person. While it is very important to be able to empathise, sympathy is not beneficial at all times. This is because sympathy puts a person at the receiving end in a mental frame of being a 'victim' of a situation or circumstances. This is not the right approach when a person wishes to deal with the situation with strength. Both the terms sympathy and empathy are often used interchangeably. However, it is important to understand the difference between the two. Empathy is when the communicator is able to place herself/himself in the receiver's situation and therefore is able to regulate her/his communication to suit the needs of the receivers. Both have their own place and are useful in different situations.

THEORIES OF INTERPERSONAL COMMUNICATION

Interpersonal communication may be viewed in a variety of ways, each of which can help us to better understand the overall communication process. There are three specific theories of interpersonal communication—functional theory, which addresses the functions of interpersonal communication; relational communication theory, which focuses on dimensions of interpersonal relationships; and the theory of the coordinated management of meaning, which addresses meanings in interpersonal relationships and the rules through which we construct interpersonal communication.

Functional Theory

According to the functional theory of interpersonal communication, we use interpersonal communication for a variety of reasons. For example, through interpersonal communication we are better able to understand our world. Talking about a problem with a friend in order to better understand a situation is an example of this function. At other times we communicate interpersonally in order to think and evaluate more effectively. We also communicate interpersonally in order to change behaviour in some way, whether that behaviour is our own or someone else's. More specifically, it

- provides a linking function between a person and her/his environment
- allows us to conceptualise, remember and plan
- serves to regulate our own and others' behaviour (the regulating function)

As infants we are nurtured physically, emotionally and intellectually through interpersonal communication. We develop cultural, social and psychological ties with the world through interpersonal communication. In short, interpersonal interactions allow us to function more practically in life.

Relational Communication Theory

Relational communication theory addresses interpersonal communication by examining dimensions of interpersonal relationships. According to communication theorists Edna Rogers-Milar and Frank Millar, three dimensions of interpersonal relationships are important: control, trust and intimacy. Created and sustained primarily through interpersonal messages, these three dimensions reflect and define the nature of the relationship (Barker 1990).

The first dimension, control, focuses on the distribution of power in a relationship, particularly the power to direct the nature of the interaction. This dimension is usually reflected in the number of messages we use to exert relational control. For example, a message such as the following exerts control: 'I am really tired to go out this evening. Let's stay home and watch a movie.'

The second dimension, trust, involves a belief that the other person will not exploit us. The third dimension, intimacy, is the degree to which two people can uniquely meet each other's needs. For example, if your partner meets all your needs and you don't feel the need for any additional relationships, then that relationship would be defined as an intimate one. However, if your partner is unable to meet all your interpersonal needs the relationship would be described as lower in overall intimacy.

Coordinated Management of Meaning Theory

Unlike the other two theories, the coordinated management of meaning (CMM) theory is a meaning-centred theory of communication. Its primary focus is on meanings in interpersonal communication and on how we coordinate and manage meanings in everyday life. CMM theorists are of the view that all communication is best viewed as coordination—primarily the coordination of each of our individual rules and the meanings that we assign to resulting behaviours. For example, if you and I were to meet for the first time, we both might include the following rules about interaction:

- When meeting someone for the first time, I should smile and say, 'Hello'
- When one meets another person, it is generally considered polite to shake hands
- If I am interested in that person, I should maintain a fair amount of direct eye contact

In addition to the above mentioned theories of interpersonal communication, there are several theories which offer insight into why and how we develop and dissolve our relationships. We will discuss some of them here.

Equity Theory

According to this theory, we develop and maintain those relationships in which the ratio of our rewards compared to the costs is approximately equal to our partner's. For example, if you and your friend start a business in which you put two-thirds of the money and your friend puts one-third, equity would demand that you get two-thirds of the profits and your friend gets one-third. Similarly, an equitable relationship is one in which each party derives rewards that are proportional to their costs. If you contribute more towards the relationship than your partner, then equity requires that you should get greater rewards. Inequity would exist in a relationship if one pays more of the costs; for example, you do more of the unpleasant tasks but your partner enjoys more of the rewards (DeVito 2000).

All of us seek equity in our interpersonal relationships. If we feel under-benefited because we get less than what we put in, we might feel angry and dissatisfied. This theory puts into focus the reasons for dissatisfaction in relationships seen in our day-to-day lives. For example, in a marital relationship, both the husband and wife may have full-time jobs but the wife may be expected to do most of the household work. In this case, the wife may be dissatisfied because of lack of equity. The greater the inequity greater the dissatisfaction and greater would be the likelihood that the relationship will deteriorate.

Social Exchange Theory

This theory is based on the economic model of profits and losses. It is based on the equation: Profits = Rewards – Costs. It claims that you develop relationships that will enable you to maximise your profits. Rewards can include money, status, love, information, goods and services. For example, to get the reward of money, you might have to work rather than play. Costs are those things that you normally try to avoid since they are considered unpleasant and difficult to do. For example, working overtime, washing dishes and clothes, and doing favours for those you dislike.

This theory claims that you seek to develop relationships which will give you the greatest profits in which rewards are greater than the costs. Those relationships which give you the greatest rewards with the least costs are the most preferred ones. You may also leave your current relationship for a new relationship which seems more profitable to you.

INTERPERSONAL COMMUNICATION AND CONVERSATION

Conversation is the essence of interpersonal communication and relationships. The process of conversation occurs in stages and examining each stage will give us an overview of what goes on when two people talk.

The Opening

The first step to conversation is to open the conversation with some kind of greeting like 'Hi, How are you?' These greetings can be verbal or non-verbal and even both. Non-verbal greetings include waving, smiling, winking and shaking hands. Usually, we greet another person both verbally and non-verbally. For example, we smile when we say 'hello'.

Feedforward

In the second step we usually give the other person a general idea of what the conversation will focus on. For example, 'I have to tell you something about him' or 'I am really depressed and need to talk to you'.

Business

The third step is the business or focus of conversation. Most conversations are goal-directed. We converse to fulfill one of the general purposes of interpersonal communication—to learn, relate or influence. This is the longest part of any conversation and the reason for both opening and feedforward.

Feedback

The fourth step is the reverse of the second. Here we send the signal that business is complete from our side. The other person may not agree that the business is complete. In that case, we may go back a step and continue the business.

Closing

This last step is the opposite of the first step. It is also called as the 'Good bye' step. This may also be verbal or non-verbal and is usually a combination of both. It signals the end of conversation. Here, we may also express our pleasure in interaction. The closing may also summarise the interaction.

Figure 10.4: The Process of Conversation

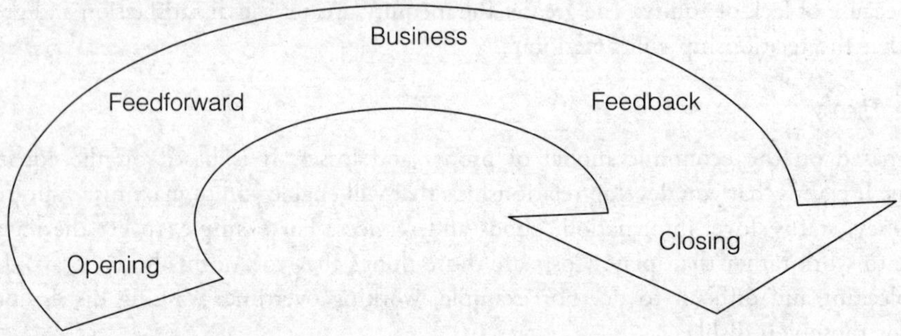

Source: Created by the authors.

INTERPERSONAL COMMUNICATION AND CONFLICT

As we experience more interpersonal relationships, we are going to experience some level of conflict. Conflict is an argument, disagreement or a fight. Conflicts may occur face-to-face or online. Conflicts can arise between two people over something as simple as which television programme to watch. They can also arise over decisions that have long-term implications, like whom to marry, where to live or whether to have children or not. We often feel negativity about engaging in conflicts. But, conflicts can also reveal areas that need to be resolved. They can actually be useful in interpersonal growth and personal development. The creative energy that can come from exploring, expressing and resolving conflicts can be channelised towards improving self-esteem, developing greater social skills and improving relationships. After the conflict, it is important to assess what we have learned, let go of the negative feelings and increase the positivity in the relationship. We will discuss more about conflicts in the next chapter on small group communication.

BUILDING INTERPERSONAL COMPETENCE

At a glance interpersonal competence seems simple. But it involves not only a person's relationship-making and keeping skills but also emotional competence. According to Daniel Goleman (1998), interpersonal competence builds on emotional skills such as:

- Monitoring your own expressions of your feelings
- Being able to read people's reactions and feelings even when people don't express them in words
- Adjusting social interaction based on the interaction you are having with another person or a group of people

This competence is not easy, especially since some people's emotions are easier to read than others'. Yet, people who practice the skills of being in touch with their own needs and feelings and know how to appropriately express their feelings are more likely to understand and deal with the needs and feelings of others. Building interpersonal competence is a lifelong process. Each relationship and each interaction matters. Each relationship and each interaction allows people to practice, learn and master the skill of empathy, sensitivity and friendship-building.

SUMMARY

- Interpersonal communication is sharing of feelings and ideas with other people.
- Most interpersonal messages are informal exchanges in dyads.
- Revolution in communication technology has brought about a shift in the way we communicate, rather than face-to-face interaction we are tending to prefer interacting in the virtual world. Over the years the definition of interpersonal communication has changed but the basic concept that communication is a fundamental aspect of our lives and an integral part of our needs as human beings has held consistent.
- Communicating with others allows us to meet basic needs for survival and safety as well as more abstract human needs for inclusion, esteem and self-actualisation for effective participation in a socially-diverse world.
- The five phases of growth in relationships are initiating, experimenting, intensifying, integrating and bonding. The five phases of relationship disintegration are differentiating, circumscribing, stagnating, avoiding and terminating.
- Skills related to self-disclosure, trust, feedback and feedforward, non-verbal communication, clarity, listening and empathy combine to determine how successfully meaning will be conveyed in interpersonal communication.
- Functional theory addresses the functions of interpersonal communication, while relational theory focuses on three specific dimensions of interpersonal relationships. These dimensions are control, trust and intimacy.
- The coordinated management of meaning theory focuses on meaning in interpersonal communication, as well as on the concept of coordination.

- Equity theory claims that we develop and maintain relationships in which rewards are distributed in proportion to costs.
- Social exchange theory claims that we seek relationships in which rewards exceed the costs and are more likely to end relationships when the costs exceed the rewards.
- Conversation is an important aspect to establish and maintain interpersonal relationships. The process of conversation consists of five stages: opening, feedforward, business, feedback and closing.
- Conflict is an argument, disagreement or a fight which may occur face-to-face or on the internet. They are considered as negative but sometimes can actually be useful in interpersonal growth, personal development and increasing positivity in a relationship.
- People who practice the skills of being in touch with their own needs and feelings and know how to appropriately express their feelings are more likely to understand and deal with the needs and feelings of others and build better interpersonal competence.

KEY WORDS

Interpersonal communication: It involves sharing of experiences with family, friends and even strangers. It occurs in different environments, formal or informal and can be direct face-to-face interactions or mediated through technologies like telephone and the internet.

Transactional view of interpersonal communication: It emphasises the importance of feedback and role reversal between the speaker and the listener.

Psychological function of interpersonal communication: It includes helping us relate to others and to form meaningful relationships whether it is face-to-face or online. It helps us to share our joys and pleasures and make us feel more positive about ourselves.

Social function of interpersonal communication: It includes being able to begin and sustain relationships. It helps to remove the feelings of isolation, fulfilling our desire to feel needed, loved, wanted and capable.

Information function of interpersonal communication: It is to help us learn, to better understand the world of objects, events and people.

Influence function of interpersonal communication: It involves communicating interpersonally in order to change behaviour in some way, whether our own or someone else's.

Maslow's hierarchy of needs: It refers to the various interpersonal needs Maslow organised into a hierarchy: physiological, safety, belongingness, self-esteem and self-actualisation needs. According to Maslow, the basic needs must be satisfied before we can focus on those that are more abstract.

Types of interpersonal relationships: It can be defined in terms of relational contexts of interaction and the types of expectations that communicators have of one another. These include: friendship, family, romantic and professional relationship.

Relationship development and disintegration: According to Mark Knapp, relationships follow typical patterns of development and disintegration.

Relationship development: When a relationship begins to develop, it occurs in stages which include: initiating, experimenting, intensifying, integrating and bonding.

Relationship disintegration: When a relationship begins to fall apart, it goes through the following five stages: differentiating, circumscribing, stagnating, avoiding and terminating.

Empathy: When we empathise with someone, we are able to experience what the other person is experiencing from that person's point of view.

Sympathy: To feel sorry for the other person.

Theories of interpersonal communication: Functional theory addresses the functions of interpersonal communication; relational communication theory focuses on dimensions of interpersonal relationships; and the theory of the coordinated management of meaning addresses meanings in interpersonal relationships and the rules through which we construct interpersonal communication.

Conversation: It is the essence of interpersonal communication and relationships. The process of conversation occurs in stages: opening, feedforward, business, feedback and closing.

Conflict: It is an argument, disagreement or a fight. As we experience more interpersonal relationships, we are going to experience some level of conflict.

EXERCISES

1. 'Over the years the definition of interpersonal communication has shifted and evolved.' Discuss.
2. 'We communicate to meet a range of human needs.' Justify the statement using Maslow's hierarchy of needs and its relationship with interpersonal communication.
3. Explain how phases of development and disintegration evolve in interpersonal relationships.
4. How does interpersonal communication enhance our lives?
5. Elaborate on the various aspects affecting interpersonal communication.
6. How can theories of interpersonal communication help us to better understand the complexities of interpersonal communication and relationships?

REFERENCES

Barker, Larry L., *Communication*, fifth edition, New Jersey: Prentice-Hall, 1990.

DeVito, Joseph A., *Human Communication: The Basic Course*, eighth edition, New York: Longman, 2000.

Goleman, Daniel, *Working with Emotional Intelligence*, London: Bloomsbury, 1998.

Knapp, Mark, *Interpersonal Communication and Human Relationships*, Boston: Allyn & Bacon, 1984.

Maslow, Abraham, *Motivation and Personality*, second edition, New York: Harper & Row, 1970.

Mohan, Krishna and Meera Banerjee, *Developing Communication Skills*, second edition, New Delhi: Macmillan Publishers India Ltd, 2009.

Schutz, William C., *The Interpersonal Underworld*, California: Science and Behavior Books, 1966.

Shookla, M. S., *A Handbook of Human Relations with Structured Experiences and Instruments*, New Delhi: Macmillan Publishers India Ltd, 2004.

Steinberg, Sheila, *An Introduction to Communication Studies*, Cape Town: Juta & Co. Ltd, 2007.

West, Richard and Lynn H. Turner, *Understanding Interpersonal Communication: Making Choices in Changing Times*, second edition, Boston: Wadsworth Publisher, 2011.

Wood, Julia, T., *Interpersonal Communication: Everyday Encounters*, seventh edition, Boston: Wadsworth Publisher, 2013.

Zeuschner, Raymond F. *Communicating Today*, Boston: Allyn & Bacon, 1997.

11

SMALL GROUP COMMUNICATION

HIGHLIGHTS

- Characteristics of small group communication
- Theories of small group communication
- Functions of small groups
- Stages of group formation
- Group processes
- Communication apprehension in small groups
- Conflict resolution

As individuals, we find ourselves interacting with different groups of people every day. Family, close friends in college, the sports team, a special office unit are all examples of small groups we may be a part of. At different junctures we come across diverse groups of people with whom we interact and become part of mostly willingly; or at times when we are obliged or duty-bound or forced to do so. By becoming part of small groups, people collectively perform practical tasks with the common goal of accomplishing an agreed desired result.

Image 11.1: A Small Group of Students

Source: Authors.

Small group communication offers distinct advantages to the members individually and the group as a whole. Small groups augment the availability and access to resources like expertise, time, money, information, and talent or ability. They provide members with enhanced feedback and self-understanding and support a better awareness and comprehension of concepts being examined by the group. The processes in the group foster greater commitment and satisfaction among members and stimulate creativity of ideas as members communicate with each other. This chapter explains what a small group is, the characteristics and functions of small groups, the stages of small group development and how the dynamics between the group members influence the effectiveness of communication.

First, let us understand what a small group is. Would a congregation of religious devotees, people gathered to attend a political rally or people travelling in a bus be called a small group? Usually small group communication is defined as three or more people working interdependently for the purpose of accomplishing a task. Thus a residents' welfare group, a study tour group travelling in a bus, members of a yoga class, a coaching class group, are all examples of small groups. In all these groups the members are in some way linked to each other (interdependence), as they together work towards a common goal. Let us discuss some key distinguishing characteristics of small groups now.

CHARACTERISTICS OF SMALL GROUP COMMUNICATION

Size

One of the primary characteristics of small groups is their unique group size. Lot of debate exists about what is the correct size of a small group. While some researchers are of the opinion that the size does not really matter when task is common, others believe that the ideal group size is 5 to 7 members. Another school of thought suggests that there should be a minimum of 3 group members but it should not go beyond 15 group members—two members make a dyad and more than 15 group members makes it a large group. So, there is some flexibility in the size of the group, but for our purposes, let us assume that its size can range from 3 to 15.

Interdependence

According to this characteristic, the action of one member of the group affects others. That is, group members cannot work without ever having an effect on each other and the members are dependent on each other, i.e. group members cannot function without being in the presence of each other. Thus small group members directly and indirectly influence each other for accomplishing their common goal. The systems theory could help us understand the interdependence dynamics in a small group. A small group can be viewed as a system—a collective whole—where all the members are working in coordination to strive for a common goal; the performance of one affects the other. If one group member is affected, it impacts the performance of the other group members and of the group as a collective. The primary feature of interdependence only suggests that groups are formed to achieve results collectively which individuals otherwise cannot achieve on their own.

In small groups, members usually perform two types of tasks to achieve their common goal—additive tasks and conjunctive tasks. Tasks initially performed and completed individually by group members and later combined are called as additive tasks, while tasks done collectively by members where they coordinate their efforts are called conjunctive tasks. For example, in a class, if a teacher divides a complex topic into smaller separate units that students are asked to work on independently which are later collated and presented together is an example of additive task while a class working together on one project is a conjunctive task. Regardless of whether the group does additive or conjunctive tasks, ensuring that all the group members participate and put in their efforts towards the goal is essential.

Norms

Each small group has certain norms that all the members follow. A norm is a guideline or rule designed to regulate the behaviours of group members. Norms decided by groups include a range of aspects from behaviour patterns, eating preferences to observances of rituals and celebrations. Norms powerfully govern how we communicate within a group. For example, traditional families have norms defining how younger members communicate with the elders in the family; similarly, in formal organisations, managers and their subordinates have clear hierarchies that determine who can communicate with whom and the protocols that need to be followed. Norms affect even the order of communication.

Identity

Small group members usually have a distinctiveness and display characteristics that enable them to be distinguished from non-members. The identity traits of group members refer to the psychological and/or physical boundaries that distinguish a group member from a non-member. Psychological boundaries refer to the feelings experienced by group members based directly on their group membership. This psychological identity sometimes is referred to as 'we'-ness and can result in both positive and negative feelings. Positive feelings include pride, cohesion, inclusion and superiority. Negative feelings include disappointment, disgust, disapproval and perhaps even embarrassment. Although these psychological boundaries are intangible, they play an important role in whether (and how) group members participate in group tasks, interact with one another, and perceive the group experience as enjoyable and worth their time.

Physical boundaries refer to the use of artefacts to indicate whether an individual belongs to a group. These boundaries include such things as clothing (e.g. wearing clothes of a colour or a blazer with a distinct logo), seating arrangements in a social setting or the workplace (e.g. group members sitting next to each other in class when they are assigned a group project) and living arrangements (e.g. members of a fraternity sharing an apartment).

> Characteristics of Small Group Communication
> - Small size
> - Interdependence
> - Common purpose
> - Norms
> - Identity

THEORIES OF SMALL GROUP COMMUNICATION

We develop theories about our environment to help organise and interpret our experiences. No single perfect, all-encompassing theory of small group communication exists. We will discuss four theories of small group communication: functional theory, symbolic convergence theory, structuration theory and naturalistic paradigm.

Functional Theory

The functional approach to small group communication is concerned with the results or outcomes of group behaviours and structures. This perspective sees communication as the tool used by the group members to solve problems and make decisions. Communication helps group members by promoting rational judgments and critical thinking, as well as preventing group members from faulty decision-making and flawed problem-solving. Therefore, since it provides the means by which group members can achieve their goals, communication is instrumental.

Research conducted from this perspective suggests that several conditions must exist for group members to make appropriate decisions and effectively solve problems. For example, group members must:

- commit to making the best decision
- identify resources needed to carry out the group's charge
- determine procedures for the group to follow
- articulate procedural rules and interaction practices
- review the decision-making process and make any necessary adjustments to the decision

According to the functional perspective, groups follow systematic procedures to accomplish their tasks. So, group members must:

- demonstrate that they understand the charge
- establish criteria with which to evaluate possible solutions
- develop alternative solutions
- evaluate those alternatives by comparing them to each other and the previously-established criteria
- use the evaluation to choose between the alternatives

The functional approach to small group communication has several strengths. First, it suggests that critical thinking, sound logic, informed discussion and systematic procedures are essential to effective decision-making and problem-solving. Second, this approach emphasises the purpose communication serves in small groups, and makes it clear that without communication group members cannot accomplish their goals.

Symbolic Convergence Theory

Symbolic convergence theory examines the sense-making function of communication. 'Symbolic' refers to verbal and non-verbal messages and 'convergence' refers to shared understanding and meaning. In small groups, members develop private code words and signals that only those inside the group understand. When groups achieve symbolic convergence, they have a sense of community based on common experiences and understandings.

Symbolic convergence theory is very different from the functional theory of group communication. The strength of symbolic convergence theory is the focus on group identity and the development of group consciousness. Symbolic convergence theory helps us understand how group members interact and provides a way of examining small group culture. We can also determine who is a group member and who isn't depending on whether they are familiar with the groups' inside jokes.

Structuration Theory

Structuration theory distinguishes between systems—such as small groups—and structures, practices, rules, norms and other resources the system uses to function and sustain. It views small groups as systems that both produce structures and are produced by structures. This means that group members follow particular rules in their interactions that produce some sort of outcome. That outcome eventually influences the group's future interactions.

Structuration refers to the processes group members employ as they work together. For example, suppose a committee decides to meet every second Wednesday of the month from 2:30 PM to 4:00 PM. This regular meeting is a rule that the group produced (and is thus an outcome of group interaction) as well as an instrument for producing the group. Other structures include methods of voting, norms of interaction and rules for distributing the group's workload.

Naturalistic Paradigm

Naturalistic paradigm is a general approach that is applicable to many communication contexts and academic disciplines. It focuses our attention on 'real life' groups. In small group communication research this means that researchers study real small groups in their natural settings. For example, a researcher might study work team culture in a local organisation, or multiple teams or groups in an organisation to focus on group identity. The naturalistic paradigm encourages researchers to venture outside corporate settings and examine self-help groups, families, religious groups and children's groups. The greatest strength of the naturalistic paradigm is its focus on naturally occurring small groups. We learn about the similarities of communication practices and norms as group members coordinate their interactions in everyday life.

FUNCTIONS OF SMALL GROUPS

Communication experts Isa Engleberg and Dianna Wynn (2003) have identified different types of groups to which you can belong—primary, social, self-help, learning, service, work, public and virtual. Each group has definite commonality of purpose that brings its members together. Ask yourself, when you join any group does it satisfy any of your needs? Or, in other words, what makes you join a particular group and why do you want to join it? You are part of many groups today and you chose to be with these groups because you seek certain benefits out of them. For example, you may have joined a yoga class because you want to keep yourself fit. Similarly, in your school or college, you join a students' activity group like dramatics, dance, literary or fine arts because you have a keen interest in any one of these. Thus, you may join a group because you have a specific need that you see getting fulfilled by becoming part of the group. At times you may join a group because of peer pressure, because you want to be with certain peer groups and be identified with them. Groups are not only instrumental in making you achieve your goals, they also satisfy and strengthen your interpersonal relationships and define your identity. Nowadays social media is becoming an effective tool in group formation to accomplish desired goals. For example, a group of university teachers, a batch of students, a group of fitness enthusiasts, all come together as powerful small groups on social networking sites like Facebook, and exchange information, share updates and mediate with each other; they share a common goal and have come together to achieve it.

Instrumental and Information Function

Groups fulfill both the instrumental and information needs of an individual. As a member of a group we seek to fulfill some of our instrumental needs which lead to our goal. Take the example of a student's union which is demanding for a canteen for students in the college premises. All students who participate as a member of this group have a stake in it and are striving together for a canteen. Group formation has led to fulfillment of instrumental needs. Alternatively, this group also shares information related to updates on this or other issues like admission updates, availability of reading material, standard of tutorial centres or how students in other colleges are handling college administration.

Image 11.2: Members of a Small Group Interacting with Each Other

Source: Authors.

Interpersonal Function

We join groups because we want to be part of that group which has members whose proximity you like or have a desire for and develop a close relationship with; groups help in meeting our interpersonal needs. The very phenomenon of inclusion in a group strongly defines our interpersonal needs. We want to be included in a group because we want to be associated with its members. We strive to adhere to the group norms so that our group inclusion status is maintained. The fear of avoidance and parting with the group keeps us in awe. We may also join groups because we want to be the decision makers in that group and influence others with our opinions and strive for having better results for the group. The interpersonal need of control becomes dominant here. Alternatively, groups also provide support during special events, emergencies, distress and mishaps in the lives of its group members.

Group membership helps meet our interpersonal needs by providing an opportunity for affection and inclusion, e.g. chapter meetings of an alumni association are a popular way to keep in touch with other students. Another important role is to connect with the institute they owe their growth to and volunteer time and provide direction to groom its students for the contemporary job market. For some others, who have done well for themselves professionally, they may find acknowledgement for their achievements by attending alumni meetings.

Identity Function

Identity is how people around us perceive us. In order to have a positive image of our identity we join certain groups that ensure a promising identity portrayal. The higher the number of our affiliations and recognitions, higher is the identity impact we have. Joining a group helps us use reference groups for social comparison, leaving us a mark ahead of the other groups. People often join groups with members who have the same affiliations or those who are from the same culture and have the same beliefs and values. For example, joining a prayer group may be essential to your grandparent because all the group members belong to her/his age group. Similarly, a parent of a growing child would like her/his child to be part of a theatre workshop group, as most of her/his friends' children would be enrolling for that too. Making her/his child join this group not just strengthens her/his relationship with her/his friends or relationship between the children but also provides a platform for these children to shed inhibitions and gain confidence through theatre.

Image 11.3: Women of a Small Group of Health Workers in Haryana

Source: Authors.

STAGES OF GROUP FORMATION

Groups, like individuals, are unique with their own experiences and expectations. However, many researchers studying group development and dynamics have recognised that group development is more predictable than individual behaviour. Thus many theories of group stage development have been cultivated, some linear, others cyclical, and it must be stressed that no definitive model of group stage development exists.

One of the most useful theories of group stage development is that discussed by Tuckman (1965). Tuckman's theory proposes that as groups develop and change they pass through stages which could be conceptualised.

Tuckman's model is an excellent model for attempting to analyse individual and group behaviour. A brief synopsis of each stage is outlined below.

Figure 11.1: Bruce Tuckman's Stages of Group Development

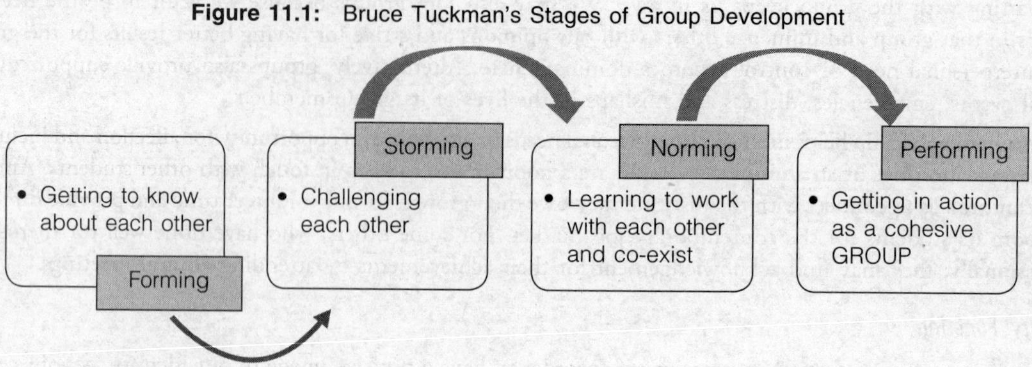

Source: Adapted by the authors based on inputs from http://lamidiadijatpatricia.wordpress.com (accessed 3 August 2015).

Forming

In the first stage of group development, the forming of the group takes place. The individuals' behaviours are driven by a desire to be accepted by others and avoid controversy or conflict. Serious issues and feelings are avoided, and people focus on being busy with routine, such as organising the team—who does what, when to meet each other, etc. Individuals are also gathering information and impressions about each other, and about the scope of the task and how to approach it. This is a comfortable stage to be in, but the avoidance of conflict means that not much actually gets done. The team meets and learns about the opportunities and challenges, and then agrees on goals and begins to tackle the tasks. Team members tend to behave quite independently. They may be motivated but are usually relatively uninformed of the issues and objectives of the team. The forming stage of any team is important because the members of the team get to know one another, exchange some personal information, and make new friends.

Storming

The second stage is necessary to the growth of the group. Normally tension, struggle and sometimes arguments occur in this stage. Storming can be contentious, unpleasant and even painful to members of the team who are averse to conflict. It is important to be aware that conflicts take place within all groups, and tolerance of each group member and their differences should be emphasised. Supervisors of the group may be more accessible, but tend to remain directive in their guidance of decision making and professional behaviour. If handled well effective resolution of conflict can produce benefits for the group in terms of development, objective and task setting, and the ultimate outcome. The group members will resolve their differences and be able to participate with one another more comfortably. The ideal is that they will not feel that they are being judged, and will therefore share their opinions and views without inhibition.

Norming

During this stage the group begins to work more constructively together towards formal or informal tasks. Roles begin to develop and be allocated within the group and although these may be accepted, some members may not be comfortable with the role(s) which have been allocated. During this stage sub-groups are likely to form in order that a supportive environment is once more created. Acceptable and unacceptable behaviours within the group are created and reinforced and thus the 'norms' for this group become fabricated. The storming and norming phases of group development are linked as it is often through the storming and challenging that acceptable group norms become set.

Performing

This stage sees the group performing effectively with defined roles, in fact at this stage it could be said that the group has transformed into a team. It is now that decisions may be positively challenged or reinforced by the group as a whole. The discomfort of the storming and norming phases has been overcome and the group has a general feeling of unity. This is the best stage for a group to complete tasks, assuming that task, rather than process and individuals, are the focus of the group.

Adjourning

Until around 1975, Tuckman had only four stages in the model. He later added a fifth stage and called it 'adjourning', also referred to as 'deforming and mourning'. Adjourning is arguably more of an addition to the original four-stage model rather than an extension. It views the group from a perspective beyond the purpose of the first four stages. Adjourning is the break-up of the group, hopefully when the task is completed successfully; everyone can move on to new things, feeling good about what has been achieved. This phase is certainly relevant to the people in the group and their well-being, but not to the main task of managing and developing a team, which is clearly central to the original four stages. From an organisational perspective, recognition of and sensitivity to people's vulnerabilities in Tuckman's fifth stage is helpful, particularly if members of the group have been closely bonded and feel a sense of insecurity or threat from this change.

GROUP PROCESSES

Group process refers to how members of a group work together to get things done. Understanding key elements influencing group dynamics can be useful in understanding group behaviour, conformity and deviance among group members, decision-making process in groups and the groups' realisation of their common goal. Key aspects influencing group processes are the nature of group structure, roles and leadership.

Group Structure

Structure of a group refers to the way the elements of a group interact; that is either they are horizontal in interactions or vertical.

According to Barker (1990), there are primarily five types of group structures—the circle, the wheel or X, Y network, chain and star or all-channel network. All these structures are distinguished by concepts of distance among members and centrality of information flow as shown in Table 11.1.

Image 11.4: Horizontal Group Structure

Source: Authors.

Table 11.1: Types of Group Structures

Structure	*Description*
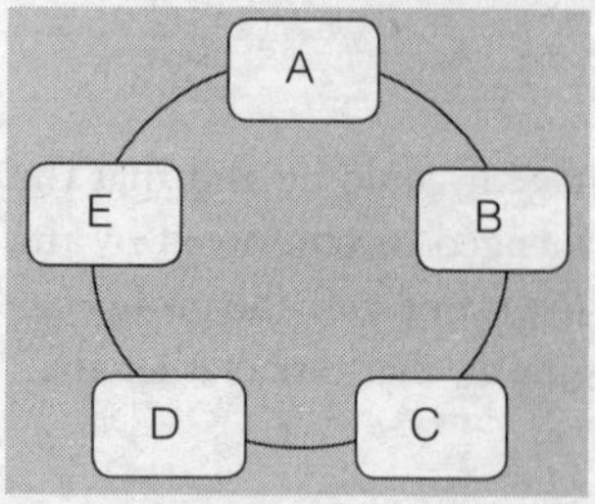 Circle	The circular group structure shows that each group member is connected to two other members. This can make coordination easy when only one or two people need to be brought in for a decision. The circle can be an effective structure for groups in which members are passing along a task and each member is expected to progressively build on the others' work. The circle is a decentralised group format where participants get more freedom to communicate among themselves and do not necessarily follow the leader in charge. For example, a group of friends engaged in any adventure activity.
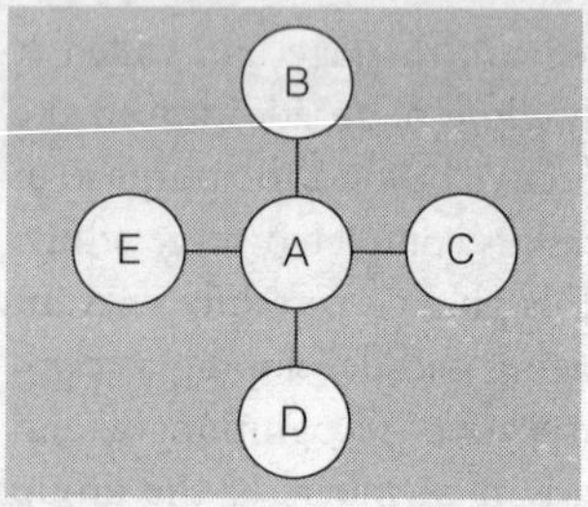 Wheel	The wheel structure in a group has one person who is in the centre around which other members are dependent for opinion and approval. The other members, like spokes of a wheel, seek to this leader or task master with high expertise for each group task. The wheel structures are mostly centralised. For example, a specialist doctor and her team of doctors while conducting a surgery. They all have a specific role, communicate regularly days prior to the surgery about taking decisions and yet wait for the final call from the senior expert.
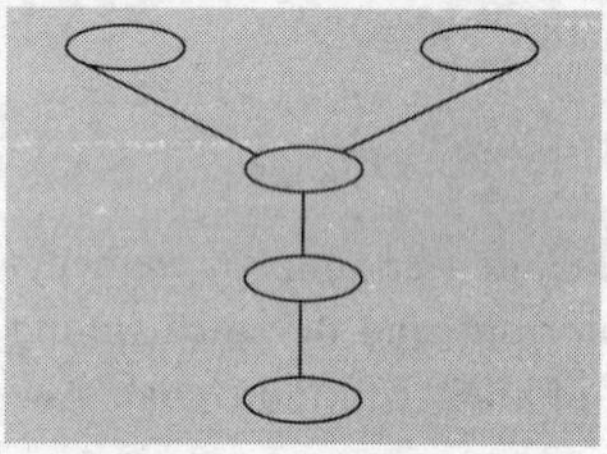 Y Network	The Y network is more centralised than the wheel. The person in the centre is viewed as the leader, due to the flow of information that (s)he sends or receives. Perhaps the most interesting part of the Y structure is its ability to identify coalitions. This network, like the wheel, is more accurate and speedy and is more adaptable in solving problems. The example of a Y network is that of a cricket team or a hockey team; wherein the captain (leader) receives information from the coach and sends it to his team members.
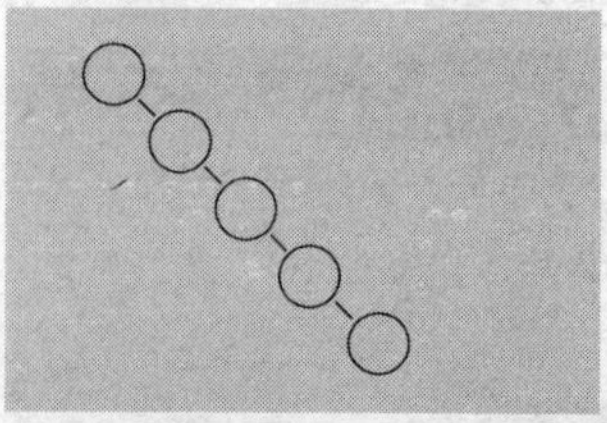 Chain Network	The chain network too is centralised like the wheel and Y network. Due to the flow of communication, again, the person in the centre is viewed as the leader. This communication network is more adaptable to solving problems of the group. Again, speed and accuracy are important here. Take an example of a director of a college, who in this case may be identified as the leader of the institute; now this leader gets direction from the administration and then networks it to her/his team of teachers in the college.
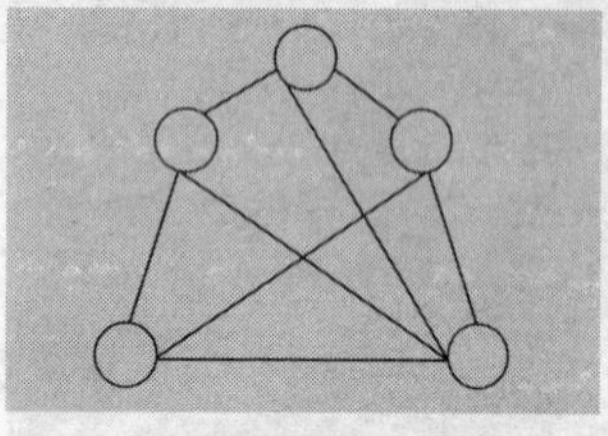 Star or All-channel network	Initial group meetings aiming to set out a group agenda may be an all channel network when everyone has an equal opportunity to contribute. No leader may emerge during the initial meeting of such group. Over time, however, another communication network will emerge (like a circle or a wheel). In short, the all channel network may be considered to be a 'no network' at all. In fact, it may be used to describe the initial group discussion. E.g. a resident welfare association group formed in a newly established housing society.

Source: Adapted by the authors from Barker (1990).

Group Roles

Every individual has some roles to perform. On a daily basis we switch between our varied roles to meet the social normative behaviours at different social settings. At one time, we are an individual at the other we are a part of a family; at another we are a part of a professional group. At all times our identity is the same, but our roles get transformed as we adapt to the respective social norms. As a part of a group formed towards seeking a particular goal, a member of that group has yet another role to perform, that of a group mate. The roles may again vary depending on the situation the group demands. Kenneth Benne and Paul Sheats proposed a classification of members' roles in small group communication that still provides the best overview of this important topic. (quoted in DeVito 2002: 264–65)

Group Task Roles

Group task roles are those roles which are intended towards achieving the group goals. Effective group members are often found multi-tasking. In an ideal group situation, however, efforts must be made that the roles are evenly spread and are interchanged too among the group members. When a single group member focuses too much on a specific task, the result can be counter-productive.

Examples of group task roles as explained by DeVito (2002) are:

1. The information seeker or giver and the opinion seeker or giver asks for or gives facts and opinions, seeks clarification of issues being discussed and presents facts and opinions to group members.
2. The evaluator-critic evaluates the group's decisions, questions the logic or practicality of the suggestions, and provides the group with both positive and negative feedback.
3. The procedural technician or recorder takes care of various mechanical duties such as distributing group materials and arranging the seating, writes down the group's activities, suggestions, and decisions, and/or serves as the group's memory.

Group Building and Maintenance Roles

A group cannot solely survive on just working towards a goal, the group members have social needs as well. Healthy interpersonal communication within the group members fosters a positive relationship leading to a satisfying and harmonised co-existence in the group, which ultimately leads to a more productive group performance.

Group-building roles as explained by DeVito (2002) are:

1. The encourager or harmoniser provides members with positive reinforcement through social approval or praise for their ideas and mediates the various differences between group members.
2. The compromiser tries to resolve conflict between her/his ideas and those of others and offers compromises.
3. The follower goes along with members, passively accepts the ideas of others and functions more as an audience than as an active member.

Individual Roles

While the group task roles and group maintenance roles are productive in nature, individual roles are counter-productive because of its very nature of anti-collectivism. Individual roles at times act like a barrier and hinder the process of group task. Examples of individual roles as explained by DeVito (2002) are:

1. The aggressor or blocker expresses negative evaluation of members and attacks the group, is generally disagreeable, and opposes other members or their suggestions regardless of their merit.

2. The recognition seeker and self-confessor tries to focus attention on her/his own self, boasts about her/his accomplishments rather than the task at hand and expresses her/his own feelings rather than focus on the group.
3. The dominator tries to run the group or members by pulling rank, flattering members or acting the role of boss.

Group Leadership

A leader plays an important role by effectively channelising the dynamics within a small group. Leadership is a primary foundation in a small group and it is often in such group environments that true leaders get an opportunity to emerge. As we have seen in the last section, different group members may act differently, hence it becomes very important that a leader is able to manage these individual behaviours in order to achieve group goals and resolve conflicts.

Today leadership is one of the most emphasised concepts in communication theory. Leader, as the word suggests, is the one who leads a group through the task. The leader leads and the others follow. But who decides who shall lead and who becomes the leader. In most cases it's a group's common call to decide on their leaders. A leader must be a person who has a command and has a high status. Status of high order may come through her/his qualifications, seniority and the nature of her/his role in the group.

How and Why of Leadership

The earlier portrayals of leadership suggest power as a deciding factor for becoming leaders. Those who were powerful became leaders; this old school thought of leaders being born is less relevant in today's time. Leaders are now made; they are either appointed or elected because of their previous leadership experiences and a set of leadership traits they possess.

There are two types of leaders—designated leaders and emergent leaders. Designated leaders are officially chosen and elected by the group members to lead them through the group task. Emergent leaders are the ones who prove their mettle in handling the task to such perfection that people tend to follow them. The latter category of leaders literally emerge through the situation dynamics and rise above others.

Understanding How Leaders Emerge

Distinctive qualities or personality traits of leaders: Leaders get identified for their distinctive set of personality traits that set them apart. Group members tend to follow them because of the uniqueness of their traits and attractive persona. Usually a leader is one who is impressive and has excellent communication skills and interpersonal techniques and a high intelligence quotient. Group members obviously would want a leader who they can look up to, with whom they can communicate without any hindrance and who can provide intelligent and practical solutions to a problem. Personality traits of leaders stand out in most cases; they are assertive, more passionate about their task, and put across their ideas in an affirmative way, expecting group members to adhere to them.

Excelling in situations: Different situations give rise to different leaders. Leaders emerge in different situational contexts—structured or semi-structured or unstructured situations. Chances of leaders emerging with a high interpersonal orientation are the highest in the unstructured and semi-structured situational contexts. On the other hand, leaders who are highly goal-oriented tend to emerge in a structured situation. They surpass their counterparts in the way they deal with the situation and aid in providing a common ground for interaction.

High level of communication and competence skills: The functional communication by a leader makes her/him a leader in true way. A high level of communication skills and competence is what all group members look up to in a leader. In all the three roles of groups—group task roles, group maintenance roles and individual roles—one who communicates more effectively and displays more competence becomes the star of the situation. Often leaders seek and contribute new ideas, involving creative methods as brain storming, evaluate ideas and decide upon in the group on choosing one of them. A leader must effectively be involved and take the primary role in goal and agenda setting, problem solving, resolving conflict and promoting a positive behaviour within the group.

Leadership Styles

Leadership has many styles. There are many theories and models that have roots into defining the leadership styles. We discuss the most relevant ones here.

The first classification of type of leadership styles is given by Barker (1990). He identifies three kinds of leadership styles:

Democratic Leadership

These leaders guide, rather than direct, a group. Receptive to group members' suggestions, these leaders leave most of the actual decision making to the group itself. Though a popular style, some groups feel lost when left on their own to such an extent. The effectiveness of this type of leadership depends on the power the leader has, the nature of task at hand and the interpersonal relationship between the leader and group members. These types of groups are shown to fare better in terms of creativity and consistency but fall behind in efficiency.

Authoritarian Leadership

These leaders are more directive than democratic leaders. They are strongly goal oriented and have firm opinions on how to achieve these goals. If their competency is respected by the group, the group works well and efficiently; if not, conflict is likely to arise within the group.

Laissez-faire Leadership

These leaders do not direct the group at all. As potential source of information and feedback on group interaction, they function as observers and recorders, available for advice when the group wants it. This kind of leadership is especially appropriate for groups engaged in creative activity, where direction would limit or stifle creativity.

The second classification is based on the path-goal theory of leadership, according to which four leadership styles are directive, participative, supportive and achievement oriented. The term 'path-goal' reflects the belief that effective leaders clarify the paths necessary for their subordinates to achieve the goals (Martin 2009). The path-goal theory thus suggests that leaders use different motivation styles to increase the work performance of their team. Let us understand these styles and find common points in these two classifications of styles of leadership.

Directive Leaders

Directive leadership, as the name suggests, has a leader that directs her/his team to comprehend group action. The directive leader clearly articulates the goal, the agenda and the expectations; provides specific guidance as group members work towards the completion of their task. (S)he takes the lead on setting and communicating group rules and procedures. This model of leadership is similar to the standard autocratic style of leadership where leaders set policies and make decisions primarily on their own, taking advantage of the power present in their title or status to set the agenda for the group. However, today it is argued that a leader can be directive without being seen as authoritarian. Effective motivation and encouragement are instrumental in seeking a positive behaviour from the group rather than threat or punishment as in the autocratic style.

Participative Leaders

Participative leaders involve group members in the decision-making process by soliciting and considering their opinions and suggestions. Inclusion of group members in the decision-making process makes them see that their personal goals align with the group goals, as a result of which they feel motivated and perform better. Participative leadership promotes a healthy social climate for interaction and interpersonal relationship development. The participative leaders try to inculcate a feeling of belonging in the members which strengthens their conformity to the group norms and behaviours. This type of leadership allows for more freedom and independence for the group members, so they can work individually and excel in their expertise. This style of leadership is similar to the standard style of democratic leadership where leaders facilitate group discussion and like to take input from all members before making a decision.

Supportive Leaders

Supportive leaders provide support to the group members when required. (S)he empathises with her/his group members' needs and emotions. (S)he tries to reduce friction within a group, and eliminates feelings of stress and frustration. These types of leaders prove most competent in groups which have frequent outbursts of conflicts. By promoting positive behaviours (s)he tries to shun negativity in the group and elicits healthy interaction. Such leaders criticise constructively in such a way that the motivation of the performers is not affected and they contribute effectively. These leaders are more successful in relational roles of the group rather than task-oriented group roles.

Achievement-oriented Leaders

Achievement-oriented leaders are driven by high-performance results. They want to achieve results at all costs and at all times. They try to instil this drive for perfection in all of their group members by setting challenging goals, constantly seeking improvement and exhibiting confidence in them so that they can meet their high expectations. They are well informed and aware of groups of similar high-performance category and try to surpass their standards. A rare species of leaders, achievement-oriented leaders work towards bringing change that is significant and hence derive respect for their unique persona.

> All the above leadership styles have their own pros and cons, yet none can be called the best or the worst style of leadership. It is to be noted that the true leader is one who adapts her/his leadership style as per the situation.

COMMUNICATION APPREHENSION IN SMALL GROUPS

Communication apprehension is the fear or anxiety associated with either real or anticipated communication with other person(s). This apprehension may stem from our basic personality, be a function of the type of communication expected, be attributed to the person or group with whom we are to communicate, or be unique to specific circumstances of the interaction (McCroskey and Richmond 2013). From whatever source it comes it causes us discomfort, may result in our behaving in a shy manner and is likely to result in our being ineffective in our communication (ibid.). The potential of communication apprehension in a small group context may be an important factor as it can create the effects as have been elaborated further:

Amount of Talk

Group members with low communication apprehension tend to speak more and participate more intensively and extensively in a small group. On the other hand, members with high communication apprehension hardly speak and their participation is infrequent and often limited. They are apprehensive to speak even when they are forced to do so.

Choice of Seats

Communication apprehension in a group member can be easily demonstrated by choice of seats. According to McCroskey and Richmond, in most seating arrangements, there are positions which are the focus of attention and positions which are relatively obscure and people with low communication apprehension regularly choose seats which are the focus of attention, while people with high communication apprehension generally prefer choosing seats which are more obscure.

Communication Content

The content generated by people with high communication apprehension is less and they often try to be submissive in the group communication. As a result, they prefer to go with the majority since they find it a safe way out. On the other hand, people with low communication apprehension dominate the interaction and generate numerous ideas; they give out relevant content and are proactively disagreeing with the group if they don't think the same way.

CONFLICT RESOLUTION

Conflict is a difference of opinion which leads to difficulty in arriving at a decision. Conflict can arise in direct or indirect forms within a group. It could be visible, loud and at the same time subtly hidden. Just as conflict commonly appears in interpersonal interactions, group interactions too get bouts of conflict. Group members may openly question each other's ideas or express frustration towards or dislike for another person. On the other hand, group members may also indirectly engage in conflict communication through critiquing, punning or passive-aggressive behaviour. Although we often perceive conflict negatively, conflict can be good for many reasons. Conflict can help realise an individual's and a group's potential. However, it can also lead to lower group productivity and stress.

After reading this chapter, you must have identified yourself as a part of some of the small groups you have been associated with. It is important to know and identify the structures that your group adapts and the role that you assume in the group. Equally impetrative it is to shed communication apprehension and choose a right leader. A leader must be participative and employ a combination of leadership styles to get the best out of the group and effectively accomplish the group task. Small groups can be effective and become the starting point of a group action that can lead to the desired change at a societal level.

SUMMARY

- A small group is a group of people usually small in numbers (3 to 15) who interact with each other in order to achieve a common goal. Because small groups have a common goal they are interdependent.
- All small groups are characterised by their typical group size, interdependence of the members, a common goal, norms set by the members and a shared identity.

- Small group communication can be understood in different ways if it is studied through different theories. Four theories that provide insight into some features of small group communication are functional theory, symbolic convergence theory, structuration theory and the naturalistic paradigm.
- Groups perform several functions of which information, interpersonal and restoring group identity are primary.
- Tuckman's (1965) model is an important theory that discusses group stage development. It proposes that as groups develop and change, they pass through four stages—forming, storming, norming and performing. Groups are structured and all group members have designated roles. The roles may again vary depending on the situation the group demands.
- There are primarily five types of group structures or networks—the circle, the wheel or X, the Y network, the chain and the star or all-channel network.
- Leadership is essential in directing group to its task fulfillment. With different leadership styles leaders often set the path to goal accomplishment.
- Conflict is the difference of opinion which leads to difficulty in arriving at a decision. The leader must be able to tackle conflicting situations.

KEY WORDS

Small group: A small group is a group of people—usually 3 to 15—who interact with each other in order to achieve a common goal. Because, small groups have a common goal, they are interdependent.

Functional approach to small group communication: It is concerned with the results or outcomes of group behaviours and structures. This perspective sees communication as the tool used by the group members to solve problems and make decisions.

Symbolic convergence theory: It examines the sense-making function of communication. 'Symbolic' refers to verbal and non-verbal messages and 'convergence' refers to shared understanding and meaning. In small groups, members develop private code words and signals that only those inside the group understand. When groups achieve symbolic convergence, they have a sense of community based on common experiences and understandings.

Structuration theory: It distinguishes between systems such as small groups and structures, the practices, rules, norms and other resources the system uses to function and sustain. It views small groups as systems that both produce structures and are produced by structures.

Group task roles: These are those roles which are intended towards achieving the group goals. Effective group members often multi-task. In an ideal group situation, however, efforts must be made that the roles are evenly spread and are interchanged among the group members. When a single group member focuses too much on a specific task, the result can be counter-productive.

Leadership: It is one of the most emphasised concepts in communication theory today. A leader must be then a person who has a command and a high status within the group. Status of high order may come through his qualifications, seniority and the nature of her/his role in the group.

Democratic leadership: In a democratic leadership leaders guide, rather than direct, a group. Receptive to group members' suggestions, these leaders leave most of the actual decision making to the group itself. Though a popular style, some groups feel lost when left on their own to such an extent.

Authoritarian leadership: In an authoritarian leadership leaders are more directive than democratic leaders. They are strongly goal-oriented and have firm opinions on how to achieve these goals. If their competency is respected by the group, the group works well and efficiently; if not, conflict is likely to arise within the group.

Laissez-faire leadership: In a laissez-faire leadership leaders do not direct the group at all. As potential source of information and feedback on group interaction, they function as observers and recorders, available for advice when the group wants it. This kind of leadership is especially appropriate for groups engaged in creative activity, where more direction would limit or stifle creativity.

Path-goal theory: The path-goal theory suggests that leaders use different motivation styles to increase the work performance of their team. According to this theory the four leadership styles are directive, participative, supportive and achievement-oriented.

Communication apprehension: It is the fear or anxiety associated with either real or anticipated communication with other person or persons.

EXERCISES

1. What is a small group? Discuss with examples the dynamics related to group roles in a small group.
2. Enlist and explain in detail the functions of a small group.
3. Discuss in detail the primary characteristics of a small group.
4. What do you understand by communication apprehension? What are the effects of communication apprehension on a small group?
5. Provide an insight into the importance of leadership in a small group. Delineate and elaborate on the various styles of leadership.
6. Why is conflict common in small group settings?

REFERENCES

Alison, Burke, 'Group Work: How to Use Groups Effectively', *The Journal of Effective Teaching Volume* 11 (2011): 2.

Barker, Larry L., *Communication*, fifth edition, New Jersey: Prentice-Hall, 1990.

DeVito, Joseph A., *Essentials of Human Communication*, fourth edition, Boston: Allyn & Bacon, 2002.

Engleberg, I. and D. Wynn, *Working in Groups: Communication Principles and Strategies*, third edition, Boston: Houghton Mifflin, 2003.

James C. McCroskey and Virginia P. Richmond, 'Communication Apprehension and Small Group Communication' in *Group Communication: Performance and Practice*, available at http://www.jamescmccroskey.com/publications/bookchapters/006_1984.pdf (accessed on 12 April 2015), 2014 [1984].

Larry, Barker, Kathy J. Wahlers and Kittie W. Watson, *Groups in Process: An Introduction to Small Group Communication*, sixth edition, New York: Pearson, 2008.

Martin, Robin, 'Path Goal Theory of Leadership', *Encyclopedia of Group Processes and Intergroup Relations*, edited by John M. Levine and Michael A. Hogg, 636–37, California: Sage, 2009.

Richmond, V. P., J. C. McCroskey and L. Powell, *Organizational Communication for Survival*, fifth edition, New Jersey: Pearson, 2013.

Scott A. Myers and Carolyn M. Anderson, *The Fundamentals of Small Group Communication*. California: Sage, 2008.

Steinberg, Sheila, *An Introduction to Communication Studies*, South Africa: Juta and Co., 2007.

Tuckman, B., 'Developmental Sequence in Small Groups', *Psychological Bulletin* 63 (1965): 384–99.

ONLINE SOURCES

http://2012books.lardbucket.org/books/a-primer-on-communication-studies/ (accessed 1 July 2015)

http://2012books.lardbucket.org/books/beginning-human-relations/s05-00-what-is-human-relations.html (accessed 14 May 2015)

http://lamidiadijatpatricia.wordpress.com (accessed 3 August 2015)

http://www.mcae.k12.mn.us/ahs/academics/SmallGroupDiscussion.pdf (accessed 14 May 2015)

http://www.utexas.edu/tip/pdf/Small%20Group%20Communication.pdf (accessed 8 March 2015)

12

ORGANISATIONAL COMMUNICATION

HIGHLIGHTS

- Concept of organisational communication
- Role of organisational communication
- Characteristics of organisational communication
- Approaches to understanding organisational communication
- Functions of communication in an organisation
- Aspects of organisational communication
- Communication flow in organisations
- Factors affecting organisational communication
- Achieving Effective Communication in an Organisation

The last century witnessed profound changes characterised by greater mobility, interconnectivity and complexity of environments. Rapidly changing technology, forces of globalisation and the rise of large transnational organisations have deeply impacted our communication. Communication technologies have redefined not only how we interact with various organisations but also their very nature. Apart from the emergence of a host of new types of organisations, today's organisations differ in structure, employers and employees relationships with virtual and multicultural teams within them. There are options of flexible timings and work from home. These changes have drastically changed work lives and personal lives. The nature of communications within an organisation is both technological and human, and consequently, the demands on individual communication abilities and competencies required have led to the growing importance of the field of organisational communication.

We begin to explore the relationship between communication and organisations by first identifying what an organisation is and what it does.

Concept of Organisation

An organisation is essentially a group of people working towards a common goal, for example, our family or a cricket team. Look around and you will see that there are various kinds of organisations that we interface with. The Resident Welfare Association (RWA) of your colony, the school or college you are enrolled in, the students union in your college, are all examples of different kinds of organisations. Now think what according to you is common among them? According to Baird (1977), organisations can be defined as collective groups of individuals constructed and reconstructed to strive for specific goals that could not be met by individuals alone.

Organisations differ in size and scale, they can be formal or informal, small or large, yet all organisations are social units of people that are structured and managed to meet a need or to pursue collective goals. They are dynamic entities constantly changing and adapting in order to pursue their goals. This process occurs through communication behaviours. Thus, understanding what an organisation is and how it works requires an understanding of the communication process of organisations. The study of nature and type of communication that takes place within organisations is called organisational communication.

CONCEPT OF ORGANISATIONAL COMMUNICATION

We have learned about the concept and characteristics of communication in Unit 1 and have understood communication as a process whereby one person tries to create understanding and meaning in the mind of another. Similarly, organisational communication has been defined in the context of communication within organisations by a few scholars. Koontz (2001) defines organisational communication as the transfer of information from the sender to the receiver provided the information is well understood by the receiver. Hybels and Weaver (2001) see communication as 'any process in which people share information, ideas and feelings, and that it involves not only the spoken and written word but also body language, personal mannerism and style', i.e. anything that adds meaning to a message. Thus organisational communication definitions largely focus on building relationships or repeated interpersonal interactions with internal organisational members and interested external public. They emphasise on sending and receiving of messages among interrelated individuals within a particular organisational setting to achieve individual and common goals.

Goldhaber (1990) identified a number of common characteristics in the variety of definitions of organisational communication: Organisational communication (*a*) occurs within a complex open system which is influenced by and influences its internal and external environments, (*b*) involves messages and their flow, purpose, direction and media, and (*c*) involves people and their attitudes, feelings, relationships and skills. Thus, organisational communication helps us to: (*a*) accomplish tasks relating to our specific roles and responsibilities within an organisation, (*b*) get used to changes through individual and organisational creativity and adaptation, (*c*) complete tasks through the maintenance of policy, procedures or regulations that support daily and continuous operations, (*d*) develop relationships with people of varying abilities, attitudes and motivations for greater satisfaction and fulfillment, and (*e*) coordinate, plan and control the operations of the organisation.

ROLE OF ORGANISATIONAL COMMUNICATION

The following are key roles of organisational communications.

Coordination

The foremost role of organisational communication is coordination. Just as the brain sends signals to the nervous system and the nervous system coordinates with the other parts of the body by responding to the stimuli and the signals, communication coordinates the actions of various components within an organisation to achieve the goals.

Sharing Organisational Goals

The second role of organisational communication is sharing of information about the goals and objectives of an organisation, about task directives and the end results. Members of an organisation should know the objectives the organisation is striving for, the job duties and responsibilities, and how their tasks fit in and help in achieving those objectives. Further, it is equally important that the members are communicated about the results of their efforts in a timely manner. Decision making of all these requires effective communication. How well a decision regarding any task or situation has been made and how effectively it has been communicated is of immense importance.

Communicating Emotions

It is only though communication that one is able to express feelings and emotions. An organisation is made up of individuals who are social beings and need to communicate their feelings and emotions such as anger, frustration, happiness and confidence in various situations while working together. An effective communication between and within various departments is vital in improving organisational effectiveness. There are ample studies (Locke 1976; Fielder 1981; Jothi 1986) which prove that personal feedback and a pleasant manner in which a supervisor communicates to her/his team members could result in higher levels of job satisfaction and work performance.

CHARACTERISTICS OF ORGANISATIONAL COMMUNICATION

The various kinds of organisations differ in terms of the purpose they serve, their size and structure, scope, etc. However, they all share a few similar characteristics which explain the differences between casual and organised groups.

Division of Labour

The divisions or departments are created to help the organisation function more efficiently. As the size of the organisation increases, so does the number of necessary departments.

Presence of Power Centres

An organisation is executed through managers who provide leadership by exercising control over day-to-day functioning of the organisation.

Substitutions of Personnel

Organisations are characterised by substitution of personnel, so that the organisation continues to function properly. For this, people may be fired, promoted, moved or get retired.

Interdependence

Various organisational components are interdependent on each other as departments do not work in isolation.

Coordination

Coordination amongst various departments is made possible through communication. Information can be communicated to various departments either through word of mouth which is an interpersonal channel of communication or through phone calls, formal letters or emails.

FUNCTIONS OF COMMUNICATION IN AN ORGANISATION

You are aware that communication serves some or all of these four functions—informative, regulatory, persuasive and integrative. Within an organisation also the functions remain the same and can be understood in the context of how they facilitate the smooth functioning of an organisation.

Informative Function

As we know informative function is one of the basic functions of communication. Within an organisation also, people at various levels have to communicate in order to obtain information. They may want to have information regarding the organisation's goals and objectives, its policies and procedures, rule and regulations. In addition, information regarding the success of an organisation in terms of the benefits, profits and work standards expected is of importance. For example, superiors need to inform subordinates about duties they need to perform. Similarly subordinates need to give constant feedback about their work to their superiors.

Regulatory Function

Use of communication to exercise control has been well understood. Communication of the orders, perceived expectations, organisations' ideologies and philosophy, rules and regulations in relation to a particular task/situation is done on a regular basis to maintain its effectiveness. For example, superiors need to control and regulate the work and behaviour of their subordinates.

Persuasive Function

Communication serves an end function of persuading the receiver of the message. In organisations also persuasive function can be seen to be reflected in the form of interpersonal compliance-gaining interactions which are often done face-to-face to convince the other person of one's viewpoints or opinions. For example, the job of the marketing and public relations department of a company.

Integrative Function

Communication within an organisation serves an important integrative function whereby it helps in providing a feeling of unity and cohesion, identity and uniformity among its members. Establishing provisions for channelling information and authority, training, and scheduling of activities and their coordination are all examples indicating the integrative function that communication does in any organisation.

ASPECTS OF ORGANISATIONAL COMMUNICATION

There are several areas that communication scholars focus upon within the field of organisational communication. However, there are five major areas of organisational communication: (*a*) leadership, (*b*) teams, (*c*) communication networks, (*d*) organisational culture and (*e*) organisational learning.

Leadership

Leadership is defined as a communicative process where ideas articulated are recognised by others as progressive tasks. The definition of leadership suggests that leadership can take different forms and can very well be associated with different styles of communication present within an organisation. Nevertheless, for an effective leadership communication the following are important.

- Allowing leaders to connect with values, attitudes and commitments considered important by their followers, thereby helping her/him to connect directly with the hearts and minds of the followers.
- Reducing tensions and rivalry by making the environment conducive to building of strong interpersonal relationships by means of using rewards and punishments.

Teams

Teams can be defined as a group of two or more people working towards a specified objective and predefined goal. Coordination among the team members is of utmost importance in order to accomplish any task. LaFasto and Larson (2001) have enumerated three important qualities that teams must have.

- A clear understanding of the goal to be accomplished and belief that the set goal embodies an important result for the same, participatory goal setting must be encouraged since it is more effective and calls for higher commitment by the team members.
- Appropriate result-driven structures should be put in place depending on the nature of tasks to be accomplished; for example, in advertising agencies, creative teams require out-of-the-box thinking whereas in others tactical teams are required.
- Have appropriate technical competencies like substantive knowledge, technical experience and good personal competencies including the skills required to identify, address and resolve socio-emotional issues.

Communication Network

Communication networks exist within every organisation in terms of who talks to whom, about what, when and where. A centralised network is said to exist when information is funnelled through a small number of individuals within an organisation. On the contrary, in a decentralised network, information is shared widely among its members and flows through many individuals. Autonomous and self-managed task teams and local units can manage emerging crises quickly rather than needing to receive permission from a centralised location.

Organisational Culture

Organisational culture can be defined as a set of knowledge, ideology, values and rituals that individuals working within an organisation share. Organisational leaders are majorly concerned with creating organisational cultures that can emphasise high performance. Several important characteristics of high performing organisational cultures as given by Eisenberg, Goodall and Trethewey (2007) are as follows:

- In organisations where participation and dissent are compromised, and there are no clear-cut directives of holding anyone responsible for a given task or decision, unethical practices emerge easily.
- High-performing cultures can be characterised on the basis of their commitment to action, the habit of maintaining close relationships, emphasising autonomy and entrepreneurship, achieving productivity, fostering strong values and focusing on what they do best.
- High-performing cultures are the ones who along with preserving their core purpose and strong identity are simultaneously open to change. For this, organisations must explicitly articulate their ideology to employees, select potential employees based on their fit with the existing culture and emphasise the special qualities of the culture.

Organisational Learning

Organisational learning refers to enhancing the capacity of organisational members' to think collectively in new and innovative ways that can help in fostering coordinated activity. From a communication perspective, dialogue is central to fostering learning and is guided by several principles.

- Inquiry and advocacy needs to be balanced. Individuals must be encouraged to ask questions that challenge existing assumptions and beliefs.
- It is important that unstated assumptions and beliefs be brought to the surface. It becomes pertinent that we dialogue and discuss, and together reach a consensus on how a certain situation needs to be looked at.
- Suspending one's beliefs and opinions in front of others through dialogue must be encouraged since it allows for introspecting at the best way a situation needs to be understood.

- For having open discussions, there should be an assurance that one's own statements will not be used against them. This helps in creating a safer environment where people will trust each other and share their thoughts and opinions fearlessly.

COMMUNICATION FLOW IN ORGANISATIONS

For understanding the communication flows in organisations we need to understand (*a*) the medium of communications and (*b*) the network within which information flows.

Medium of Communication

You are already familiar with the fact that channel is a key element of communication. The channel or the means that is chosen to send a message is very important. The decision of which channel to choose for communicating is very important not only because it influences the efficiency with which the message is communicated but also because it affects the way in which the message is interpreted by the recipient. Many communication scholars believe strongly in the fact that medium itself is the main message which implies that the message is embedded within the medium you choose to communicate and is often responsible for the perception about the message. In an organisation also, the selection of channel is crucial in determining information flow among individuals. For example, in order to call a meeting of stakeholders, a formal invitation letter sent through mail with due time notice is more appropriate whereas a meeting of the team members may convene after receiving a short notice over an SMS. The choice of channel will not only determine the speed of message dissemination but also who is able to access the message and interpret it to take action in response. A host of receiver- as well as sender-related aspects influence the selection of a channel. However, the following factors should be kept in mind while choosing a channel.

- *Cost*: Before deciding a channel, it is important to consider the cost involved. Suppose one wants to communicate about a new policy or rule within a university, a printed copy would work the best. However, if the number of departments are many then probably sending an email to all the department heads or sending a fax would work best. Further, a mention of posting it on the website can be done.
- *Confidentiality*: Depending upon the confidentiality of the message, a communication channel for conveying a particular message can be chosen. An internal memo enclosed within an envelope can be used if the message is highly confidential. Similarly a choice can be made between post or courier.
- *Urgency*: At times, when one requires speedy communication, the cost incurred in communicating a particular message is justified by the urgency of communicating a particular message.
- *Distance*: Both within and across, the organisation determines whether one will land up using an electronic medium like email or written medium like letter based on the distance involved.
- *Time*: Time of the day when the message is being communicated will directly affect the type of channel used.
- *Resources*: While deciding to communicate anything written or electronically all the available resources must be taken care of.

Networks of Organisational Communication

How communication flows within organisations is also influenced by the network used for communicating the message. Networks represent the patterns or paths along which information flows within an organisation. Communication network links are established within an organisation to guide the members in doing their day-to-day job and seek coordination from others while working. Communication networks within organisations differ in patterns of structure and formation.

Messages that flow within an organisation can be through formal or informal structures. Each organisation creates its own set of definite rules and regulations that govern the pattern of communications to be followed by each individual. These rules and regulations act as directives—i.e. norms and protocols—to people working at all levels within an organisation. These well-defined procedures enable smooth functioning of the various departments. This kind of communication generally takes place in already-specified directions. For example, if a student wants to complain about ragging in colleges then there is a definite procedure to be followed, or if a junior executive wants to suggest changes to the top management then her/his proposal will have to be routed through the given hierarchy of her/his superiors before it reaches the top. Thus, formal communications are governed by a predefined set of rules and regulations. These formal channels give rise to formalised networks. These formalised networks can further be categorised as vertical or horizontal or diagonal in nature.

On the contrary, in an organisation whenever and wherever people meet and interact a kind of informal communication network is also created. This type of communication is based on friendship, relationship, proximity and shared interests between co-workers or the so-called 'personal networks'. These informal bonds created between co-workers are very powerful and aid in making communication more effective. These often result in generation of new ideas amongst co-workers. Thus, effectiveness of informal networks significantly influences the overall communication. Examples of such informal networks include a group of employees gathering at the office canteen everyday during lunch hour or sharing a cab service irrespective of the departments they belong to. Informal networks serve the following organisational functions: provide a sense of belongingness, security; provide an opportunity to discuss in an open sphere, reduce stress and tension and most importantly facilitate formal communication. For an organisation to function effectively, it is necessary that both formal as well as informal structures exist simultaneously.

Types of Organisational Communication Networks

Within an organisation, the manner in which communication flows from one member to another creates and determines the shape and structure of the networks of communication. Understanding these structures will help us understand how a message or information is communicated and is helpful in gaining insights about the organisation as a whole.

Vertical Communication

Vertical communication takes place between members at different levels in an organisation. It can be downward or upward in nature. Downward communication network is generally the most frequent form of vertical communication and takes place from top to bottom. Mostly members who are in powerful positions convey messages to their subordinates. For example, messages sent from the principal of a college to the various heads of departments. Assisting communication of specific task directives, informing subordinates about the procedures and practices, updating them about their performance and facilitating coordinated functioning within an organisation are basic purposes of downward communication. Effectiveness of the downward communication relies largely on print or oral channels of communication. Downward communication provides an advantage of maintaining discipline within an organisation. Misinterpretation of the message and ignoring the characteristics of the receiver are common challenges faced while communicating downwards.

Figure 12.1: Downward Communication

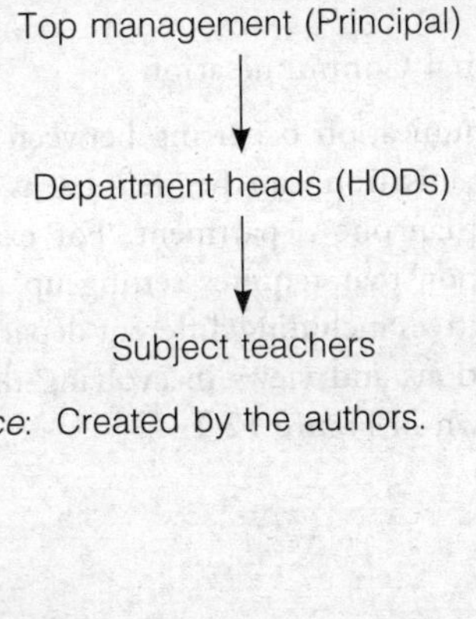

Source: Created by the authors.

Upward communication takes place when feedback is provided from the lower level to a higher level. For instance, if a university is proposing to follow a new student evaluation system, teachers may decide to oppose the new system due to various reasons, and they may prepare a feedback and state the problems faced by students and the teachers in doing so. This kind of upward communication helps in keeping the top management and the immediate senior updated of how one feels about her/his work or assigned task; peers and the organisation in general and informs them of the problems or challenges faced if any. It is done using progress reports, suggestions, explanations, appeal, grievances, feedback questionnaires and complaints. Some personal information about the ideas, attitudes and performance are the basic information and facts that can be collected using upward communication networks.

Figure 12.2: Upward Communication

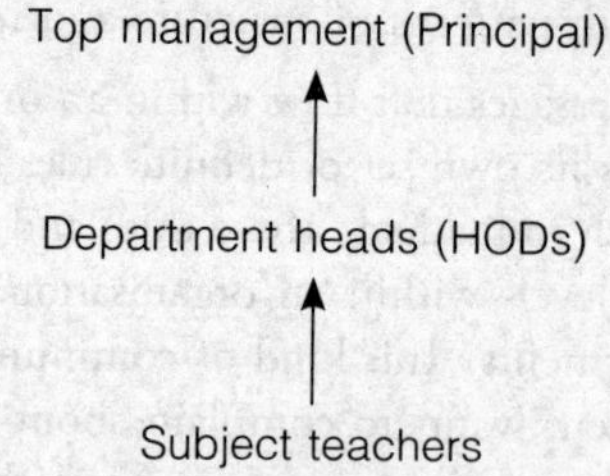

Source: Created by the authors.

Horizontal or Lateral Communication

Apart from upward and downward communication networks, communication is often seen to happen laterally or horizontally. Lateral communication takes place between individuals who are working at the same level. Messages that flow horizontally typically involve exchange of information or data necessary to complete daily routine tasks and this can be done either face-to-face or via telephone. Kumar and Thakur (2008) have given four key purposes of lateral communication—task coordination, problem solving, information sharing and conflict resolution. Horizontal communication within the same department helps facilitate coordination and results in stronger emotional and social bonding between peers.

Figure 12.3: Horizontal or Lateral Communication

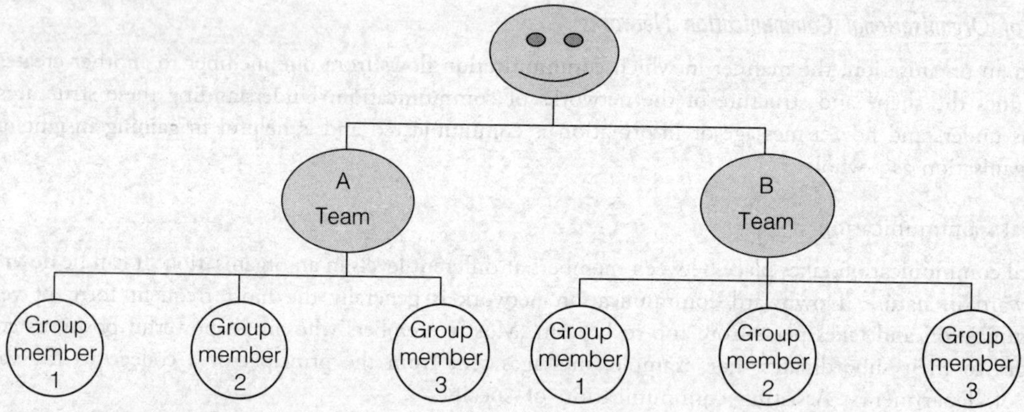

Source: Created by the authors.

Diagonal Communication

Communication occurring between people who work in different departments and at different levels within an organisation can be defined as diagonal communication. At times there are situations which involve more than one department. For example, when a university wants to implement a new system of student evaluation that requires setting up new systems and protocols, to facilitate a smooth transition inter-college committees including different department heads/in-charges can be formed to understand the process, give their suggestions and views in evolving the system and implementation. This can diagrammatically be represented as shown in Figure 12.4.

Figure 12.4: Diagonal Communication

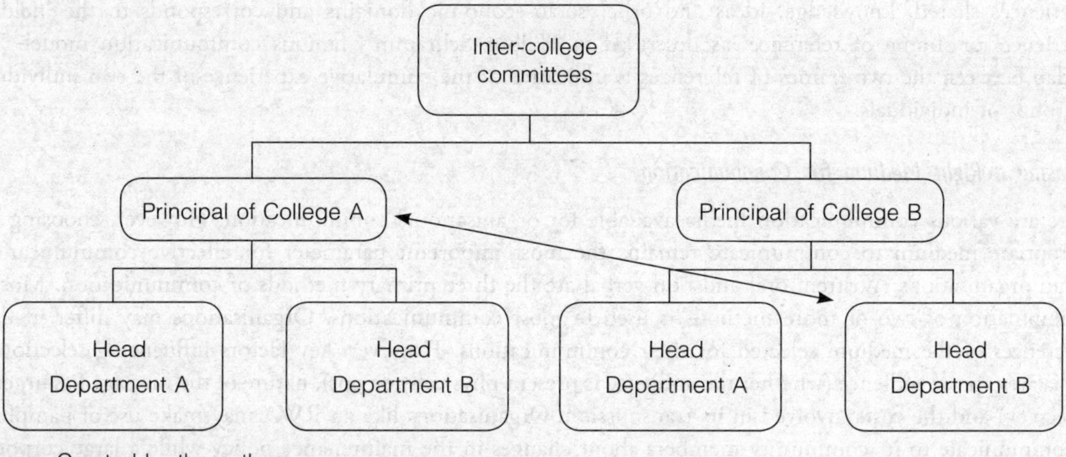

Source: Created by the authors.

Similarly, while organising an annual fund raising event for a charity, a team may be formed from different departments of the organisation for facilitating the process and participation of their department members in the event.

Grapevine

'Grapevine' is the unstructured or the informal communication network that exists within an organisation. It can be considered synonymous to rumour, and has its own advantages and disadvantages. If the correct lines of communication are not used in an organisation, it always results in the formation of grapevine. Grapevines are formed generally because people in the groups have something in common that links them together. A person can belong to one or more groups. For example, a manager can belong to a group of women that go to lunch together. (S)he can also belong to a group of people who travel together by the official transport. (S)he could have a third group of people scattered throughout the organisation with which (s)he shares other common interests outside of work. In this example, the manager is likely to pass information across her/his three main informal networks in order to verify the accuracy of the rumours (s)he hears.

There are some intrinsic problems in relying on informal organisational channels. The main problem is that much of the information that gets spread through the grapevine is not verified. Some of the information is likely to be false. However, all grapevine communication is not bad. At times, grapevine communication can help in creating social bonds. Whatever people may talk about through the grapevine, it helps build new ties and connections. Teams tend to become more unified when members talk outside of the domains of project work or assignment they may be working on. Grapevine is an integral part of all organisations and can never be completely removed. Thus managers should try and reduce its influence by considering carefully the ways in which information needs to be communicated in the organisation, both formally and informally. They must remember that whatever is being communicated, it should be communicated accurately, completely and using appropriate channels of communication which are accessible and approachable.

FACTORS AFFECTING EFFECTIVE ORGANISATIONAL COMMUNICATION

As we have learnt in Unit 1 for the transfer of knowledge, facts or opinions to take place adequately and completely, the presence of a 'common ground' is one of the basic and most essential requirements. Common ground is usually defined on the basis of the similarity between the sender and the receiver in terms of the experiences shared, knowledge, ideas and other socio-economic domains and corresponds to the 'field of experience' or 'frame of reference' as described in Wilbur Schramm's famous communication model. The overlap between the two frames of references is indicative of the cumulative experience of the two individuals or groups of individuals.

Choosing a Right Medium for Communication

There are various communication media available for organisational communication. However, choosing the appropriate medium to communicate remains the most important parameter for effective communications within organisations. Written, oral and non-verbal are the three primary methods of communication. Mostly, a combination of two or more methods is used in most communications. Organisations may differ in their preferences of the medium selected for their communications. However, key factors influencing selection of media are type of audience (whether the audience is present physically or not), nature of the message (its urgency or secrecy) and the costs involved in its transmission. Organisations like an RWA may make use of pamphlets to communicate to its community members about changes in the maintenance policy while a large corporate house may send email to its employees about a policy change directive.

It has been seen that a majority of the corporate organisations make use of written communication for any kind of orders, directives, policies and events or even for getting feedback. Written communication of this kind is authentic in nature and is helpful in promoting uniformity in policy and procedure. Very frequently reports that showcase the performance of the organisation or talk about any of their projects is used as a preferred medium by organisations to communicate with shareholders and public at large. In order to avoid noise and reduce physical, socio-psychological and technical barriers that can impede the process of communication, knowledge about the usage, availability, need and necessity as well as the potential benefits of various media used for communication is essential. The effectiveness of media used for communication is dependent upon two factors—information richness and complexity of the messages being communicated.

Information richness is usually defined as 'the potential information carrying capacity of data'. If a medium is capable of conveying great deal of information, the medium is said to be high in richness like telephone or radio. On the contrary, if it is able to transmit only a little information it is said to be low in richness; for instance, a formal letter or memorandum. The four factors that can be used to measure information richness are—feedback, channel, type of communication and language source being used for communication. Thus, whether the medium used has high degree of information richness or not can be measured by determining the amount of feedback obtained and can range from immediate to very slow.

A message comprises words, ideas, concepts which can be formal or informal, short or long, concise or redundant/unnecessary. For a message to be effective, the message must be clear, concise and simply stated without any technical jargon and should be of reasonable length as per the ability of the listener or audience to comprehend and may vary for different subsets of audiences. In absence of these, a message becomes complex and hard to follow. For instance, in a review meeting in an organisation, the messages communicated must be specific in nature. Any ambiguity caused by the message being too long or with several redundant messages may result in adding complexity to the message. The team leader must focus on communicating clearly the stated objectives of the task and methods to achieve those objectives. (S)he also ought to mention very clearly the indicators for measuring performance against the stated objectives, the timeframe available and outcomes expected. Likewise, for organising an event which involves many people of the organising committee like the annual fest in a college, the college head needs to provide clear details of date and time, events expected, people responsible, etc. during the planning meetings. Both these situations exemplify simple and effective communication.

ACHIEVING EFFECTIVE COMMUNICATION IN AN ORGANISATION

An organisation comprises hierarchal structure with defined communication lines. Successive transmission of messages through the hierarchy dilutes the message and affects communication. For effective organisational communication, the right information has to be given to the right person at the right time and in the right form. The following steps can be adopted by management in order to achieve effective communication in an organisation:

- The message to be communicated must be comprehensive, adequate and complete.
- Every organisation must ensure smooth and effective communication amongst its various departments and within each department as well. For the same the organisation must make the work environment more conducive towards facilitating open and free communication. For effective communication, the subject matter and the purpose of communication must be clear. Thus, there should be clarity in idea and the specific steps that should be taken to achieve the intended end.
- The information should be transmitted at the right time and should reach the receiver at the right time.
- Communication is a cyclic process. Feedback should be encouraged to look for responses of the employees. It provides the sender with the opportunity to suggest, verify, accept, criticise and initiate any further action.
- Empathy plays a crucial role in communication and to be mindful of other people's situations, attitudes, needs and interests. This will help in strengthening interpersonal relationships between superiors, subordinates and will boost the motivation to achieve organisational objectives.
- Selection of proper channels consistent with the type of information being transmitted, the urgency or secrecy of information and the degree of media richness each medium can afford to provide.
- Informal communication is as important as formal communication. Performance appraisal and reward meetings should be used to encourage frequent, unscheduled communication. This will be helpful in enhancing mutual understanding and will minimise the effect of status differences.
- Organisations should develop elaborate and balanced information systems to cope with the problem of information overload and time pressure.

SUMMARY

- Communication forms the essence of human life. Within an organisation too, communication serves as a lifeline for its effective functioning. There is defined division of roles and responsibilities along with the presence of well-defined power centres. However, it is only the coordination between and among the various organisational departments which make an organisation work.
- To achieve coordinated action, communication serves four major functions—exchange of information, regulation, persuasion and integration.
- Communication serves these functions through the use of formal and informal networking structures. The formal structures are intentionally produced to introduce clarity in the roles, duties and responsibilities. Informal structures co-exist and perform major functions which are unofficial paths, flexible in nature, speedier and serve to fill in the possible gaps in the formal communication.
- For efficient organisational communication, the selection of channel and use of existing network should be done appropriately.
- Important and urgent messages must be communicated through oral channels. They can or cannot be combined with the written channels.

- Various types of networks operate in downward, upward or lateral directions in an organisation.
- Various organisational barriers exist pertaining to organisational policy being followed, rules and regulations, hierarchical positions and status differences, etc. By ensuring timely dissemination of information, empathy, proper feedback and fostering informal communication, an organisation can easily overcome these barriers.

KEY WORDS

Organisation: It refers to a group of people working towards a common goal.

Organisational communication: It involves sending and receiving of messages among interrelated individuals within a particular organisational environment.

Organisational structure: It is created when individuals within an organisation interact with one another. They do so in accordance with certain predefined rules and norms and can be of different type and messages flow within an organisation through formal or informal structures.

Organisational culture: It can be defined as a set of knowledge, ideology, values and rituals that individuals working within an organisation share.

Communication networks: It refers to the lines of communication existing within an organisation and are often described in terms of who talks to whom, about what, when and where.

Vertical communication: It takes place between members at different levels in an organisation. It can be downward or upward in nature.

Horizontal or lateral communication: It takes place between individuals who are working at the same hierarchical levels within an organisation.

Diagonal communication: It occurs between people who work in different departments and at different levels within an organisation.

Grapevine: This is the unstructured or the informal communication network that exists within an organisation and has its own set of advantages and disadvantages.

EXERCISES

1. Define the term 'organisation'.
2. Explain the concept of organisational communication?
3. Explain the purpose and functions of communication within an organisation.
4. What are the various communication networks prevalent in an organisation?
5. Explain the various factors that determine effective organisational communication.
6. How can communication within an organisation be made more effective?

REFERENCES

Aggarwal, R., *Communication Today and Tomorrow*, Jaipur: Sublime Publications, 2000.

Baird, J. E., Jr, 'Some Nonverbal Elements of Leadership Emergence', *Southern Speech Communication Journal* 42 (1977): 352–61 as cited in S. M. Ketrow, 'Communication Role Specializations and Perceptions of Leadership', *Small Group Research* 22 (November 1991): 492–514.

Barker, Larry L., *Communication*, fifth edition, New Jersey: Prentice-Hall, 1990.

Barnard, C., *The Functions of the Executive*, Harvard: Harvard University Press, 1938, as cited in S. S. Khanka, *Organizational Behavior: Text and Cases*, fourth revised edition, New Delhi: S. Chand and Company Ltd, 2007.

Eisenberg, E. M., H. L. Goodall and A. Trethewey, *Organizational Communication: Balancing Creativity and Constraint*, fifth edition, Boston: Bedford/St. Martin's, 2007.

Fielder, 'Die Fuehrung den Arbeitswillen (Management Determines Will to Work)', *fortshrittlich Betriesfuehrung and Industrial Engineering*, 30 (1981): 4.

Goldhaber, G., *Organisational Communication*, fifth edition, Dubuque: Wm. C. Brown, 1990.

Hybels, S. and H. R. Weaver, *Communicate Effectively*, sixth edition, Boston: McGraw-Hill, 2001.

Jothi, S. S., *Human Research Management in Co-operative Sector: A Study on Selected Units in Visakapattinam District*, New Delhi: Inter India Publication, 1986.

Khanka, S. S., *Organizational Behavior: Text and Cases*, fourth revised edition, New Delhi: S. Chand and Company Ltd, 2007.

Koontz, H., *Management: A Global Perspective*, tenth edition, New York: McGraw-Hill, 2001.

Kumar, P. and K. S. Thakur, *Textbook of Organisational Behavior*, Delhi: Academic Excellence, 2008.

LaFasto, M. J. F., and C. Larson, *When Teams Work Best: 6,000 Team Members and Leaders Tell What it Takes to Succeed*, California: Sage, 2001.

Locke, E. A., 'The Nature and Causes of Job Satisfaction' in *Handbook of Industrial and Organizational Psychology*, edited by M. D. Dunnette, 1297–349. Chicago: Rand McNally, 1976.

Miller, K., *Organizational Communication: Approaches and Processes*, Belmont, CA: Wadsworth, 2003.

Zeuschner, Raymond F., *Communicating Today: The Essentials*, New Jersey: Pearson, 2002.

ONLINE SOURCE

http://web.mit.edu/allanmc/www/mcluhan.mediummessage.pdf (accessed 10 April 2015)

UNIT IV

COMMUNICATING WITH THE MASSES

This unit is dedicated to understanding human communication at the highest levels in the hierarchy of communication transactions—public communication and mass communication. These communications involve a large group of audience. The first chapter of the unit begins with a description of the personal, professional and public benefits of learning about public speaking. We get familiar with the basic concepts of public communication and examine the process of public speaking. The next three chapters define mass communication, media, society and the culture and explore the relationships among them and how they define us and our world. We delve into how mass communication works, how it changes when technology is introduced into the process, and how differing views of communication and mass communication can lead to different interpretations of their power. These chapters deal with the process, nature, and elements of mass communication. The goals and the effects of mass communication are also outlined. We also discuss the changing nature of contemporary mass communication and its implications for both communication industries and consumers.

13

PUBLIC COMMUNICATION

HIGHLIGHTS

- Everyday public speaking
- Benefits of public communication
- Process of public speaking
- Models of public speaking
- Ethics in public speaking
- Apprehension in public speaking
- Developing public speeches and speech delivery
- Presentation aids and public speaking

Our ability to communicate using formalised systems of language sets us apart from other living creatures on the earth. We spend a lot of our time in formal and informal oral communication. The most successful and powerful people have mastered the ability to communicate effectively. Any kind of oral communication requires us to think, reflect and compose our thoughts choosing the right words, tone, pronunciation and body language. This is more so in formal communication situation where one needs to convince or persuade listeners to be receptive and accept our idea, product or service. Formal oral communication includes all forms of public speaking and interpersonal communication situations like interviews (face-to-face or telephonic), meetings, workshops, trainings, seminars, conferences, lectures, business presentations, speeches, etc.

Public speaking, also termed public communication or presentational speaking, is an essential level in the transaction of human communication (Wrench, Goding, et al. 2011). Through public communication, others inform and persuade us. And we in turn, inform and persuade others-to act, to buy, or to think in a particular way (DeVito 2012). The listeners may range in size from several people to hundreds, thousands and even millions. Public speaking is the process of designing and delivering a message to an audience. Effective public speaking involves understanding our audience and why we want to address them. It also involves choosing elements for the speech that engage our audience and delivering the message skilfully. Good public speakers understand that they must plan, organise and revise their material in order to develop an effective speech. In public speaking a speaker presents a relatively continuous message to a relatively large audience in a unique context.

According to Aristotle, 'The three important elements of speechmaking are—speaker, subject, and person addressed—it is the listener that determines the speech's objectives and end' (Beebe and Beebe 2005). Public speaking as a form of communication can be used for large groups of people. When one-on-one communication will not be an effective way to communicate our information, we use public speaking. It is generally believed that in public speaking, as in any form of communication, there are five basic elements, often expressed as '*who* is saying *what* to *whom* using what *medium* with what *effects*?' (Nikitina 2011). Good orators should be able to change the emotions of their listeners, not just limit themselves to merely informing them. Public speaking can be used in the fields of leadership and personal development, business, customer service, public relations, large group communication and mass communication.

Some people have the ability to effectively speak in front of others. It is true that natural talent does play a role in public speaking, however there is no evidence that suggests that only those who have a natural talent for public speaking can give effective presentations. This is a skill we can develop with practice, just as riding a motor cycle or mastering another language. Speaking effectively in public is something that can be learnt regardless of a person's innate talent. It is important to know that each element in the public speaking process depends on and interacts with all other elements. For instance, the way we organise a speech depends on factors such as the topic, the audience, our purpose and the time available. When we give a public speech we do most of the speaking and the listeners do most of the listening. The listeners also send messages in the form of feedback; for example, applause, bored looks, nods of agreement or disagreement and focused squints. The audience also impacts how we prepare and present our speech. It influences our arguments, language and method of organisation and in fact, every choice we make. For example, we would not present to an audience of women's groups a speech on saving money prepared for middle school students.

EVERYDAY PUBLIC SPEAKING

To help us further understand why public communication is important, we will first examine public speaking in everyday life.

Informative Speaking

One of the most common types of public speaking is informative speaking, i.e. to share one's knowledge of a subject with an audience. Reasons for making an informative speech vary widely and it has become a common part of numerous jobs and other everyday activities. You may have been asked to instruct a group of co-workers on how to use new software or present a report on your latest project to a group of managers; physicians lecturing about their areas of expertise to medical students, other physicians and patients; fire-fighters giving demonstrations on how to effectively control a fire.

Persuasive Speaking

A second common reason for speaking to an audience is to persuade others. In our everyday lives, we are often called on to convince, motivate or persuade others to change their beliefs, take an action or reconsider a decision. Convincing clients to purchase a company's products involves influencing other people through public speaking. For some people, such as elected officials, giving persuasive speeches is a crucial part of attaining and continuing career success. Other people make careers out of speaking to groups of people who pay to listen to them. Motivational authors and speakers, such as the Dalai Lama motivate people to do better in their lives.

Entertaining Speaking

Entertaining speaking involves an array of speaking occasions ranging from introductions to wedding toasts, to presenting and accepting awards. Entertaining speaking has been important since the time of the ancient Greeks; in fact, Aristotle identified epideictic speaking (speaking in a ceremonial context) as an important type of address. Anyone who has watched an awards show on television understands well that it requires preparation and practice to be effective. The rising popularity of comedy shows in India bears testimony to the effectiveness of entertaining speaking. There are professionals—from religious leaders to comedians—who make a living simply from delivering entertaining speeches.

BENEFITS OF PUBLIC SPEAKING

Oral communication skills have been skills that college graduates have found useful in their professional lives. It makes learning about public speaking worthwhile. Let's take a look at some of the personal benefits you'll get from public communication and from giving public speeches.

Personal Benefits

Developing Critical Thinking Skills

One of the very first benefits from public communication is an increased ability to think critically. Problem-solving is one of the many critical thinking skills that people engage in. For example, when preparing a persuasive speech, you'll have to think through real problems affecting your campus, community or the world and provide possible solutions to those problems. You'll also have to think about the positive and negative consequences of your solutions and then communicate your ideas to others. Being able to think through problems and analyse the potential costs and benefits of solutions is an essential part of critical thinking and public speaking aimed at persuading others. These skills will help one not only in public speaking but also throughout one's life.

Improving Verbal and Non-verbal Skills

Public communication helps you fine-tune verbal and non-verbal communication skills. The skill to make public speeches can be acquired by practising. When you prepare to speak publicly for the first time, having the opportunity to actively practice communication skills and receive professional feedback will help you become a better communicator. Enhancement of speech-making skills is also possible through short-term certificate courses.

Overcoming Fear of Public Speaking

An additional benefit is that it helps reduce fear of public speaking. Whether a person has spoken in public a lot or is just getting started, most people experience some anxiety when engaging in public speaking. One explanation for this anxiety is that people often have little exposure to public speaking.

Professional Benefits

We can all recognise a good public speaker as a person who has a special talent or ability to speak in front of others with ease in an engaging manner. It offers several benefits to enhance our professional prospects:

Employment Opportunities

In the workplace, we need to be able to clearly and concisely communicate with co-workers, clients and supervisors. Employers always look for candidates with five major skills and qualities—verbal communication skills, strong work ethics, teamwork skills, analytical skills and initiatives. Public speaking is related to verbal communication skills. As we acquire the skills of public speaking, we also develop and refine our general communication abilities such as developing a more effective communication style, giving and responding appropriately to criticism, improving listening skills and refining our interpersonal communication skills. Our verbal communication can be a great asset to forming a positive image about ourselves in the minds of others.

Increased Confidence

Knowing how to communicate effectively in interpersonal or group settings will increase our confidence in what we say. This will lead to better performance in job interviews, professional group presentations and meetings, and even casual conversations with our seniors, co-workers or peers.

Educational Benefits

Public speaking teaches us to develop a strong introduction, body and conclusion for a variety of speaking engagements. While we learn public speaking we also learn a wide variety of academic and career skills—conducting research, explaining complex concepts, organising a variety of messages, evaluating the validity of persuasive appeals, and supporting an argument with logical, emotional and ethical appeals.

Enhanced Personal and Social Abilities

Public speaking provides training in a variety of personal and social competencies. It enables us to manage our fear of communication situations in general and of public speaking in particular. As we master the skills of public speaking, we will grow in power, i.e. we will become more effective in influencing the thinking and behaviour of others. As organisational managers, political leaders, older siblings or members of any group, power enables us to empower others (DeVito 2012).

Leadership Skills

In the workplace public communication skills are increasingly essential if you have to be an effective leader. People always come to know us best through our communications skills. As we rise in the hierarchy, we will need leadership skills to enable ourselves to lead groups and teams in informative, problem-solving, decision-making and brainstorming sessions. No leader succeeds merely by possessing the best information. True leaders use that information to motivate and activate employees and followers.

THE PROCESS OF PUBLIC SPEAKING

Getting your message heard depends on three fundamental components—message, skill and passion. When what we are saying is clear and coherent, people are more likely to pay attention to us. When our message is vague or ambiguous, people will often stop paying attention to us. We may have very good ideas but if we do not possess basic public speaking skills, we are going to have great difficulty in getting anyone to listen to us (Wrench, Goding, et al. 2011).

Finally, if we want our message to be heard, we must communicate with passion. Passion is the extra spark that attracts people's attention and makes them want to listen to a message. We must believe in the message that we want to communicate. Only when we have an emotional connect and faith in our message, will we be able to communicate it passionately and convincingly.

Figure 13.1: Process of Public Speaking

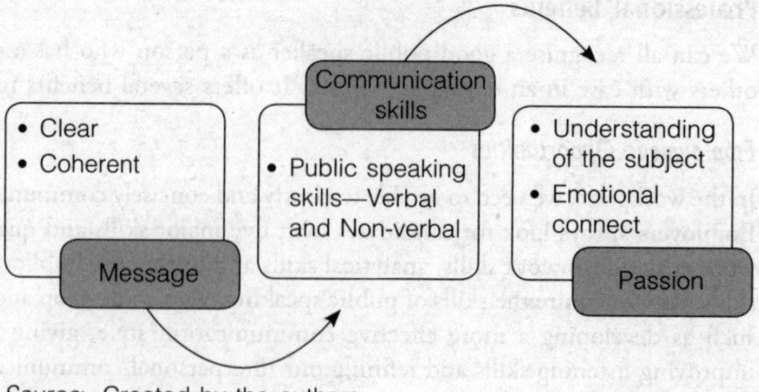

Source: Created by the authors.

MODELS OF PUBLIC SPEAKING

There are two models of public speaking that are widely discussed in communication—interactional model and transactional model.

Interactional Model

The interactional model of communication was developed by (Schramm 1954). Schramm identified encoding and decoding as two basic processes of communication. The encoding process involves preparing and delivering a speech. The decoding process involves sensing (for example, hearing or seeing), interpreting, evaluating and responding to the source's message. In public speaking decoding is done by the audience when they listen to the words of the speech, pay attention to non-verbal behaviours of the speaker and attend to any presentation aids that the speaker uses. Thus they are able to interpret what the speaker is saying.

Many problems can arise in the decoding process. A speaker's verbal message, non-verbal communication and mediated presentation can all make a message either clear or hard to understand. For example, use of new or technical terms, speaking too fast or too softly, or small print on presentation aids may make it difficult for the audience to understand what the speaker means. On the other hand, by providing simple definitions of technical terms, using well-timed gestures, or displaying charts and graphs of quantitative information, the speaker can help the audience interpret and understand the message.

The communication process becomes complete when a receiver responds to the speaker's message and encodes it suitably. This process is called feedback. According to Schramm there are three types of feedback—direct, moderately direct, and indirect. Direct feedback occurs when the receiver directly talks to the source during or after a speech, for instance, during a question-and-answer session. Moderately direct feedback focuses on non-verbal messages sent while a source is speaking, for instance, audience members smiling and nodding their heads in agreement or looking at their watches or mobile phones. Indirect feedback involves a greater time gap between the actual message and the receiver's feedback. For example, suppose you go door-to-door in a colony to inform the residents about a health check-up camp you are organising and you do not find many people participating in it on the day of the camp. Your audience (the residents you spoke to) have offered an indirect feedback on your message through their non-participation. One of the challenges public speakers face has to do with responding effectively to audience feedback, especially the direct and moderately direct forms.

Transactional Model

According to the interactional model individuals engage in the role of either source or receiver and the meaning of a message is sent from the source to the receiver. To address the weaknesses of the interactional model of communication, Barnlund (2008) proposed a transactional model of communication based on the premise that individuals send and receive messages simultaneously. The transactional model assumes that the meaning of a message is correlated by both people interacting by sharing a common field of experience. For meaning to occur, we must have some shared experiences with our audience. A common field of experience is created by the speaker and the audience sharing a common culture and socio-political environment. It is challenging to speak effectively to audiences with very different experiences from our own. We must build shared fields of experience so that we can assist audience members in interpreting our message.

Dialogic Theory

The dialogic theory is based on three main principles:

1. Dialogue is more natural than monologue.
2. Meanings are in people not words.
3. Contexts and social situations impact perceived meanings.

Often people think of public speaking as engaging in a monologue—the speaker stands and delivers information and the audience passively listens. However, we must understand that all communication including public speaking can be viewed as a dialogue between the speaker and audience (Arnett and Arneson 1999).

Let us understand the three principles related to dialogic theory of public speaking.

Dialogue is More Natural than Monologue

A speech should be a dialogue between a speaker and the audience. The speaker should endeavour to be attentive and actively engage the audience by asking questions and giving answers. Non-verbal behaviour of the audience (for example, fidgeting of feet or maintaining eye contact) function as feedback for speakers and makes the interaction two-way or reciprocal. This improves the quality of the communication process.

Meanings are in People, not Words

A speaker and audience may differ in how they see and understand the speech. It is not easy to predict how audience will interpret specific words. Yet, the speaker and the audience must mutually agree upon and share the meanings of words. For instance, the word 'food' may mean vegetarian food to one person and non-vegetarian food to another. Communication will only be successful if we know our audience well and choose a language that will be most appropriate for the context. For example, using an urbanised language when speaking to a rural audience would certainly act as a barrier and affect our ability to convey meanings clearly.

Contexts and Social Situations Impact Perceived Meanings

How we address people, the words we choose and how we deliver a speech is all dependent on different speaking contexts and social situations. There has to be a marked difference in the manner in which we address the different audience. This is necessary because the audience have different experiences, levels of knowledge and cultural backgrounds. A good public speaker takes into account the cultural background of her/his audience and tries to engage the audience in a dialogue from their perspective.

ETHICS IN PUBLIC COMMUNICATION

Speech is a powerful communication process and can be used to influence a large number of people simultaneously. Therefore, every public speaker should know how to use this power for the public good. A public speaker has the moral responsibility to be ethical at every stage of the speech-making process. Ethical public speaking requires knowledge, honesty, integrity, credibility and giving proper credit for all ideas and words that are not our own. Ethics deals with issues of what is right or wrong in our interactions. For example, Adolf Hitler and Osama bin Laden are examples of eloquent and persuasive speakers whose intentions were were considered unethical by many. Ethical public speakers are more important today than ever.

Speech is a powerful communication process and can be used to influence a large number of people simultaneously. Therefore, every public speaker should know how to use this power for public good.

APPREHENSION IN PUBLIC SPEAKING

You have already studied about communication apprehension in the chapter on small group communication. While preparing for a public speech people experience mild to severe apprehension due to several reasons. Several factors contribute to a speaker's apprehensions. By removing these factors or lessening their impact, we will be able to reduce our anxiety. These factors are described here.

New and different situations make one anxious. Therefore, gaining as much experience in public speaking as possible can make it less new and different will lessen one's anxiety. Rehearsing in the room in which one will give speech, or standing in the front of the room before the actual presentation, as if one was giving the speech will boost confidence. Thinking positively about oneself and preparing thoroughly also reduces anxiety. Visualising an audience as enlarged small groups also makes speakers more comfortable. Identifying the similarities between speaker and the listeners also helps speakers to see themselves as part of the audience and not as standing in front of strangers. Developing a positive attitude and a positive self-perception helps in overcoming apprehension. Visualising oneself in the role of being an effective public speaker helps in anticipating one's actions and audience reactions to the speech. Visualising oneself walking to the front of the room, fully and totally confident shall give one the confidence and feel in control of the situation. Seeing and analysing film clips of speeches made by effective public speakers helps speakers to model their performance on those speakers. This gives an opportunity to emulate competent speakers and develop self-confidence.

Systematic desensitising is a useful technique for dealing with a variety of fears including those involved in public speaking. In this technique the speaker creates a hierarchy of behaviours leading up to the desired but feared behaviour of, for example, giving a speech before a large audience. Speakers can take some small efforts to overcome their apprehensions. For instance, the speaker can begin by asking a question or giving an answer to a question in class. The speaker can also practice speaking in front of a group, class or introduce another speaker to the class. The speaker can finally give a small and simple speech in the class.

Achieving each small step will motivate the speaker to move to the next step above. Each successful step makes the next step easier to achieve. Imagining oneself successfully achieving each step enhances the self-confidence and reduces apprehension. Physical activity, gross bodily movements and movements of the hands, face and head before giving a speech eases apprehension. Using a visual aid temporarily diverts the audience's attention from the speaker and allows them to get rid of their excess energy. By breathing deeply a few times before getting up to speak, our body is relaxed. Our fear increases when we feel that the audience's expectations of us are very high. Therefore, we should maintain realistic expectations from our self as a speaker. We should compete with ourselves. We should aim that every speech we give is better than our previous one.

DEVELOPING A PUBLIC SPEECH AND SPEECH DELIVERY

Before beginning our preparation for a speech, we need to understand the context in which the speech will be delivered. We should be aware of the physical, temporal, social-psychological and cultural contexts in which the speech will be delivered. Each of these contexts is often a challenge to the speakers and affects their success.

Physical Context

The physical context of a speech includes the environment in which a speech will be given. A speech may be given in a small room in a school or a community centre, in a hall or in an open amphitheatre. Speakers generally do not have much control over the physical environment in which they will give a speech. However, they should familiarise themselves with the physical space in which the speech will be delivered. This will also determine whether they will need an audio-visual aid or mike system. The seating arrangement and location of the podium on stage, the kind of decoration within the room, lighting and temperature in the room, furniture, etc. will all affect the speech delivery process.

Temporal Context

The temporal context of a speech has to do with the time of the day, moment in history and the sequence of communication events in which a speech is made (DeVito 2009). An audience's attention and alertness varies according to the time of the day. Audience's are more attentive in the morning than in the evening or near lunch time. Sometimes, certain topics become more relevant to the audience, and during certain situations they pay attention to the speech. For instance, a speech on dengue management will be more relevant to audiences during monsoon season when the mosquitoes breed than during winters. Speakers must also consider the content of speeches made by speakers just before them so that they are aware of what has been spoken and do not repeat the same points or examples.

Socio-psychological Context

The social profile of the audience, their roles and interpersonal relationships with each other, their social norms, values and practices, psychological states, etc. all affect audience's participation and response to a speech. Speakers should try to know their audience in advance so that they can anticipate their response to the message given in the speech.

Cultural Context

When a speaker interacts with an audience from different cultural backgrounds, misunderstandings can sometimes occur due to differing cultural beliefs, norms and practices. A public speaker must try to understand the cultural makeup of their audience so that we can avoid misunderstandings or misconceptions. Speakers must try to create an environment of trust, mutual respect and understanding (DeVito 2009).

> **Activity**
>
> View a speech on TV or internet. Identify the strengths and weaknesses of the speaker's content and delivery style? What did you like about the speaker? What could the speaker do to improve? If you were to deliver the speech, how would you do things differently?

Developing Public Speeches

Preparing and developing public speeches can take eight steps. A speaker may or may not follow these steps in a sequence. However, all the steps are important and necessary. Speakers may go from one step to another or even to a previous step to review their speech building and delivery process. Following all the steps will help speakers deliver effective speeches and achieve their objectives.

Step 1: Select the Topic and Purpose of Speech

A suitable speech topic should be worthwhile and deal with matters of substance. It should be appropriate to the needs of the audience. It should be sensitive to the culture, environment and occasion in which the speech is given. The topics we select must be worth the time and attention of the audience. There are certain taboo topics and subjects in every culture. These should be avoided.

Step 2: Audience Analysis: Analyse Your Audience

Being aware of your audience is important when we select a topic and identify the objectives of our speech. Knowing our audience's needs, interests, previous knowledge and existing opinion about the subject of the speech helps adapt the message to their needs and sensibilities in ethical ways. The objective of a speaker is to be successful in persuading the audience. However, sometimes even if speakers are able to make the audience think with an open mind towards the message in their frame of reference rather than having a negative or positive attitude towards it, then also they can consider themselves successful. Public speakers should respect cultural differences and group affiliations of their audience.

The cultural backgrounds, ethnic ties and religious traditions of an audience may vary widely. A speaker needs to learn more about the backgrounds and attitudes of the audience. This will help in selecting a topic, defining a purpose and developing an outline of the speech. The audience can be analysed in terms of their demographic characteristics, psychological frame and their situational circumstances at a given point of time with reference to the speech. The demographic characteristics of an audience include characteristics like their age, gender, educational level, occupation, income, culture, ethnicity, race and religious views. One should also be careful of the language, illustration, humour and examples being used to avoid offending and alienating the audience. As far as possible we should make our language as inclusive as possible. We should also be mindful of using a sexist language and making assumptions based on demographic characteristics of the audience. It is very essential for public speakers to avoid an ethnocentric mindset, that is, assuming that their cultural approach is superior to the audience. Public speakers should never assume that their audience's ways of doing things is backward, inferior or ineffective in comparison to their own ways.

Step 3: Research Your Speech Topic

After we have decided the main idea or the central theme of our speech, we need to do some research to gather factual information on the topic. The information should be accurate, reliable and relevant. Information should be presented truthfully in an unbiased manner. This helps a speaker to be ethical and develop credibility. There are several sources and materials which can be referred to for developing a speech. Several printed (newspapers, books, magazines, journals and encyclopaedia) and digital sources (TV, radio, websites and blogs) can be used to gather information. Speakers can seek information through personal interviews, surveys and focus group discussions.

While writing our speech we must also be careful not to plagiarise. Plagiarism means to represent someone else's ideas and words as our own. We must give due credit to people and sources from where we write words and ideas by duly quoting them. This helps avoid copyright infringement and the resultant embarrassment on being called a copycat or thief of somebody's intellectual property.

Step 4: Formulate Your Thesis and Major Propositions

This step involves development of the main body or message of a speech. This is the most important part of a speech. This part of the speech can be substantiated by using a testimony in the form of a direct quote or a paraphrase of what was actually said or written. Testimonies help to develop, support and clarify ideas. They add depth to what is being said and build a holistic perspective on the topic of the speech. Testimonies can be sought from peers and professionals in the relevant subject or field.

Step 5: Construct the Introduction, Transition and Conclusion

The introduction sets the tone of a speech and also the speaker's goodwill with the audience. If we have not been formally introduced by someone, we must introduce ourselves to establish our credentials. This assists the audience to decide whether we are worthy of their attention and time. The introductory remarks also establish whether the speech is on a light-hearted topic or something serious. An introduction should be short and it should gain the audience's attention. It should be able to establish the relevance of our topic to the audience, and state the main theme and points. A good introduction establishes our credibility regarding our knowledge and experience regarding the topic of the speech. The introduction is usually about 10 per cent of the length of the entire speech. For example for a ten-minute speech, our introduction should be about one minute long. An effective introduction arouses curiosity within the audience and encourages them to continue listening to the speech. We can grab the attention of the audience by using interesting statements, questions, humour, anecdotes, quotations, stories and pictures in the introduction.

Step 6: Organise Your Speech

The next step is to make an outline of the speech in a sequence of sentences establishing relationships between the various points and subpoints, its introduction, conclusion and the list of references used. We can organise the main points of a speech in several ways. The main points may be presented in a sequential or chronological order, in a logical pattern giving a rationale for our main theme or message. The speech outline may also be written in a narrative format where there are stories, characters, settings/situations told in a dramatic manner using emotional appeals.

Step 7: Word Your Speech

For a speech to appeal to a diverse audience, it is imperative for the speaker to select words carefully. The idea is to sound credible, truthful, knowledgeable, passionate and confident. The words should be clear, unambiguous and non-offensive. Words with more than one meaning and technical jargons should be strictly avoided. The speaker can choose to speak in one or more languages in the same speech for better impact.

Step 8: Rehearse and Deliver Your Speech

A speech can be delivered in different styles. Based on the method or style of speech delivery, a speech can be classified into four types—impromptu, extemporaneous, manuscript and memorised.

1. *Impromptu*: An impromptu speech involves delivering a message on the spur of the moment without preparation. This kind of speech occurs when someone is asked to 'say a few words' or give a speech on a special event or occasion. Impromptu speeches are informal, spontaneous and conversational. They are usually short and focus on a single theme or idea and employ an engaging tone.
2. *Extemporaneous*: Extemporaneous speaking involves delivering a speech in a conversational manner using some notes consisting of keywords, paraphrases or sentences. Most public speeches are delivered in this style. They are carefully planned and well-rehearsed. They help the speaker maintain eye contact with the audience and clarify any doubts or queries. This kind of speech draws the attention of the audience and engages them verbally and non-verbally. Therefore, this style of speech delivery requires exhaustive preparation and rehearsal on the part of the speaker.
3. *Manuscript*: In this style of speech the speaker reads the entire speech word by word from a paper. The speaker repeats the exact words and is usually not able to make eye contact with the audience. This kind of speech is very precise and can be timed to the nearest second. This makes such speeches suitable for broadcast on radio or TV. However, speech given in this style can become very monotonous and boring. A speaker can use presentation aids like charts, presentations, films, audio recordings, etc. to sustain the interest of the audience. The speaker should also practice voice modulation and gestures to provide expression and emotion in the speech.
4. *Memorised*: This type of speech involves reciting a scripted speech from memory. Memorised speaking requires the recitation of a written message that the speaker memorises fully. It enables the speaker to move freely and use body language to maintain eye contact with the audience throughout the speech. This form of speech requires immense practice to appear natural and not sound unnatural. To be able to successfully deliver such a speech a speaker must plan and memorise the use of pitch, tone, volume, pace, pause, gestures and facial expressions. Else the speaker may end up making a monotonous and uninteresting speech with poor audience response. Sometimes the speaker can make the speech too informal, forget the exact words, may fumble or mix up or forget to emphasise key words. This spoils the effect of the speech. At other times, the speaker may be conscious or over dramatic and make the speech too formal and mechanical. Effective delivery, however, is conversational, that is, our audience

feels we are talking *with* them, not *at* them. Our speech shouldn't sound 'rehearsed', 'memorised', or 'read out', no matter how many times we have practiced it.

PRESENTATION AIDS AND PUBLIC SPEAKING

Presentation aids, especially the visual aids, are powerful tools that help audience to remember a speech while allowing speakers to engage, prove and reinforce their ideas. They help in delivery of the main message of a speech even more effectively. It is important to remember that visual aids do not replace good public speaking skills of a speaker. The speaker should carefully select visual aids to be used in a speech. A visual aid should have accurate content, be well designed and easy to use. Speakers should not assign too much attention to them and should not read verbatim from the visual aid, or else the speaker may be perceived as being less knowledgeable and credible. The aid should only highlight the keywords or main points. The speaker should be able to elaborate on the points suitably.

The visual aid should be checked before any speech for accuracy, sequential order, spelling or grammatical errors or missing parts. Speakers should duly rehearse the use of the aid prior to giving the speech so that the speech sounds fluent. Before using digital media as visual aids the speaker should check for availability of power supply, availability of appropriate technology to get display and audio output, and other compatibility issues. We must remember to use the visual aid only as a support material and not a substitute for our well-planned and rehearsed speech. A speaker should have backup plans available just in case the visual aid does not work properly or there is a technical failure. Having the main prints of a speech written on a paper or a printout of our computer presentation can be very useful for successful speech delivery. Some guidelines for preparing and using visual aids are listed below.

Guidelines for Preparing Presentation Aids

- Select the right presentation aids
- Adapt to your audience
- Be aware of your specific purpose
- Consider your own skill and experience
- Take into account the room in which you will speak
- Make your presentation aids easy to see and use
- Keep your presentation aids simple

Guidelines for Using Presentation Aids

- Rehearse with your presentation aids
- Maintain eye contact with your audience, not your presentation aids
- Explain your presentation aids
- Time your presentation aids to coincide with your discussion of them
- Do not pass objects or visual aids or other small items among a large audience
- Use handouts effectively

We all need to acquire the art of public speaking. Public speaking is not just talking or saying anything in our mind in front of a large audience. It is a formal process that requires meticulous search, planning, rehearsing and delivery of content. It also requires the speaker to be skilled at both verbal and non-verbal communication.

Good public speakers can not only sensitise and inform the audience about an issue but also persuade them to action in a direction desired by them. Public speaking can be used to influence a large number of people within a short span of time. Thus, it requires a speaker to be knowledgeable, credible and ethical.

SUMMARY

- Public speaking is the process and act of speaking or giving a lecture to a group of people in a structured, deliberate manner intended to inform, influence or entertain an audience. Generally public speaking is used to inform and persuade the audience.
- The three important benefits of public speaking are developing critical thinking skills, verbal and non-verbal communication skills and overcoming fear of public speaking.
- Public speaking depends on three fundamental components—message, skill, and passion.
- The dialogic theory of public speaking is based on three main principles—dialogue is more natural than a monologue, meanings are in people not words, contexts and social situations impact perceived meanings.
- There are four styles of speech delivery—impromptu, extemporaneous, manuscript and memorised.

KEY WORDS

Public speaking: The act of delivering a speech in front of a live and usually large audience.

Impromptu speaking: An impromptu speech involves delivering a message on the spur of the moment without advance preparation.

Extemporaneous speaking: Extemporaneous speaking involves delivering a speech in a conversational manner using some notes consisting of keywords, phrases or sentences.

Manuscript speaking: In this style of speech the speaker reads the entire speech word by word from a paper. The speaker repeats the exact words and usually will not be able to make an eye contact with the audience.

Memorised speaking: This type of speech involves reciting a scripted speech from memory that is without any notes. Memorised speaking requires rote recitation of a written message that the speaker memorises fully.

EXERCISES

1. Identify the three components of getting your message across to an audience.
2. Describe the ways to overcome speaker's apprehension in public speaking.
3. Explain the three principles discussed in the dialogical theory of public speaking.

REFERENCES

Arnett, R. C. and P. Arneson, *Dialogic Civility in a Cynical Age: Community, Hope, and Interpersonal Relationships*, Albany, NY: SUNY Press, 1999.

Barnlund, D. C., 'A Transactional Model of Communication' in *Communication Theory*, second edition, edited by C. D. Mortensen, 47–57. New Brunswick, NJ: Transaction, 2008.

Beebe, S. A. and S. J. Beebe, *Public Speaking Handbook*, Boston, MA: Allyn & Bacon and Pearson, 2005.

DeVito, Joseph. A. *Human Communication: The Basic Course*, New York: Pearson, 2012.

———, *The Interpersonal Communication Book*, twelfth edition, Boston, MA: Allyn & Bacon, 2009.

Morreale, S. P. and J. C. Pearson, 'Why Communication Education is Important: The Centrality of the Discipline in the 21st century', *Communication Education* 57 (April 2008): 224–40.

Nikitina, A., *Successful Public Speaking*, Denmark: Ventus Publishing, 2011.

Schramm, W., 'How Communication Works' in *The Process and Effects of Communication*, edited by W. Schramm, 3–26, Urbana, IL: University of Illinois Press, 1954.

Wrench Jason S., Anne Goding, Danette Ifert Johnson and Bernardo A. Attias, *Stand Up, Speak Out: The Practice and Ethics of Public Speaking* 1, New York: Pearson, 2011.

14

MASS COMMUNICATION

HIGHLIGHTS

- Key aspects and definitions
- Elements of mass communication
- Mass communication as the fourth estate
- Effects of mass communication
- Functions of mass communication

KEY ASPECTS AND DEFINITIONS

Mass communication is a term which comes from the combination of two words—'mass' and 'communication'—meaning communicating to the masses. This term can be used to explain the process of disseminating information to large segments of the population, simultaneously with the help of mass media. Stanley Baran (2002) defines mass communication as the process of creating shared meaning between the mass media and their audience. Similarly, R. Bitner (1989) also defines mass communication as messages communicated through a mass medium to a large number of people. Mass communication can also be defined as a process by which a group of people working together transmit information to a large heterogeneous and anonymous audience simultaneously.

Key to the concept of mass communication is sending multiple sets of information to the large masses at the same time. The 'heterogeneous' characteristics of mass communication audience makes them imperative in nature because the audience are the masses formed by the individuals coming from different backgrounds, class, castes and religions. They are also 'anonymous' as they do not know each other. The sender/source and the receiver of a message in mass communication have no physical contact, nor do they know the individual members of the masses and therefore are not united.

Features of Mass Communication

Since mass communication is about communicating with large masses of population, therefore, there is a need to use a medium or several media to reach the audiences. It also necessitates the presence of some kind of mediators to connect with the audiences and to regulate the information being sent out. Let us discuss some of the characteristic features of mass communication here.

Features of mass communication:

1. Mass medium
2. Presence of gatekeepers
3. Delayed feedback
4. Limited sensory channels
5. Impersonal *vs* personal communication

Mass Medium

Mass communication is a mediated process and requires a potent medium for communication. Internet, radio, TV and newspapers are all examples of how mass media can reach out to a heterogeneous audience at the same time. In mass communication, the nature of the medium involved in the process defines the outreach and influence of mass communication. For example, the audiences of internet are going to be very different from those of radio, with the former being few, literate and resourceful as compared to radio audiences who can be a very large number, illiterate and resource-poor.

Presence of Gatekeepers

Gatekeepers have always existed in the process of mass communication. An interesting aspect of gatekeeper is that they are often present even when media is not involved. A gatekeeper can be an individual, a dyad, a small group or a large group organisation through which messages get passed from a source to the receiver. When various mass media are involved, the gatekeeper performs important functions within the mass communication system like screening, filtering, rejecting and selecting messages. This functioning of the gatekeepers permit the passage of messages through mass media and at times also stops the message. Thus, when a mass communication system is concerned with the broadcast, telecast or printing of a news item, the gatekeeper decides which news will or will not be aired or published. Since all the messages sent through mass communication are usually passed through the gatekeepers, there is usually no guarantee that what the receiver gets, is exactly what was originally sent by the source.

> The concept of gatekeeper was first coined by Kurt Lewin who described 'gatekeepers' as individuals or groups of persons who govern the travels of news items in the communication channels.

Any person or formally-organised group directly involved in relaying or transferring information from one individual to another through a mass medium can be referred to be a gatekeeper. A gatekeeper can exist in any form of organisation, either formal or informal. A gatekeeper can be a news editor in the newspaper office who edits one section of report from the original report, the censor board which deletes scene from the films before it goes to the audience or any government official who doesn't subscribe its audiences to the realities of its policies. Any individual who controls the processing of messages before being disseminated to the audiences through mass media can be considered as a gatekeeper. A gatekeeper performs three functions:

1. Limiting the information through editing before dissemination to the audiences.
2. Expanding the amount of information by injecting additional views or angles.
3. Reorganising or reinterpreting the information gathered before disseminating it.

Delayed Feedback

Mass communicators are usually subject to additional feedback in the form of criticism in other media, such as a TV critic writing a column in a newspaper (Baran 2002). Mass communication is a process of communication which has indirect and, at times, delayed feedback. A source or any government scheme having communicated a message regarding family planning through radio, TV or print either has to depend on indirect means like survey of audience reaction, census, letters and telephone calls from audience members or a review of the programme by columnists to know the reaction of audience.

Limited Sensory Channels

In the process of mass communication, only the two senses work—eyes and ears, as one can only either see the visual images and hear the voice of the speaker or see and hear both together. This process of mass communication limits the number of sensory channels from which audience can draw inferences unlike interpersonal communication, where the sender and receiver are in physical proximity to each other and have no limitation in the use of sensory channels. That is, there are limited sensory channels as compared to interpersonal communication where touch and other non-verbal messages can have a profound effect on the outcome.

Impersonal and Personal Communication

Mass communication is completely impersonal. As explained in the last feature about the limited sensory channels used in the process, participants in mass communication are usually strangers and, hence, messages are impersonal. We as receivers can appreciate a film or a show, but we can't personally call the director of a film or a show and tell her/him how we really felt for her/his production. Hence, mass communication lacks the feeling of proximity.

ELEMENTS OF MASS COMMUNICATION

Sources

We have understood the concept of 'source/sender' in the process of communication and that the source can be multiple people at times. However, in the process of mass communication, the end result or product is decided by 'many' people's efforts. For example, a newspaper—reporters gather news, writers draft editorials, a cartoonist draws an editorial cartoon, the advertising department lays out ads, editors lay out all these elements on a sample page, technicians transfer this page to a master, printers print the final paper, the finished copies are given to the delivery staff, and, of course, behind all this is the publisher who has the money to pay for a building, the press, staff, trucks, paper, ink and so on. This proves that the nature of mass communication is institutional as well as organisational. The new technological advent has further changed the mass communication situation drastically.

Encoding/Sending

The process of encoding in mass communication is always multistage. For example, a film producer has an idea and explains it to a screenwriter. The writer then produces a script. The script goes to a director, who translates it for the camera. Cinematographers capture the scenes. The raw film goes to an editor, who splices together the final version. The film is copied and sent to theatres where a projector displays it on the screen, and the audience watches it.

Decoding/Receiving

The messages in mass communication process are always public. Anyone who can access and afford the medium of media such as internet, newspaper or a TV set can receive the message. Mass communication is addressed 'to whomsoever it may concern', as the same message is sent to all the receivers. Termination of message is easiest in mass communication. The TV set or laptop or radio goes off at the click of a button and the newspaper can easily be put aside. And the sender or source cannot do much to prevent these sudden terminations of message by the decoder.

Audience

Herbert Blumer (1946) was the first to define the 'mass' formally as a new type of social formation in modern society, by contrasting it with other formations, especially the group, crowd and public. In the mass communication process, all its members don't know each other, are not aware of their common membership, don't share the same values, don't have a certain structure of relationships and above all don't interact to achieve some purpose. The crowd is much larger and restricted within observable boundaries in a particular space. But the audience remains this way temporarily and at times re-forms with the same composition. Audience possess certain identity and is an essential element in democratic politics within an open political system and often comprising of the better informed section of the population.

Feedback

The feedback in mass communication is typically one-way and in most instances, more difficult than in the interpersonal setting. But now the situation of delayed feedback is rapidly changing because of the technological facilities like internet. Newspapers have begun including email addresses of reporters to encourage readers' feedback that too immediate. Producers of TV shows scan websites, tweets and blogs to know the reaction to their telecasted episodes. People these days tweet about any newsworthy events they attend. However, still the institutional, systematic, large-scale feedback conducted by media research companies, such as the Audit Bureau of Circulations for newspapers and MRI for magazines, tend to be more delayed.

Noise

Noise in the mass communication setting can be semantic, environmental, or mechanical (as already discussed in Chapter Four) and when there is more than one machine involved in the process of mass communication, mechanical noise can be compounded. This creates a barrier in the mass communication act.

MASS COMMUNICATION AS THE FOURTH ESTATE

Mass media are everywhere and from the moment you get up in the morning till the time you go to bed, mass media are available to keep you well acquainted with the information, and they make sure you're entertained in every way. They also try to sell products to generate revenue for the manufacturers. The influence of mass communication in our lives is so profound and it is more so in urban areas and may be to a lesser extent in the rural and tribal regions.

More than any other cultural institution in the world, mass media influence our daily lives the most. The amount of time we spend on mass media today is way larger than any other thing. Information and entertainment are the main sources on which mass media thrive. They define our purchase decisions, voting behaviour and academic achievements. We are informed of the policies of our governments through newspapers and electronic media. Likewise, we people need mass media to express our needs, complaints and wishes to the authorities Because of this all-encompassing impact of the mass media, politicians, businessmen and government agencies depend on media to influence people. During the Indian parliamentary elections of 2014, we witnessed politicians spending millions of rupees on political campaigns through mass media. Business firms across the world spend a lot of money to market their products with the help of advertisements on mass media. Mass media is also considered as a tool by the political parties to get to the masses. Mass communication and the mass media have contributed immensely in strengthening democracies across the world. As Wilbur Schramm writes,

> By making one part of a country aware of other parts, people, arts, customs, and politics; by permitting the national leaders to talk to the people, and people to the leaders and to each other; by making possible a nation-wide dialogue on national policy; by keeping the national goals and national accomplishments always before the public—thus modern communication, widely used, can help weld together isolated communities, disparate subcultures, self-centered individuals and groups, and separate developments into a truly national development. (Schramm 1964).

EFFECTS OF MASS COMMUNICATION

How does mass communication play a key role in changing our way of life? It affects our lifestyles and ways of thinking? Are mass media's effects on today's society good? The effects of mass communication on society are explained in four specific ways by John Vivian (2002).

Lifestyle Effects

The role of socialising is very vital in today's society and mass communication plays an important role in this context. The access to the information through the channels of mass communication is very rapid and almost everywhere and the mass communication has significant role in initiating and changing the lifestyles of society.

Socialisation

The acculturation and socialisation process initiated by the mass media influence children, elders and the young alike. What the elders and siblings do, children copy and learn the values by listening and observing and this gradually expands to include the influence of mass media at large. Up to the early childhood socialisation, the mass media play a very modest role but their impact grows with age. With the changing times and technological advancements, children spend more time watching television than in any other activity except sleep. TV and the internet have replaced and displaced all the socialising influences in today's times.

> New shows on television like *Doremon*, *Umi Zumi* are giving more skills-based learning to children and *Gali Gali Sim Sim* came out as a show which imparted more information on the value of nutrition than parents. MTS India, the mobile network service provider, advertising campaign features a newborn who is familiar with technology and is exploiting the internet right from birth. The campaign sign off—'Born for the Internet'—is a reference to socialising effect and today's digital natives for whom the internet is a way of life.

Living Patterns

The lifestyles we follow in everyday life is both reflected and shaped up by the mass media. The mass communication and the lifestyle are very much knotted with each other. In the mid-1950s, the advent of TV in the developed nations took over the socialising role and keeping people up-to-date. TV kept people at home in the evening and influenced as well as persuaded them. Even the advertisement and campaigning of the products were also telecasted according to the audiences. The timings of the campaigning are also adjusted by the media companies to find and keep audiences updated with the latest. The programmes are scheduled as per the time with the audiences for example many radio and TV programmes are scheduled in the afternoon to be available when the homemakers are relatively free and same is for school-going children.

Intergenerational Eavesdropping

The internet revolution and TV—the advent of mass media—have diffused the boundaries among the generations of today's society. The impact of mass media has not let go even the social institutions. Topics such as sex which were considered taboo by parents in India a few years ago, even in urban homes, are being 'eavesdropped' by children, i.e. they learn it through mass media without having to talk about it.

Attitude Effects

Influencing Opinion

Mass media exposure affects people's choices and also influences them. Hence it's very important to understand the effect of mass media as a tool and the impact it has on the attitudes and behaviour. We all know that people adjust their thought process, opinions and attitudes, gradually at times and suddenly too. The media messages are very important in the processes of change. And political opinions and consumer buying power are also very much decided by the way the media presents the messages.

Role Models

Every individual is different and the way we perceive the media messages depends on our individual perceptions. Hence, the extent of mass media messages influence on individuals is very difficult to gauge and depends completely on the individual. As each individual is distinct and the access to the mass media messages decides the influence its messages have on them. The role models being considered especially with respect to the Hindi film industry in India are a good example of this. The media has maximum exposure to three units in Indian society—films, crickets and politics. People associated with these units influence the people mostly. Especially, young people groom themselves in conformity with the latest and popular styles of film actors or other role models. This imitation, called 'modelling', even includes speech mannerisms from whoever is considered to be 'stylish' at that moment. This is the biggest reason why Salman Khan was nominated as the Goodwill Ambassador from India for Rio Olympics 2016.

Stereotypes

Stereotypes are the other side of mass media and they flow naturally along with mass media. Stereotyping is a kind of shorthand that can facilitate communication. Working women are always portrayed as dressed in western outfits and this holds a generalisation about women, and housewives are always portrayed as decked up in sarees in the TV serials. In popular TV serials the women in negative characters are always shown as home wreckers with loud make-up, dress or mannerisms. These are a few typical Indian TV stereotypes.

Agenda-setting

Mass media set the agenda for political parties and issues. The mass media have been quiet about the significant social development initiatives that have been taking place in the country. The picture projected by the media is not always parallel to the real situation, as it lends legitimacy to events, individuals and issues according to its own perception. This brings to fore the agenda-setting role of media. For example, the coverage of the anti-corruption movement led by Anna Hazare is an example of the media agenda-setting and status conferral.

Cultural Effects

A collective name for all behaviour patterns socially acquired and socially communicated by means of symbols is known as culture. And communication has a large impact on the cultural behaviour of the society. Culture means the values, beliefs, social behaviour, material objects that form people's lives. The cultural impact of mass communication messages to large audiences is culturally unifying. Cultural values are passed from one generation to another through communication. Communication is at the core of the society in unifying with respect to the cultural values. Different people behave differently because they perceive and organise their cultural values differently. And mass communication is an important factor in shaping and reflecting contemporary values through the content they transmit to the people.

Behavioural Effects

Motivational Messages

The day we try a new chocolate, just after watching the advertisement proves the power of the mass media. The persuasion power to motivate peoples to go ahead and get going is unmatchable. Even the advent of religious channels in India depicts the impact mass media creates. The amount of religious spaces created by the mass media reflects the norms of the society. However, the effect of mass media is not equal for all and can also be short lived depending on the products. It all ends up on the individual perception and how the perception differs.

FUNCTIONS OF MASS COMMUNICATION

Mass communication can be a teacher and entertainer. Mass communication could be a potent force for mass enlightenment, supplementing and continuing new and old ideas and spreading information, exposing political corruption and also providing entertainment. Political and social reformers saw a positive potential and hailed mass communication for its educational and cultural benefits in making a contribution to progress. Mass communication is also feared for its disturbing influence. The potential for communication technology to promote enlightenment has been invoked once again in respect of the latest communication technologies, based on the computer and telecommunications. At the same time media have also been appreciated for its effort to preserve global peace and to solve environmental problems.

Thus, mass communication has come to stay in our lives as a permanent companion. It serves various purposes and has specific goals.

The functions of mass communication are:

1. Information
2. Education
3. Entertainment
4. Entertainment-education
5. Persuasion
6. Surveillance of the environment
7. Transmission of heritage
8. Interpretation of information
9. Prescription for conduct
10. Catalyst for development

Information Function

Mass media carry a lot of information which is essential for our day-to-day life. We know exam results, weather forecasts, current affairs, traffic regulations, last dates, precautions, government policies, etc. from mass media. The core of media's information function is performed by the media content called news. The place or time dedicated for news in a mass media is called a news hole. News is the most consumed item of any media. News can be defined as reports on things that people want or need to know. Information should be accurate, objective and complete. Biased or incomplete reports will keep the audience away from the media. Advertising is also mass media's information function since we get much useful information from classified advertisements.

Image 14.1: Media Showcases Violent Political Protest, Demonstration and International Terrorism

Source: 'Protests at India Gate' by Ramesh Lalwani (Flickr; CC BY 2.0).

Education Function

Information is different from education. Education is systematically organised information with predefined objectives. The primary sources of education in our society are schools or colleges. Media also perform the functions that educational institutions do. Media are lifelong educators for the society. They give us comprehensive knowledge of selected topics. Non-news content or news-based content like editorials, articles, columns in newspapers provide us with complete idea of a subject. Health magazines, IT magazines are also examples for education through media. More recently, mass media in India have started directly participating in our educational system by publishing and broadcasting the educational supplements for school-going children. Moreover, we also have a number of TV channels dedicated for mass education. Vyas Channel of Consortium of Educational

Communication under the University Grants Commission and Gyandarshan of Doordarshan are some such efforts.

Image 14.2: Media also Portrays Issue-based Programs

Source: 'Shahrukh Khan From The NDTV Greenathon at Yash Raj Studios' by BollywoodHungama (Wikimedia Commons; CC By 3.0).

Image 14.3: Aamir Khan's show Satyamev Jayate: Using TV as a Medium of Educating People on Serious Issues

Source: 'Secretary Clinton and Bollywood Star Aamir Khan' by Sandra Jacobs (Wikimedia Commons; CC0 Public Domain).

Entertainment Function

Irrespective of their type, mass media are wonderful entertainers. All media have entertainment content and the internet has the largest content compared to other media. Newspapers publish cartoons, comics, puzzles, special weekend supplements for amusing people. Movies are another big stock for entertainment.

Entertainment–Education

Entertainment-education is an approach in which social messages are incorporated into entertainment programmes. The strategy is to combine the efforts of a creative team that designs the storyline, incorporating socially informative messages, and an evaluation team that uses communication and behavioural theories to achieve and measure behavioural change. According to Bouman (1999), 'Entertainment-Education is the process of purposively designing and implementing a media message both to entertain and educate, in order to increase audience member's knowledge about an educational issue, create favorable attitudes, and change overt behavior.'

An actor in a radio or TV soap opera or a cartoon may serve as a role model who demonstrates the positive or negative consequences of her/his character's actions. A role model's greatest impact occurs when the audience identifies with the character and follows the character's positive example. People often want to emulate a role model's behaviour. By following a character through a storyline, a listener can be motivated to adopt prevention techniques, and can learn the importance of education, getting tested for STDs and so on.

Entertainment-education comes in many forms including serial dramas broadcast on TV and radio, cartoons, interactive 'talk' shows and folk media. It allows the audience to make decisions on their own without being preached to. Framing messages in a popular, entertaining format helps create an environment where people of all ages can carry on conversations about topics discussed in the latest episode of their favourite soap opera or cartoon. In some cases such as reproductive health, entertainment-education is used to legitimise sensitive topics for public discussion, giving people the positive reinforcement they need to talk about the issues with family and friends. Interpersonal communication becomes more feasible and acceptable, and positive learning and decision-making are more likely to follow. These programmes which use the 'talk show' format allow questions to be asked and talked about freely. They may inspire listeners to advocate for change, increase their knowledge or change their attitude towards a topic, and empower audiences to change their own behaviour.

Persuasion

Persuasion means influencing attitudes or opinions. Mass media have many ways to persuade people. Most people form opinions from the information they get from mass media. Media have direct and indirect methods for persuasion. For public opinion formation, mass media use editorials, news analysis and commentaries. In such cases, the purpose is clear and direct. The most obvious method of persuasion is advertising. Advertisements are direct methods to influence purchasing behaviour of the public. Some media report events hiding their vested interests in news. Such biased, subjective reports are for persuading people to form favourable attitudes towards them or their interests. Opinionated news is an indirect method of persuasion. It is against the ethics of responsible journalism. News and opinion should be given separately.

Image 14.4: Persuasion: Indian Parliamentary Elections 2014 Revolved Around the Persuasion Power of Three Men—Modi, Kejriwal and Rahul Gandhi

Source: 'PM Modi Portrait(cropped)' by Narendra Modi (Wikimedia Commons; CC BY SA 2.0); 'ArvindKejriwal2' by TY (Wikimedia Commons; CC BY SA 3.0); 'Rahul Gandhi in Ernakulam, Kerala' by Hibi Eden (Wikimedia Commons; CC BY SA 3.0).

Surveillance of the Environment

Mass media observe the society and its activities and report them to make people aware of their socio-cultural environment. In other words, we as social animals are always under the close observation of mass media. Media are our watchdogs. They always watch people indulging in good and bad deeds and report them to encourage or correct deeds. Reports about corruption are good examples considering this watchdog function of mass media.

Transmission of Heritage

Mass media are the bridges between our past and present. They report day-to-day affairs which will become history tomorrow. The best records of modern history are newspapers of the past.

Interpretation of Information

Mass media provide us with information from every nook and corner of the world. They do not just report facts and figures of the events, rather they interpret events to make us aware of what happens, and why, where, when and how it happens. Media interpretation may be biased or not. But, it helps develop our views towards an event or object or personality.

Image 14.5: Media Interpretation: The Interpretation by Media that Fair is Beautiful as Seen in Ads Aimed at Men

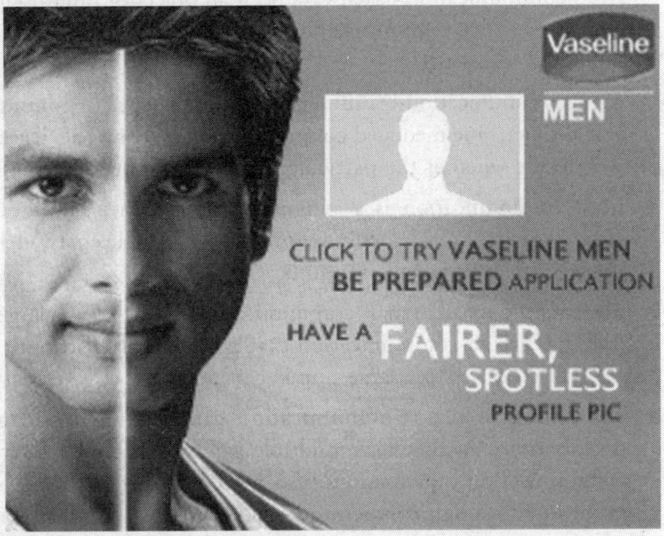

Source: 'Vaseline Ad' by Amit Agarwal (Flickr; CC BY 2.0).

Prescription for Conduct

How should we behave in a society? What is good for social life? As a member of a larger social system, we face these questions every now and then. In most cases, mass media provide us the answers. During election time, if we are confused about choosing a candidate, news coverage of policies and leaders of various parties may give us an insight that helps us take decisions. This is how media prescribe our political conduct.

Catalyst for Development

Image 14.6: Malala Yousafzai: Positive Portrayal of Issues by Media

Source: 'Remise du Prix Sakharov à Malala Yousafzai Strasbourg 20 novembre 2013 04' by Claude Truong-Ngoc (Wikimedia Commons; CC BY 3.0).

In a country like India, media's role in national development is highly important. Media's contributions to national development are mainly in two ways—as advocates for development and as the carriers of development messages. Mass media find out problems faced by people in different walks of their life and make the administrators aware of them. Most often, media report such events and further campaign to get the grievances redressed. On the other hand, media make people aware of their rights, government subsidies, development policies and the merits and demerits of adopting or practicing them for better life. This development-oriented function of media is termed as development communication. Development communication has been recognised as a special area in communication study and research. For example, 'Main Kuch Bhi Kar Sakti Hoon', a television show aired through Doordarshan, India on the weekend talks about the gender equality and empowerment.

SUMMARY

- Mass communication has always been an object of interdisciplinary study, but it is gaining greater degree of autonomy. Mass communication is directed towards a relatively large, heterogeneous audience. It is public, rapid and transient.
- Mass communication is different from other types of communication such as interpersonal communication and also machine mediated communication system. The degree of 'masses' involved in any particular situation will decide whether the particular communication process is mass communication or not.
- Mass communication is distinguished from other kinds of communication by a number of features or characteristics—mass medium, presence of gatekeepers, delayed feedback, limited sensory channels, and impersonal vs personal communication.
- The concept 'mass' in mass communication is defined as a large, heterogeneous, assorted, anonymous audience. The channels of communication that produce and distribute news, entertainment content, visuals and other cultural products to a large number of people.
- The nature of mass communication can be understood by considering them as complex and formal organisations. As they have multiple gatekeepers which filter the information reaching the audiences. Mass communication organisations also need a great deal of money to operate and completely exist to make a profit due to tough competition.
- Mass communication is considered to be a purposeful commodity. And it fulfills the functions of informing, creating awareness, educating, persuading and entertaining. Mass media carry a lot of information which are essential for our day-to-day life. Advertising is also mass media's information function.
- Mass media or communication through media has long-term cumulative effects. It impacts the society in four prominent ways, which range from lifestyle effects, attitudinal effects, behavioural effects, and cultural effects. All these effects impact the society with a cumulative force which leads to changes in the decision makings and the way of living.

KEY WORDS

Mass communication: Mass communication refers to the process by which a complex organisation with the aid of one or more machines produces and transmits public messages that are directed at large, heterogeneous and scattered audiences.

Audiences: Audiences generally are self-selected; people who tune in to a particular TV or who read a particular magazine. Mass audiences also are heterogeneous, meaning that they are both large and diverse. They actually are made up of groups of people with dissimilar background, demographics and socio-political characteristics; they are spread over a vast geographic area.

Gatekeepers: A gatekeeper is any person who has control over what material eventually reaches the public. Gatekeepers exist in large numbers in all mass communication organisations. This filtering processing is called gatekeeping.

One-to-many systems: This is the most common form of mass communication. In such a system, there is just one source but many receivers. The source in this system can be an individual, a dyad, a small group or a large group.

Many-to-one system: In the many-to-one system there is only one receiver and many sources.

Many-to-many system: In this system there can be number of sources and number of receivers. The process of news diffusion in India is one of the prominent examples of this system. All of the people, dyads, and groups within the society serve as the receivers and all the mass media (television, radio, newspaper, magazines, internet and so on) serve as sources.

EXERCISES

1. Explain the concept of 'mass communication' with examples and discuss its characteristics.
2. How does mass communication functions as a system?
3. With reference to the 2014 elections in India, discuss the growth and impact of mass media on elections in India.
4. 'Mass communication and society are two sides of the same coin.' Discuss this statement with reference to the effects of mass communication on the society.
5. Do you believe the media is solely responsible for children's violent behaviours? Why?

REFERENCES

Aggarwal, B. V. and S. V. Gupta, *Handbook of Journalism and Mass Communication*, New Delhi: Concept Publishing Company, 2001.

Baran, S. J. *Introduction to Mass Communication*, New York: McGraw-Hill, 2002.

Biagi, S., *Media Impact: An Introduction to Mass Media*, sixth edition, Belmont CA: Wadsworth, 2003.

Bitner, R., *Mass Communication: An Introduction*, New Jersey: Prentice-Hall, 1989.

Blumer, Herbet, 'Collective Behaviour' in *Outline of Sociology*, edited by A. M. Lee, 167, New York: Barnes & Noble, 1946.

Bouman, M. P. A., *The Turtle and the Peacock: Collaboration for Prosocial Change; The Entertainment-Education Strategy on Television*, The Netherlands: University of Wageningen, 1999.

Dominick, J. R., *The Dynamics of Mass Communication: Media in the Digital Age*, seventh edition, Boston: McGraw-Hill College, 2001.

Kumar, K., *Mass Communication in India*, New Delhi: Jaico Publishing House, 2000.

Mathur, P. and J. Yadav, *Issues in Mass Communication: The Basic Concepts*, New Delhi: Kanishkha Publishing House, 2008.

McQuail, D., *McQuail's Mass Communication Theory*, New Delhi: Vistaar Publications, 2004.

Sardesai, R., *The Election That Changed India*, available at www.internetlivestats.com/internet-users/india/ (accessed 15 March 2016), 2015.

Schramm, W., *The Process and Effects of Mass Communication*, Urbana, IL: University of Illinois Press, 1964.

Vivian, J., *The Media of Mass Communication*, sixth edition, Boston: Allyn & Bacon, 2002.

15

MODELS AND THEORIES OF MASS COMMUNICATION

HIGHLIGHTS

- Models of mass communication
- Paradigm shift in mass communication theories
- Theories of mass media and governance
- Mass communication in transition

In the last chapter we have discussed the concept of mass communication as a study of how individuals and entities transmit information through mass media to large segments of the population at the same time. Mass communication is usually understood with respect to the various mass media and how people relate to these mass media. And the sources of mass communication are the most important means of persuasion, framing public opinion, creating influence. The media contents have a direct impact on public opinion. Now the concept of mass communication needs to be understood through its evolution over the years and the proposed models and theories to understand the process of mass communication. In the earlier chapters we have studied about the models of human communication process, now we will understand more about the new models describing mass communication. Each model represents mass communication's distinctive features and helps us to understand the mass communication process. And the chapter explains the basic structures of the models and theories. The significant changes in the models and theories of mass communication with time are also being traced.

MODELS OF MASS COMMUNICATION

We have all studied in the earlier chapters about the models of human communication process. There is a need to construct new models when we talk about mass communication. So, there are different models that explain the process of mass communication. Each constructed model adequately represents Mass Communication's distinctive features and helps us to understand the Mass Communication process.

The One-Step Approach Model

In early analyses of mass communication, a simple speaker-audience model was used. One of the biggest limitations of this model was the analysis of the people's reactions towards the message because people react to media messages in a delayed manner. Due to this delay, people are affected not just by the message received but also by other sources around them. This observation led to the evolution of the one-step view to a more complex model known as the two-step flow of information and influence model.

Figure 15.1: The One-Step Approach Model

Source: Created by the authors.

The Two-Step Flow of Information and Influence Model

This concept was given by Paul Lazarfeld, Berelson and Gaudet (1948: 151). According to this model, the flow of communication to the individual is often directed through an opinion leader who plays a vital role in both spreading and interpreting the information. In highlighting the importance of the social context of the receiver in the process of interpretation of mass communication messages, this model differs significantly from earlier ones. It presents the mass audience as being composed of interacting and responsive individuals rather than of the socially isolated and passive atoms.

1. One-step approach model
2. Two-step flow of information and influence model
3. Multi-step approach or diffusion of innovation model
4. HUB model
5. Westley and MaCleans' model

According to Lazarfeld and his fellow researchers, communication flows in two directions—horizontal and vertical. Horizontally, opinion leaders are cultivated and the information is passed from the various mass media to certain opinion leaders and vertically message is passed on from these opinion leaders to the other people within the population. But before we start discussing this model, we need to understand the concept of 'opinion leaders'. Opinion leaders are the heart and soul of mass communication. Opinion leaders are similar in many dimensions but they tend to have more competence or information on any given topic than the general public. These people have major influence on the decisions and these opinion leaders may come from business, politics, religious, civic or community groups. They may also be employees of media organisations. If they are the opinion leaders, they are probably communicating their opinions through the media. A mass communication source initiates the process of communication by sending the message. The message could fall outside the realm of common experience for the ultimate receiver but fall into the realm of common experience for the opinion leader. For example, the first speech given by Narendra Modi in the Parliament was about the economic difficulties and crisis in the nation. As a citizen of India, every citizen was the target audience but not all could have understood given the varied educational levels and interest in understanding economic issues. Thus, a few people may turn into opinion leaders who translate or interpret some complex issues as per a common person's understanding. They may be part of the mass communication system in talk shows and debates on TV wherein the issues are discussed at length, or may be part of interpersonal communication systems like family, friends and neighbours.

'*Chai pe Charcha*', chat over tea at the bus stops, street corners, etc. in small towns and villages are examples of how opinion leaders influence the interpersonal communication systems and inform and influence general public. Hence, the impact of the mass communication process is felt not as a result of the message presented by the mass communication source, but as an effect of the interpersonal communication between the opinion leaders and their followers.

Like other models, two-step flow has its shortcomings too. It diminishes the direct influence of mass media on the audiences. This model isn't applicable in today's day and age where TV and internet are rampant as its effects are evident only in political studies that were conducted decades ago when there was no TV influence.

Figure 15.2: Two-Step Flow of Communication

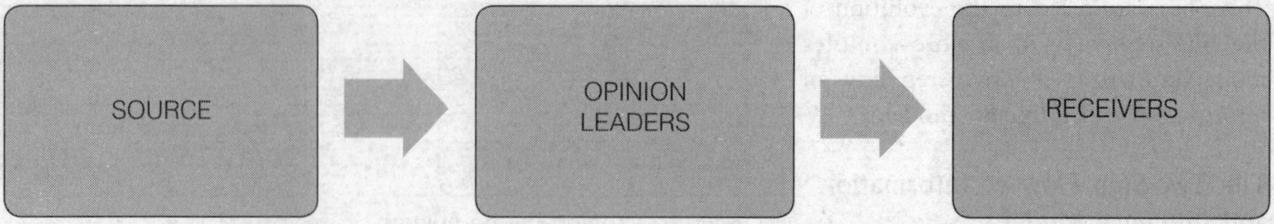

Source: Created by the authors.

Multi-Step Flow of Communication Model or Diffusion of Innovations Model

Diffusion research goes one step further than the two-step flow model. The original diffusion research was done as early as 1903 by the French sociologist Gabriel Tarde who plotted the original S-shaped diffusion curve. Tardes' 1903 S-shaped curve is of current importance because 'most innovations have an S-shaped rate of adoption' (Rogers 2003/1995: 221). Diffusion is the 'process by which an innovation is communicated through certain channels over a period of time among the members of a social system'. An innovation is 'an idea, practice, or object that is perceived to be new by an individual or other unit of adoption'. According to Rogers, 'Communication is a process in which participants create and share information with one another to reach a mutual understanding' (ibid.). So, the essence of communication lies in sharing but it may take many persons or processes to share information with a large mass of population.

Studying how innovation occurs, Rogers argued that it consists of four stages:

1. Invention
2. Diffusion (or communication) through the social system
3. Time
4. Consequences

Any innovation that goes through the right social system network at the right time, will have the positive consequences with respect to the acceptance of the innovation with the audiences/receivers. In other words, the information flows through networks. The nature of networks and the roles opinion leaders play in them determine the likelihood that the innovation will be adopted. Innovation diffusion research has attempted to explain the variables that influence how and why users adopt a new information medium, such as the internet.

In the multi-step model, there are five adopter categories which exist in the social system. They are—innovators, early adopters, early majority, late majority, and laggards. These categories follow a standard-deviation curve, very few people adopt the innovation

Figure 15.3: Model of Diffusion of Innovation

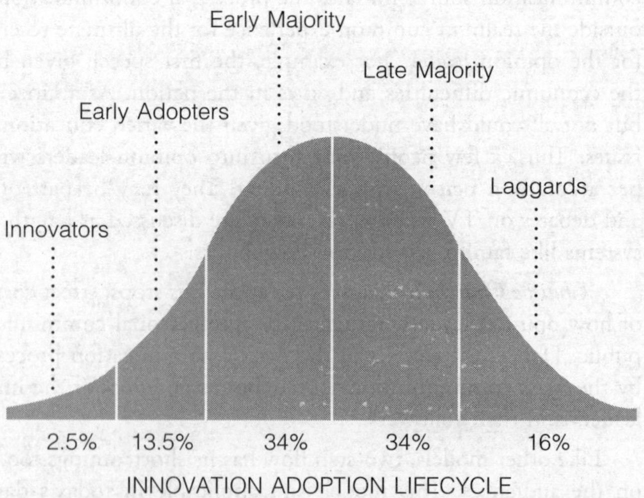

Source: 'Diffusion of Innovation' by Pnautilus (Wikimedia Commons; CC BY SA 3.0).

in the beginning (just about 2.5 per cent of all exposed to new idea or technology) and hence are called the innovators, early adopters make up about 13.5 per cent, they follow the innovators. Early adopters are followed by the early majority after some time and make up 34 per cent, the late majority also constitutes about 34 per cent of the population who take considerable time to make up their mind which could be because of several reasons like limited resources or limited perception about the new idea. These are followed by the Laggards who are again a few who resist change and constitute about 16 per cent.

HUB Model

Image 15.1: HUB Model Pictures Communication as a Process Similar to that of Dropping a Pebble into a Pool

Source: Image by bykst/2430 (pixabay; CC0 Public Domain).

It is the first model that visualises the process of mass communication to be interactive. The HUB (Hievert, Ungurait, Bohn) model describes the process as a set of concentric elements always involved in a series of actions and reactions. HUB model pictures communication as a process similar to that of dropping a pebble into a pool. This action causes ripples that expand outward until they reach the sides of the pool, and then a few bounce back towards the centre. The content of communication is like a pebble dropped into the pool of human affairs. Many factors affect that message as it ripples out to its audience and bounces back—such as the codes used to transmit the messages, the gatekeepers impacting the audiences, the mass media used, the regulators of mass media, the audiences, the effect of messages on the audiences and most importantly the content. These factors are the components of the total process of mass communication. The HUB model's rings also reflect the physical process of sound conduction and electronic transmission.

Westley and MacLean's Model

Bruce Westley and Malcolm MacLean's model (1957) is an extension of Theodore Newcomb's model (1953) and specifically adapted for the mass media. Newcomb's model treats an opinion statement or an issue as an R–N (communicator–information) relationship on the assumption that the R (communicator) and N (information) are systematically related to each other. And the information or opinion or issue attains full meaning only in the light of who expresses it and the image of the speaker is influenced by the nature of the opinion or issue. On similar lines, Westley and MacLean's model introduces a new element—'channel role'. This model has the following main elements:

N – events/information

R – communicator/reporter

E – medium/channel/gatekeeper

A – Receiver/audience

This model explains that messages in mass communication pass through different check points called 'gatekeeper' before they are actually received by the receiver. This model emphasises the role of gatekeepers within the media organisation. They decide on which messages are to be transmitted and which are not to be transmitted. How much information needs to be given to the audience and how the contents are to be modified.

Figure 15.4: Westley and MacLean's Model of Mass Communication

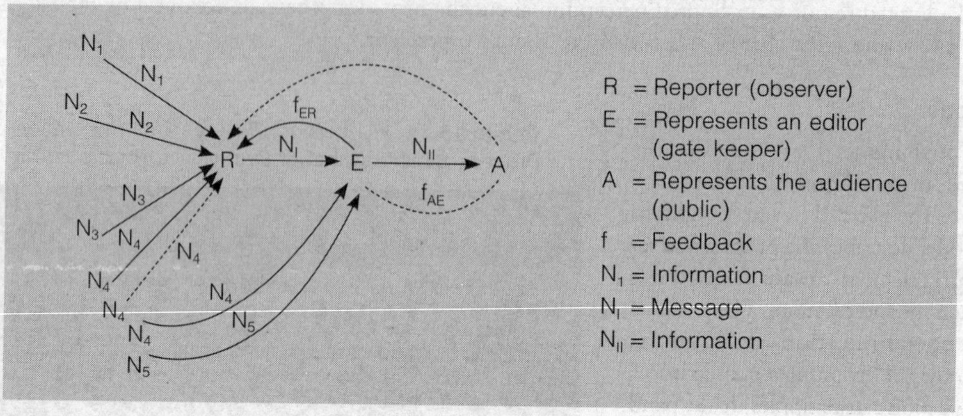

Source: Based on a concept by Westley and MacLean (1957).

Distinctive features of mass communication as per Westley and MacLean's model are:

1. The several stages at which selection/filtering (gatekeeping) takes place.
2. The self-regulating nature of the system, since a large number of E roles compete for A's.
3. The importance of feedback in the total process.
4. It does not portray the relationship of the communicators and audience members.

PARADIGM SHIFT IN MASS COMMUNICATION THEORIES

The paradigm shift in mass communication refers a transformation from one organising theoretical perspective to another, from one world view or groups of beliefs that researchers adopt to look at issues concerning mass communication to another. Thomas Kuhn in *The Structure of Scientific Revolution* (1962) argues that scientific advancement is not evolutionary, but rather is a series of peaceful interludes punctuated by intellectually violent revolutions, and in those revolutions one conceptual world view is replaced by another. Though paradigm shifts require rejection of one view of reality in favour of a radically new order, most of these theories are not entirely new but were built on existing ones. They are for the most part updated versions of old ones. Shift therefore occurs when it becomes increasingly difficult for one paradigm to answer all the questions posed by changes in society due to new technologies and increase in knowledge and understanding about the process of mass communication about the process of mass communication.

The paradigm shift in the history of mass communication is as follows:

Table 15.1: Paradigm Shift in the History of Mass Communication

Paradigm in Mass Communication	*Theories under the Paradigm*
The All Powerful Media Paradigm	1. Magic bullet theory 2. Propaganda theory

(*Table 15.1 contd.*)

(*Table 15.1 contd.*)

The Limited Effects Paradigm	1. Dissonance theory 2. Personal influence theory 3. The uses and gratifications theory
The Moderate Effects Paradigm	1. Agenda setting theory 2. Social learning theory 3. Play theory
The Powerful Media Paradigm	1. Public opinion theory/Spiral of silence theory 2. Dependency theory 3. Cultivation analysis theory 4. Individual differences theory

Source: Adapted from Dominick (2010).

The All Powerful Media Paradigm

This perspective was the dominant paradigm when print was the dominant medium; that is, around the nineteenth century. People believed that the media were all powerful and the messages were likened to a bullet released at an audience member; it had immediate and direct impact on the audience. The media were considered to have the power to profoundly shape people's perceptions of the social world and to manipulate their actions in subtle but highly effective ways.

This era was characterised by two dominant perspectives:

1. One argued for the positive effects of the all powerful media
2. Other branded effects of the all powerful media as negative

Scholars challenged this theory, arguing that it has no scientific basis, but they contended that no single theory could cover all media effects. The all powerful media theory eventually collapsed under its own weight (Baran and Davis 2000), ushering in the Limited Effects Paradigm.

Theories under the All Powerful Media paradigm are:

1. Magic bullet theory
2. Propaganda Theory

Magic Bullet Theory

This theory is considered to be a behaviour and attitudinal change theory. The mass media in the period between the 1930s and 1950s was perceived as having a powerful influence on people's behaviour. Several factors contributed to a strong effect of media use on this theory of communication which included the fast rise and popularisation of radio and TV, the emergence of the persuasion industries such as advertising and propaganda, and Hitler's monopolisation of the mass media during WWII to unify the German public behind the Nazi party.

Image 15.2: Media Theorists have Classified Orson Welles *War of the Worlds* Broadcast on 30 October 1938 as the Archetypal example of the Magic Bullet Theory

Source: 'War of the Worlds Radio Broadcast First Edition Record' by Mechanoid Dolly (flickr; CC BY SA 2.0).

This theory works by injecting the message directly into the 'bloodstream'

of the public, attempting to create a uniform thinking. It is also known as the hypodermic-syringe model and transmission-belt model. This theory suggests that media texts are closed and audiences are influenced in the same way. The Magic Bullet theory assumes that the media's message is a bullet fired from the 'media gun' into the viewer's 'head' (Berger 1995). It suggests that the media injects its messages straight into the passive audience. This passive audience is immediately affected by these messages. The public essentially cannot escape from the media's influence, and is therefore considered a 'sitting duck' (Croteau and Hoynes 1997). People end up thinking what they are told because there is no other source of information. Both models suggest that the public is vulnerable to the messages shot at them because of the limited communication tools and the studies of the media's effects on the masses at the time (Davis and Baron 1981).

Harold Lasswell's Propaganda Theory

Harold Lasswell is a prominent author in the area of propaganda research (1946, 1948). According to him, the way we humans behave brings up our conditioned response to external environmental stimuli. He was particularly interested in examining the effects of the media in creating public opinion within a democratic system. In *Democracy through Public Opinion* (1941), Lasswell examines the effects of propaganda on public opinion, and the effects of public opinion on democracy. Lasswell claims, 'Democratic government acts upon public opinion and public opinion acts openly upon government' (ibid.: 15). Lasswell rejected simplistic behaviourist notions about propaganda effects. He argued that propaganda was more than merely using media to tell a lie to people in order to gain temporary control over them. But people need to be slowly prepared to accept radically different ideas and actions coming towards them from the mass media.

Communicators or senders require a well-planned and developed strategy or long-term campaign in which new ideas and images are carefully introduced and then cultivated in the minds of the audiences. Symbols must be created and people must be gradually taught to associate specific emotions such as love or hate with these symbols. If these cultivation strategies are successful, they create what Lasswell referred to as master (or collective) symbols. Master symbols are associated with strong emotions and possess the power to stimulate beneficial large-scale mass action if they are used wisely, for example, the colour saffron signifies strong reactions in the Indian political circles.

Strengths of propaganda theory:

1. First systematic theory of mass communication
2. Focuses attention on why media might have powerful effects
3. Identifies personal, social, and cultural factors that can enhance media's power to have effects

Weaknesses of propaganda theory:

1. Underestimates the abilities of average people to evaluate messages
2. Overestimates the speed and range of media effects
3. Ignores personal, social and cultural factors that limit media effects

The Limited Effects Paradigm

This era is believed to have emerged in 1938 when actor-director Orsen Welles pulled a Halloween joke that creatures from Mars had invaded Earth. This made about one million Americans flee their homes. Some scholars thought that it was because of the all powerful media but Lazersfeld and his colleagues conducted a research which showed that, another 5 million Americans remained undisturbed. They were able to prove that the limitation was due to individual differences such as intelligence and educational levels, social categories such as religion and political affiliations and personal relationships such as friends and family. They argued that media were no longer feared as instruments of political oppression and manipulation because the public itself was viewed as very resistant to persuasion and extremist manipulation. This perspective dominated the 1950s, 1960s and 1970s, and its influence echoes even today.

> Some of the theories of the limited effects paradigm are:
>
> 1. Cognitive dissonance theory
> 2. Personal influence theory
> 3. The uses and gratifications theory

Cognitive Dissonance Theory

This theory was coined by L. A. Festinger in 1957. The theory predicts that people will seek out information which confirms existing attitudes and views of the world or reinforces other aspects of behaviour. Similarly, it predicts that people will avoid information which is likely to increase dissonance/conflict. If someone dislikes a person, (s)he will dislike her/his views, what (s)he says is unlikely to cause cognitive dissonance. Dissonance is acute when a liked person says something seemingly 'out of character' or is not as per the expectations or the image held of her/him.

> Cognitive dissonance is when you have two conflicting beliefs and you adjust one belief to fit the other belief.

Image 15.3: Some Believe that Eating Fast Food is Unhealthy. Yet, every week they would stop by McDonald's or KFC for a quick lunch. In order to get rid of this dissonance, one could do several things: deny ('These are healthy; they're made with real chicken.'), weigh positives and negatives ('I'd rather have fast food than go hungry.') or procrastinate ('I won't go to KFC next week.')

Source: 'Mcdonalds Gaisano Mall Butuan' by Historyadororoig (Wikimedia Commons; CC BY SA 3.0); 'HK KFC' by Terence Ong (Wikimedia Commons; CC BY SA 3.0).

The problem with this theory is that it makes people rationalise their mistakes, it takes away the sense of personal accountability and there is no way of measuring dissonance.

Personal Influence Theory

This theory is the outcome of a classic study of the 1940 presidential elections in the US. This study was conducted by Lazarsfeld, Berelson and Gaudel in 1948. They were interested in the general impact of mass media on voting behaviour and especially in the people who changed their voting intention during the course of the political campaign. Their findings were that broad coverage of the campaign by the mass media simply reinforced the initial preferences of the voters. It was only the personal influence or interpersonal relationships that changed the voting behaviour of the voters.

Researchers suggest that within the group to which we belong certain people have a particularly strong influence. These people have been called opinion leaders—'individuals who, through day-to-day personal contacts, influence others in matters of decisions and opinion formation' (Bandura, Jeffery and Wright 1974). These opinion leaders can come from any social, economic or occupational level. It was this discovery that generated a two-step flow of communication model as has been explained in the earlier section for example, the political campaigning during the Indian general elections of 2014. Followers of Baba Ramdev voted for Narendra Modi as Baba Ramdev himself canvassed for Modi. The followers of Baba Ramdev did not go for any further persuasion from any other source except from their own opinion leader.

Uses and Gratification Theory

Uses and gratifications theory states that the audience members choose the programmes that they feel gratified by, and discard or avoid other content in media. For example, the hourly sale advertisements we receive on our mobile phones from online retailers like Flipkart, Amazon and Snapdeal. We as receivers may at times be gratified by the message (if we were waiting for a sale) and go for immediate shopping during the sale hour and at times completely ignore the message. This theory has emerged out of the studies which shifted their focus from what 'the media do to the people' to what 'people do with the media' (Katz 1959). The uses approach assumes that audiences are active and willing to expose themselves to media and that the most potent of mass media content cannot influence an individual who has 'no use' for it in the environment in which (s)he lives. The uses of mass media are dependent on perception, selectivity and previously-held values, beliefs and interests of the people. The term 'gratification' refers to the rewards and satisfaction experienced by audiences after the use of media. It helps explain motivations behind media use and habits of media use or the actual need satisfaction by the media. In a nutshell, this theory deals with individual functions and dysfunctions views that mass media audience make active use of what the media have to offer arising from a complex set of needs which the media gratify.

Moderate Effects Paradigm

When TV joined radio, everything changed because everyone has almost equal opportunity to consume media content first-hand and the 'no effect' verdict was revisited. This attitude gave rise to the moderate effects paradigm.

> Some of the theories of moderate effects paradigm are:
>
> 1. Agenda setting theory
> 2. Social learning theory
> 3. Play theory

Agenda Setting Theory

The study carried by Maxwell McCombs and Donald Shaw on the 1968 on the American Presidential elections showed that the media were quite powerful in setting the agenda for the public. This led to the development of the agenda setting theory which positions that the mass media predetermine what issues are regarded as important at any given time. An agenda is a selection of items arranged to give some items more importance than others. This theory says that the news media present the public net with of the world as it is but with an agenda of their own—a selection of reports about what is happening in the world.

> Some of the theories of the powerful media paradigm:
>
> 1. Public opinion theory/Spiral of silence theory
> 2. Dependency theory
> 3. Cultivation analysis theory
> 4. Individual differences theory

Agenda theorists try to describe and explain:

1. how the stories are selected, packaged and presented a process known as gate keeping,
2. the resulting agenda, and

3. how this agenda affects what people think about the relative importance of the issues presented.

The theory also 'predicts' that if a particular news item is presented prominently and frequently by the press, the public will come to believe that it is important. Jeffers (1997) and Folarin (2003) say that the 'Agenda Setting Theory' does not ascribe to the media the power to determine 'what people actually think', but it does ascribe to them the power to determine 'what to think about'. A host of research studies of newspapers, TV and other news sources have confirmed that our personal agendas are indeed set in this manner. McCombs and Shaw (1972) found substantial correlation between the agendas set by the media and the public's beliefs about the importance of the issues. It was found that audience had different sets of beliefs depending on their social categories. That is, young people's receptions of the important issues differed from other people and men's patterns were different from women's. Differences in attention to issues and evaluations of their importance also varied among people with different income levels and different political preferences. But the authors did find strong support for the agenda setting theory.

Image 15.4: Modi in Media: Agenda-Setting is an Important Influence on our Political Process

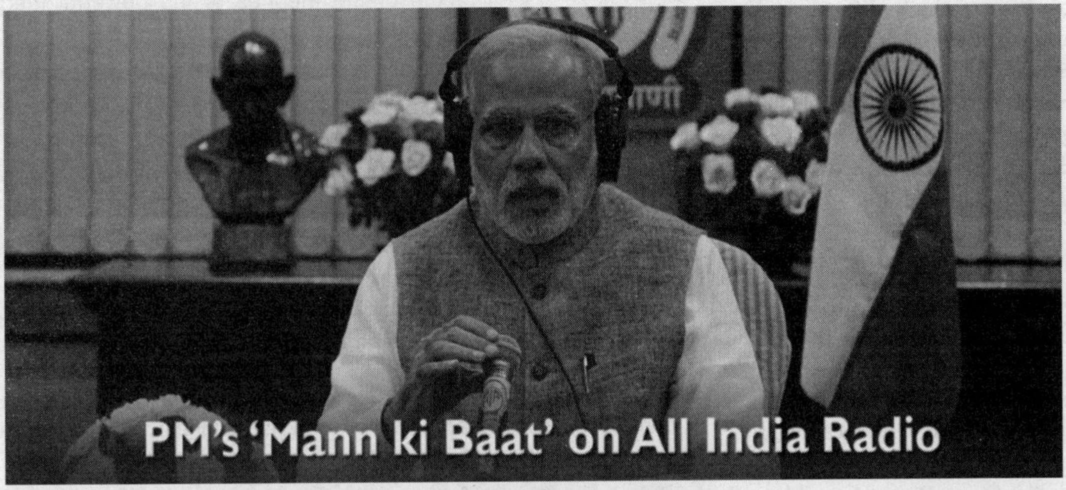

Source: 'Prime Minister Narendra Modi during his "Mann ki Baat" on All India Radio' (Wikimedia Commons; CC BY SA 2.0).

At the same time, the researchers concluded that the influence of the media's agenda must be interpreted in long-range terms and depends on social categories, changing patterns of media use and frequency of media exposure. Generally then, agenda-setting appears to be one indirect way in which the media can change society over a long period of time.

Social Learning Theory

It is one of the most widely used theories in mass communication. According to this theory given by Albert Bandura in 1977, the media are active but subtle educators in teaching readers, viewers and listeners about the world. Due to audiences, frequent exposure to TV, the medium is deemed capable of teaching viewers a number of both positive and negative social behaviours and attitudes that they might not personally come into contact with. An important component of this theory is that it explains how people can learn from observations alone. The Swachch Bharat Abhiyan launched by the Indian Prime Minister Narendra Modi is an example of social learning theory as the Government of India is expecting people to learn from the observations in mass media about the issue and also from the social system in which they live.

Play Theory

This theory of mass communication was developed by William Stephenson (1987) who counters those who speak of the harmful effects of the mass media by arguing that first and foremost the media serve audiences as play experiences. Even newspapers are read for pleasure rather than information and enlightenment. He sees media as a buffer against conditions which would otherwise be anxiety producing. The media provide communication pleasure. Stephenson argues that what is most required by people within a national culture is something for everyone to talk about. For him mass communication should serve two purposes—it should suggest how to maximise the communication-pleasure in the world and indicate how far autonomy for the individual can be achieved in spite of the weight of social controls against him. It is this theory which created the nomenclature of 'infotainment' in the Indian TV news channels history. As the Indian TV news channels are promoting themselves as the agents of providing the information/news along with the entertainment.

The Powerful Media Paradigm

With the birth of TV and new technologies it has become increasingly difficult to ignore the media and their increasing influence especially in the areas of socialisation, perception of social reality and knowledge of public and political issues due to agenda setting by the mass media, acquisition of cognitive and motor skills, and satisfaction of individual needs for entertainment diversion (Baran 2006).

Some of the theories of the powerful media paradigm:

1. Public opinion theory/Spiral of silence theory
2. Dependency theory
3. Cultivation analysis theory
4. Individual differences theory

Public Opinion Research Theory

Walter Lippmann says our individual opinions can differ from those that are expressed in the outside world. He develops the idea of propaganda, claiming that 'In order to conduct propaganda, there must be some barrier between the public and the event'. With this separation, there is the ability of the media to manipulate events or present limited information to the public. This information may not match the public's perception of the event. In this way Lippmann (1922) showed how individuals use tools such as stereotypes to form their opinions.

Lippmann argues 'the way we see things is a combination of what is there and of what we are expected to find'. In order to make intelligent decisions about public affairs and politics, knowledge of the subject matter is necessary, but 'few can be expert'. Noelle-Neumann (1973) presented the power of the media in her article

Image 15.5: Conflict Over Child Vaccinations: There are numerous conspiracy theories around the world that suggest vaccines are a western conspiracy to sterilise Muslims

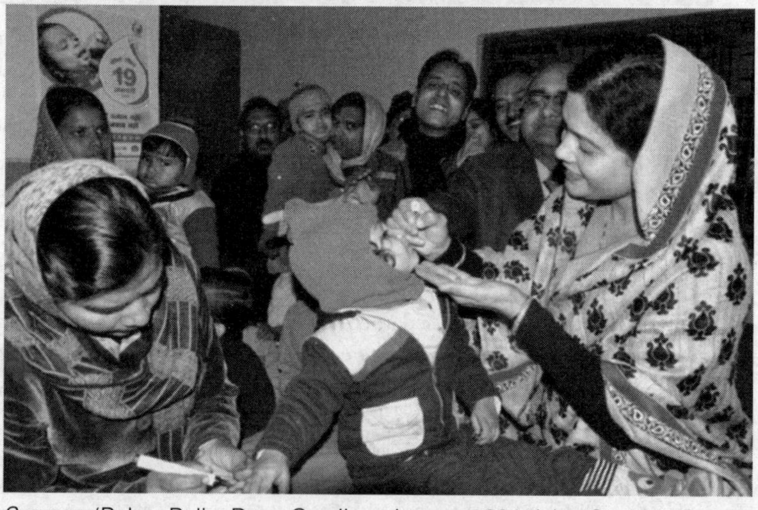

Source: 'Pulse Polio Day, Gwalior, January 2014' by Shobhit Gosain (Wikimedia Commons; CC BY SA 3.0).

'Return to the concept of Mass media' and her spiral of silence theory. Spiral of science theory is a public opinion theory which positions that the mass media are the most readily available sources for assessing the prevailing public opinion climate and whatever view predominates in the media will tend to be magnified in the subsequent stages of personal opinion formation and expression. Neuman argues that truly certain parts of the society can make their opinion known and thus have greater influence over public policy, consequently, the news media are a prominent source of information about public opinion and even a formulator are quite powerful. The phrase 'spiral of silence' actually refers to how people tend to remain silent when they feel that their views are in the minority. The model is based on three premises:

1. People have a 'quasi-statistical organ', a sixth-sense if you will, which allows them to know the prevailing public opinion, even without access to polls,
2. People have a fear of isolation and know what behaviours will increase their likelihood of being socially isolated,
3. People are reticent to express their minority views, primarily out of fear of being isolated.

Dependency Theory

This theory relates to the degree to which audiences are dependent upon the mass media. S. J. Ball-Rokeach and Melvin De Fleur (1976, 1989) believe 'the potential for mass media messages to achieve a broad range of cognitive and behavioral effects will be increased when media systems serve many unique and central information systems.' The fewer the sources of information in a media world, the more likely the media will affect our minds and thoughts, our attitudes and how we behave. Further, that influence will have increased potential 'when there is a high degree of structural instability in the society due to conflict and change.'

However, just as the audience may be changed by information/messages it receives, in turn the media systems themselves are changed according to audience response. In the words of De Fleur and Rokeach, both the media and their audiences are integral parts of the society. At critical decision-making times such as elections, people become increasingly dependent on the media, especially TV, for election information and guidance. Rokeach and De Fleur argue that the greater the uncertainty in society, the less clear are people's frame of reference, consequently there is greater audience dependence on media communication.

Image 15.6: Cultivation Theory Examines TV's Cumulative Effects on Human Attitudes and Behaviour

Source: 'Brij Kothari speaking to group' by Howcheng (Wikimedia Commons; CC BY SA 3.0).

Cultivation Theory

> The cultivation hypothesis states that the more television people watch, the more likely they are to hold a view of reality that is closer to television's depiction of reality. (Zaharopoulos 2001)

People in society conceive certain social realities through their exposure to the mass media, especially the TV.

Cultivation theory tries to explain this influence of TV on people's conceptions of social reality and the extent of exposure to TV and its impact.

> Cultivation, as defined by Gerbner, is concerned with the cumulative pattern communicated by television over a long period of exposure rather than any particular content or specific effect. Among the questions this research seeks to answer is whether such effects are visible in a smaller community and whether there are similar effects among heavy newspaper readers. Many of the cultivation's theories claim about heavy media use and its relationship to feelings of fear are connected to the tenets of a public health model of reporting crime and violence. (Chang and Reber 2000)

After conducting several research projects on the effects of TV on viewers, cultivation theory was founded by George Gerbner in 1976 as he compared TV's socialising force to that of religion, claiming that it defines social roles, standardises behaviour and homogenises communities much like religion did in early human history.

Assumptions: Cultivation theory has the following assumptions:

1. Because TV content is mass produced and occupies a central role, it is more influential than other forms of mass media. TV has become a major part of our life. We spend more time watching TV than at any other activities except sleep and occupational duties (Kubey and Csikszentmihalyi 2002). On an average, persons in the developed world watch about 21 hours per week, which translates into nine years in front of the TV in a regular lifetime (Burroughs, Rindfleisch and Shrum 2003).
2. TV shapes people's attitudes and beliefs about society and other people. And also TV cultivates the values and attitudes which are already present in the culture of the people. It also serves to strengthen the status of the values and attitudes and at times even challenges it.
3. According to this theory, if a viewer watches the TV for more than four hours in a day this can lead to Mean World Syndrome.
4. TV does not reflect reality; rather, it creates an alternate reality. TV deeply influences our life. Our life has dramatically changed with TV. As TV went into each household, there were many positive and negative phenomena. Although TV has positive aspects, it also has negative effects for our life.

Criticism: When the concept of content analysis, the cultivation theory criticises the lack of categorisation in TV programming. As theorists of cultivation theory make no distinction between different genres or types of violence they view cartoon violence in the same light as realistic violence.

Individual Differences Theory

This theory proposes that each of us has unique qualities that result in our reacting differently to media messages.

Image 15.7: An Individual's Needs, Attitudes, Values, Prior Beliefs and other Cognitive and Emotional States Play an Important Part in Screening and Selecting Media Exposure and Interpretation

Source: 'Aero India Press Conference' by US Consulate Chennai (flickr; CC BY ND 2.0).

In other words, the reaction to media content differs according to the motivation of audience members, their position to accept or reject a given message, intelligence, beliefs, opinions, values, needs, moods, prejudices, perceptibility, etc. In *Theories of Mass Communication*, De Fleur and Rokeach (1982) state that individual differences perspective implies that media messages contain particular stimulus attributes that have differential interaction with personality characteristics of audience members. Since there are individual differences in personality characteristics among such members, it is natural to assume that there will be variations in effect which correspond to these individual differences.

THEORIES OF MASS MEDIA AND GOVERNANCE

Theories of the press describe an ideal way for media systems to be structured and operated. Normative theories do not describe things as they are, nor do they provide scientific explanations; instead, they describe the way things shall be if some ideal values or principles are to be realised. They help explain the way in which social communication rules impinge on mass media structures, conventions and performance, and highlight the consequences of non-convergence between societal communication principles and mass communication principles. Based on the work of American researchers Fred Siebert, Theodore Peterson and Wilbur Schramm (1956) the following are the theories:

Normative theories or the theories of the press are:

1. Authoritarian media theory
2. Libertarian media theory (Free press theory)
3. Soviet-communist media theory
4. Social responsibility media theory
5. Democratic-participant media theory
6. Development media theory

Authoritarian Media Theory

This is the oldest of the press theories. It is an idea that placed all forms of communication under the control of a governing elite or authorities. Authorities justified their control as a means to protect and preserve a divinely ordained social order. It actually began in sixteenth century Europe when feudal aristocracies exercised arbitrary power over the lives of most people. It derived from the state's philosophy of absolutism in which recognition of truth was entrusted to only a small number of 'sages' who were able to exercise leadership in a top-down approach. Media professionals are therefore not allowed to have any independence within the media organisation. Also foreign media are subordinate to the established authority, in that all imported media products are controlled by the state. Authoritarian media still operate today in countries where the press is largely owned or controlled by government. The instruments of authoritarian control include repressive legislation and decrees, heavy taxation, direct or subtle control of staffing and of essential production inputs like newsprints, prior censorship and suspension of production. The 1975 Emergency established by then Prime Minister Indira Gandhi showcases the control of the government over the functioning of the press. Many parts of Pakistan are still under this authoritarian rule by its army and also the government.

Libertarian Media Theory (Free Press Theory)

Libertarian thought emerged out of the authoritarian theory when some social movements—including the Protestant Reformation—demanded greater freedom for individuals over their own lives and thoughts. It prescribes that an individual should be free to publish what (s)he likes and to hold and express opinions freely. It sees the press as a free 'market place' of ideas—that all ideas should be put before the public, and the public will choose the best from that 'market place'. Libertarian theory does not advocate media immunity to the rule of law but asserts that people should be seen as rational beings able to distinguish between good and bad, truth and falsehood—which renders prior censorship of media unnecessary. As a matter of fact, in the libertarian system, attacks on the government's policies are fully accepted and even encouraged. Moreover, journalists and media professionals ought to have full autonomy within the media organisation. It also advocates that the press be seen as partner in progress with the government in the search for truth, rather than a tool in the hands of government. It is hard to find intact examples of libertarian media systems in today's world in a democratic country, the mass media are very free to do whatever they like and cover.

Soviet-communist Media Theory

The Soviet theory is closely tied to a specific ideology—communism. Siebert, Peterson and Schramm (1956) trace the roots of this theory back to the 1917 Russian Revolution based on the postulates of Marx and Engels. The media organisations in this system were not intended to be privately owned and were to serve the interests of the working class. It advocates the complete domination of media by a communist government for the purpose of forcing those media to serve the party. According to this theory, the main task of the press is to promote the socialist system and maintain the sovereignty of the proletariat (working class) via the communist party. While the Soviet-Communist theory seeks to use the media to support development and change towards the attainment of the communist stage, the authoritarian seeks to use the media to maintain the status quo. But they are similar in subjecting the media to direct state control. Every issue in communist Soviet union must be seen and interpreted in favour of the communist party.

> The four working principles of Soviet press are:
>
> 1. Truthfulness
> 2. Partiality
> 3. Commitment to the people
> 4. Mass culture

Libertarian and social responsibility theories assign economic function to the press while the Soviet press removes the profit motive since it is an arm of government and financed by the government. Libertarian and social responsibility theories expect the media to raise social conflict to the level of discussion but Soviet theory forbade organisation of press structure along the lines of political conflicts since social societies aspired to become 'classless societies'.

Social Responsibility Media Theory

Social responsibility theory emerged as a result of conflict between professionalism and self-regulation of the press and pressure for greater regulation of the media. This theory states that the media can be used by anyone who has an idea to express but they are forbidden to invade private lives or disrupt social structures. It calls on the media to be responsible for fostering productive and creative 'Great Communities' (Davis and Baran 2003), and that media should do this by prioritising cultural pluralism by becoming the voice of all the people and not just elite groups or groups that had dominated national, regional or local culture in the past. It also points out that the media, in carrying out their obligations, must adhere to the highest ethical standards. The basic principles of the theory, summarised by McQuail (1987), include:

- To serve the political system by making information, discussion and consideration of public affairs generally accessible.
- To inform the public to enable it to take self-determined action.
- To protect the rights of the individual by acting as watchdog over the government.
- To serve the economic system; for instance, by bringing together buyers and sellers through the medium of advertising.
- To provide 'good' entertainment, whatever 'good' may mean in the culture at any point in time.
- To preserve financial autonomy in order not to become dependent on special interests and influences.

Democratic–participant Media Theory

This theory advocates media support for cultural pluralism at the grassroots. The media are to be used to stimulate and empower pluralistic groups. It calls for development of innovative 'small' media that can be directly controlled by group members. In other words, the existing bureaucracy, commercialisation and professional hegemony in media system should be broken down to allow or guarantee easy media access to all potential users and consumers. The theory reflects disappointment with libertarian and social responsibility theories for failing to deliver social benefits expected of them. It condemns the commercialisation and monopolisation of private-owned media and the concentration and bureaucratisation of government-owned media. It also criticises the public media for being too elitist, too susceptible to the whims of the government, too rigid and too slavish to professional ideals at the expense of social responsibility; it therefore calls for greater attention of the media to the needs, interests and aspirations of the receiver in a political society. Also, the media conglomerates must be replaced or mixed with small-scale media enterprises. It also calls for 'horizontal' in place of top-down communication to ensure feedback and complete communication circuit.

Development Media Theory

Development media theory advocates media support for an existing political regime and its efforts to bring about national economic development. It argues that until a nation is well established and its economic development well underway, media must be supportive rather than be critical of government. Journalists must not tear apart government efforts to promote development but, rather, assist government in implementing such policies. The duty of the press practicing this theory is to promote development. It also emphasises grassroots participation. The tenets of this theory as pointed out by McQuail (1987) are:

1. Media must accept and carry out positive development tasks in line with nationally-established policy.
2. Freedom of the media should be open to economic priorities and development needs of the society.
3. Media should give priority in their content to the national culture and language(s). The media should also give priority of coverage to other development countries.
4. Media should give priority in news and information to link with other developing countries that are close geographically, culturally or politically.
5. Journalists and other media workers have responsibilities as well as freedoms in their information gathering and dissemination tasks. In the interest of development ends the state has a right to intervene in, or restrict, media operation; and devices of censorship, subsidy and direct control can be justified.

MASS COMMUNICATION IN TRANSITION

Today's Indian society has inherited the wisdom, mistakes, creativity and vision of the people who work in the mass media industries and the society that regulates and consumes what the mass media produce. Mass media's journey is significantly different than they were five years ago. A combination of technological, economic and social factors have made some traditional business models obsolete and several media are struggling to re-invent themselves for the digital era. Other media are dealing with a fundamental shift in the ways they reach their audiences. The different ways in which the transitions have occurred in the mass media are described below.

Mass Communication and Technology

At the technology level, the emergence of the internet has created a new channel for mass communication. The rapid increase in mobile and wireless connections has led to the growth of internet penetration in India.

Key beneficiaries are emerging new media segments, which include internet advertising, online classifieds and gaming, all of which are on a rapid growth path. The primary reason behind this growth in competition is easy to see: 'The Internet brings down the cost of mass communication to a level at which almost anybody can afford it. A single individual can start a website for a relatively small sum (Facebook started in a Harvard dorm, Flipkart started by bunch of passing out friends), and the websites can reach a potential audience of millions' (Dominick 2010). Furthermore, low cost implies that individual sites can be supported solely by those who create them, thus removing the profit consideration from the equation. It's probably fair to say that the vast majority of bloggers, for example, blog for reasons other than profit.

With the increasing proliferation of digital platforms, technology will play an even more important role in the mass media industry in the near future. As the number of 'connected consumers' rises, a host of opportunities and challenges will arise for mass media players, as these consumers will not expect flexibility and choice in their content consumption experience but also generate a wealth of data through their behaviours. Further, the competitive scenario of the mass media industry has also started to change with the entry of traditional technology players such as Google.

Mass Communication and Economics

An important aspect of mass communication is economics. Mass communication is expensive. They operate corporately as businesses that exist to make a profit, or by non-profit organisations that must obtain funding elsewhere to subsidise the media costs. It is a global business in which profits are huge. For example, Sony which owns Sony Records, Sony Worldwide/SW Radio, Columbia Tristar Pictures and Columbia Records had sales in billions of rupees over the last couple of years. The Indian media industry exhibited robust growth in the past few years with the revenues increasing from about Rs 805 billion in 2011 to Rs 965 billion in 2012, representing a year-on-year increase of about 20 per cent. This growth was achieved in spite of a relative slowdown in the broader economy, underlying the resilience of the mass media industry (CII 2013). Digitisation has been a significant driver for the growth of both Indian TV and film sectors. Competition is another aspect of the economic reality. Researchers scientifically calculate the size of television and radio audiences, which directly impacts the advertising rates those media charge. The Indian media industry is expected to continue its strong growth momentum over 2012–17 to reach total revenues of Rs 2245 billion (ibid.).

Mass Communication and Social Trends

Social change has also hastened the transition. Consumers became accustomed to receiving their information and entertainment for free, and efforts to charge for the internet content met with resistance. Net neutrality is a big question for today's generation. Traditional passive media exposure replaced by active participation in new social media such as Facebook, Linkedin and Twitter. The recording industry CDs have been replaced by person-to-person file sharing. People began to spend their time creating media content (more than half of the world's teens have created a social networking site; more than 100 million people have started blogs) and less time-consuming media content.

Mass Communication and Culture

Mass communication and culture are two sides of the same coin. As we all know culture defines our realities, but who contributes to the construction and maintenance of culture? Because culture is constructed and maintained through communication, it is in communication that cultural power resides. And because mass media are such a significant part of

> Three dichotomies which shape the debate between mass communication and culture:
>
> 1. Micro vs macro level effects
> 2. Administrative vs critical research
> 3. Transmission vs ritual perspective

the modern world, more and more attention is being paid to the interaction between mass communication and culture. Since the introduction of the first mass circulation newspapers in the 1830s, media theorists and social critics have argued about the importance and power of the media industries and mass communication. Stanley Baran (2006) has underlined three dichotomies which shape the debate between mass communication and culture.

Micro vs Macro Level Effects

As long as we debate the effects of media only on individuals, we remain blind to media's greatest influences (both positive and negative) on the way we live. For example, the horrific events of Nirbhaya rape case in 2012 once again brought public debate on the issue of media effects. Even the gruesome shootout at Littleton, Colorado's Columbine High School in 1999 brought public debate on the issue of media effects; USA Network co President Steve Brenner was forced to defend his industry: 'Every American has seen hundreds of films, hundreds of news stories, hundreds of depictions, thousands of cartoons ... Millions don't go out and shoot people' (as quoted in Albiniak 1999).

Image 15.8: What are the Effects of Media on Sensitive Issues? This scene is from protest march after the 16 December 2012 gang rape in India.

Source: 'Delhi protests-India Raped, says one young woman's sign' (Wikimedia Commons; CC BY-SA 3.0).

Most people believe media have relatively few direct effects at the personal or micro level. The hidden but much more important impact of media operates at the cultural or macro level. Violence on TV contributes to the cultural climate in which real-world violence becomes more acceptable. Sure, perhaps none of us have gone out and shot people.

Administrative vs Critical Research

Administrative research asks questions about the immediate, observable influence of mass communication. Does a commercial campaign sell more cereal? Does an expanded section increase newspaper circulation? Did a party chief's quotes inspire the now legally-confined rapists in India? For decades the only proof of media effects that science (and therefore the media industries, regulators and audiences) would accept were those with direct, observable, immediate impacts. Sixty years ago, however, Lazarsfeld warned of the danger of this narrow view. He believed in critical research—asking larger questions about what kind of nation we are building, what kind of people we are becoming and what would serve our culture better. Administrative research concerns itself with direct causes and effects; critical research looks at larger, possibly more significant cultural questions.

Transmission vs Ritual Perspective

Last is the debate that led Professor Carey (1989) to articulate his cultural definition of communication. The transmission perspective sees media as senders of information for the purpose of control; that is, media either have effects on our behaviour or they do not. The ritual perspective, Carey wrote, views media not as a means of transmitting 'messages in space' but as central to 'the maintenance of society in time'. Mass communication is 'not the act of imparting information but the representation of shared beliefs'. In other words, the ritual perspective is necessary to understand the cultural importance of mass communication.

Image 15.9: The Transmission Message in this Ad is Obvious: Buy Kingfisher. The ritual message is another thing altogether. What is it?

Source: 'Kingfisher beer ad in Goa' by Olexdj (Wikimedia Commons; CC BY-SA 3.0).

What message is being transmitted in Kingfisher beer? Buy Kingfisher beer, of course. So people either do or do not buy Kingfisher beer. The message either controls or does not control people's beer-buying behaviour. That is the transmission perspective. But what is happening culturally in ad? What reality about alcohol and socialising is shared? Can young people really have fun in social settings without alcohol? What constitutes a good-looking man or a woman? What does it mean to be a successful person in a cosmopolitan city? Reflection on these questions can surely lead us to understand better how potently media impacts our culture and living.

SUMMARY

- Normative theories or theories of the press describe an ideal way for media systems to be structured and operated. They are authoritarian, communist, libertarian and social responsibility theories, democratic-participant media theory and development media theory.
- An important aspect of mass media is economics. Mass media are expensive. They operate corporately as businesses that exist to make a profit, or by non-profit organisations that must obtain funding elsewhere to subsidise the media costs. Mass media is a global business for which profits are huge.
- Communication is a symbolic process whereby reality is produced, maintained, repaired and transformed (Carey 1989: 23). Communication has the potential to be a practical discipline in the first place because 'communication' is already a meaningful concept. In a diverse society like ours, the mass communication has responsibility to fill the cultural gaps in the society. Mass communications has the power to disseminate information and ideas across several societies and get the people talking and thinking about varied issues. Mass communication enforces these basic norms and values of the society through reportage of

cultural issues and events. It is mainly through the different types of mass media that the cultural products are exhibited.

KEY WORDS

Magic bullet theory: The theory suggests that the mass media could influence a very large group of people directly and uniformly by 'shooting' or 'injecting' them with appropriate messages designed to trigger a desired response.

Propaganda theory: The theory says: 'Behaviorism brings up the notion that all human action is a conditioned response to external environmental stimuli.'

Uses and gratification theory: This theory has emerged out of the studies which shifted their focus from what the media do to the people to what people do with the media.

Agenda setting theory: This theory posits that the mass media predetermine what issues are regarded as important at any given time.

Spiral of silence: The phrase 'spiral of silence' actually refers to how people tend to remain silent when they feel that their views are in the minority.

Authoritarian media theory: It is an idea that placed all forms of communication under the control of a governing elite or authorities. Authorities justified their control as a means to protect and preserve a divinely ordained social order.

Development media theory: It argues that until a nation is well established and its economic development well underway, media must be supportive rather than critical of government.

EXERCISES

1. Using an appropriate theory, construct the relationship between mass media and society.
2. 'Normative theory seeks to locate media structure and performance within the milieu in which it operates.' Explain.
3. Money plays a very important role in media. Explain this with reference to media economics.
4. What do we mean by mass media as cultural storyteller?
5. What do we mean by mass communication as cultural forum?

REFERENCES

Abelman, R. and D. Atkin, 'What Children Watch When They Watch TV: Putting Theory into Practice', *Journal of Broadcasting and Electronic Media* 44 (2000): 143–61.

Albiniak, Paige, 'FCC: Hands Off Broadband', *Broadcasting & Cable*, 18 October 1999, 20.

Ball-Rokeach, S. J. and M. L. DeFleur, 'A Dependency Model or Mass-media Effects', *Communication Research* 3 (1976): 3–21.

———, *Theories of Mass Communication*, fifth edition, White Plains, NY: Longman, 1989.

Bandura, A., R. W. Jeffery and C. L. Wright, 'Efficacy of Participant Modeling as a Function of Response Induction Aids', *Journal of Abnormal Psychology* 83 (1974): 56–64. Reprinted in *Annual Review of Behavior Therapy and Theory and Practice* 3, edited by C. M. Franks and G. T. Wilson, New York: Brunner/Mazel, 1975.

Baran, S., *Introduction to Mass Communication: Media Literacy and Culture*, fourth edition, London: McGraw-Hill, 2006.

Baran, S. and D. Davis, *Mass Communication Theory: Foundations, Ferment and Future*, Belmont, CA: Thomson Wadsworth, 2000.

Berger, A., *Essentials of Mass Communication Theory*, London: Sage, 1995.

Burroughs, J. E., A. Rindfleisch and L. J. Shrum, 'Does Television Promote Materialsim? Cultivating the Desire for the Good Life', *International Communication Association* (2003): 1–36.

Carey, J. W., *Communication as Culture: Essays on Media and Society*, Winchester, MA: Unwin Hyman, 1989.

Chang, Y. and B. H. Reber, 'Assessing Cultivation Theory and Public Health Model for Crime Reporting', *Newspaper Research Journal* 21.4 (2000): 99.

Confederation of Indian Industries (CII), *India Entertainment and Media Outlook*, 2013, available at https://www.pwc.in/assets/pdfs/india-entertainment-and-media-outlook/india-entertainment-and-media-outlook-2013.pdf (accessed May 2016).

Croteau, David and William Hoynes, *Media/Society: Industries, Images and Audiences*, London: Pine Forge Press, 1997.

Davis, D. K. and S. J. Baran, *Mass Communication Theory: Foundations, Ferment, and Future*, Belmont: Wadsworth Publishing, 2003.

Davis, D. K. and S. J. Baron, 'A History of Our Understanding of Mass Communication' in *Mass Communication and Everyday Life: A Perspective on Theory and Effects*, edited by D. K. Davis and S. J. Baron, 19–52, Belmont: Wadsworth Publishing, 1981.

Dominick, J., *The Dynamics of Mass Communication: Media In The Digital Age*, New Delhi: Tata McGraw Hill, 2010.

Folarin, B., *Theories of Mass Communication: An Introductory Text*, Abeokuta: Link Publications, 2003.

Gerbner, G., 'Cultivation Analysis: An Overview', *Mass Communication & Society* l.3–4 (1998): 175–94.

Gerbner, G. and L. Gross, 'Living with Television: The Violence Profile', *Journal of Communication* 26.2 (1976): 173–99.

Jeffres, L. W., *Mass Media Effects*, second edition, Illinois: Waveland Press Inc., 1997.

Katz, E., 'Mass Communication Research and the Study of Culture', *Studies in Public Communication* 2.1 (1959): 1–6.

Kubey, R. and M. Csikszentmihalyi, 'Television Addiction Is No Mere Metaphor', *Scientific American* 286 (2002): 74–80.

Kuhn, Thomas S., 'Section IX: The Nature and Necessity of Scientific Revolutions', *The Structure of Scientific Revolutions*, first edition, Chicago, IL: University of Chicago Press, 1962.

Lasswell, H., *Democracy through Public Opinion*, USA: George Banta Publishing Company, 1941.

———, 'Describing the Contents of Communication' in *Propaganda, Communication and Public Opinion*, edited by B. L. Smith, H. D. Lasswell and R. D. Casey, 74–94, Princeton, NJ: Princeton University Press, 1946.

———, 'The Structure and Function of Communication in Society' in *The Communication of Ideas*, edited by L. Bryson, 37–51, New York: Harper & Row, 1948.

Lazarsfeld, P., B. Berelson and H. Gaudet, *The People's Choice*, second edition, New York: Columbia University Press, 1948.

Lippmann, W., *Public Opinion*, New York: Harcourt, Brace and Co., 1922.

McCombs, M. and D. Shaw, 'The Agenda-Setting Function of Mass Media', *Public Opinion Quarterly* 36 (1972): 176–87.

McQuail, D., *Reader in Mass Communication Theory*, London: Sage, 1987.

Morgan, M, and N. Signorielli, 'Cultivation Analysis: Conceptualization and Methodology' in *Cultivation Analysis: New Directions in Media Effects Research*, edited by M. Morgan and N. Signorielli, Newbury Park, CA: Sage Publications, Inc., 1990,

Newcomb, Theodore M., 'An Approach to the Study of Communicative Acts', *Psychological Review* 60 (1953): 393–404.

Noelle-Neumann, E., 'Return to the Concept of Powerful Mass Media', *Studies of Broadcasting* 9 (1973): 66–112.

Rogers, Everett M., *Diffusion of Innovations*, fifth edition, New York: Free Press, 2003 [1995].

Siebert, F., T. Peterson and W. Schramm, *Four Theories of the Press*, Urbana: University of Illinois Press, 1956.

Stephenson, W., *The Play Theory of Mass Communication*, Classics in Communication and Mass Culture, NJ: Transaction Publishers, 1987.

Westley, Bruce and Malcolm MacLean, 'A Conceptual Model for Mass Communication Research', *Journalism Quarterly* 34 (1957): 31–38.

Zaharopoulos, T., 'Traditional Family Relationships and Television Viewing in Greece', *Transnational Broadcasting Studies*, Archives 6 (2001).

16

MEDIA FOR MASS COMMUNICATION

HIGHLIGHTS

- Classification
- Broadcast media
- Mass media professions
  - Advertising
  - Public relations
  - Journalism

For mass communication to work, media are the means. Let us understand the concept of 'mass media'. Dutton (1986) breaks down the term 'mass media' into its constituent parts. Mass means 'many' and what we are interested in here is, 'how' and 'why' different forms of media are required and used by a large number of people (the audience). A medium is a 'channel of communication', a means through which people send and receive information. The printed word, for example, is a medium; when we read a newspaper or magazine, something is communicated to us in some way. Similarly, electronic forms of communication TV, telephone, film and such like are media. Mass media, therefore, refer to channels of communication that involve transmitting information in some way, shape or form to large numbers of people. Although the question of exactly how many a 'large number' will qualify as a 'mass' is something that's generally left undefined.

CLASSIFICATION

Various communication scholars have approached media studies from several different perspectives, each focusing on a different aspect of the media. These diverse view points are helpful to gain a fuller understanding of mass media.

Mass Media and Interpersonal Media

'Mass' means 'many', thus mass media refers to channels of communication that involve transmitting/disseminating information or message to large, anonymous and scattered heterogeneous masses. One of the main factors in the process of mass communication is technology. Mass communication represents the creation, designing and sending of messages to a large heterogeneous audience with the help of technology. Thus a mass medium (such as TV, film, newspaper) is generally classified as 'one-to-many' communication system wherein 'one' person (such as the reporter of a newspaper, the director of a film) communicates with many people (the audience) in a manner that it is largely impersonal and one-way with no simultaneous feedback from that audience.

The interpersonal media refer to person-to-person communications involving direct and indirect methods, i.e. they may take place in face-to-face settings or through media platforms. When members (audience) of a team (small group) in an MNC watch a motivational film (media) by the HR department (communicators) to improve group performance, it is an example of direct interpersonal media use. When the manager of a company makes a telephone call to an employee to give her/him a feedback on performance appraisal, it is an indirect method of interpersonal media use. Interpersonal media are any form of media intended for use in dyadic or small group communications contexts. Existing as highly impersonal on one end and deeply intimate on the other, the crux of interpersonal communication is the interconnectedness of people involved in it. Thus a range of media forms can be used to communicate with people within an interpersonal context.

Entertainment and Information Media

Another way of categorising media is through their intended use. Entertainment media such as books, magazines and television dramas are significantly different than information media such as newspapers and television news programmes because they appeal to different audiences and serve different functions.

Technology Involved Media

Another and perhaps the most accepted classification of media is according to the physical form and characteristics of the technology involved. This is further classified into different subcategories:

Print Media, Non-print Media, Electronic Media

Print media uses the printing technique and includes books, journals, magazines, newspapers, workbooks and textbooks. Non-print media do not use the printing software or hardware and can include projected and non-projected media; for example, documentaries, TV, radio, etc. Electronic media is media that uses any form of technology and needs an electrical supply to access. Different forms of audio media, visual media and audio-visual including the internet, blogs, social media, TV, radio are all examples of electronic media.

Projected Media and Non-projected Media

Projected media require a light source for projection; for example, film projector slides. Non-projected media do not require any light source; for example, 3-dimensional objects, 2-dimensional objects, prints, charts, models, etc.

Audio Media, Visual Media and Audio-visual

Audio media involves forms of media that carry sounds alone; for example CDs, MP3, audio tapes, record player, radio, etc. Visual media are the ones that can be seen; for example, computer, white board, etc. Audio-visual refers to those instructional materials which provide students with audio and visual experiences by appearing to the hearing and seeing senses at the same time; for example, TV, video tapes, films, documentaries, etc.

Localite and Cosmopolite

Media can be understood in terms of the socio-cultural context of the receivers and the senders. Cosmopolite media link individuals with communicators outside their socio-cultural system. Localite media on the other hand link individuals with local communicators or those within their socio-cultural environment. According to Evret Rogers (2003) the cosmopolite media are suitable for spreading awareness and knowledge about specific issues while the localite media help in persuading and convincing people to alter their ideas and behaviours. Interpersonal channels may be localite or cosmopolite, while mass media channels are mostly cosmopolite in nature. Thus a national newspaper or a general entertainment TV channel is a cosmopolite channel as people from different regions, cultural and ethnic groups and urban/rural parts of India read the same newspapers.

Alternative and Mainstream Media

Mainstream media refers to all types of media that reach out to large groups of people, i.e. newspapers, radio, television, magazines, movies, internet, etc. Mass media can be both alternative and mainstream media. Alternative differs from mainstream mass media, as it provides information which is different, 'independent' or 'alternative' to the mainstream media and also differs along one or more of the following dimensions—content, aesthetic, modes of production, modes of distribution and audience relations. Alternative media often aim to challenge existing powers, to represent marginalised groups and to foster horizontal linkages among groups and communities of interest. Advocates of alternative media consider it to be a media tool that challenges traditional hegemonic power relations via their selection of content and their rhetorical and structural framing of news and information.

All media forms have immense potential to promote or perpetuate an ideological framework, however, alternative media aim to provide a critical perspective and promote counter-hegemonic discourse. Because the term 'alternative' has connotations of self-marginalisation, some media outlets now prefer the term 'independent' over 'alternative'. For example, *Ujala Chadi*, a rural newspaper in Rajasthan serves villages with news they can use because even regional language papers often do not serve the needs of rural readers.

Public, Private and Community Media

Media can also be understood in terms of its ownership and control. Structures of media ownership can take the form of public, private or community enterprise. 'Public' refers to those media that are largely funded out of general public revenues. Public media can be state-owned or state-managed, i.e. controlled by the government in power. For example, Doordarshan and All India Radio, are owned by the Government of India. On the other hand 'private' media are enterprises whose financing is provided by individuals, groups and/or corporations and are guided by commercial and profiteering interests. Also, private media is run by certain ideology and beliefs; for example, Zee TV, *The Times of India* newspaper, the channel Radio Mirchi, etc. Community media, such as community radio or community newspapers, are usually community-owned and controlled and give access to voices in the community and encourage diversity, creativity and participation. Community media ensure media pluralism, diversity of content and representation of a society's different groups and interests. Community media encourage open dialogue and transparency of administration at the local level and offer a voice to the voiceless. They are established on the concepts of public access and sharing experiences and information.

Now let us understand how media are classified according to the physical form and the technology involved. Given below are the major categories of mass media in this view:

> Types of media according to technology involved are:
>
> 1. Print media
> 2. Broadcast media
> 3. Narrowcast media
> 4. New media

Print Media

In 1457, Johannes Gutenberg invented movable metal types. This paved the way for mass production of printed materials. Resultantly, presses and publications spread rapidly first across Europe, and then in the other continents. Mass production of printed documents led to democratisation of knowledge. In other words, it made knowledge and education accessible to common people. It was exactly a revolution because till then knowledge was considered the property of the elite.

Types of Print Media

The three popular forms of print media are books, magazines and newspapers. These forms of print media are different in their binding, regularity, content and timeliness, though the means and methods for production are similar to certain extent.

Newspapers

Newspapers are periodically published documents that carry current information about the society. The first newspaper was *Publick Occurrences* published by Ben Harris in 1690. The first newspaper published in India was the *Bengal Gazette* by James Augustus Hicky in 1780. It is also called Hicky's Gazette. Newspapers are the primary mass medium from which people receive news. And, by every measure, newspaper industry overpowers all other media, be it in advertising revenue or the size of audience.

Characteristics of newspapers: Primarily newspapers are print media even though digital age offers online newspapers and e-papers. That is why it has all the features that any print medium has.

Major features of these mass media are given below:

- **Predominance of news-oriented content**: There are three types of content in newspapers—news; views and advertisements.
- **Regular periodicity**: Newspapers may be published daily or weekly.
- **Future reference**: Being a print medium, newspapers can be kept for future use.
- **Choice of the time of use**: Unlike TV and radio, a newspaper can be read at any time.
- **The literates' medium**: Unlike TV and radio, newspaper demands literacy on the part of the audience.
- **Low cost**: Compared to other media, newspaper is a cost-effective medium.
- **Multiple users**: Many readers can read a copy of the newspaper simultaneously or separately.
- **Textual medium**: Text is the soul of newspapers, though they do carry images and graphics.

Classification of Newspapers

Newspapers can be categorised into various types based on their page size/format, content type, periodicity, time of publication, area of circulation and type of the users.

1. **By page size or page format:** By size, newspapers can be divided into three—broadsheet, tabloid and berliner.
   - *Broadsheet* is the largest of the various newspaper formats and is characterised by long vertical pages (typically 22″ × 559 mm or more). The term derives from types of popular prints usually just of a single sheet, sold on the streets and containing various types of material, from ballads to political satire.
   - *Tabloid* is a smaller newspaper format per spread mostly used for a weekly or semi-weekly alternative newspaper that focuses on local-interest stories and entertainment. The tabloid newspaper format

is particularly popular in the UK. *Tehelka* and *Mint* are well known Indian weeklies in the tabloid format.

- *Berliner* is a newspaper format with pages normally measuring about 470 mm × 316 mm (18.5″ × 12.4″). The Berliner format is used by many European newspapers, including dailies such as *Le Monde* in France and *The Guardian* in the UK.

2. **By time of publication:** Morning dailies, evening dailies.
3. **By content:** Newspapers are mainly classified as general newspapers, political newspapers, and financial/business newspapers.
4. **By periodicity:** Dailies and weeklies are two type of newspapers based on the periodicity. Dailies are newspapers that are published at least five times a week and weeklies are those published once a week.
5. **By circulation area:**
   - *National dailies*: Their primary area of circulation is across the nation. The *Wall Street Journal* and *USA Today* are national dailies of the US. *The Hindu*, *Times of India* and *Hindustan Times* are national dailies in India.
   - *Hometown newspapers*: Town-centric newspapers focusing issues on that particular city is called hometown newspapers. *Midday* of Mumbai is an example.
   - *Metropolitan dailies*: These dailies concentrate on the affairs of a metro city. Examples: *Metro Vartha* of Malayala Manorama.
6. **By audience:**
   - *Community newspapers*: Newspapers published on and by a community; for example *Newsday* based in New York, *Adyar Times* and *Anna Nagar Times* in South India.
   - *Religious newspapers*: Newspapers published by religious organisations, focusing on religious news with a mission of propagation; e.g. *Punybhoomi*.
   - *Immigrant and ethnic newspapers*: Newspapers published by ethnic groups living in alien lands as expatriates like Indians in the Gulf countries. Benjamin Franklin's *Philadelphische Zeitung* in 1732 is the first of its kind. *Gulf Madhyamam* published from the Middle East is first full-fledged ethnic media in Malayalam.
7. **By language:** English newspapers, vernacular newspapers (the newspapers in regional languages). Also, braille newspapers published for the visually-challenged.

Image 16.1: Regional Newspapers of India

Source: 'Punjabi language newspapers' by Shemaroo (Wikimedia Commons; CC BY 3.0).

Magazines and Periodicals

Unlike newspapers, magazines are periodical publications carrying non-news items. In the past magazines were as expensive as books. So they could be afforded only by the wealthy. And during this time, they were not considered mass media since they served only a small section of the society. And these magazines focused on political and literary affairs. But now magazines are considered as mass medium as they are much cheaper, with wide circulation and are involved in spreading the varied cultures in society and create a sense of belonging among people.

Classification of Magazines

Magazines are of different types. Five major categories are

1. *General interest magazines*: These are magazines that cover a wide variety of topics and are aimed at reaching a broad audience. Some examples are *The Week*, *Outlook*, *India Today*, *Readers' Digest* and *National Geographic*.
2. *Business magazines*: These are also called trade magazines. They focus on topics related to a particular occupation, profession or industry. The *Forbes*, *Business World*, *Business Today* and *Silicon India* are some of trade magazines.
3. *Consumer magazines*: Consumer magazines also aim at reaching the general public and they are called so because their readers are prompted to consume products and services advertised in them. In the modern age, most of the women's magazines have ended up as consumer magazines. Health tourism and IT magazines are no exceptions either. *Vision Plus*, *Black Book*, *Right Choice* are some examples of consumer magazines in India.

Image 16.2: Magazines on Display

Source: 'Zeitschriften' by Christian Bohr (Wikimedia Commons; CC BY-SA 3.0).

4. *Literary reviews*: Those magazines which publish content about books, both fiction and non-fiction, are literary reviews. *Time Literary Survey* and *Bhashaposhini* are two examples.
5. *Academic reviews*: These are publications of a serious nature that focus on academic research articles and are available mainly through subscription or mail order. For example, the *Economic and Political Weekly* and *Seminar*.
6. *News magazines*: News magazines stress on news-based content and analysis. Some examples are *Time*, *News Week* and *Tehelka*.

Books

Books are bound pages of written or printed messages of considerable length, mostly on one topic meant for circulation. They are produced using durable materials and in a portable form.

Classification of Books

Books are categorised according to their content type and target audience. Based on the nature of the content, books can be categorised generally as fiction and non-fiction. Fiction books include novels, collections of short stories, anthologies of poems, etc. Non-fiction books comprise of academic and reference books.

As commercial commodities books can also be categorised according to their uses and users and they are as follows.

Trade books: Trade books target general readers and are mainly categorised as adult books and children's books. They include hardbound and paperback books and are sold at retail outlets. Adult trade books include fiction, current non-fiction, biographies, literary classics, hobby books, and books on self-help, popular science, travel, technology, etc. Children's book categories range from preschool picture books to young readers books, drawing/colouring books, cartoon books, comic books, children's fiction are subcategories of children's books.

Professional books: Professional books target occupational groups such as engineers, doctors, managers, lawyers, technicians, etc. These books are not for general readers and are mainly sold through direct mail order to the publishing houses or distributors.

Textbooks: Textbooks are for academic community. Because of their mass production, textbooks are low-priced books.

Paperbacks: Paperbacks are low-priced books having cheaper, flexible covers and pages. They lack durability as they are meant for 'use and throw'.

Religious books: The purpose of religious books is propagation of religion and these include holy texts, hymnals and inspirational books. The Bible is the bestselling book of all times.

Reference books: Reference books include encyclopaedias, dictionaries, atlases, handbooks, almanacs, etc.

University-Press books: University-Press Books are non-commercial books and these aim at the academic world. Oxford University Press, Chicago University Press, Harvard University Press are leading university presses.

BROADCAST MEDIA

Broadcast media is the distribution of audio and video content to a dispersed audience via radio, TV, films and others. The mass media which uses electronic or electromechanical energy for transmission of messages are called electronic media. The radio and TV messages are transmitted via air waves or radio signals.

Types of Broadcast Media

Radio

Origin and growth of radio: Guglielmo Marconi is credited as the inventor of radio. In fact, long-distance electronic communication existed since the middle of the nineteenth century. The telegraph communicated messages through a series of long and short clicks. Cables across the Atlantic Ocean connected even the far-distant USA and England using this technology. By the 1870s, telegraph technology had been used to develop the telephone, which could transmit an individual's voice over the same cables used by its predecessor. When Marconi popularised wireless technology, contemporaries initially viewed it as a way to allow the telegraph to function in places that could not be connected by cables. Early radios acted as devices for naval ships to communicate with other ships and with land stations; the focus was on person-to-person communication. However, the potential for broadcasting—sending messages to a large group of potential listeners—wasn't realised until later in the development of the medium.

The idea came to be known as broadcasting. The first radio stations were set up in Pittsburg, New York and Chicago in the 1920s. Radio broadcasting is everywhere as the signals reach everywhere. Indian government radio broadcaster 'All India Radio' reaches 98.25 per cent of the population of India. John Vivian (2002), describing the ubiquity of radio, says: 'People wake up with clock radios, jog with headset radios, and party with boom boxes and commute with car radios. People listen to sports events on the radio even if they are in the stadium.'

Characteristics of radio as a mass medium: The radio is a powerful mass medium and has a lot of advantages, both technical and message wise, to reach maximum number of people. The following are the characteristics of radio which differentiate it from other forms of mass media:

1. Radio is a cost-effective medium when compared to the other media.
2. Radio is a public medium as it can be accessed by any number of people simultaneously and together without too much technical glitches.
3. Radio is accessible to the illiterate people and doesn't require its audiences to be literate. As radio is just an audio medium and does not require literacy skills and hence it is very useful tool for community media. Radio is accessible to the visually-challenged also.
4. Radio is a mobile medium and can be carried away by its receiver anywhere and everywhere.
5. Radio is a background medium as it can be used while doing other jobs. Nowadays with new technological innovations, radio is now available with home appliances like refrigerator, geysers, washing machine, etc. as an inbuilt gadget.
6. Radio is the fastest and a speedy medium. It is an instant explanation of the things that are happening in the studio or outside. It transmits the messages and these messages can be picked up by anyone who has a radio set or receiver which is tuned into a radio station. Nowadays through the satellite connection, we can also receive radio signals of various AIR stations on our TV set-top box. On the other hand, other mass media like a newspaper give the previous day's news and of course television too can cover events instantly. But TV is more complex medium as compared to radio for production and transmission of news.

Types of radio stations

I. *Commercial stations*: Commercial stations broadcast for profit. The broadcasting in the commercial stations is normally interrupted by the advertisements, commonly called 'commercials'. This is the dominant type of broadcasting in USA and also in India. This kind of stations are common elsewhere, and exist alongside public broadcasting where programming is largely funded by broadcast receiver licenses, public donations or government grants. These stations support themselves financially by selling airwaves to advertisers. In India, vast majority of stations come under this category along with government-funded ones. Some of the commercial stations in India are Radio Mirchi, Red FM, Oye FM and many more.

II. *Non-commercial stations*: Non-commercial stations are broadcasting for the community and don't belong to the profit making sectors. The community radio fall into this category. Community radio is owned and operated by community or members of community. Community radio stations are supported by the state, individuals, corporate or even international bodies. The main aim of these stations is to become the voice of people and help develop the community. It can be defined as a vibrant community broadcasting system to enhance pluralism and diversity. Community radio is distinguished by three essential principles: non-profit; community ownership, management; and community participation.

Community radio is always confined to a small community and caters to a particular geographical area. Community radio serves a community which uses common resources for livelihood, has common development issues and concerns, which are relatively localised but nevertheless connected to national and provincial development goals (UNDP 2002). Some of the examples of community radio are Alfaz-e-Mewat run by an NGO in the Mewat region about 100 kms from Delhi, Radio Jamia run by MCRC Jamia, Delhi and DUFM run by University of Delhi are examples of an educational institutional-run community radio and Rudi no Radio run by SEWA organisation in Ahmedabad, Gujarat is operated exclusively by women. So, community radio offers opportunities to people to raise issues of concern to small community groups.

Radio programming: Radio programmes can be mainly categorised into two: news and non-news (entertainment) programmes. However, the nature of the radio programmes is completely determined by the policy of the country or the individual organisations. In USA, radio is more an entertainment medium than a news channel. In India, it has a perfect mix with AIR running the pure news programmes along with traditional and modern music and coverage of current political and development issues and there are several private radio channels serving mainly the entertainment function. The following are the different types of radio programmes:

1. **News** is an important format of radio programme because it keeps us informed as to what is happening in our own community and other communities.
2. **News bulletins** have assumed greater importance in radio broadcasting in recent years. Only AIR stations in India can give the news and have several long bulletins interspersed with hourly or even half-hourly news summaries.
3. **Newsreel**, a popular form of news broadcasting, is of fifteen or more minutes' duration. It contains eye-witness accounts, extracts of speeches and reports of other events, commentaries, short talks and interviews in much the same way as a newspaper includes pictures and feature articles.
4. The radio **interview** is a lively variation of the talk among the people and about the people who are involved in the news affair or events. Talk programmes were the earliest form of spoken word broadcasting as the talk programmes were the simplest and most effective.
5. The regular radio **magazine programme**, derived from the newsreel, is a useful outlet for a great deal of informational and soft news material which cannot be programmed elsewhere. Magazine programmes can be of either 16 or 30 minutes duration. They are a combination of various formats of radio programming such as short talks, interviews, on-the-spot reports and eye-witness accounts of events, commentaries, music.
6. The **documentary** programme is a story of something between 16 and 60 minutes in length. But the exact length of any radio documentary is related to the subject and its treatment.
7. The **discussion** programme provides a platform for the exchange of ideas on issues and events. The discussion can be serious or light-hearted. However, the main purpose of the discussion programme is to get us thinking.
8. Light **entertainment** is a rather loose term used by many stations to cover a wide field of programming including book and short-story readings; serialised drama, particularly light and humorous drama; variety programmes featuring light musical entertainment, comics, letter programmes; quizzes and panel games.
9. **Music** is one category of programme which occupies maximum air time on stations.
10. **Radio drama**: There are three ways the radio plays are presented:

    (a) Complete self-contained plays of 30, 45 or 60 minutes in length,

(b) Serial dramas of 16 or 30 minutes in length and in these dramas the action goes forward from one episode to another;

(c) Series drama of 30 minutes and completes in one whole episode; the principal characters of the series reappear in new situations in each new drama in the series.

Television

Origin and Growth of TV

The Bell Telephone Labs and AT&T was the first company which gave the USA public a mechanical television demonstration over both wire and radio circuits on 7 April 1927. But it further took eight years more for the actual beginning of television broadcasting pictures and sound were sent by wire from Washington D.C. to New York City. Cable television was introduced in Pennsylvania, 1948. Cable TV is the process of sending TV signals to subscribers through wires or fibre optic cables. With its inception in 1948, cable TV became a means of bringing TV to rural areas. By 1950s, TV gained widespread acceptance in USA and also in some European countries. In 1970s, the development of satellite television allowed more channels and also encouraged businessmen to target programming toward specific audiences. This also enabled the rise of subscription television channels, such as Home Box Office (HBO) and Showtime in USA, and Sky Television in the UK. A digital mode of transmitting TV channels through a set-top box (STB) is now a reality in India too. This has only taken place due to satellite transmission for Conditional Access System (CAS). Satellite transmission is all about sending television signals using satellites in the orbit.

Characteristics of TV as a Mass Medium

1. **Audio-visual medium**: TV is audio-visual medium which carries moving pictures and sound.
2. **Live medium**: TV enables the live transmission of the events happening anywhere and everywhere in the world.
3. **Popular medium**: It is a very popular medium among the masses. A person need not be literate to watch TV while newspaper reading requires literacy, thus making it one of the most powerful mass medium influencing lives of people across the globe.
4. **Expensive medium**: As compared to other mass media, it is relatively a more expensive medium. The cost of television set and the cable connections are expensive for the poor people in our country. In addition, there are huge costs involved in setting up TV studios and stations and cost of transmission.

Types of TV Transmission Systems

The mode of delivery of television messages is being defined and redefined by the technological advancements. The prominent ways of television transmission are given below.

TV broadcasting: It is over-the air transmission of audio-visual signals from towers owned by television stations on frequencies allotted to them by the Ministry of Information and Broadcasting like Doordarshan (DD). People don't have to pay for these channels and they are free to air as the signals of these channels can be by simply turning on a TV set. This is true only for government-run TV channels like DD National, DD News and DD Metro.

Cable TV: The process of sending TV signals to subscribers through a wire is known as Cable TV. Cable TV system was popularised in India during the Gulf War in 1991. There has been speedy transmission of signals without losing picture quality with the help of optical fibres.

Satellite transmission: The transmission of television signals through satellites is known as satellite transmission. It enables the households to receive signals directly from the satellites using dish antennas. This is also called Direct-to-Home (DTH) Satellite Services. It is a purely digital technology that delivers channels to a receiver that is set top box placed in subscriber's house. The set top box converts digital signals received by the antennas into audio-visual format. And now the Government of India has made it compulsory for every household to have set top boxes to receive transmission. And Indian audiences have plenty to choose with respect to DTH like Tata Sky, Dish TV, Videocon, Airtel and many more.

Film and Cinema

A film can be simply defined as a sequence of images of moving objects photographed by a camera and providing the optical illusion of continuous movement, when projected onto a screen. Film, both as a medium and as an art, is very different from other media of mass communication. In 1873, the development process of film started. Films are largely independent and are always pre-recorded. Adams Sitney (1979) identified four formal characteristics common in structural films, but all four characteristics are not usually present in every film:

- Fixed camera position (an apparently fixed framing)
- Flicker effect (strobing due to the perception of still image by the audience in a motion picture)
- Loop printing
- Re-photography (off the screen)

Movies are 'larger than life' and movie stars are more glamorous. This makes films one of the most popular entertainment media. Film has cinema audience and the success of any film is simply rated through its box office returns. Film is more expensive to produce as compared to other mass media.

Growth of Film

Films started to attract millions of people world over as it grew as an independent entertainment industry. This trend started getting explored as soon as potential of cinema as a medium was expanded. The need for a realistic treatment of the stories leads to the concept of the feature films. This style of filmmaking was also the narrative structure of earliest feature films. Colour films revolutionised the medium further as the audiences were hugely attracted to colour film as the colours provided a real-life visual experience. The re-release of cult film—'*Mughal-e-Azam*' is a fine example of black-and-white Hindi classic turned into coloured film. The film still made mullah at the box office in spite of a re-release after decades.

Earlier history of cinema can be divided into Silent Era and the Era of Talkies.

1. **Silent Era** refers to the period during which films were produced without sound due to the absence of adequate technology. The power of the cinema during the silent era was the power of their stories. '*Raja Harishchandra*' was the first silent film released in India in 1913.
2. **Talkies** refers to films with sound. Another categorisation of the history of cinema was on the basis of the colour of visuals. Earlier films were produced in black-and-white. '*Alam Ara*' is the first sound film released in India.

The film industry of US is the biggest one in the world with its brilliant technical quality.

Types of Films

Films can be mainly categorised into two—documentaries and feature films. Documentary is a realistic film based on a specific topic or an issue and it sheds light on the various aspects of the subject matter.

It is informative and educative in nature. It is a non-fiction narrative, at times without actors. Typically a documentary is a real time record of an event, person, or a place. On the other hand, feature films are movies released for commercial success and the duration is at least 40–45 minutes (2 reels) long intended for theatrical release.

Film Genres

Apart from this division in general nature, films can be segmented according to the treatment of the content. The main genres of films are: Comedy, Drama, Romance, Action/Adventure, Mystery/Suspense, Horror, Fantasy, Science Fiction, Musicals. Main companies producing the films all over the world in the Movie Industry are Warner Brothers, Walt Disney, Columbia Pictures, Twentieth Century Fox, Paramount and Universal.

New Media

Mass media have witnessed changes that are technical, textual, conventional and cultural. Since the mid-1980s and with some changes over the period, a number of features have been observed. The emergence of new Information and Communication Technologies (ICTs) such as the internet brought the phenomenon of the new (online) media. The online media is otherwise known as the new media because it is a departure from the old or the conventional media of radio, TV, newspaper and magazine. New media can be defined as interactive forms of media that use the internet, including podcasts, blogs, vlogs, social networks, text messaging, wikis, virtual worlds and all other computer-aided communication formats available online. The main terms used in discourses about new media include digital, interactive, hyper-texual, virtual, networked and simulated.

Characteristics of New Media

Mark Poster (1999) was one of the first theorists to provide an insightful discussion about the emerging communications revolution of 'new media'. He argued that the main difference between old broadcast media and new media was that new media were 'active', whereas old media were 'passive'. According to him, new media have the following advantages over other mass media:

1. Although the new media may face limitations of screen size, downloading time, server capacity, they still score over other media with respect to the capacity to overcome the lack of time and space.
2. New media are very flexible. These can handle variety of forms for the information presented—words, pictures, audio, video and graphics.
3. New media are speedy and immediate; deliver information speedily.
4. Not just the speed, new media cover different aspects of news at one time.
5. New media can connect one format of information with other formats and sources of information through hyperlinks.
6. New media are interactive with a human-machine communication system with immediate feedback many times.
7. Unlike traditional media, new media are multi-task media, as they may include various types of media formats in one single platform; for example, we can watch television and listen to radio, and read newspapers on a webpage.
8. New media are very cost effective when compared to other media.
9. Access to new media is expansive. As we can get access to the web or new media sources wherever we are through any smart phone or laptop.

The Internet

The internet has become an inseparable part of our lives especially the urban and cosmopolitan life. The internet can simply be described as the collection of networks that link computers and servers together. It is a computer network consisting of a worldwide network of computer networks and cables that use the TCP/IP network protocols to facilitate data transmission and exchange. An official definition was made by the Federal Networking Council in the US in 1995:

> The Federal Networking Council agrees that the following language reflects our definition of the term "Internet". "Internet" refers to the global information system that (i) is logically linked together by a globally unique address space based in the Internet Protocol (IP) or its subsequent extensions/follow-ons; (ii) is able to support communications using the Transmission Control Protocol/ Internet Protocol (TCP/IP) suite or its subsequent extensions/follow-ons, and/ or other IP-compatible protocols; and (iii) provides, uses or makes accessible, either publicly or privately, high level services layered on the communications and related infrastructure described herein.

Internet can be described by four major characteristics:

1. Interactivity, that is, ICTs are effective two-way communication channels.
2. Permanent availability, the new ICTs are available 24 hours a day.
3. Global reach; they bridge the geographic distances.
4. Reduced costs for many; relative costs of communication have shrunk to a fraction of previous values.

Growth of internet: Internet was considered just a simple network of computers until the early 1990s, and it was used to transmit government data and enable academic research and conversations. But with the evolution of the World Wide Web by Tim Berners Lee in early 1990s and online subscription service providers such as America OnLine (AOL), CompuServe and Prodigy, the internet traffic began to explode universally.

Internet and the global village: McLuhan's idea (1968) of a global village is made possible by the emergence of the internet. Global village is the idea that the new communication technologies will permit people to become increasingly involved in one another's lives. McLuhan believed that electronic media would permit 'the human tribe' to become 'one family'. The net transforms every user into a potential mass communicator, making freedom of the press a reality for everyone. But freedom has been criticised because individuals are not bound by the kinds of economic and legal restraints that tend to impose responsibility on larger, commercially-oriented media.

Social Media Networks

Andreas Kaplan and Michael Haenlein (2010) define social media as 'a group of Internet-based applications that build on the ideological and technological foundations of Web 2.0 and that allow the creation and exchange of user-generated content'. Kietzmann, Hermkens, et al. (2011) say that social media employ mobile and web-based technologies to create highly interactive platforms via which individuals and communities share, create, discuss and modify user-generated content. It introduces substantial and pervasive changes to communication between organisations, communities and individuals.

As of 2015, social media has become one of the most powerful sources for news updates through platforms such as Face book, Blogger, Twitter, WordPress, LinkedIn, Pinterest, Google+. Tumblr, MySpace and Wikia. Social media is different from traditional media in many aspects such as quality, reach, frequency, usability, immediacy and permanence. Kaplan and Haenlein (2010) created a classification scheme of social media:

1. **Blogs**: A blog is basically a journal that is available on the web. It is derived from the term 'Web Log'. The activity of updating a blog is 'blogging' and someone who keeps a blog is a 'blogger'.
2. **Vlogs**: A video blog or video log, sometimes shortened to vlog is a form of blog for which the medium is video, and is a form of web television. The word derived from the term 'Video Web Log'.
3. **Podcast**: A podcast is a type of digital media consisting of an episodic series of audio radio, video, PDF, or ePub files subscribed to and downloaded through web syndication or streamed online to a computer or mobile device. The word is derived from 'broadcast' and 'pod' from the success of the iPod, as podcasts are often listened to on portable media players.
4. **News portals**: A web portal is a web site that brings information together from diverse sources in a uniform way. Usually, each information source gets its dedicated area on the page for displaying information (a portlet); often, the user can configure which ones to display.

MASS MEDIA PROFESSIONS

Advertising

The word advertising comes from the Latin word advertere meaning 'to turn the minds towards'. According to William J. Stanton, 'Advertising consists of all the activities involved in presenting to an audience a non-personal, sponsor-identified and paid-for message about a product or an organization.' According to Philip Kotler, 'Advertising is any paid form of non-personal presentation and promotion of goods, services, or ideas by an identified sponsor.' The American Marketing Association (AMA) defines advertising as 'any paid form of non-personal presentation and promotion of ideas, goods or services by an identified sponsor.' So, what comes through is that it is a paid for pitch created to sell an idea, product or service. However, it also must be understood that it need not always be a commercial product or a service for profit. Beautiful advertisements have been created to enthuse people to contribute to social change like adopting a child, education of the girl child, conservation of energy and other resources and environment protection. In India these are either funded by government agencies, bilateral agencies or the corporate houses.

Ek Boond Zindagi Ki.

Can you recall something?

Polio eradication program! The Polio Eradication Program of the Government of India. It is easy to remember the name of this popular programme only because of advertising. This is the power of advertising. It is persuasive, informative and designed to influence behaviour or thought patterns. It could also be defined as a one-way communication through a medium in which the sponsor is identified and the message is controlled by the sponsor. Every major medium is used to deliver these messages, including TV, radio, movies, magazines, newspapers, video games and the internet.

Let's think of these—print advertisements in newspapers telling us about the sale of the week; big hoardings telling us which car to buy; the RJ, or radio jockey, asking us to go for a public event in the city over the weekend; the huge mural wall at the metro station carrying the name and address of the local eating joint. The world of advertisements is fascinating due to its powerful appeal across generations and very subtle ways of nudging our behaviour towards the idea or a product advertised.

Classification of Advertisements According to Various Media

According to various media:

1. Print media advertising
2. Electronic media advertising
3. New media advertising

Print media advertising: Newspapers and magazine advertisement, bills, wall posters, banners, calendars are all different forms of print advertisements. The rise of the newspaper industry is directly related to the rise of print advertising industry. As the process of printing became cheaper, quicker and better, the first ad agency also came into being around the same time. All this took place after the successful installation of the first linotype printing machine by the Statesman in Calcutta in 1907. Print ads can be categorised as classified and display ads.

1. *Classified ads*: The weekly ads that you see in the newspapers asking us to buy a new house, rent a house or seeking matrimony are all considered to be classified ads. These ads provide valuable information in a very direct manner. The matter in these ads is projected in a very dry manner as they contain only basic facts and generally there are no designs and illustrations involved. Information about property markets, shares, matrimonial, detective agencies, housing, births and deaths in the classified pages of most national dailies are all classified ads.

Image 16.3: Classified Ads in India

Source: 'For Sale—Classifieds' by Khantipol (Wikimedia Commons; CC BY 2.0).

2. *Display ads*: These are complete opposite to the classified ads. These ads are bigger, fancier, colourful and also contain attractive images. Display ads also take more space in the newspapers and magazines. Weekend newspapers and glossy magazines usually carry many display ads. The display ads give away the information with respect to the products in a grandeur scale. The ads of sale in big stores, lifestyle products, and government schemes are all considered to be display ads.

Electronic Media Advertising: The advertisements through the electronic media are very vibrant and these advertisements can be heard on radio as well as seen on television. The rise of the TV industry has provided

Image 16.4: Print Ad: Pears Soap Display Ad in 1900 in British Media

Source: 'Pears Soap 1900' by VAWebteam (Wikimedia Commons; CC0 Public Domain).

Image 16.5: Electronic Advertisement on a Road

Source: '(1) Darlinghurst Road-7' by Sardaka (Wikimedia Commons; CC BY 3.0).

a great impetus to the electronic advertising industry. This impact of growing television media industry is so much that people watching TV find electronic ads more interesting than the television programmes.

The electronic ads can also be displayed and seen as the text and image on big monitors and light boards in the shopping malls, roads and various public places. In big cities and metros, there are many text boards at the traffic signals giving away the information with respect to safe traffic rules and regulations.

New media advertising: As soon as you go to any website on your smart phone or laptop, you find ads popping up, asking you to download popular film songs or vote for your favourite candidate during election time! The new media advertising brings in the new phase in advertising with the coming of the internet and extreme popularity of smart android phones. The new media have created a huge platform for advertisers who are reaching the unreached. The new media advertising is the advertising for the twenty-first century.

Image 16.6: Advertisements on Internet that keep popping up

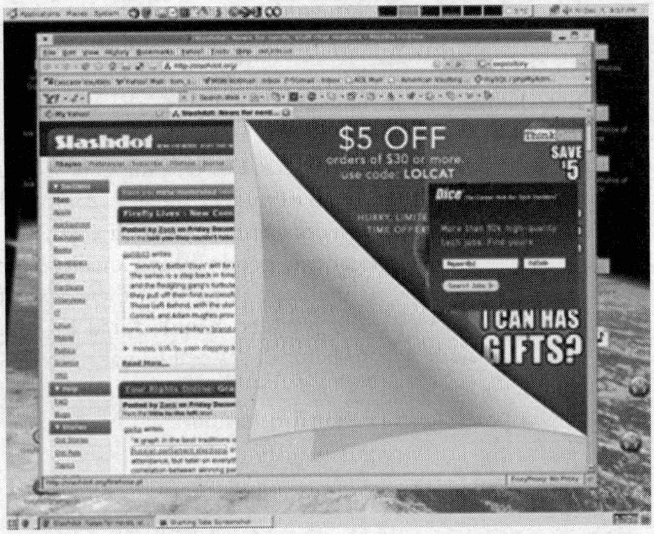

Source: 'Slashdot Ad Overlay Error' by Tom Sayles (flickr; CC-BY SA 2.0).

Classification of Advertisements According to Theme or Content

According to theme or content:

1. Product advertising
2. Service advertising
3. Public service advertising
4. Institutional advertising

Product advertising: The re-launch of 'Maggi' noodles after a six-month ban in India and the people's response to it. Maggi ads were in surplus in mainstream mass media and so were the sales of Maggi at stores all across India. This is the impact of product advertising and is the most common type of advertising. The main focus of the ad in this case is the product and not the company or manufacturer. These ads are all out to sell the product with high style irrespective of the company. They don't carry too much information also. Ads of soft drinks, shoes, cars, cell phones and food products belong to this category of ads.

Service advertising: This type of advertising only focuses on the service provided by the company or organisation rather than the manufactured item or product. The ads of the phone networks, national or private banks, the railways, or a hotel are examples of the service ads. The ads simply show the company as a leading service provider in its particular field. Let us consider the example of a national bank. The banks advertise their saving schemes and loan facilities that they offer for buying homes and vehicles. Similarly, the Indian Railways advertisements may boast of its wide network and service to the nation. Everyone knows about the railways but in order to keep the public interested in the railways, the service ads keep coming in to familiarise the people about the railway services. These ads are issued in the newspapers and websites of Indian Railways.

Public Service Advertising (PSA): This is also called social service advertising or development advertising. This type of advertising is completely focused on the social issues that impact society on a larger scale.

The issues such as family planning, national integration, polio eradication, pollution control, child education, sports, etc. The main aim is to create public awareness through direct messages. And the main difference between these ads when compared to other types of ads is that these ads do not sell products and service. They sell only the ideas. Polio eradication campaign is an example of PSA. These ads are issued through various mainstream mass media such as newspapers, radio and TV. These ads try and reach out to the masses to create awareness on polio eradication and also motivate parents to take their children for polio drops on the specified day like 'Polio Ravivar'. The campaign was successful in fixing one Sunday of a month for a social cause and popularised through such ads to associate a day for a very important social responsibility of parenting and protecting the nation (all vulnerable children in the age group of 0–5 years) from polio infection.

Institutional advertising: The concept of creating good public image is through the institutional advertising. Any organisation, company or government today is completely dependent on institutional advertising as the institutional ads represent the organisation in good sight. Institutional ads focus on the organisation's work in areas of research, development, goodwill and quality control. Many times institutional ads concentrate on the social work done. As the main purpose of these ads is to promote a positive image of the organisation rather than only focus on the product manufactured by them. TATA Steel ads in the 1980s with the tag line—'Ispat bhi hum banate hain' or 'We also make steel'—is a good example of institutional advertising. Similarly, the 'jaago re' ad by Tata Tea—this institutional ad relates tea with the democratic right to vote and displaying responsible and rational behaviour.

Public Relations

> Public Relations is a distinctive management function which helps establish and maintain mutual lines of communication, understanding, acceptance and cooperation between an organization and its publics; involves the management of problems or issues; helps management to be updated with and be responsive to public opinion; defines and emphasizes the responsibility of management to serve the public interest; helps management keep abreast of and effectively utilize change, serving as an early warning system to help anticipate trends; and uses research and sound and ethical communication as its principal tools. (Harlow 1976)

The American Public Relations Association, described public relations as 'The management function which evaluates public attitudes, identifies the policies and procedures of an organization with the public interest, and executes a programme of action to earn public understanding and acceptance.' The International Public Relations Associations (IPRA), meeting in Hague in May 1960, arrived at a definition of PR as

> A management function of a continuing and planned character through which public and private organizations and institutions seek to win and retain the understanding, sympathy and support of those with whom they are or may be concerned, by evaluating public opinion about themselves, in order to correlate as far as possible their own policies and procedures to achieve by planned and widespread information more productive co-operation and more efficient fulfilment of their common interests.

Functions of Public Relations

- Establishment of the relationship among the two groups (organisation and public): this is the prime functions of the public relations.
- The notion of public relation is directly related to the art or science of developing reciprocal understanding and goodwill among the people.
- One of the essential functions of public relations is to analyse the public perception & attitude, identify the organisation policy with public interest and then execute the programmes for communication with the public.

Elements of Public Relations

- Public relations are planned effort or management function in an organisation as well as society.
- Public relation develops the relationship between an organisation and its publics.
- Public relations evaluate the public attitudes and opinions.
- Public relations also decide the organisation's policies, procedures and actions in order to relate to the organisation's publics.
- Public relations also takes the necessary steps to ensure that policies, procedures and actions are in the public interest and are socially responsible.
- Public relations execute the actions or communication programme.
- Public relations develop rapport, goodwill, understanding and acceptance among the organisation.

The Components and Tools of Public Relations

> The components and tools of public relations are:
> 1. Public
> 2. Relations
> 3. Propaganda
> 4. Campaigns
> 5. Lobbying

To perform the above mentioned functions, the public relations process needs to use the following tools:

Public: A group of similar individuals; an assortment of persons having the same interests, problems, circumstances, goals; it is from such persons that opinion emanates. Every public has its own desires, wants; it has its likes and dislikes, many times, strong likes and strong dislikes.

Relations: Public relations develops the relationship between an organisation and its publics through the evaluation of the public attitudes and opinions. All human beings wish to establish relationships with one another.

Propaganda: Propaganda is the manipulation of symbols to transmit accepted attitudes and skills. It describes political application of publicity and advertising, also on a large scale, to the end of selling an idea, cause or candidate or all three.

Campaigns: These are concerted, single-purpose publicity programmes. The campaign is usually on an elaborate scale, employs coordinated publicity through various media, aimed at a number of targets, but focused on specific objectives. A campaign objective may be to make a particular individual or a party win an election or promotion of political cause or an issue, the reaching of a sales goal, or raising quota of funds for a particular development concern.

Lobbying: It entails the exertion of influence, smooth and measured pressure on other, exercise of persuasion cum-pressure. In essence, it means a group putting its points of view forward in an attempt to win the other groups' support.

Journalism

Curtis (2011) defines journalism as the practice of investigating and reporting events, issues and trends to the mass audiences of print, broadcast and online media such as newspapers, magazines and books, radio and TV stations and networks, and blogs and social and mobile media. Journalism includes the desire to write, the desire to be known, the desire to influence for good and the desire for knowledge. The press, or journalism, is referred to as the fourth estate as it acts as the watchdog for a democracy. The idea of journalism is to inform the citizens about the happenings and the journalists cover everyone in the society including individuals, organisations, institutions, governments and businesses also the cultural aspects of society such as arts and entertainment. But the news media are the main sources of information and opinion about public affairs.

Journalism comes in several different forms:

a) News
   (i) Breaking news: Telling about an event as it happens.
   (ii) Feature stories: A detailed look at something interesting that's not breaking news.
   (iii) Enterprise or Investigative stories: Stories that uncover information that only a few people know.

b) Opinion
   (i) Editorials: Unsigned articles that express a publication's opinion.
   (ii) Columns: Signed articles that express the writer's reporting and his conclusions.
   (iii) Reviews: Such as concert, restaurant or movie reviews.

c) Online, journalism can come in the forms listed above, as well as:
   (i) Blogs: Online diaries kept by individuals or small groups.
   (ii) Discussion boards: Online question and answer pages where anyone can participate.
   (iii) Wikis: Articles that any reader can add to or change.

The ten absolutes of journalism according to Reuters (2014) are:

1. Always hold accuracy sacrosanct
2. Always correct an error openly
3. Always strive for balance and freedom from bias
4. Always reveal a conflict of interest to a manager
5. Always respect privileged information
6. Always protect their sources from the authorities
7. Always guard against putting their opinion in a news story
8. Never fabricate or plagiarise
9. Never alter a still or moving image beyond the requirements of normal image enhancement
10. Never pay for a story and never accept a bribe

Reporting

The way to get the information from varied sources is through reporting. And accuracy and fairness are the hallmarks of journalism reporting. Neither accuracy or nor fairness must ever be sacrificed for speed in the profession of journalism. Accuracy is also more than just getting the facts right—it is getting the right facts, and backing up our interpretation of the facts with authoritative and unimpeachable sourcing. The people or documents used in reporting a story are called 'sources'. There are three main ways to gather information for a news story:

Interviews: Today's reporting is restrained by the interviews. The interviews are all about talking with people who know something about any story that is happening around and which the reporter is reporting.

Observation: It is the most important source for information. As watching and listening to people and visiting places where news is taking place can really make news. And nowadays what you see in the mainstream Hindi news channels is a good example of news from sheer observations by the producers.

Documents: These form the secondary source of information. They include reports, public records, and stories from the past and also other printed material.

Writing

The ABC of Writing is: Accuracy, Brevity and Clarity. Here are the keys to writing for good journalism:

- Get the facts. All the facts you can.
- Tell your readers where you got every bit of information you put in your story.
- Be honest about what you do not know.
- Don't try to write fancy. Keep it clear.

> As rightly asserted by Harold Laswell, whenever you are interviewing someone, observing something happening or reading about something, write down the answers to the 'Five Ws' about that source:
>
> - Who are they?
> - What were they doing?
> - Where were they doing it?
> - When do they do it?
> - Why did they do it?

Start your story with the most important thing that happened in your story. This is called the 'lead'. It should summarise the whole story in one sentence. From there, add details that explain or illustrate what is going on. Again, write the story like telling it to a friend. Start with what is most important and then add background or details as needed. Each time one introduces a new source, a new paragraph must start. Each time one brings up a new point, a new paragraph must start.

Writing Style: Inverted Pyramid: A news story attempts to answer all the basic questions about a particular event in the first two or three paragraphs Who? What? When? Where? Why? and occasionally How? ('5 Ws' and 1 H).

Inverted pyramid technique helps to answers these questions by deciding the structure of the story. This is used to write a report. The first paragraph gives the most important information of the story. The second and third paragraphs, follow up on the information by expanding on the lead and adding information that is less important.

News

News is the timely report of events, facts, opinions and interests. It is a news piece of information about a significant and recent event that affects the audience and is of interest to them.

Joseph Pulitzer, publisher of *New York World*, defined news as, 'Original, distinctive, dramatic, romantic, thrilling, unique, curious, humorous, odd and apt to be talked about.' Walter William, Founder of First School of Journalism, said, 'news in the broadcast sense is that which is of interest to the reader public.'

Figure 16.1: Basic Inverted Pyramid Writing Style

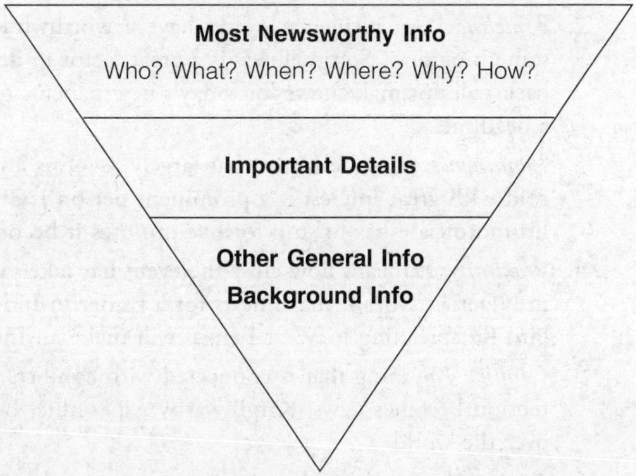

Source: 'Inverted pyramid 2' by The Air Force Departmental Publishing Office (Wikimedia Commons; CC0 Public Domain).

> Definition of a news item is dependent on:
>
> - Size of the community
> - Periodicity of publication
> - Social character and economic base of the community
> - Focus of attention of the community

Hard news and Soft news: Stories of primary and urgent importance rate the 'hard' news classification. Examples would include articles concerning a key vote in the parliament, approval or rejection of crucial legislation, the police department's certain activity, natural calamities, etc. These situations would provide 'must' stories that readers would expect to see.

News of secondary importance is labelled as 'soft' news and might concern items as a film release, minor crimes, sports news, entertainment news, mishaps, etc.

Image 16.7: Content is the King in Journalism

Source: 'Content is like water' by Stéphanie Walter (Wikimedia Commons; CC By-SA 3.0).

News Values

1. *Impact*: It is the consequence a story has on the people. When the tsunami waves struck several parts of the world, thousands of people were affected. It became major news for the whole world. But if a cyclone kills 50 people in Bhutan, it may not have any impact on other parts of the world.
2. *Timeliness*: An incidence would have a worthwhile exercise soon after it has been reported. News is something new. So timeliness is a great factor in deciding news. An incident that happened one month back will not make news for today's newspaper. For a 24-hour television news channel, every second is a deadline.
3. *Prominence*: It is the factor that largely revolves around prominent people. Even the trivial actions are read with great interest if a prominent person is involved. If the prime minister's car breaks down and his motorcade has to stop for five minutes it becomes news.
4. *Proximity*: It means how close the event has taken place. 'Ebola virus flu spreading and hundreds dying in Nigeria.' Does it make news for a reader in India? One may read it but do not worry about it. But bird flu spreading in West Bengal will make an Indian living in Delhi alert.
5. *Conflict*: Anything that is connected with conflicts, arguments, charges and counter-charges, fights and tension becomes news. Kargil war was a conflict between India and Pakistan. It became great news all over the world.
6. *Bizzare*: Unusual incidents always attract readers. This is an old fact of journalism. If a dog bites a man, it is not news but if a man bites dog, it surely becomes news e.g., a man pulls a car by his hair, a woman gives birth to triplets.
7. *Currency*: It has somewhat similar appeal like timeliness. These are ongoing events but have continuity. Issues that have the value of currency come and go, but there are always such several events being discussed by people. When the Commonwealth Games were held in Delhi, India it became news because everybody was interested in it. Likewise when SAARC leaders meet in Delhi to formulate future action plans, it becomes the current news.

Individually or collectively, all these can give you opportunities to write great stories. One needs to know how to structure the story, so that the most important and interesting information gets to the reader in most efficient manner.

SUMMARY

- Mass media that use electronic or electromechanical energy for transmission of messages are called electronic media. Major broadcasting media are radio and TV.
- Advertising is a public announcement to inform and persuade people to buy a product, a service or an idea. An advertisement would include any notice, circular, label, wrapper or any other document or any announcement made orally, or by means of producing or transmitting light, sound or smoke.
- Public relations is the deliberate, planned and sustained effort to establish and maintain mutual understanding between on organisation and its publics. Investing on Public relations will help the organisation to achieve its objective effectively and smoothly.
- Journalism is the practice of investigating and reporting events, issues and trends to the mass audiences of print, broadcast and online media such as newspapers, magazines and books, radio and television stations and networks, and blogs and social and mobile media.

KEY WORDS

Mass media: Mass media refer to channels of communication that involve transmitting information in some way, shape or form to large number of people.

Newspapers: Newspapers are periodically published documents that carry current information about the society.

Community Radio: Community Radio is radio owned and operated by members of community.

Social Media: Social Media is a group of Internet-based applications that build on the ideological and technological foundations of Web 2.0, and that allow the creation and exchange of user-generated content.

Advertising: Advertising: is a public announcement to inform and persuade people to buy a product, a service or an idea.

Public Relations: Public Relations is the deliberate, planned and sustained effort to establish and maintain mutual understanding between an organisation and its publics.

Journalism: Journalism is the practice of investigating and reporting events, issues and trends to the mass audiences of print, broadcast and online media.

EXERCISES

1. Classify the different mass media for mass communication.
2. Outline the growth of advertising and public relations as professions.
3. What is the difference between advertising and public relations?
4. Define news and discuss the factors that determine the news value.
5. Discuss the inverted pyramid approach in news writing with relevant illustrations.

REFERENCES

Curtis, A., *What is Journalism*, available at http://www.uncp.edu/home/acurtis/Courses/ResourcesForCourses/Journalism/JournalismWhatIsIt.htm (accessed May 2016), 2011.

Dutton, B., *The Media*, London: Longman, 1986.

Harlow, Rex F., 'Building a Public Relations Definition', *Public Relations Review* 2 (1976): 36.

Kaplan, Andreas M. and Michael Haenlein, 'Social Media: Back to the Roots and Back to the Future', *Journal of Systems and Information Technology* 14.2 (2012): 101–04.

———, 'Users of the World, Unite! The Challenges and Opportunities of Social Media', *Business Horizons* 53.1 (2010): 59–68.

Kietzmann, J. H., K. Hermkens, I. P. McCarthy and B. S. Silvestre, 'Social Media? Get Serious! Understanding the Functional Building Blocks of Social Media', *Business Horizons* 54.1 (2011): 241–51.

Lister, M., J. Dovey, S. Giddings and K. Kieran, *New Media: A Critical Introduction*, second edition, London: Routedge, 2009.

Lule, J., *Understanding Media and Culture: An Introduction to Mass Communication*, London: Sage, 2012.

McLuhan, M., *Understanding Media*, London: Sphere, 1968.

Pearce, C. Sims, 'God and Go A Conversation with Will Wright', available at http:/ /www.gamestudies.org/0102/2002 (accessed May 2016), 2002.

Poster, Mark, *The Mode of Information*, Cambridge: Polity Press, 1990.

———, 'Underdetermination', *New Media and Society* (1999).

Public Broadcasting Service (PBS), 'Guglielmo Marconi', *American Experience: People & Events*, available at http://www.pbs.org/wgbh/amex/rescue/peopleevents/pandeAMEX98.html (accessed May 2016).

Reuters, *Reuters Handbook of Journalism*, available at http://handbook.reuters.com/extensions/docs/pdf/handbookofjournalism.pdf (accessed May 2016), 2014.

Rogers, E., *Diffusion of Innovation*, fifth edition, New York: Free Press, 2003.

Sitney, P. Adams, *Visionary Film: The American Avant-Garde 1943–1978*, second edition, Oxford: Oxford University Press, 1979.

United Nations Development Programme (UNDP), *Community Radio in India: Step by Step; A Resource Guide for Community Radio*, available at http://www.undp.com (accessed May 2016), 2002.

Vivian, J., *The Media of Mass Communication*, sixth edition, Boston: Allyn & Bacon, 2002.

ABOUT THE EDITORS AND CONTRIBUTORS

THE EDITORS

Sarita Anand is associate professor at the Department of Development Communication and Extension, Lady Irwin College, University of Delhi. Her research interests include communication for development using community radio and ICTs, positive deviance approach for BCC in health, gender and development. She has been involved in research studies with UN agencies, government institutions and non-profit organisations. She has published in peer-reviewed journals and has co-authored two books, *Facilitating Dialogue: Enhancing Results* and *A Handbook of Researches in Media and Communication*.

Archna Kumar is associate professor at the Department of Development Communication and Extension, Lady Irwin College. Her academic and research interests include development issues, participatory communication and management of development programmes. She has published in a number of peer-reviewed journals. She has worked on issues of gender, national resource management, ICTs and community radio for development as well as use and building capacities for the most significant change techniques for M&E of C4D programme.

THE CONTRIBUTORS

Shweta Anand taught at the Department of Development Communication and Extension, Lady Irwin College. She is currently pursuing her PhD in community radio for development at the University of Delhi. She has also worked as a researcher and project coordinator at the Centre for Media Studies, New Delhi.

Sunaina Batra teaches at the Department of Development Communication and Extension, Lady Irwin College. Her research interests include public health, positive deviance and BCC. She has worked with Public Health Foundation of India (PHFI), New Delhi.

Tinny Dawar has taught at the Department of Development Communication and Extension, Lady Irwin College. She is currently pursuing her PhD in gender and education at University of Delhi.

Komita Dhanda teaches development communication and media studies at Lady Irwin College. She is a theatre practitioner and has been working with Jana Natya Manch since 2004. She is also a part of the administration team that runs a small alternative theatre space called Studio Safdar in Delhi.

Ruchi Gaur teaches at the Department of Development Communication and Extension, Lady Irwin College. Her research interests include gender and development, and programme monitoring and evaluation. She has worked with the planning commission.

Aparna Khanna is associate professor at the Department of Development Communication and Extension, Lady Irwin College. Her interests are in designing and evaluating media, ICTs for development including new and convergent media, and training and advocacy.

Swati Kwatra teaches at the Department of Development Communication and Extension, Lady Irwin College. She has worked with TERI on a number of research projects related to environment education and awareness. She is pursuing her PhD at TERI.

Nilanksha Sachdev has taught at the Department of Development Communication and Extension, Lady Irwin College. She has worked in the field of education, training and communication planning in NIIT Foundation, PVR Nest, Ideosync Media Combine and PHFI.

Sonia Sain teaches at the Department of Development Communication and Extension, Lady Irwin College. Her interests are training and advocacy, and development of innovative communication media for creating awareness about development issues.

Neha Sharma has taught at the Department of Development Communication and Extension, Lady Irwin College. She is currently pursuing her PhD in community ownership and participation in health at the University of Delhi. She has worked with NIOS, PHFI and is trained in qualitative research for health.

Anjali Singh teaches at the Department of Communication and Extension, Institute of Home Economics, New Delhi. Her interests include ICTs for development, and training and advocacy. She has had short teaching assignments with Lady Irwin College, Guru Gobind Singh Indraprastha University, Delhi, and NOIDA International University.

Sweta Suman teaches at the Department of Development Communication and Extension, Lady Irwin College. She is currently pursuing her PhD in media, gender and politics from Ambedkar University, Delhi.